PERFORMING ZIMBABWE

Thinking Africa is an imprint of the University of KwaZulu-Natal Press, published in association with the Department of Philosophy at the University of Pretoria. Most volumes published under the imprint represent research produced by the department's Thinking Africa project, although any manuscript judged by the imprint editor to meet its criteria and objectives may be accepted for publication. The imprint represents a transdisciplinary interrogation, not only of central themes such as memory, alterity, African humanism, emancipation, identity and violence, but also of Western modernity and the legacy of its disciplinary grid of intelligibility. Volumes that appear under the imprint will be of interest to all scholars who recognise the possibility and imperative of thinking Africa from a position that is at once post-Area Studies and post-disciplinary.

Imprint editor: Leonhard Praeg
Email: leonhard.praeg@up.ac.za

Previous Thinking Africa volumes:
Afrikaner Identity: Dysfunction and Grief by Yves Vanderhaegen (2018)
NGOs and Social Justice in South Africa and Beyond, edited by Sally Matthews (2017)
A Report on Ubuntu by Leonhard Praeg (2014)
Ubuntu: Curating the Archive, edited by Leonhard Praeg and Siphokazi Magadla (2014)
Violence in/and the Great Lakes: The Thought of V-Y Mudimbe and Beyond, edited by
    Grant Farred, Kasereka Kavwahirehi and Leonhard Praeg (2014)
On African Fault Lines: Meditations on Alterity Politics by V-Y Mudimbe (2013)
The Return of Makhanda: Exploring the Legend by Julia C. Wells (2012)

PERFORMING ZIMBABWE
A Transdisciplinary Study of Zimbabwean Music

Edited by
Luis Gimenez Amoros and Maurice T. Vambe

UNIVERSITY OF KwaZulu-Natal Press

Published in 2018 by University of KwaZulu-Natal Press
Private Bag X01
Scottsville, 3209
Pietermaritzburg
South Africa
Email: books@ukzn.ac.za
Website: www.uknpress.co.za

© 2018 University of KwaZulu-Natal

All rights reserved. No part of this publication may be reproduced or transmitted in any form or by any means, electronic or mechanical, including photocopying, recording, or any information storage and retrieval system, without prior permission in writing from University of KwaZulu-Natal Press.

ISBN: 978-1-86914-396-1
e-ISBN: 978-1-86914-397-8

Managing editor: Sally Hines
Editor: Alison Lockhart
Proofreader: Cathy Munro
Typesetter: Patricia Comrie
Indexer: Christopher Merrett
Cover design: Marise Bauer, M Design
Cover image: *Mbira*, ILAM Archive / ILAM / Africa Media Online

CONTENTS

List of Illustrations — xi
Acknowledgements — xii
Preface: Understanding Zimbabwe: The Shona and Ndebele in
   Zimbabwe and Beyond — xiii
Barbara Mahamba and Luis Gimenez Amoros

Introduction: The Study of Zimbabwean Music by Zimbabwean Scholars — 1
Luis Gimenez Amoros

Part I: Indigenous Music and Its Transformations — 11

1. *Mbira* in Urban Spaces: *Mbira*-making and the Multiple Contexts of Zvirimudeze Mbira Ensemble Performances in Zimbabwe — 13
Perminus Matiure

2. The Shangwe and Tsonga Idioms in *Xinombela* Musical Arts for the Adolescents in Gokwe and Chiredzi, North-West and South-West Zimbabwe — 43
Renias Ngara and Doreen Sibanda

3. Performing Subversion: Negotiating Social and Political Space in Zimbabwe through *Chinyambera* Traditional Dance — 56
Innocent Tinashe Mutero

4. Shangwe *Mukwerera*: Systems and Hierarchies of Communication in Gokwe, Zimbabwe — 76
Renias Ngara

5. *If Vagina Had Teeth*: Song, Film and the Reshaping of Female Identities through Rituals of Rainmaking Ceremonies among the Shona People of Western Mozambique — 93
Maurice T. Vambe

6. Doing the 'Serious Business of Older People' Correctly: Zimbabwean *Mbira* Popular Adaptations — 111
Vimbai Chamisa

Part II: Zimbabwean Urban Popular Music across Time 141

7 The Middle Class and the Popularisation of Musical Concerts in Harare Township, Salisbury, from the 1940s to 1970 143
Barbara Mahamba and Azon Twala

8 The Promotion of Popular Music in the Major Cities of Zimbabwe: A Contested Terrain by Musicians and Promoters 167
Victoria Blessing Butete

9 *Chimurenga* Music and Narratives of Zimbabwe's Liberation Struggle[s]: Rethinking Simon Chimbetu's 'Zimbabwe Iyoyi', 'Ndarangarira Gamba' and 'Pane Vasipo' 194
Urther Rwafa

10 Music and Violence: Discordant Siblings? A Study of Political Music in the Land Reform Programme of Zimbabwe, 2000–10 216
Bridget Chinouriri and Munyaradzi Nyakudya

Part III: The Rise of Dancehall in Zimbabwe: Regarding Transdisciplinary Studies 229

11 Dancehall Music in Zimbabwe: Youth Activism or Subalternity? Some Notes on the Politics of Music Based on Select Songs at the 2014 Zimdancehall Awards 231
Rekopantswe Mate

12 Performing Manhood in Zimdancehall: Music as Patriarchised Space in Zimbabwe 251
Manase Kudzai Chiweshe and Sandra Bhatasara

13 The Depiction of the Unsung African S/hero or Heroine in Post-2000 Zimdancehall Music Lyrics: A Critical Analysis 274
Ruby Magosvongwe

14 The Political Underpinnings of Zimdancehall Music: Analysing Selected Songs of Winky D and Tocky Vibes 288
Itai Muwati, Tinotenda Mwamuka and Charles Tembo

15 Patterns of Ndebele Zimdancehall Music 309
Zifikile Makwavarara and Albert Nyathi

Conclusion   325
    Luis Gimenez Amoros

Contributors   328
Index   333

In memory of Sheasby Matiure and Benita Tarupiwa

ILLUSTRATIONS

Figure 1.1:	*Nyunganhare*	18
Figure 1.2:	*Karimbamutatu*	19
Figure 1.3:	*Mbiragita*	20
Figure 1.4:	*Karimbashauro*	21
Figure 1.5:	*Karimbaduriro*	22
Figure 1.6:	*Karimbanhovapasi*	23
Figure 1.7:	Pitch range for the keys belonging to the three *mbiras*	23
Figure 1.8:	Range of *nyunganyunga*	23
Figure 1.9:	Sharpening of *mbira*	27
Figure 1.10:	Flattening keys of *mbira*	27
Figure 1.11:	Amplification of *mbira*	29
Figure 1.12:	Flyer advertising *mbira* show by Zvirimudeze and Mawungira Enharira	35
Figure 1.13:	*Nyunganyunga* with numbered keys	38
Figure 1.14:	Transcriptions of 'Chemutengure'	38
Figure 1.15:	Notation for 'Nhemamusasa'	39
Figure 1.16:	Transcription of 'Nhemamusasa' using staff notation	40
Figure 1.17:	Zvirimudeze Mbira Ensemble performing at a wedding	40
Figure 6.1:	'Taireva' standard *kushaura* and *kutsinhira* parts, as performed by Fradreck Mujuru	124
Figure 6.2:	'Taireva' standard *mbira* lines in 'Chamunorwa', 0:29–0:36	125
Figure 6.3:	*Kudeketera* tune and text traditionally sung for 'Chaminuka Ndimambo'	132
Figure 6.4:	*Kudeketera* text from 'Chaminuka Ndimambo' performed on 'Ancient Voices', from 3:36–3:51	132

ACKNOWLEDGEMENTS

We would like to thank the scholars who have participated in this book, as well as Kirk Helliker, Unit of Zimbabwean Studies' director, Rhodes University. This book is the result of valuable conversations about Zimbabwean musical culture with many scholars mainly at Zimbabwean universities.

Our special thanks to the International Library of African Music (ILAM) at Rhodes University, and particularly to Lee Watkins, Elijah Madiba and Diane Thram for their support in conducting the sound repatriation of ILAM's Zimbabwean recordings at Zimbabwean universities. The sound repatriation became the main motor behind the publication of this book.

Our most sincere thanks to all the music artists who appear in the book for their contribution to Zimbabwean musical culture.

PREFACE

Understanding Zimbabwe
The Shona and Ndebele in Zimbabwe and Beyond

Barbara Mahamba and Luis Gimenez Amoros

Zimbabwe is a country that was geographically mapped by British colonial institutions in the 1890s, which saw the formation of various artificial boundaries used to classify the country and its inhabitants. The country was called Southern Rhodesia from 1896 to 1964, when the 'Southern' was dropped. There are two main linguistic groups in Zimbabwe; namely, Shona and Ndebele. However, the Zimbabwean Constitution also recognises Chewa, Chibarwe, English, Kalanga, Khoisan, Nambya, Ndau, Shangani, Sotho, Tonga, Tswana, Venda and Xhosa, as well as sign language, as official languages.

The Shona-speaking people
According to Gerald Mazarire (2009: 3), the term 'Shona' was not in use prior to the nineteenth century and even then it was seen as a great insult, a term used by one's enemies. There was no homogenous linguistic group of people who called themselves Shona and no one considered themselves Shona. Instead, there existed groups of people who spoke similar languages and had similar beliefs and institutions, spread over an area larger than present-day Zimbabwe, stretching into present-day South Africa, Zambia and Mozambique. Within this zone, there was a constant movement of people, goods and ideas, with varied notions of self-identity. The Shona languages borrowed words such as *gomo* (mountain), *hwai* (sheep) or *zamu* (breast) from the Khoisan who had settled on the plateau before 900 AD.

The first time that the word 'Shona' was contextually applied by the Ndebele and Europeans, according to David Beach (1980: 18), was in the nineteenth century to refer to the people from the south-west of the Zimbabwean plateau, especially the Rozvi. The word 'Shona' was gradually extended, first in reference to the central Shona and then to the rest of the people presently known as the Shona, even though in many cases their ancestors did not use that name to describe themselves. Before this, they were variously described as '*vaNyayi*', '*abeTshabi*', '*Karanga*' or

'Hole' (Mazarire 2009: 3). The term 'Shona' began to gain gradual prominence in the late nineteenth century, carrying over into the twentieth and twenty-first centuries.

Terence Ranger (1985: 16) notes that precolonial African societies were characterised by pluralism, flexibility and multiple identities and that African notions of tribe, gender and generation were bounded by the rigidities of invented tradition. Colonialism effectively brought this perpetual movement of people to a halt, thereby freezing the geopolitical and ethnolinguistic maps the Europeans had created (Chimhundu 1992). Ranger (1985) further asserts that ethnicity was a colonial creation, arguing that colonial administrators and missionaries invented tradition to suit their vision of a more comprehensible colonial administration, with units that could be easily managed as 'tribes'. Therefore, the term 'Shona' to denote a tribe or a regional grouping is artificial, although it has come to be used to refer to people who speak different but interrelated dialects in Zimbabwe (Mazarire 2009: 3). In its modern political context, the term 'Shona' refers to the country's most populous ethnic group. The Shona people occupy most of contemporary Zimbabwe, except the Matabeleland region in the south-west of the country. Shona is widely spoken in Mashonaland, Masvingo and Manicaland provinces and some parts of the Midlands province, constituting more than 80 per cent of the Zimbabwean population. The ethnic and linguistic category of Shona people encompasses different subcategories and dialects, such as Karanga, Korekore, Zezuru, Ndau and Manyika. Beach (1980) also includes Kalanga, Shanga and Nyanga.

The creation of the Shona language

The formation of the Shona language was the result of two processes: the codification of dialects by missionaries and the creation of a unified standard by the colonial regime. It emerged originally in the translations of the Bible into African languages by the missionaries, but ended up as a search for a common system of writing for all Shona-speaking areas (Chimhundu 1992: 87). In eastern Zimbabwe, the missionaries created the term 'Manyika' as a regional tribal identity, yet it originally referred to the people under Chief Mutasa (Chimhundu 1992: 88; Ranger 1985). The Shona language was divided into the different dialects of Zezuru, Manyika, Korekore, Karanga and Ndau. In 1929, the Southern Rhodesian administration tasked a commission of missionaries, colonial officials and a leading South African linguist, Clement Doke, to bring together these dialects into one single language. Sinfree Makoni, Janina Brutt-Griffler and Pedzisai Mashiri (2007: 28) argue that the different Shona groups were classified according to the various missionary stations located in Mashonaland: the Zezuru had the Roman Catholic Church and Wesleyan Methodist Church; the Manyika had the Anglican Church and United Methodist; the Ndau had the American Board Mission (American Methodist); the Kalanga had the London Missionary Society; and the Karanga had the Dutch Reformed Church. The Korekore had no particularly influential missionary denomination. The five different dialects brought together became known as 'standardised Shona'. However, this version of standardised Shona was mainly composed of Zezuru and Karanga (29). These artificial regional-tribal formations continued into postcolonial Zimbabwe and remain a factor in the politics of the country and, for some Zimbabweans, this artificially created ethnolinguistic divide between Shona and Ndebele people has been further accentuated in the postcolonial era.

The Ndebele-speaking people
The roots of the Ndebele-speaking people of south-western Zimbabwe can be traced back to about 1820 when Mzilikazi, driven by the desire to maintain the autonomy of the Khumalo clan, migrated from Zululand (Ndlovu-Gatsheni 2000: 60). Mzilikazi moved with some women, children and livestock, backed by a handful of soldiers. According to oral tradition, Mzilikazi managed to create alliances around himself with the best families of the Khumalo clan (Rasmussen 1977: 14). Battles with the Zulu had seriously depleted the Ndebele population and so when Mzilikazi's group migrated through the Transvaal, they embarked on massive raids and incorporated vulnerable groups and adversaries, mainly the Pedi, Tswana and Sotho (Ndlovu-Gatsheni 2000: 60). Constant warfare with adversaries, mainly the Griquas and Boers, stopped Mzilikazi from establishing a permanent settlement south of the Limpopo River.

In about 1840, according to Beach (1980: 16), the Ndebele migrants, probably numbering more than 23 000, settled in what had been the Shona-speaking Changamire state in the south-west of the plateau. Mzilikazi, as the leader, was able to build the foundation of his society out of people from diverse ethnic backgrounds, modelling it on the Zulu kingdom. It is also vital to note that Nguni migrants had shattered the centre of Rozvi power and caused widespread scattering of the Rozvi people, making them an easy target for the Ndebele, who then incorporated most of them into what later emerged as the Ndebele state in western Zimbabwe. Mazarire (2009: 32) postulates that by the 1850s Ndebele control stretched as far as the Zambezi River, the Mapfungautsi plateau and Gokwe, with chiefs Chireya, Pashu and Nkoka paying tribute to the Ndebele as a sign of allegiance. The Ndebele state subsequently grew into one of the strongest in southern Africa.

Later, after settling on the Zimbabwean plateau, Mzilikazi began consolidating his power by attacking, conquering and assimilating the Rozvi, Kalanga, Nyubi, Venda, Birwa and Tonga groups. These groups became known as the amaHole. The Ndebele state, which started as a migrant kingdom, ultimately became a multinational state, led by the abeZansi, those from the south, who were at the apex of the Ndebele political and social ladder (Ndlovu-Gatsheni 2000: 60). Occupying the immediate lower level were the abeNhla from the north, comprising mostly the Sotho and Tswana. Together, these two groups represented the population of the Ndebele whose ancestors originated south of the Limpopo River. The amaHole were at the bottom. Given this high level of assimilation of groups of people who had never identified themselves as Ndebele, to talk of a fully fledged Ndebele tribe existing independently from this intermingling and dilution by incorporated groups would be misleading and ahistorical. Therefore, the question of who is really Ndebele and who is not remains an ongoing debate.

The language and culture of immigrants formed the bedrock of the language and culture of the Ndebele, even though the immigrants were in the minority – about 33 per cent (Beach 1980: 16). In terms of religion, the Ndebele assimilated the Kalanga belief in the Mwari cult. Mzilikazi and, subsequently, his son Lobhengula, honoured the Mwari cult.

Present-day Ndebele ethnicity can therefore best be described as being the result of self-conscious membership of a multi-ethnic state in the nineteenth century, as well as a twentieth-century invention. Ranger (1985: 25) identifies the the colonial administrators from Natal as the twentieth-century inventors of this ethnicity and says they viewed 'the Ndebele' in the colonial image of 'the Zulu' and paid Ndebele chiefs, who were only too ready to accept such a glamorous and authoritarian identity. In Ranger's opinion, although the Rhodesian government did not seek to create some form of Ndebele 'homeland', the settlers' invention of 'the Ndebele' contributed to the imposition of the colonial hegemonic state. Therefore, the emergence of the Ndebele to prominence as an ethnic grouping in historiography has its roots in the colonial machinery's invention of tradition and tribalism in the land stretching between the Limpopo and Zambezi rivers.

The Shona and the Ndebele in the postcolonial period

Zimbabwe attained its independence in 1980. The two main groups of people who participated in the Zimbabwean war of liberation were the Shona and the Ndebele. The first local nationalist political movement formed with the aim of liberating

Zimbabwe was the Zimbabwe African People's Union (ZAPU). However, as a result of ideological differences, two distinct political movements were formed; namely ZAPU, which was almost entirely Ndebele, and the Zimbabwe African National Union (ZANU), which had a large following of Shona people. They shared the same vision of liberating Zimbabwe. ZANU later split in 1975 into two wings: ZANU–PF (Zimbabwe African National Union – Patriotic Front), loyal to Robert Mugabe, and ZANU–Ndonga, loyal to Ndabaningi Sithole. At independence, most Shona closely identified themselves with ZANU–PF and most Ndebele with ZAPU. The postcolonial state had the daunting task of bridging the ethnic and regional disparities created by colonialism. However, before the government could attain this, there was a gradual growth of discontent among the Ndebele, who were disillusioned by what has been termed the 'politics of exclusion', especially in the political administration of the newly formed state of Zimbabwe.

The serious ethnic and regional divisions that characterised 1980 to 1997 cascaded into what was then referred to the Gukurahundi, which was an effort by the incumbent government to flush out the dissidents (the name comes from chiShona, roughly translating as 'early rain that washes away the chaff before spring rains'). James Muzondidya (2009) asserts that no episode in the history of Zimbabwe better represents the broad failure of the government's coercive tactics than the ZAPU-ZANU–PF conflict that broke out in Matabeleland. Though it started out as a political conflict between two nationalist parties with different visions, the conflict later assumed ethnic and regional dimensions as a result of the number of events and processes (Ranger 1985: 184).[1] Thus, the invention of ethnicity and tribalism, which is largely a legacy of colonialism, has continued in the postcolonial era to dictate the relations between the Shona and Ndebele. The contestations over regionalism and ethnicism are no longer as hostile as they were soon after independence, mainly as a result of the Unity Accord signed between ZAPU and ZANU–PF in 1987. However, former members of ZAPU withdrew from the Unity Accord in 2008, thus dissolving their alliance with ZANU–PF, and reformed ZAPU.

---

1. Gukurahundi is now widely regarded as a state-sanctioned massacre – more than 20 000 people were killed. https://www.theguardian.com/world/2015/may/19/mugabe-zimbabwe-gukurahundi-massacre-matabeleland.

The resignation of former president Robert Mugabe in November 2017 has opened up a new period for Zimbabwe. However, the fact that the current president, Emmerson Mnangagwa, is believed to be one of the architects of the Gukurahundi massacre remains a problem in Ndebele-Shona relations, as well as affecting the responses of the people of Matabeleland to the Mnangagwa presidency.[2] While Mnangagwa reportedly denies involvement in the massacre, the Gukurahundi remains an issue that he cannot wish away.[3] Besides the issue of the Gukurahundi massacre, certain international sources claim that he will begin a neo-liberal period in the country. However, it is uncertain how this will affect the Zimbabwean population.[4]

References

Beach. D.N. 1980. *The Shona and Zimbabwe, 900–1850: An Outline of Shona History*. Gweru: Mambo Press.

Chimhundu, H. 1992. 'Early Missionaries and the Ethnolinguistic Factor during the "Invention of Tribalism" in Zimbabwe'. *Journal of African History* 33(1): 87–109.

Makoni, S., J. Brutt-Griffler and P. Mashiri. 2007. 'The Use of "Indigenous" and Urban Vernaculars in Zimbabwe'. *Language in Society* 36(1): 25–49.

Mazarire, G.C. 2009. 'Reflection on Pre-colonial Zimbabwe *c.*850–1880s'. In *Becoming Zimbabwe: A History from the Pre-colonial Period to 2008*, edited by B. Raftopoulos and A. Mlambo, 1–38. Harare: Weaver Press.

Muzondidya, J. 2009. 'From Buoyancy to Crisis, 1980–1997'. In *Becoming Zimbabwe: A History from the Pre-colonial Period to 2008*, edited by B. Raftopoulos and A. Mlambo, 167–200. Harare: Weaver Press.

Ndlovu-Gatsheni, S.J. 2000. 'The Post-colonial State and Matabeleland'. In *Violence & Memory: One Hundred Years in the 'Dark Forests' of Matabeleland*, edited by J. Alexander, J. McGregor and T. Ranger, 17–38. Oxford: James Currey.

Ranger, T.O. 1985. *The Invention of Tribalism in Zimbabwe*. Gweru: Mambo Press.

Rasmussen, R.K. 1977. *Mzilikazi of the Ndebele*. London: Heinemann.

---

2. https://mg.co.za/article/2017-11-24-00-gukurahundi-ghosts-haunt-mnangagwa.
3. https://www.biznews.com/thought-leaders/2017/11/29/mnangagwa-zimbabwe-gukurahundi-killings/.
4. http://www.aljazeera.com/news/2018/01/eyes-zimbabwes-mnangagwa-wef-davos-180124125748504.html.

INTRODUCTION

The Study of Zimbabwean Music by Zimbabwean Scholars

Luis Gimenez Amoros

This book provides a transdisciplinary approach to Zimbabwean music by Zimbabwean scholars. It not only covers aspects of Zimbabwean music from a musicological point of view, but also opens up a wide range of subjects of broad academic interest in Africa and elsewhere. Themes of interest include music and land reform; nationalism in relation to musical culture in Zimbabwe; music with regard to the youth (such as dancehall music); the use of gospel music for religious and political purposes; the interrelation of specific types of music (for instance, *mbira*) in rural and urban spaces; the relationship between people living across borders (for instance, Shona-speakers along the border of Zimbabwe and Mozambique); current understandings of the liberation struggles since 1980; historical approaches to Zimbabwean music during colonial times; and music and gender.

The importance of a transdisciplinary study on Zimbabwean music

This book aims to provide a solid foundation for future studies on Zimbabwean music, either historically (in the precolonial and colonial eras) or in the contemporary (postcolonial) period. Departing from a purely musicological perspective, this book also analyses the different musical realities in Zimbabwean musical culture, such as Zimdancehall, *mbira*, *sungura* and *chimurenga*. Furthermore, it provides a study of the functionality of traditional dances such as *chinyambera*, *jichi* and *xinombela* in both a traditional and a contemporary context. Sociologically, these musical cultures in Zimbabwe reflect the political and economic texts in which music is produced. The importance of this book is perhaps its ability to provide various perspectives on Zimbabwean music from different disciplines in the humanities by Zimbabwean scholars, and its exploration of relevant and contemporary aspects of music that have not been studied by international scholars, such as certain historical approaches, gender studies, sociological aspects of music in urban and rural areas, or the music industry in Zimbabwe.

The editors of this book believe that a transdisciplinary book on Zimbabwean music written by local scholars is important for the study of Zimbabwean music because it offers a valuable contribution to postcolonial studies. Furthermore, the transdisciplinary study of music functions to demonstrate the importance of music in its social context in Zimbabwean studies. The book examines music as an artistic and social form of expression and, thus, it examines Zimbabwean music from two perspectives; namely, the participant (musicians) and observer (audience). This dual perspective is highlighted with reference to rural or urban spaces, and gender. As a result of this duality, the semiotic relationship between music and society is addressed throughout the book. The book also provides perspectives on musical cultures that reignite debates on topics that would not normally be accessible to international scholars in the Global North. Therefore, this book breaks new ground essential for the study of Zimbabwean music.

International scholars writing on Zimbabwean music since the sixteenth century
The first reference to Zimbabwean music by a Westerner is found in 1586 – the Portuguese missionary Father João dos Santos writing about *mbira* music (Tracey 2015: 130). Andrew Tracey (132) also makes a reference to the German explorer Carl Mauch, who attempted to transcribe three *mbira* tunes performed near Great Zimbabwe in 1872. These references feasibly help us to prove the existence of *mbira* music for more than 430 years, but they do not provide any information about the musicological study of *mbira* music or its semiotic interaction with society.

Since the 1940s international scholars have regularly published academic studies on Zimbabwean music. In particular, general studies of lamellophones (*mbiras*) have been extensive, as evidenced by the work of international scholars such as Arthur Morris Jones (1949), Hugh Tracey (1961), Gerhard Kubik (1964, 1965), Robert Kauffman (1969, 1972); Andrew Tracey (1970, 2015); Paul Berliner (1975); John Kaemmer (1989); Ernest Brown (1994); Thomas Turino (1998), Johannes Brusila (2002); Banning Eyre (2015) and Tony Perman (2015). These scholars have written on different aspects of *mbira* music, although, according to many academics, the most popularised study of *mbira* music is *The Soul of Mbira* (Berliner 1978). Berliner offers extensive research on the *mbira* and its social context in rural areas, where it functioned to connect families with their ancestors through all-night *bira* ceremonies.

INTRODUCTION

In contrast to the ethnographies on Zimbabwean music by international scholars, this transdisciplinary study offers a specific study of *mbira* music in different rural and urban contexts from insiders' points of view by scholars such as Perminus Matiure (Chapter 1) or Vimbai Chamisa (Chapter 6). Matiure is an *mbira* performer and the head of the Music Department at Midlands State University in Gweru. He offers a new musicological perspective on *mbira* music from a practical and creative point of view, given that he is able to provide a self-reflectivity about the migration of *mbira* music into urban spaces in postcolonial Zimbabwe.[1] Matiure provides new views on *mbira* music in rural and urban spaces from his position both as an academic and as a Zimbabwean, and from this particular context, contests Berliner's popularised *mbira* studies.

Apart from the studies on lamellophones in Zimbabwe, there have been other aspects international scholars have focused on – for example, Turino's (1998) work on the notions of nationalism, cosmopolitanism and globalisation in Zimbabwean music from the 1950s to the late twentieth century. Turino's study is mostly based on urban spaces in an attempt to focus on different forms of music that portray Zimbabwean identity in colonial and postcolonial times. The author uses cosmopolitanism and globalisation to examine the influence of external musical genres in Zimbabwe since the 1960s, such as jazz, kwela, Congolese rumba and Kenyan benga. Turino also discusses *chimurenga* music through the influence of *mbira* and electric ensembles in the post-1980 era. However, most of Turino's work focuses on Harare and not other cities in Zimbabwe, such as Bulawayo and Gweru. In contrast, this book is a combination of various studies on Zimbabwean music in different urban contexts, including popularised music genres such as Zimdancehall.

In relation to the study of music in Harare, Barbara Mahamba and Azon Twala's work on the history of Mbare (a township in Harare) from its genesis in 1907 to the 1970s (Chapter 7) serves to draw a comparison with Turino's study on the music in Harare. Mahamba and Twala emphasise the importance of the black middle-class population in sustaining the musical culture in the historical township of Mbare during colonial times. The middle-class black population rented venues or helped

---

1. With regard to the rural and urban context of *bira* ceremonies, Andrew Tracey made a documentary entitled *Mbira Dzavadzimu: Urban and Rural Ceremonies with Hakurotwi Mudhe* (1975). This documentary is a valuable resource to understand the different aspects of *bira* ceremonies in urban and rural Zimbabwe.

to provide income to artists, so that within the oppressed black population, the richest ones tended to help to sustain the local culture economically and through venue provision.

Another relevant aspect studied by international scholars on Zimbabwean music is music censorship during postcolonial Zimbabwe and more specifically after 2000 (Eyre (2001, 2004, 2015; Thram 2006). Eyre, for example, analyses the different forms of music censorship by the postcolonial Zimbabwean state. Eyre's book (2001) mostly concentrates on the post-2000 era when the new agrarian reform took place in the country and many artists served to promote the state policies as a response to the political threat of the Movement for Democratic Change (MDC). As a result, Eyre offers a reflection on how state politics was able to control musical expression in Zimbabwe. In relation to the discussion on music censorship in Zimbabwe, this book offers different points of view from insiders on music during the land reform process. In Chapter 3 Innocent Tinashe Mutero offers an in-depth analysis of how *chinyambera* dance in Gweru provides a criticism of the Zimbabwe African National Union – Patriotic Front (ZANU–PF) policy and a form of artistic resistance towards censorship law in Zimbabwe. In Chapter 10 Bridget Chinouriri and Munyaradzi Nyakudya offer valuable criticism of how land reform policy structured music production during the 2000s in order to promote the state's view of new forms of equality through land redistribution.

Zimbabwean scholars writing on Shona music

Since independence in 1980, several books essential for music education in Zimbabwe have been written and published by Zimbabwean scholars – for example, *Music Rocking from Zimbabwe* (Zindi 2013), *Women Musicians of Zimbabwe* (Makwenda 2013), *Songs That Won the Liberation War* (Pongweni 1982) and *Zimbabwe Township Music* (Makwenda 2005). A more recent publication is Mhoze Chikowero's *African Music, Power, and Being in Colonial Zimbabwe* (2015). Chikowero's book is a detailed description of how local music was contested in colonial Zimbabwe by Rhodesian forces. The author addresses the importance of music during the liberation struggle, from its genesis in the 1890s to the independence of Zimbabwe. Chikowero points out the representation and sovereignty of Zimbabwean culture as a social form of resistance during colonial times and as the representation of national culture after independence. Our transdisciplinary book offers a wider array of opinions of Zimbabwean scholars with regard to the different historical periods mentioned above. Together,

Chikowero's contribution and this book will offer new academic literature on Zimbabwean music by local scholars.

The narratives of Zimbabwean scholars on the study of Zimbabwean music have been extensive in academic journals from the Global South, such as *Muziki: Journal of Music Research in Africa* or the *Journal of the Musical Arts in Africa*. One of the most published scholars has been Maurice Vambe. Although Vambe's discipline is based on English literature in Africa, he has been able to cover many issues regarding Zimbabwean music, such as the notion of *chimurenga* (2004, 2011); music and gender in post-independence Zimbabwe (Rwafa and Vambe 2007). In particular, it is important to mention that the notion of *chimurenga* (from the Shona, 'revolutionary struggle') covers three main periods in the music of resistance and independence in present-day postcolonial Zimbabwe: the first liberation war between Zimbabweans and the British in the 1890s; the war of independence against the Rhodesians during the 1970s and the agrarian reform in the 2000s as a revolutionary input promoted and implanted by the state. The notion of *chimurenga* has been used and contested by different Zimbabwean scholars to describe the various historical periods – see, for example, Andrew Manyawu (2014), Vongai Nyawo (2012) and Memory Chirere (2008).

There have also been Zimbabwean scholars who have concentrated on other aspects of music – for instance, Blandina Makina (2009) on the music of Sam Monro as a white Shona-rapper regarding his criticism towards the state and Ezra Chitando, Masiiwa Ragies Gunda and Joachim Kügler's (2007) edited collection on the use of Christian religion in the social discourse of Zimbabwean music. Furthermore, one has to emphasise the various doctoral dissertations and Master's theses – for example, Mickias Musiyiwa's (2013) doctorate, 'The Narrativization of Post-2000 Zimbabwe in the Shona Popular Song-Genre: An Appraisal Approach', offers an in-depth analysis of the uses of history and musical culture by the political elite in Zimbabwe in order to produce new music that emphasises the goals of the government, thereby providing an insider's perspective on a topic previously only written about by international scholars such as Eyre (2004). Vimbai Chamisa's PhD is an examination of the music industry in Zimbabwe in relation to popular musical styles such as *jiti*, *mbira* and *chimurenga*. Laina Gumboreshumba's (2009) Master's thesis offers a unique analysis of Andrew Tracey's contribution to the analysis of *mbira* music by providing an organised and concise study of the *mbiras* found in Zimbabwe.

Chapter summary
The chapters in this book have been organised into parts as follows: (1) Indigenous ('traditional') music and its transformations; (2) Zimbabwean urban popular music across time; and (3) The rise of dancehall in Zimbabwe: regarding transdisciplinary studies.

Part I: Indigenous music and its transformations
This part is made up of various transdisciplinary chapters that analyse the continuum of traditional music and its transformations in Zimbabwe through education, the music industry, gender studies and film.

In Chapter 1 Perminus Matiure offers an analysis of *mbira* music in urban spaces, mostly focusing on Gweru and to a lesser extent Harare. Matiure covers the historical period from 1980 to 2015 and shows how *mbira* music migrated from rural to urban spaces. The chapter provides a criticism of other literature on *mbira* music by international scholars with regard to the use of *mbira* and how the urban context affects the way in which *mbira* performances are different, depending on whether they are in rural or urban areas. The urban performances are meant for entertainment; therefore, the spiritual cosmos of *mbira* based on calling the spirits is restricted to rural areas.

With regard to rural areas, in Chapter 2 Renias Ngara and Doreen Sibanda offer a study of the Karanga and Tsonga people in relation to the educational codes of certain dances that promote gender equality and virginity as a social value among adolescents in Chiredzi and Mberengwa in southern Zimbabwe. These dances are the *xinombela* in Tsonga and the *jichi* in Karanga.

In Chapter 3 Innocent Tinashe Mutero analyses how *chinyambera* dance is used to build criticism against the Zimbabwean state. He exposes *chinyambera* dance as a form of resistance in relation to the different forms of music censorship by the Zimbabwean state. Mutero provides a musical and social analysis of the *chinyambera* dance band, Tavirima, and its performances as a form of necessary rebellious expression in urban spaces such as Gweru.

In Chapter 4 Renias Ngara examines the gender roles in Shangwe dances among adolescents in the Gokwe region. This chapter provides insight into the functionality of dance and its various messages related to the period before entering into adulthood for teenagers. It both values and questions the hierarchical systems of the elders in the Gokwe region.

In Chapter 5 Maurice Vambe explores the film *If Vagina Had Teeth* and the rainmaking ceremonies of the Shona people of western Mozambique. He analyses the notion of Shona identity and its similarities and differences in Zimbabwe and Mozambique, through the Manyika and Ndau people respectively. In addition, he also touches on the power of Shona women to control men's actions in a patriarchal society through rainmaking ceremonies. In general, this chapter provides a valuable view on Shona culture with reference to the borders imposed during colonialism that separate the Shona people in Mozambique and Zimbabwe.

In this part of the book, a study of the Zimbabwean music industry provides a valuable criticism of the values and representations of national music, as well as the sustainability of this industry in a national context. Vimbai Chamisa's Chapter 6 examines the use of *mbira* music by contemporary artists, such as Oliver Mtukudzi, Chiwoniso Maraire and Thomas Mapfumo. The musical arrangements by these artists are often based on the polyrhythmic variations of *mbira* music and the influence of certain traditional songs such as 'Nemamusasa', 'Nyamaropa', 'Taireva' and 'Bangidza'. The artists mentioned above are promoted internationally as 'Made in Zimbabwe' because their music is based on traditional *mbira* variations or, at the very least, on the use of lamellophones during live performances.

Part II: Zimbabwean urban popular music across time

In this part of the book the semiotic understanding of music during the colonial and postcolonial period is brought out and Zimbabwean culture along the southern African borders and is also considered.

In Chapter 7 Barbara Mahamba and Azon Twala provide an in-depth analysis of the township of Mbare in Harare from 1907 when the first residential area of black people was established in the capital. Mahamba and Twala emphasise the importance of the black middle class in sustaining musical culture from the beginning of the twentieth century until independence.

Victoria Butete's Chapter 8 is a deep analysis of the Zimbabwean music industry in relation to the interaction of musicians and promoters. Butete's chapter addresses the challenges for Zimbabwean artists, including (but not exclusively) the economic problems since 2000. In addition, Butete provides a valuable critique of the interactions between musicians and the music industry's agents in Zimbabwe, portraying the difficulties Zimbabwean musicians have in sustaining themselves through music.

Urther Rwafa's Chapter 9 examines Simon Chimbetu's lyrics as representations of the voiceless in colonial and postcolonial Zimbabwe in both urban and rural areas. Chimbetu is not only a respected musician in Zimbabwe, he also participated in the liberation struggle during the 1970s. Thus, Rwafa's analysis of Chimbetu's lyrics provides an important analysis of a Zimbabwean's sentiments during the different phases of independence and post-independence. According to Rwafa, Chimbetu's lyrics portray a nationalist sentiment as much as a valuable criticism of the Zimbabwean government.

As part of historical research on Zimbabwean music, in Chapter 10 Bridget Chinouriri and Munyaradzi Nyakudya examine the use of music during the land reform from 2000 to 2010. The redistribution of the land in Zimbabwe has been one of the most extensively discussed academic topics in Zimbabwe and generally in Africa. This chapter offers an examination of how the government used music to promote the land reform in Zimbabwe. Given that after independence most of the land was occupied by 4 500 white farmers, the necessity to redistribute the land was clear, but was also used as a form of control by the government in the 2000s. This chapter provides an account of the first ten years of the agrarian reform programme and shows how music played an important role during this period.

Part III: The rise of dancehall in Zimbabwe – regarding transdisciplinary studies
In Chapter 11 Rekopantswe Mate offers an analysis on Zimdancehall as a musical style that connects the artists with the people who live in the townships around Harare. Mate analyses the socio-economic context of the 2000s and how it affected the Zimdancehall industry as a system of piracy, promoters, fans and media.

On the theme of music and gender studies in urban spaces, this book offers two chapters on Zimdancehall in relation to manhood and the objectification of women. In Chapter 12 Manase Kudzai Chiweshe and Sandra Bhatasara examine the hegemonic masculinities of Zimdancehall, such as certain attitudes by male artists towards the control of women's agency. This chapter also provides an explanation of the social conditions of male Zimdancehall artists, with regard to unemployment and the patriarchal forms of survival in harsh economic conditions in Zimbabwe.

In Chapter 13 Ruby Magosvongwe examines songs in Shona by some of the emergent Zimdancehall artists, such as Tocky Vibes, Shinsoman and Killer T. In Chapter 14 Itai Muwati, Tinotenda Mwamuka and Charles Tembo critique the stereotype of African women as docile and explore how their agency is portrayed in Zimdancehall lyrics.

Finally, Zifikile Makwavarara and Albert Nyathi provide an analysis of Zimdancehall in Bulawayo produced in Ndebele. The authors observe that Zimdancehall in Ndebele has been highly influenced by South African kwaito, given its close relationship to Tswana, Zulu and Sesotho.

In total, the different parts of this book provide an analytical overview of Zimbabwean music that could become the foundation of further studies on the subject. It is hoped that this books shows Zimbabwean music as a legitimate terrain in postcolonial literature for local and international scholars and also proves the value of Zimbabwean scholars' offerings on this and other related themes.

References

Berliner, P. 1975. 'Music and Spirit Possession at a Shona *Bira*'. *African Music* 5(4): 130–9.

———. 1978. *The Soul of Mbira: Music and Traditions of the Shona People of Zimbabwe*. Chicago: University of Chicago Press.

Brown, E.D. 1994. 'The Guitar and the "Mbira": Resilience, Assimilation, and Pan-Africanism in Zimbabwean Music'. *The World of Music* 36(2): 73–117.

Brusila, J. 2002. '"Modern Traditional" Music from Zimbabwe: Virginia Mukwesha's Mbira Record "Matare"'. In *Playing with Identities in Contemporary Music in Africa*, edited by M. Palmberg and A. Kirkegaard, 35–46. Uppsala: Nordiska Afrikainstitutet.

Chamisa, V. 2014. 'Commodified Versions of Shona Indigenous Music: (Re)construction Tradition in Zimbabwean Popular Music'. PhD diss., University of the Witwatersrand, Johannesburg.

Chikowero, M. 2015. *African Music, Power, and Being in Colonial Zimbabwe*. Bloomington: Indiana University Press.

Chirere, M. 2008. 'To Whom Does Oliver Mtukudzi Belong?' *Muziki* 5(1): 111–23.

Chitando, E., M.R. Gunda and J. Kügler (eds). 2014. *Prophets, Profits and the Bible in Zimbabwe: Festschrift for Aynos Masotcha Moyo*. Bamberg: University of Bamberg Press.

Eyre, B. 2001. *Playing with Fire: Fear and Self-Censorship in Zimbabwean Music*. Copenhagen: Freemuse.

———. 2004. 'Playing with Fire: Manipulation of Music and Musicians in Zimbabwe'. In *Shoot the Singer! Music Censorship Today*, edited by M. Korpe, 94–105. London: Zed Books.

———. 2015. 'Thomas Mapfumo and the Popularization of Shona Mbira'. *African Music* 10(1): 84–101.

Gumboreshumba, L. 2009. 'Understanding Form and Technique: Andrew Tracey's Contribution to Knowledge of Lamellophone (Mbira) Music of Southern Africa'. M.Mus. thesis, Rhodes University, Grahamstown.

Jones, A.M. 1949. 'African Music'. *African Affairs* 48(193): 290–7.

Kaemmer, J.E. 1989. 'Social Power and Music Change among the Shona'. *Ethnomusicology* 33(1): 31–45.

Kauffman, R. 1969. 'Some Aspects of Aesthetics in the Shona Music of Rhodesia'. *Ethnomusicology* 13(3): 507–11.

———. 1972. 'Shona Urban Music and the Problem of Acculturation'. *Yearbook of the International Folk Music Council* 4: 47–56.
Kubik, G. 1964. 'Xylophone Playing in Southern Uganda'. *Journal of the Royal Anthropological Institute of Great Britain and Ireland* 94(2): 138–59.
———. 1965. 'Transcription of Mangwilo Xylophone Music from Film Strips'. *African Music* 3(4): 35–51.
Makina, B. 2009. 'Re-thinking White Narratives: Popular Songs and Protest Discourse in Post-colonial Zimbabwe'. *Muziki* 6(2): 221–31.
Makwenda. J. 2005. *Zimbabwe Township Music*. Harare: Storytime Promotions.
———. 2013. *Women Musicians of Zimbabwe*. Harare: Storytime Promotions.
Manyawu, A.T. 2014. 'The Construction of Uhuru Party Group Identity in Zimbabwe: A Textual Analysis of Revolutionary Songs in Shona'. *South African Journal of African Languages* 34(1): 49–63.
Musiyiwa, M. 2013. 'The Narrativization of Post-2000 Zimbabwe in the Shona Popular Song-Genre: An Appraisal Approach'. PhD diss., University of Stellenbosch, Stellenbosch.
Nyawo, V.Z. 2012. 'Rhythms of Resistance: Chants That Propelled Zimbabwe's Third Chimurenga'. *Muziki* 9(2): 53–65.
Perman, T. 2015. 'A Tale of Two Mbiras'. *African Music* 10(1): 102–25.
Pongweni, J.C. 1982. *Songs That Won the Liberation War*. Harare: College Press.
Rwafa, U. and M.T. Vambe. 2007. '"Hear Our Voices": Female Popular Musicians in Post-independence Zimbabwe'. *Muziki* 4(1): 66–86.
Thram, D. 2006. 'Patriotic History and the Politicisation of Memory: Manipulation of Popular Music to Re-invent the Liberation Struggle in Zimbabwe'. *Critical Arts* 20(2): 75–88.
Tracey, A. 1970. 'The Matepe Mbira Music of Rhodesia'. *African Music* 4(4): 37–61.
———. 2015. 'The System of the Mbira'. *African Music* 10(1): 127–49.
Tracey, H. 1961. 'A Case for the Name *Mbira*'. *African Music* 2(4): 17–25.
Turino, T. 1998. 'The Mbira, Worldbeat, and the International Imagination'. *The World of Music* 40(2): 85–106.
Vambe, M.T. 2004. 'Versions and Sub-versions: Trends in *Chimurenga* Musical Discourses of Post-independence Zimbabwe'. *African Study Monographs* 25(4): 167–93.
———. 2011. 'Rethinking the Notion of *Chimurenga* in the Context of Political Change in Zimbabwe'. *Muziki* 8(2): 1–28.
Zindi, F. 2013. *Music Rocking from Zimbabwe*. Harare: Zindisc Publishing.

Part I

Indigenous Music
and Its Transformations

CHAPTER 1

Mbira in Urban Spaces
Mbira-making and the Multiple Contexts of Zvirimudeze Mbira Ensemble Performances in Zimbabwe

Perminus Matiure

This chapter explores the paradigm shift that *mbira* has experienced in its adoption and adaption in the urban environments of Zimbabwe. It is apparent that there are aspects of *mbira* that have changed to suit the contemporary environment in a postcolonial framework. The period under discussion is from when Zimbabwe attained its independence (1980) until 2015 and the chapter focuses on Harare, the capital city of Zimbabwe, as well as Gweru the provincial capital of the Midlands Province. These locations were chosen because several active *mbira* ensembles that evolved as a result of the shift of *mbira* performance from rural to urban spaces soon after independence are active in these areas.

The data that furnishes this chapter was collected through applied action research methodology, which resonates with the theory of applied ethnomusicology. Charles Keil (1982) sees applied ethnomusicology as a field whose parameters go beyond academic application. Klisala Harrison, Elizabeth Mackinlay and Svanibor Pettan (2010: 1) agree in their definition of applied ethnomusicology as 'the approach guided by principle of social responsibility, which extends the usual academic goal of broadening and developing knowledge and understanding towards solving concrete problems and working both inside and beyond typical academic contexts'. Or, as Rebecca Dirksen (2012: 2) puts it: 'In reality, applied research is central to the field and increasing in importance.'

Harrison, Mackinlay and Pettan (2010) and Dirksen (2012) outline the main concerns of applied ethnomusicology. Relevant to this chapter are artistic representation, recontextualisation and adaptation, performance practices and cosmopolitanism. Given that the core of this chapter is based on the urbanisation of *mbira* during recent postcolonial times in Zimbabwe, it mainly refers to the Zvirimudeze Mbira Ensemble on issues concerning the performance of *mbira* in the urban spaces of Gweru and Harare, although other active *mbira* ensembles are also mentioned.

The theory alluded to above advocates practical engagement by researchers in order to solve problems affecting the community, especially problems related to music. Daniel Avorgbedor (1992) calls for interventions based on applied ethnomusicology to help to resolve the cultural changes caused by modern forces such as rural to urban migration. Emphasis is on the experience and cyclic systems in which planning, followed by implementation, then evaluation and back to planning again becomes the common phenomenon.

The word *mbira*, as referred to in organology, means a type of instrument characterised by metal keys mounted on a wooden soundboard (*gwariva*). The aggregates of the keys are also called *mbira*, which is generically referred to in some texts as lamellophone. There are different *mbira* instruments in Zimbabwe and these are historically associated with particular Shona communities such as the Korekore, Manyika, Zezuru, Karanga, Ndau and Tonga groups. These instruments are known by a variety of names: *mbira huru*, also referred to as *mbira dzavadzimu* or *nhare*, which is commonly associated with the Zezuru; *mbira njari*, which is associated with the Zezuru and the Karanga; *mbira dzavatonga*, belonging to the Tonga people; *matepe* and *munyonga*, both associated with the Zezuru; and *karimba*, also commonly known as *nyunganyunga*, which is commonly taught in schools and institutions of higher learning.

During the precolonial period some of these *mbiras* were well known and used frequently in traditional ceremonies among the Shona people. However, with the passage of time, some of the instruments underwent transformations to suit modern environments. The *mbiras* that have secured a firm place in the contemporary music industry are *nyunganyunga* and *mbira huru* because these two *mbiras* are some of the instruments that were accommodated in urban spaces, schools and institutions. The other reason is that most of the teachers who introduced traditional instruments in schools were either *dzavadzimu* or *nyunganyunga* players. The adaptability of *mbira dzavadzimu* and *nyunganyunga* has culminated in the evolution of the concept of the *dandaro* ceremony in an urban context. *Mbira* players who migrated to towns occasionally met to play *mbira* as a continuation of the rural *bira* practice. These ceremonies were then named *matandaro* (plural of *dandaro*).

The *dandaro* ceremony is a modern *mbira* performance commonly practised in towns to entertain people in beer halls and restaurants. In some cases the ceremony is used to replace the traditional *bira* commonly practised in rural areas. *Matandaro* performances have enabled *mbira* to secure a space in urban areas through staged performance.

This chapter addresses issues concerning the recontextualization of *mbira* and the evolution of the contemporary *matandaro* ceremonies in urban areas of Zimbabwe. It discusses how *mbira* music has been popularised and commercialised through recording and radio broadcasting. *Mbira dzavadzimu*'s space in the contemporary *dandaro* is also interrogated by discussing the various modern contexts in which it is performed.

The chapter identifies and discusses aspects of the cultural legacy of *mbira dzavadzimu* that have changed to adjust to and accommodate contemporary styles of music. These changes are the tuning systems, the use of microphone pickups to amplify the sound of the *mbira* and also the hybridisation of *mbira dzavadzimu* by adding some keys to the common *mbiras*. It also uncovers aspects of how *mbira* is constructed in the modern environment. The general thesis overarching this chapter is that the growth of *mbira* in Zimbabwe has been as a result of researchers whose works are informed by applied ethnomusicology and also that urban *matandaro* practices have become a reliable platform for the sustainability of the legacy of *mbira* in Zimbabwe.

Evolution of *matandaro* practices

The word *dandaro* is derived from the Shona word *kutandara*, which means 'leisure/social time'. When people have nothing special to do, they occupy themselves with activities that are meant to entertain them. In the early postcolonial period family members engaged in different entertainment activities – for instance, grandfathers or grandmothers would gather and narrate folktales about the rabbit (*tsuro*) and the baboon (*gudo*) to their grandchildren. It was also during these *matandaro* that the elders taught the young about their cultural norms and values (*tsika*), proverbs (*tsumo*) and idioms (*madimikira*). It was also at times such as these that family members were entertained by *mbira* players. Thus members of a family had time to socialise either by listening to tales or music before going to sleep and even during the day when they had nothing important to do. The role of *dandaro* in this case is to provide an opportunity for family members to interact socially through singing, dancing and tales. The concept of *dandaro* is a common feature among the Shona, especially during the winter season when people take a break from intense farming activities. The use of *dandaro* as a means of entertainment for family members has been described at a micro level, but it can also be perceived from a macro level where it is used to entertain community members.

The evolution of *dandaro* in towns is attributed to the urban migration of Shona people, necessitated by the emergence of towns in Zimbabwe in the early 1890s. When the Europeans arrived in Zimbabwe, they established industries and factories and this culminated in the evolution of towns. Many Shona people, especially men, left their homes to seek employment in towns such as Salisbury (now Harare), Bulawayo, Gwelo (now Gweru) and other smaller towns such as Masvingo, Kwekwe, Kadoma, Chegutu and Marondera. Among those who moved to towns, *mbira* players and makers also migrated to work in firms and industries and this resulted in *mbira* gaining momentum in urban spaces.

Paul Berliner (1993: 187) asserts that '*mbira* music is a regular part of the most recent development of the *dandaro* or *matandaro*, which have been growing in popularity in townships'. The difference between a traditional *bira* and a *dandaro* ceremony is that *matandaro* are conducted in urban areas and focus more on social interaction than the traditional sacred function of *biras*. Berliner again: '*Matandaro* are also characterized by medium spirit manifestations similar in some respects to the *bira* but modified for compatibility with urban lifestyles.' Claire Jones (2008: 125) confirms that *mbira* ensembles were responsible for 'entertaining patrons in the beer gardens and nightclubs of Harare's townships'. Harare as an urban area is completely different from the traditional rural areas where *mbira* is performed for religious purposes during a *bira* ceremony. Even participants during shows in beer gardens and nightclubs are different in the sense that they comprise of people from different Shona communities such as Zezuru, Korekore, Karanga, Ndau and Manyika, just to mention a few. Their presence at such shows does not have a common goal with that of a traditional *bira*. *Mbira dzavadzimu* was previously performed in contexts where participants were of the same lineage and having a common religious background and common goal.

When music migrates from its area of origin to other places, it does not only get transferred, but also modified and recontextualised. The same happened to the *mbira* music of the Shona when the *mbira* players migrated to towns. It was not only their music that adapted to the new cosmopolitan lifestyle, but also their ideologies and cultural practices. The performance of *mbira* in the context of urban-based '*bira*' re-emerged and then intensified with the passage of time. What happened was that families that were highly traditional started visiting each other to perform traditional *biras* in towns, where *mbira* was performed. However, they also ended up performing *mbira* in beer gardens to entertain people on Sundays.

The majority of performances were secular, rather sacred in nature. As a result, the *mbira* players termed these urban *mbira* performances *matandaro* to distinguish them from the traditional *bira* ceremonies. The emergence of *matandaro* in urban spaces resulted in the promotion of *mbira* through the preservation of *mbira* pieces; the distribution of *mbira* music through recording and radio; an increase in *mbira* players by formalising the teaching and learning of the instrument; the transformation of *mbira* performances and monetisation; the migration of *mbira* pieces, instruments and skills to overseas countries; and, more importantly, the innovation and hybridisation of the *mbira*.

Innovation and hybridity in *mbira* construction

In precolonial times, *mbira* construction was common in rural areas where *mbira* makers relied on natural and scrap materials obtained from plant, animal and mineral resources. *Mbira* soundboards were constructed using *mubvamaropa* (bloodwood) or *mufenje* (rock cabbage) trees. The *mbira* keys were made from minerals such as copper and iron (*mhangura*). The resonator (*deze*) was made from large pumpkin gourds. The *mbira* was passed on from generation to generation and so there was very little change in how the *mbira* was constructed. The use of a model *mbira* made it easy for *mbira* makers to reproduce the *mbiras* and also enabled the easy transmission of the instrument and its tunings from one generation to another with very minor changes.

However, the introduction of *mbira* in urban spaces, especially in institutions of learning, motivated *mbira* makers and teachers to research *mbira*, leading to the production of innovative ideas meant to improve the sonic efficacy of *mbira*. This was done by adding some keys or rearranging them to come up with different hybrids of the same model. The idea was to improve and enhance the sound and also to achieve a new sonic order on the *mbira* and/ or enable it to play certain songs that were not composed for *mbira* performance. An example of *mbira* makers who improved *mbira dzavadzimu* are the Mujuru *mbira* players. The addition of keys slightly changed the tuning system of the instrument to create a hybrid, which they named *dambatsoko* or *gandanga*. A well-known *mbira* maker who improved *nyunganyunga* by adding keys is Chaka Chawasarira.

I myself am an *mbira* player, maker, teacher and researcher. I have researched both *nyunganyunga* and *mbira dzavadzimu* and my findings enabled me to come up with six innovations of *mbira*. These hybrids are presented and discussed below.

Nyunganhare

I made the *nyunganhare* in 2006. It is a hybrid of *nhare*, also called *dzavadzimu*, and the Kwanongoma *nyunganyunga*.[1] The keys on the left are for *nhare* and those on right are for *nyunganyunga*. The resultant sound on the *nyunganhare* is also a combination of the *nyunganyunga* and the *nhare*. The instrument is therefore very handy when *nhare* and *nyunganyunga* are played together.

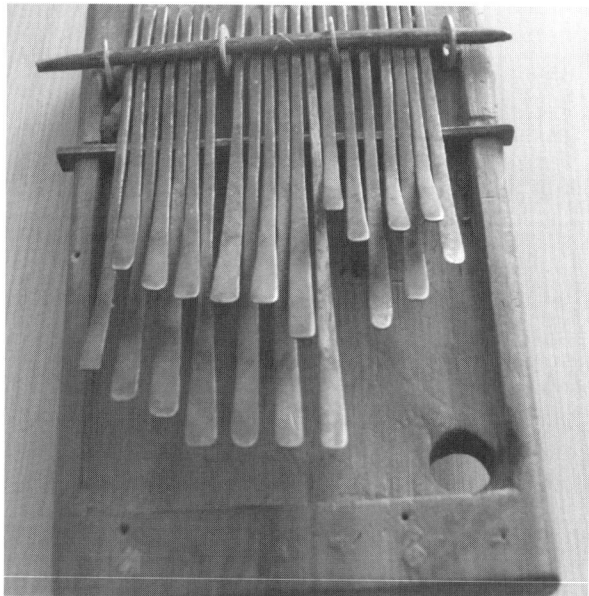

Figure 1.1 *Nyunganhare*

Karimbamutatu

Karimbamutatu is my 2010 innovation. The *mbira* has three hybrids of *nyunganyunga* mounted on one soundboard. The top *mbira* has seventeen keys added to the ordinary *nyunganyunga*. The entire *mbira* has keys belonging to the top register of the ordinary *nyunganyunga* tuned in C major (the term 'register' is taken to refer to relative highness or lowness of the pitch of the keys). The

---

1. Kwanongoma College of Music was established in 1962 in Bulawayo, the second-largest city in Zimbabwe. It was established under the directorship of Robert Simson for the purpose of reviving traditional music, which he felt was becoming extinct.

middle *mbira* is the ordinary *nyunganyunga*, but with an additional key, E flat. Usually a *nyunganyunga* in C has no E. The bottom *mbira* has fourteen keys tuned in the same way as the lower register of the ordinary *nyunganyunga*. You can play any of the *mbiras* or produce several combinations of the left and right sides of each *mbira*. This *mbira* can produce several variations by changing sides. Its construction of three-in-one also endorses Africanist philosophy, which advances the concept of communality. Having three *mbiras* on one soundboard is a symbol of collectivism, which is an important aspect of *unhu*/ubuntu. Nkonko Kamwangamalu (1999: 25–6) has this to say about ubuntu: 'Sociolinguistically, ubuntu is a multidimensional concept which represents the core values of African ontologies: respect for any human being, for human dignity and for human life, collective sharedness, obedience, humility, solidarity, caring, hospitality, interdependence, communalism, to mention but a few.'

'Collective sharedness' and 'communalism', in particular, are clearly portrayed in the *karimbamutatu*. The three *mbiras* share the same soundboard and the same resonator. Combining the left features of one *mbira* and the right of another illustrates communalism.

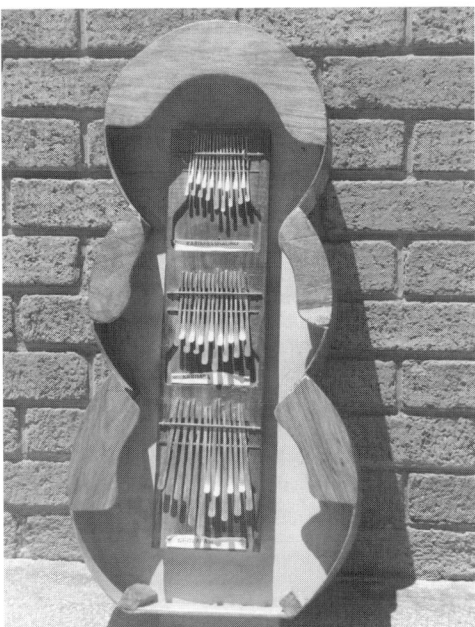

Figure 1.2 *Karimbamutatu*

Mbiragita

This is my most recent innovation, made in September 2015. The instrument was called *mbiragita* as it is a hybrid of a bass *mbira* with twelve keys tuned in C major mounted at the bottom and twelve corresponding strings, using the traditional gita form. Each *mbira* key has its own corresponding string, tuned to the same pitch. When playing this *mbira*, it is possible to play exactly the same way *mbira* keys are played on the strings. The instrument can also be played by mixing *mbira* keys and strings to give a unique sound.

Generally the motive behind the innovations presented above and others discussed below is to make the *mbira* more marketable and also to make the instrument compete with other modern musical instruments. It is also one way of perpetuating the legacy of *mbira* music.

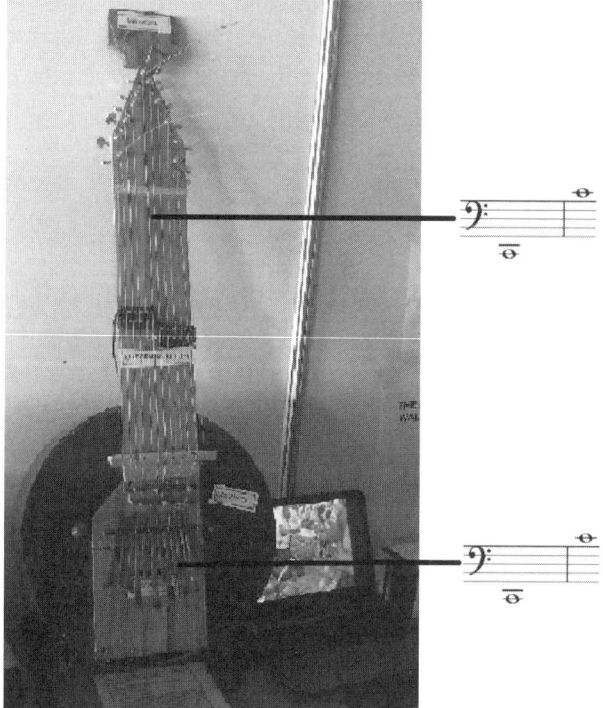

Figure 1.3 *Mbiragita*

Karimbashauro

Such a gesture was advanced by the Zvirimudeze Mbira Ensemble, mentioned earlier in this chapter. We founded the ensemble in 2012. The name translates as 'what is contained in the calabash'. I designed three *mbiras* developed from the *nyunganyunga mbira*, also known as the Kwanongoma *karimba*. They comprise the lead (*karimbashauro*), the middle (*karimbaduriro*) and the bass (*karimbanhovapasi*). The last two names were adopted from Mbira Dzenharira, a popular renowned *mbira* ensemble based in Norton, near Harare. The three *mbiras* have keys arranged in different registers, but all tuned in C major. For instance, the middle C of the lead is the highest note for the middle *mbira* and the middle C of the middle *mbira* is the highest key for the bass.

Karimbashauro has the highest register and it is responsible for playing the lead. The scale of G major was extended to complete the scale. The addition of the notes D, E, F and G made it possible for the *mbira* to play the lead line just like *dzavadzimu* and because of the ability to play the lead, I decided to name it *karimbashauro*, which means *karimba* that plays the lead.

Figure 1.4 *Karimbashauro*

Karimbaduriro

The *Karimbaduriro* has notes that range from lower C to upper C and has two additional notes – F sharp and F. This *mbira* is suitable for maintaining the main rhythm with very few variations.

Figure 1.5 *Karimbaduriro*

Karimbanhovapasi

Nhovapasi is a word derived from the Shona *kurovera pasi*, which means playing low notes. This *mbira* provides the bass line responding to the lead, *karimbashauro* above. It also communicates with the drums. *Karimbanhovapasi* has notes belonging to the lowest register and is tuned to the key of C major. In other words, the highest note has the same pitch with the middle note of the rhythm. Two additional keys not found on a normal *nyunganyunga* have been added – F and F sharp. Important to note is that the design of these *mbiras* has the advantage of extending the sound range over four octaves.

Figure 1.6 *Karimbanhovapasi*

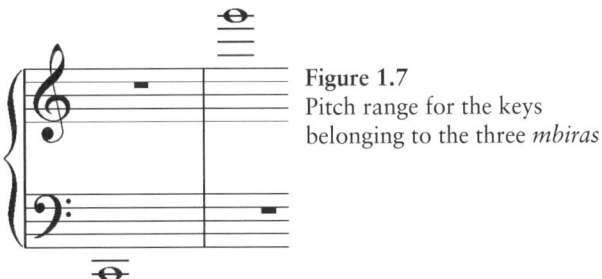

Figure 1.7
Pitch range for the keys belonging to the three *mbiras*

Compare this with the range of the common *nyunganyunga*:

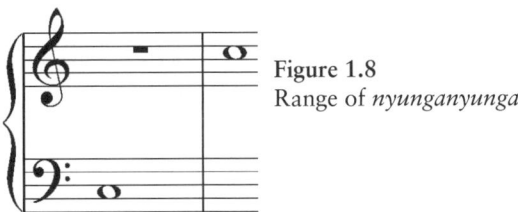

Figure 1.8
Range of *nyunganyunga*

The Zvirimudeze Mbira Ensemble has a repertoire of songs consisting of both traditional pieces, inherited with the legacy of *mbira*, and songs with lyrics composed by its members to address social and contemporary issues, but drawing the instrumentals from traditional pieces. The old pieces we play are 'Nhemamusasa' (Build a Shelter), 'Karigamombe' (Bull Defeater), 'Taireva' (We Said It), 'Chipembere' (Rhinoceros), 'Nyamaropa' (Meat and Blood), 'Dangurangu' (That Which Belongs to Me) and 'Mahororo' (Deep Sound). We also play original lyric compositions by members of Zvirimudeze, such as 'Sabhuku' (Village Head), which is accompanied by 'Dangurangu'; 'Nharo Hapana' (There Is No Argument), which is accompanied by 'Karigamombe'; 'Ndaneta' (I Am Tired), accompanied by 'Chipembere' and 'Simukayi' (Rise up), accompanied by 'Nhemamusasa'. There are also songs with both the music and lyrics composed by members of Zvirimudeze, such as 'Chembere Yawira Mugoronga' (An Old Person Has Fallen into a Ditch), 'Zvirimudeze' (That Which Is the Calabash) and 'Sabhuku Ane Nharo' (The Kraal Head Is Controversial).

The reason that Zvirimudeze plays some of the old pieces is to preserve them and keep their memory. It is apparent that some of them seem to be dying away, so playing them during weddings, modern shows and any gathering where people of different ages come together can be one way of preserving them. Some of the songs that are disappearing are 'Wangawakarara' (You Were Sleeping) and 'Saunyama' (Mr Meat). The ensemble usually performs to a public consisting of all age groups, the young and the old, women, men and children. Most of these people are urban dwellers in the cities of Harare and Gweru. The diverse collection of songs by Zvirimudeze is to cater for all age groups, although particular attention is given to the young, who are the future custodians of the *mbira* legacy.

Like many other *mbira* ensembles currently active in towns, the organisation of Zvirimudeze is a development of the rural-based ensemble *mhuri* (family). A number of the skills and characteristics of contemporary ensemble *mbira* performances can be traced back to the original rural *mbira* performances. As discussed above, the rural to urban migration of *mbira* players has resulted in a paradigm shift in the repertoire for *mbira*, the structure and context in which *mbira* is played and the type of audience that listens to *mbira* music. The changes in practices and in *mbira* music came as a result of the adaptation of *mbira to* urban spaces, which has helped to revive and sustain some of the traditional songs on the verge of extinction, as well as improving the sonic efficacy of *mbira* instruments through hybridisation.

However, from another perspective, the migration of *mbira* players from rural to urban spaces has had a negative impact on the originality and sustenance of the legacy of *mbira*. Many Shona people believe that tradition must be kept unchanged and their wish is to live like their ancestors as a way sustaining their culture. However, migration and technology have acted against this, resulting in the dilution of the indigenousness of both Shona traditional beliefs and musical instruments like *mbira*. Thus the need to address the impact of migration on the legacy of *mbira* through applied research by scholars.

This view is in line with Avorgbedor's call for applied ethnomusicological interventions in solving problems related to music emanating from rural to urban migration. Avorgbedor (1992) maintains that the movement of people from their rural homes where they grew up to towns has an impact on the originality of their music. The changes are as a result of adaption to the new environment and the adoption of a new musical style. He suggests that it is the duty of applied ethnomusicologists to design projects to reduce the intensity of change caused by rural-urban migration.

J. Clyde Mitchell (1966: 37) gives a detailed account of the impact of rural ideologies on urban practices and beliefs:

> In any nation, urban and rural represent different social systems. However, cultural diffusion or borrowing occurs as people, products, and messages move from one place to the other. Migrants bring rural practices and beliefs to town and take urban patterns back home. The experiences and social forms of the rural area affect adaptation to city life. City folk develop institutions to meet specific urban needs.

Concerning the impact of rural to urban migration on traditional music in general, Jones (1992: 27) argues that 'the influx of settlers with their own music and the introduction of new employment patterns further influenced indigenous music'. Although the move increased the popularity of *mbira dzavadzimu* in towns both locally and abroad, it left only a few *mbira* players among the Shona people in the rural areas. In other words, currently the Shona spirituality in which *mbira* is the core continues to exist in principle, but it is slowly losing space in Shona traditional practices, which are being undermined by Western ideologies and beliefs. New forms of urbanisation are driven by Western cultural consumerism, such as Zimdancehall, reggae, rock, jazz and techno-house or hip-hop. The *mbira* has had to adopt new approaches of learning the instrument, new ideas and values about *mbira* that are to be passed on to the next generation through modern means, as well as the idea of playing *mbira dzavadzimu* for commercial purposes.

Adaptation of *mbira* in urban spaces

The adaptation of *mbira* in towns has led to some significant changes in the tuning systems, the resonation system, the number of keys, the materials used to make the *mbira* and the construction methods. Most of the changes have brought positive results in that they enabled *mbira* to compete with other contemporary instruments. The changes have also helped *mbira* to secure a firm space in the modern music industry. However, to some extent the move has compromised the sacred efficacy of *mbira* and its originality. In addition the rate at which *mbira* is being influenced by modernity is so high that retarding it is not an easy task.

Most of the contemporary *mbira* players have adopted modern tuning systems of mbira, although it is true that the implication of scale was also original to African music cultures. The *mbira* is tuned to a particular tonal order based on a tonal centre common to particular mbira types. This tonal order is the same as the tonic of a Western scale. For example, an *mbira* tuned in G major has G as the tonal centre. The idea of a tonal centre was first propounded by Berliner (1993). An *mbira* maker can tune individual keys that are out of tune by making use of traditional *mbira* tuning themes, which are tested by playing 'Nyamaropa'. She or he then makes sure that each key fits perfectly in this piece. Keys that are out of tune will then be tuned by either sharpening or flattening their pitches.

Sharpening a key is done by pushing the key upwards as shown in Figure 1.9. When the key is pushed up, its length from the bridge is reduced, thereby making the part that vibrates shorter, resulting in the key vibrating with a faster frequency, thus raising the pitch. The other method for sharpening the key, which is commonly used when constructing the *mbira* and tuning the keys for the first time, is to remove the bottom part by cutting a piece off to raise the pitch. When a piece is cut off, the length and bulkiness of the key is reduced and it will vibrate with a faster frequency, thus raising the pitch.

A key that seems to have too high a pitch is pulled down until the correct pitch is reached. When reducing the pitch of a key, its length is increased by pulling down the key, as in Figure 1.10. When the key's length is increased, the frequency of the vibration becomes slower, thereby producing a lower pitch. Another way to lower the pitch is to forge the part immediately below the bridge to lengthen the key.

MBIRA IN URBAN SPACES

Figure 1.9 Sharpening of *mbira*

Figure 1.10 Flattening keys of *mbira*

Once the keys are tuned and tested with by playing 'Nyamaropa', the entire instrument is suitably tuned to play other pieces. 'Nyamaropa' is preferred because it is the oldest song used for this purpose and it makes the process easy and fast and no additional devices are needed. Another reason for using this piece of music is that the secret of *mbira* is embedded in the characteristic tone structure for *mbira* and the pieces performed on it. Using a piece of traditional music like this to test the tuning of *mbira dzavadzimu* was a traditional method of preserving the originality of temperament and tuning of the *mbira*. The implication is that once an *mbira* is in standard tuning, it continues to relate to the ancestors.

Currently some *mbira* makers combine traditional and modern methods of tuning *mbira*. Often they use the traditional method first and then fine-tune using modern electronic tuners or tuning forks, especially if they are playing with other pitch-based instruments. However, expert traditional *mbira* performers do not need such devices. They use their ears to tune their *mbira*. Once the instrument can produce a desired scalic structure, then the *mbira* is able to play other songs or be fused with other instruments. According to Thomas Turino (2000: 46), the fusion of *mbira* and guitars 'does not in itself constitute a heterogenization of the cosmopolitan sphere'. Instead, it is an indication that the music performed by these artists on guitars is borrowed from *mbira* and that Western instruments are being used to play traditional music. This dimension is hardly looked at by writers and researchers of *mbira*. They always think that *mbira* is being affected by Western music, and yet the opposite is also true.

Another significant change in the move from rural to urban space is in the amplification system of *mbira*. About 90 per cent of *mbira* ensembles that perform in *matandaro* ceremonies use *mbiras* with microphone pickups connected to an amplifier to make the sound loud enough to entertain a large audience. Microphone pickups are prepared by wrapping very thin copper wire around a magnet, as much as 7 000 times. There are different types of microphone pickups and each one is projected to receive certain signals, which are of either low or high frequency. The microphone pickups are positioned firmly under the keys of the *mbira*, leaving a space of about half a millimetre. This is meant to allow the keys to vibrate within the magnetic field of the microphone pickups. When a key is plucked, it vibrates to produce sound waves that cut through the magnetic field of the magnets in the microphone pickup, which converts the acoustic energy into an electronic signal. This signal is transmitted to the amplifier via a mixer, which receives the electronic signal and amplifies it to a certain level of adjustable loudness depending on the size of the amplifier and speakers. The sound is then received and transmitted by the speakers, making the sound of *mbira* loud enough to be heard by a big audience, as summarised in Figure 1.11.

MBIRA IN URBAN SPACES

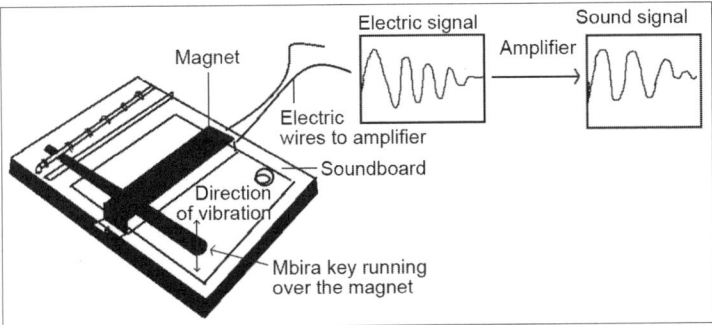

Figure 1.11 Amplification of *mbira* (Matiure 2014)

Figure 1.11 represents the amplification system of *mbira* as follows:

Vibrating *mbira* key → pickup → amplifier → speakers → audience.

To maintain the quality of *mbira* some ensembles, such as Mbira Dzenharira, make use of microphone pickups extracted from a lead guitar on lead *mbira* (*nheketo*) and pickups from rhythm guitar on rhythm *mbira* (*duriro*) and those from bass guitar are also fitted on bass *mbira* (*nhovapasi*).

The amplification of *mbira* has made it possible for *mbira* ensembles to perform to larger audiences in *matandaro* ceremonies held in big halls and stadiums, such as national functions, alongside other electric bands. The system of connecting *mbiras* to amplifiers has resulted in a reduction in the use of traditional resonators (*mateze*), but in the rural context, *mbira* was performed in a hut (*banya*) and amplified by gourd resonators, which were suitable for a small group of people. Usually the sound of *mbira* was enhanced by the acoustics of the hut.

Currently some *mbira* players opt to play the *mbira* by using external microphones to capture the sound, instead of attaching microphone pickups. Sheasby Matiure, who has performed in several shows as a resident artist in the United States, has this to say: '*Ini ndino farira kuridza mbira iri mudeze mayo asi ichitorwa ne* microphone *panze pedzakaiswa* microphone pickups', which can be translated as: I prefer playing the *mbira* amplified by a resonator placed close to a microphone rather than fitted microphone pickups'.[2]

---

2. Sheasby Matiure, interview, Gweru, 14 December 2012.

Some well-known *mbira* players who prefer using natural gourds are Cosmas Magaya and Irene Chigamba. They say that they want to retain the originality of the sound. Some *mbira* players have adopted new resonators made from fibreglass or wood, which are more durable than traditional gourd resonators.

Construction of *mbira* in towns

The introduction of *mbira* in towns saw the reproduction of *mbiras* for sale. Traditional *mbira* makers only used to make *mbiras* upon request. The idea was to provide the instrument in response to traditional and communal demands, not for business. Some of the early *mbira* makers who migrated to towns are Samuel Mujuru, Chaka Chawasarira (to Harare) and the late Eliot Ndlovu and Machinga (to Bulawayo). These *mbira* makers and many more adopted modern methods and materials to construct *mbiras*. The type of *mbiras* that were commonly made were *dzavadzimu* and *nyunganyunga*. What motivated *mbira* production after its introduction to towns was that there was a high demand for *mbiras* in urban institutions such as schools, colleges and universities, which were now teaching *mbira* or had *mbira* ensembles that performed during public events.

The population of Zimbabwe is increasing, which is impacting heavily on natural resources, a reserve of materials used to make *mbiras*. The increase in population has resulted in deforestation and indigenous trees are now endangered. In order to conserve the remaining trees, the government established the Environmental Management Agency. The agency does not condone the cutting down of trees or veld fires. *Mbira* makers are thus forced to buy processed *mubvamaropa* timber from factories in towns, which is easy to work with. The wire they use is bought from hardware shops in towns. The availability of materials used in making *mbiras* in towns has increased the availability of *mbira* makers in towns such as Gweru, Harare, Bulawayo and Mutare.

Colleges such as the Kwanongoma College of Music have also contributed to the increased demand for *mbiras* in towns. This college established a workshop for instrument construction and research in 1962, with the aim of teaching traditional music to teachers. Robert Simson introduced the teaching of traditional instruments at Kwanongoma as a way of reviving traditional music, which he felt was becoming extinct (Matiure 2008: 56). Simson's justification of the need for African music education, in conjunction with other ethnomusicologists such as Hugh and Andrew Tracey, culminated in the establishment of Kwanongoma. Many teachers were trained to teach African instruments at this institution, making possible the revival of African music. Ian Smith's government did not fully support the teaching of African music in schools during the colonial era.

The teaching of traditional music in schools was enhanced soon after independence in 1980. Jones (2008: 22) acknowledges that after independence, 'many educators had begun to encourage the teaching and performance of traditional music and dance'.

Mbira survival trends

The ability of *mbira* to secure a space in the contemporary environment can be attributed to a number of changes, some of them discussed above. Nevertheless, there are notable trends in the instrument's survival, which have played an important role in the *mbira*'s longevity and its remaining attractive to both young and old. In addition, such trends have not only enabled the instrument and its music to gain popularity in the urban cities of Zimbabwe, but also internationally in Germany, North America, Sweden and South Africa, among others.

The survival trends of *mbira* have been fundamental in maintaining its hegemony. The first is the overall tuning of *mbiras*, which has continued to include the core arrangement of the keys. Tuning systems of *mbiras* are believed to share some common structures regionally. However, there seem to be some differences in the tonal centres of the keys. Some have overall tuning systems that have a high register, while others are low. For instance, the tuning system of *mbira* in Mhondoro is definitely different from the common tuning systems in Chiota, Njanja and Makoni in terms of highness or lowness. Another survival trend has been the *mbira dzavadzimu*'s playing technique, which involves three fingers, left and right thumb and right index finger. These fingers are used to manipulate keys so that polyphonic and polyrhythmic combinations are produced. The keys of *mbira dzavadzimu* are strategically positioned on the soundboard so that each finger plays particular keys. The left thumb plays the top and bottom left manuals of the *mbira* while the right thumb and index finger play the right keys, which are the lead keys or *nhetete/nheketo*. This technique has continued to survive even after the *mbira* was introduced in urban areas.

Another surviving aspect is the traditional efficacy of *mbira*. Some families who used to perform *mbira* during traditional functions did not abandon the practice when they migrated to towns. Instead, they continued to hold some of the traditional ceremonies – for instance, healing and appeasing the ancestors. In town people may live in same street, but do not necessarily have a common historical lineage as close neighbours would in rural areas. So relatives from other parts of the town travel to gather for these ceremonies and they often hire *mbira* players for US$500.00 to US$1 000.00. I have attended one such function in Marondera, a town in Mashonaland, where *mbira* was performed for spirit mediums to evoke the spirits in the same way as in rural areas.

One more trend that continues to exist is the performance style of *mbira*. A traditional *mbira* ensemble usually consisted of a solo *mbira* player and a *hosho* (percussion gourd filled with seeds) player and the the rest of the participants, who join in singing, ululation, dancing and clapping hands. Families that conduct traditional ceremonies in town still make use of this performance style. In the case of more than one *mbira* player, one plays the lead (*kushaura*) and the rest play the backup (*kutsinhira*). Some of the *mbira* ensembles in cities still adopt this style, although the *mbiras* may be of different registers. Usually the lead will have a higher register than the bass *mbiras*, as discussed in relation to Zvirimudeze earlier in this chapter.

Mbira singing is characterised by a lead and response singing style. It must be noted that not all songs make use of this style, some are sung in unison, but lead and response is the dominant style, even in urban performances. Another singing style that has withstood time is the use of vocables (*mahonyera*) and yodelling (*huro*). Experienced *mbira* players decorate their singing with non-verbal cues, which are usually presented together with poetic utterances (*kudeketera*). It is true that some of the *mbira* ensembles performing in cities are still making use of these singing styles when playing some the *mbira* songs. In addition, respect for the *mbira* player's ancestry is still common in urban areas, as shown by the tradition of calling *mbira* players by their totems, such as Samaita, Nyamasvisva, Mhofu and so on.

Totems are used by the Shona people as a way of extending respect to the owner of the instrument and also as part of identity. The belief is that people of the same totem are descendants of the same genealogy and have a clear history of where they come from. The idea of calling each other by totems is one way of strengthening relations among *mbira* players. It is also another way of respecting the owners of the legacy of *mbira* (the ancestors).

Commercialisation of *mbira*

Commercialisation of *mbira* music started as early as the 1940s. Jones (2008: 125) confirms the shift of performances from traditional to commercial or from rural to urban, local to international: 'Performance contexts have extended from traditional to commercial settings and onto international stages'. Pickard Mackenzie (2010) underscores the various changes that took place when *mbira* was introduced on stage and how *mbira* players have adjusted their performance practices to suit the modern environment. The evolution of the *dandaro* ceremony in urban areas also led to the commercialisation of *mbira*. Several *mbira* ensembles currently found in Zimbabwe were formed with the aim of generating income. *Mbira* ensembles appear as independent groups or fuse *mbira* with other Western instruments such as guitars and keyboards. The most successful band to fuse *mbira* and guitars is Thomas Mapfumo and the Blacks Unlimited, currently based in the United States of America. Other *mbira* players – such as Stella Chiweshe, Beauler Dyoko, Sekuru Gora, Ephat Mujuru, Mhuri yekwaRwizi, Mhuri yekwaZambuko, Mhuri yekwaChigamba and Mbira Dzenharira – have become popular on the local scene.

As a result of the commercialisation of *mbira*, some *mbira* makers import *mbira* from rural areas such as Mhondoro and Hwedza for resale in Harare. Others export *mbira* to foreign individuals or institutions in countries overseas. These include Samuel Mujuru, Albert Chimedza, Chartwell Dutiro and Cosmas Magaya, to mention but a few. Samuel Mujuru, who is based in Harare, says that he sells an average of 100 *mbiras* in the United States and an average of 60 *mbiras* in Zimbabwe every year. Albert Chimedza has opened the Mbira Centre in Harare, where *mbiras* are produced in large quantities for sale in Germany and Sweden.

The other way in which the *mbira* has been commercialised is through recording *mbira* music for the radio and selling CDs. William Moylan (1992: 11) defines the recording process as 'capturing the physical dimensions of sound and then reproducing those dimensions either immediately or from a storage medium (magnetic, solid, electronic, digital), thereby returning those dimensions to their physical, acoustic state'. Moylan's definition stresses that physical sound waves are captured and converted to electronic signals that are capable of being reproduced, depending on the storage medium used. Therefore, as much as recording has contributed to the commercialisation of *mbira*, it is also a method for preserving the music. Recorded music is also helpful for transcription and analysis by music researchers. As Jones (2008: 28) points out, 'a number of players of the *mbira huru* (also called *mbira dzavadzimu*) who were committed to the preservation and popularization of the instrument became well known through recording and radio broadcast'.

Prior to Zimbabwe's independence, Teal Records, a subsidiary of Gallo Records in South Africa, was responsible for recording music (Eyre 2005: 37). Teal later became Gramma Records and a second recording company, Zimbabwe Music Company, was formed. The two later combined to operate under a single administration. However, under colonial rule, any music performed for ritual purposes was not recorded or played on the radio.

Most early recordings of *mbira* were carried out in rural areas across the country in late 1929 by Hugh Tracey. These recordings include *mbira* players from Njanja and are currently archived in the International Library of African Music in South Africa. Recording of *mbira* in studios only began in the 1950s. Jones (2008: 125) indicates that 'the pioneering musician and band leader Beauler Dyoko was the first female *mbira* player to be recorded in 1962'. This was followed by Stella Chiweshe's recording of her 45-rpm single 'Kasahwa' in 1974. Turino (1998) notes that Rhodesian radio and record companies began to broadcast and disseminate *mbira* and other indigenous music some time during the 1950s or early 1960s. It should also be noted, however, that there are several other recordings of male *mbira* players that took place earlier than the 1960s. The recording of *mbira* music on 45-rpm singles enabled the commercialisation of *mbira* music through record sales and radio broadcasting. The broadcasting of music on radio and television is one way of popularising and marketing both music genres and artists. Recording and broadcasting of *mbira* also contributed to the development of the *dandaro* ceremony in that ensembles rehearsed in nightclubs before visiting the recording studios. Johannes Brusila (2002: 37) provides a historical perspective of how *mbira* and other African music became popular:

> The recording of *mbira* has a relatively long history. From the 1940s onwards the mobile studios of the local radio companies, first Central African Broadcasting Station and later Rhodesia Broadcasting Corporation, recorded African music for their programmes. Also South African record companies and later their Zimbabwean subsidiaries released *mbira* music. In the 1960s and 1970s many *mbira* players, such as Hakurotwi Mude, Cosmas Magaya, Ephat Mujuru, Beauler Dyoko and Stella Chiweshe managed to acquire national fame with the help of such recordings.

The recording of *mbira* has increased significantly as a result of the mushrooming of various recording studios all over Zimbabwe. These include Shed Studio, Ngavongwe, Gramma Records, Metro Studios, Gospel Train Records, Dat

Studio, Tuku Music, Kingstons Music, RTP Records and Diamond Studio. The emergence of more recording studios has enabled the popularisation of traditional music, especially *mbira*, through radio, studio and live recordings of *mbira* music during national public events, such as independence celebrations, as well as live performances during *mbira* shows in nightclubs, book cafés and beer halls. *Mbira* ensembles now market themselves using fliers and posters as illustrated in Figure 1.12, advertising events by Zvirimudeze and Mawungira Enharira. The flyers clearly show how *mbira* ensembles have adopted a modern approach of marketing their shows, as well as charging a fee for their performances.

Figure 1.12
Flyer advertising *mbira* show by Zvirimudeze and Mawungira Enharira

Mbira ensembles common in towns

Currently there are more *mbira* ensembles in towns than in rural areas. It is apparent that the instrument is slowly gaining a firm space in towns and now competes with Western musical instruments such as guitars. There are several successful *mbira* ensembles active in Harare, Bulawayo and Gweru. Some of the renowned *mbira* ensembles that have spearheaded the success of *mbira* are Mbira Dzenharira, Mawungira Enharira, Zvirimudeze, Dzimbahwe, Mhembero and Matumba Emhondoro.

These ensembles usually perform in restaurants, beer halls and nightclubs, and at national events, weddings and galas. For instance, Mbira Dzenharira has a contract with Gijima sports bar in Harare and Zvirimudeze was contracted by Mhuka Huru Restaurant in Gweru from 2010 to 2012. Every Friday Mbira Dzenharira performs from seven in the evening to about midnight. The group includes the lead *mbira* (*nheketo*), which is of the *dzavadzimu* type belonging to the highest register, two rhythms (*duriro*), one *nyunganyunga* and one *dongonda* with a middle register and the last one with the lowest register, which plays the bass (*nhovapasi*). The young and the elderly visit this bar to drink and be entertained by *mbira* music. Upon my visit to the bar, I discovered that the bar is always full on Fridays. According to the manager, people travel from many parts of Harare and neighbouring towns such as Norton and Marondera. He went further to say that most of the people who frequent the bar to listen to *mbira* music are already familiar with this type of music from their lives in rural areas before they moved to towns. Others, especially the young, find the music unique and worth listening to as an alternative to contemporary music. The same ensemble is sometimes invited to perform during the opening of Zimbabwean Parliament as part of the government's policy of Black Consciousness and Afro-centrism. Mbira Dzenharira has released several albums, including *Fare Fare Tindike*, *Gonawapotera*, *Tingaputike Neshungu* and *Kumatendera*.

The breakaway ensemble Mawungira Enharira, which originated from Mbira Dzenharira, had a contract with the Book Café in Harare. The ensemble also performs every Friday to an audience of young and old, including many young artists who specialise in different genres. These artists appreciate *mbira* music, although they do not play the *mbira*. Apart from performing in Harare, the ensemble visits other cities where it teams up with other bands, though not necessarily *mbira* ensembles.

Sheasby Matiure argues that the migration of *mbira* from rural to urban areas has culminated in the expansion of *mbira* overseas, but a reduction at home. However, I disagree that there has been a decrease in *mbira* playing in Zimbabwe. While it may have decreased in rural areas, it has arguably increased in urban areas. In fact, there are now many *mbira* groups in most towns, schools and institutions of higher learning.

Zvirimudeze Mbira Ensemble

The Zvirimudeze Mbira Ensemble is based in Gweru and is made up of four lecturers and two technicians from the Department of Music and Musicology at

Midlands State University. The band members are: Perminus Matiure who plays *karimbanhovapasi*; Taona Muatengo, *karimbashauro*; Wonder Maguraushe, *karimbaduriro*; Decent Chambwera, drums; Absolom Mutavati, technician; and Elijah Chikomo, lead singer. Zvirimudeze plays three hybrids of *nyunganyunga* that I designed and that were crafted by members of Mbira Dzenharira in Norton. The *mbiras* are a combination of the lead (*nheketo*), which has a higher register, the middle register that produces the rhythm (*duriro*) and the lowest register, which plays the bass (*nhovapasi*). Most of the original compositions address social phenomena. Some keys were added to the lead so that the scale of C on the top manual is complete. In order to improve their music the ensemble has incorporated a Western drum kit, which is played by Decent Chambwera. The drum kit assists in maintaining a constant beat, as well as intensifying the rhythmic contour.

I have discovered through our performances that there are two categories of listeners. There are those that are familiar with *mbira* because of their rural experiences, and although performed in a different context with different acoustic properties and different renditions of songs, they still recognise the music. Usually such audiences prefer to contribute by singing and dancing and some even ask for shakers and play to accompany the *mbira*. The second category constitutes those who were born and bred in cities and have never attended an *mbira* performance before and the only *mbira* music they are familiar with is from radio and television.

Teaching of *mbira* in schools and institutions

The formal introduction of *mbira* in schools also characterises the prominence of *mbira* in towns. Its move from rural to urban areas culminated in the evolution of formal teachers of *mbira*, some of whom are making use of different notations to transcribe *mbira* music for teaching purposes. The idea of transcribing *mbira* songs is meant to improve the learning process. One of the most common notations used by *mbira* teachers is number notation. This notation is used to teach *nyunganyunga*. It is generally believed that the notation was designed by Dr Dumisane Maraire when he was teaching *mbira* in the United States, although some argue that the notation was designed by Chaka Chawasarira when he was teaching *mbira* to children. The notation involves numbering the keys of *nyunganyunga* from left to right, so that the top notes have even numbers (2, 4, 6, 8, 10, 12, 14) and the bottom notes have odd numbers (1, 3, 5, 7, 9, 11, 13, 15). The numbers denote the position of the key on the soundboard. The numbers have no reference to the pitch of the keys. The *mbira* in Figure 1.13 is tuned in F major and the pitch names are indicated next to the number.

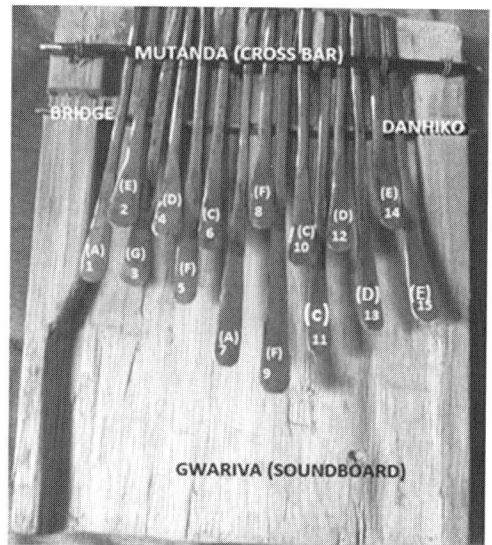

Figure 1.13 *Nyunganyunga* with numbered keys

The numbers are placed in three columns with boxes the left (L) representing the left thumb, the middle (F) the index finger and the right (R) the right thumb. Each box is ascribed to one pulse. Others use Sibelius computer software to transcribe *mbira* pieces using staff notation. The staff notation (a) and number notation (b) in Figure 1.14 are transcriptions for the basic pattern of 'Chemutengure'.

a)

b)

L	5		1		1		1	
F								
R	11		15		13		13	

L	5		1		3		3	
F								
R	11		15		11		11	

Figure 1.14 Transcriptions of 'Chemutengure'

MBIRA IN URBAN SPACES

Looking at both notations, it can noted that the total number of pulses is 24. These notations simplify the teaching of *mbira* and also enable easy distribution of pieces among *mbira* learners. Another kind of notation makes use of boxes and is used for pieces performed on *mbira dzavadzimu*. The keys are also numbered 1 to 6 or 7 from right to left on the top left manual, A to G from right to left for the keys on the bottom left manual and small 1 to 7 or 8 from the left to right on the lead keys, starting from the second key on the left. The first key on the right manual is marked X, as it does not belong to the same register as the rest of the keys. Note that the letters A to G have no connection with the pitch of the keys. The numbers and letters are written in boxes of two columns going downwards and each box is equivalent to a pulse. The left column labelled L represents the top and bottom left manuals, which are played with the left thumb and the right (R) column represents keys played by the right thumb and index finger. The box notation of 'Nhemamusasa' is shown in Figure 1.15.

L	3	C	4	E	4	G
R	4	4	3	3	2	2

L	3	C	5	E	4	G
R	1	1	4	4	2	2

L	2	D	5	E	4	G
R	5	5	4	4	2	2

L	3	C	4	E	2	1
R	1	1	3	3	1	1

Figure 1.15 Notation for 'Nhemamusasa'

When interpreting this notation the student is directed by the numbers and letters, as well as the hand signs left (L) and right (R). The notes written one after the other are separate and those in one line are played as a chord. The same piece can be transcribed using staff notation, as in Figure 1.16.

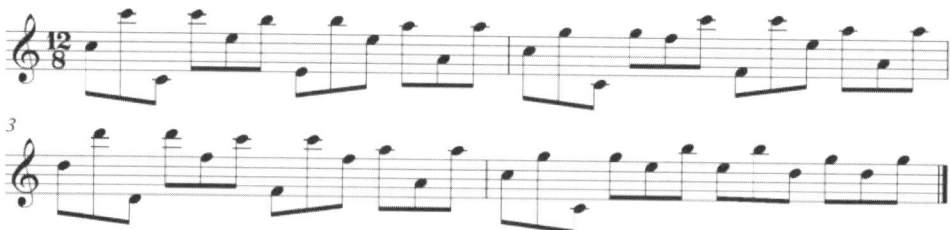

Figure 1.16   Transcription of 'Nhemamusasa' using staff notation

In addition to the use of notations, *mbira* players have adopted choreographic tendencies and the use of costumes when they perform. Some have designed their own costumes. Members of Zvirimudeze sometimes put on African attire or suits, especially when they are invited to perform during wedding ceremonies. The costumes should be suitable for the context in which the *mbira* is performed. Some ensembles put on animal skins and special clothes. Figure 1.17 shows Zvirimudeze performing during a wedding in Harare.

Figure 1.17   Zvirimudeze Mbira Ensemble performing at a wedding ceremony (from left: Perminus Matiure, Elijah Chikomo, Taona Muatengo and Wonder Maguraushe)

Conclusion

This chapter has presented the events that led to the evolution of *matandaro* ceremonies, during which *mbira* music is central, followed by a close analysis of how the traditional *bira* was transferred and recontextualised in towns where *mbira* is now performed for commercial purposes. There has been a paradigm shift in the perception and efficacy of *mbira* when it migrated from rural to urban areas. The music has managed to secure a firm space in the urban environment and to recontextualise itself for entertainment in shows staged in restaurants, hotels, national galas and beer halls. *Mbira* music has now been commercialised and several *mbira* ensembles have been formed. Ensemble members are earning a living by either performing or producing the *mbira* instrument for sale. *Mbira* has also secured space in urban schools and institutions of higher learning where it is not only taught, but also performed to entertain people during gatherings. The ability of *mbira* to secure space in urban settings has culminated in the popularisation of the instrument and its music in Zimbabwe and overseas countries. The underlying principle that cultures are vulnerable to change in a context of rural to urban migration, modernity, Christianity and education is recognised in the changes that created space for *mbira* in urban areas. It is recommended that the space for *mbira* in urban setting needs to be enhanced through seminars, workshops and festivals.

References

Avorgbedor, D.K. 1992. 'The Impact of Rural-Urban Migration on a Village Music Culture: Some Implications for Applied Ethnomusicology'. *African Music* 7(2): 45–57.

Berliner, P. 1993. *The Soul of Mbira: Music and Traditions of the Shona People of Zimbabwe*. 3rd edition. Berkeley: University of California Press.

Brusila, J. 2002. 'Modern Traditional Music from Zimbabwe: Virginia Mukwesha's Mbira Record Matare'. In *Playing with Identities in Contemporary Music in Africa*, edited by M. Palmberg and A. Kirkegaard, 35–45. Uppsala: Nordiska Afrikainstitutet, in co-operation with the Sibelius Museum/Department of Musicology, Åbo Akademi University, Finland.

Dirksen, R. 2012. 'Reconsidering Theory and Practice in Ethnomusicology: Applying, Advocating, and Engaging beyond Academia'. *Ethnomusicology Review* 17: 1–35.

Eyre, B. 2005. *Playing with Fire: Fear and Self-censorship in Zimbabwean Music*. Copenhagen: Freemuse.

Harrison, K., E. Mackinlay and S. Pettan. 2010. *Applied Ethnomusicology: Historical and Contemporary Approaches*. Newcastle upon Tyne: Cambridge Scholars Publishing.

Jones, C. 1992. *Making Music: Musical Instruments in Zimbabwe Past and Present*. Harare: Academic Books.

———. 2008. 'Shona Women *Mbira* Players: Gender, Tradition and Nation in Zimbabwe'. *Ethnomusicology Forum* 17(1): 125–49.

Kamwangamalu, N.M. 1999. 'Ubuntu in South Africa: A Sociolinguistic Perspective to a Pan-African Concept'. *Critical Arts* 13(2): 24–41.

Keil, C. 1982. 'Applied Ethnomusicology and a Rebirth of Music from the Spirit of Tragedy'. *Ethnomusicology* 26(3): 407–11.

Mackenzie, P. 2010. 'The Traditional Mbira on Stage: A Study of Contemporary Performance Practices'. Master's thesis, University of Arizona, Tucson.

Matiure, P. 2014. 'Archiving the Cultural Legacy of Zezuru *Mbira Dzavadzimu* Legacy in the Context of *Kuriva Guva* and *Dandaro* Practices'. PhD diss., University of KwaZulu-Natal, Durban.

Matiure, S. 2008. 'Performing Zimbabwean Music in North America: An Ethnography of *Mbira* and Marimba Performance Practice in the United States'. PhD diss., Indiana University, Bloomington.

Mitchell, J.C. 1966. 'Theoretical Orientations in African Urban Studies'. In *The Social Anthropology of Complex Societies*, edited by M. Banton, 37–68. London: Tavistock.

Moylan, W. 1992. *The Art of Recording*. New York: Van Nostrand Reinhold.

Turino, T. 1998. 'The *Mbira*, Worldbeat, and the International Imagination'. *The World of Music* 40(2): 85–106.

———. 2000. *Nationalists, Cosmopolitans, and Popular Music in Zimbabwe*. Chicago: University of Chicago Press.

CHAPTER 2

The Shangwe and Tsonga Idioms in *Xinombela* Musical Arts for the Adolescents in Gokwe and Chiredzi, North-West and South-West Zimbabwe

Renias Ngara and Doreen Sibanda

The Shangwe and Tsonga people are found in Gokwe and Chiredzi districts, situated in north-west and south-west of Zimbabwe, respectively. In the social contexts of Gokwe and Chiredzi, teenagers and the young in general present various challenges to their parents in relation to expected traditional behaviours. Social problems relating to premature marriage and intermarriage with other groups are some of the possible factors that fuel divorce among young couples. We argue that the problem could be alleviated through the use of *xinombela* musical arts and idioms.

This chapter investigates how the Shangwe and Tsonga in the Gokwe and Chiredzi districts use idioms and music to pass on indigenous knowledge to adolescents. It has three main objectives: firstly, it attempts to discuss how music is employed as a vehicle for the transference of indigenous knowledge and heritage with regard to marriage practices; secondly, it examines how the two communities employ idioms as another mode of dispensing knowledge about the significance of maintaining virginity among adolescents until they are officially married; and thirdly, the chapter reconceptualises the theory of cultural conditional gender equality in *xinombela* dance.

We argue that *xinombela*, which is a fertility dance of the Tsonga, is also comparable with the Shangwe fertility dance, *jichi*. The *xinombela* dance is characterised by two formations: *mitila*, a single line, and *kurhendzeleka*, a circular formation.

Culture experts Kokwani Mbiza, N'waSalani Baloyi and N'waLisimati Mbanyele from Haisa village provided the data for this chapter in 2014.

Application and analysis of the *xinombela* dance model
Mitila

According to culture experts Kokwani Mbiza, N'waSalani Baloyi and N'waLisimati Mbanyele, the word '*mitila*' is the plural of *ntila*.[1] The English equivalent of *ntila* is 'line'. So in *mitila*, one line is for boys and the other one for girls and as soon as they get onto the stage, the dancers stand in these two distinct lines, facing partners of the opposite sex. Mbiza noted that the dance is a moment when girls are free to seduce (*kukhinya*) the boys. Upon identifying a boy as her dance partner, the girl turns her back and moves her *xibabela* (traditional skirt), signalling that the boy should follow her. The duo then swiftly moves inside the dance arena. Baloyi further explained that each dancer endeavours to display his/her ability to move the waist. A boy turns around so as to come closer to the girl and stretches his hands out to signal that she should not go away from him. Mbiza says:

> *Mufana wa cina a karhi a khinga nhwanyana leswaku a n'witshinelela leswi kombaka ku n'wi rhandza.*
> A boy dances coming closer to the girl as a sign of showing that he loves her.[2]

Girls and boys naturally fall in love with each other to enjoy the dance. They do not dance with the same partner until the end of the dance. A boy dances towards a girl as a sign that he loves her. In the past, a girl could date a boy during the dance and such a relationship could result in genuine marriage.

When we asked why the girls would not face the boys during the *xinombela* dance, Mbiza indicated that it is a sign of honouring the boys, just as Tsonga wives are expected to respect their husbands in marriage. Mbiza said: '*Xinombela a xidyondzisa vafana kugiya*' (*xinombela* teaches boys how to dance).[3] According to Baloyi: '*Ku cina ka vafana ni vanhwanyan a ku ri ndhavuko wa xikhale wa VaTsonga*' (It is our Tsonga culture and tradition to dance in pairs. There is nothing

---

1. Kokwani Mbiza, N'waSalani Baloyi and N'waLisimati Mbanyele, interviews, 15 October 2014, Haisa village.
2. Mbiza, interview.
3. Mbiza, interview.

hidden about the dance model).[4] This notion is comparable with the Shangwe game song entitled 'Sarura Wako', which literally means 'Choose one for yourself'. In this game song, one girl at a time moves inside a circular formation of seated boys and girls and sings:

> *Sarura wako*
> *Kadeyadeya ane ndoro chena*
> *Wangu mutsvuku*
> *Kadeya-deya ane ndoro chena*
> *Simuka hande*
> Choose yours
> Kadeya-deya with a white mark[5]
> Mine is light in complexion
> Kadeya-deya with a white mark
> Rise up and let us go

In this context, one after the other, each of the girls is given the freedom to make a choice from the boys seated in a circle, the one she admires and loves.

Kurhendzeleka/circular formation

Kurhendzeleka dances are performed in pairs and dancers move in a circular formation on the stage. In the Tsonga tradition, this is the time when boys and girls concentrate on showcasing their styles as they attempt to stroll all over the arena. According to Mbiza, the girls are free to lead in the fast clockwise dance. However, the lead singer and the drummers remain on the stage until all the performers have moved off the stage. The circular dance symbolises the round huts in which they live. The circle is also an expression of the Tsonga's belief in continuous life after death. The Tsonga performers get into a deep moment of singing, drumming and dance, with the aim of developing a sense of unity as they dance around. Dancers sometimes reduce their pace, allowing themselves some time to refresh since the whole performance is on stage and can take a long time.

---

4. Baloyi, interview.
5. 'Kadeya-deya' is just a nonsense word, which is part of the game.

Examples of *xinombela* songs: Song texts and the application of idioms

The passing on of indigenous knowledge systems to adolescent girls with regard to marriage practices is the primary aim of *xinombela* musical arts. The first song presented below provides a testimony of how the Tsonga attempt to pass on indigenous lore on marriage to teenage girls:

> *Xinombela vatekana hi vuxaka*
> *Aaa aye iye manane hi leximakwenu*
> *Hi leximakwenu, hi leximakwenu*
> *Xinombela vatekana hi vuxaka.*
> In *xinombela* we marry within our culture
> Relatives, let me pass it to you
> Let me pass it to you, let me pass it to you
> In *xinombela* we marry within our culture.

Baloyi and Mbanyele said that this is one of the songs sung by Tsonga girls who have reached puberty and are ready to marry. In practice, the Tsonga and the Shangwe educate their children about expected marriage practices. *Ngano* (folktales) are one of the models for passing on indigenous knowledge regarding marriage. *Xinombela* musical arts are also utilised to pass on marriage lore when participants engage in singing and dancing. The Tsonga and Shangwe believe that if their adolescents want to engage in premarital sexual activities, the teachings reflected in *xinombela* may remain in their memories and discourage them from acting against tradition. The Shangwe and the Tsonga reckon that adherence to and observation of proper marriage practices could be one way of reducing the rate of unexpected teenage pregnancies. Scholars in Malawi, working on issues of unwanted pregnancies among adolescents, note: 'The experience of pubertal changes may be associated with excitement, anxiety, distress and other psychological problems depending on the expectations and understanding of what the changes signify and mean' (Munthali and Zulu 2007: 151).

The need to reduce unexpected pregnancies among teenagers is not only a concern of the Malawian community, but also of the Shangwe and Tsonga of Zimbabwe, and arguably across southern Africa. An attempt to apply songs and idioms to impart expected sexual practices and reduce the rate of unwanted pregnancies among adolescents is their concern. The Shangwe and Tsonga expect teenagers to retain and cherish the African philosophy of ubuntu. The lack of respect for virginity is seen as disregarding humanity, as implied in *xinombela* ritual performances.

In rites of passage such as *xinombela*, teenage girls play a principal role, since they are the ones who initiate the dance. Mbiza posits that the song text quoted above shows that the Tsonga believe that it is a taboo to marry outside their ethnic group. Interviews revealed that their inherited knowledge informs young girls and boys that marrying within their community helps to preserve and sustain their marriages. The Tsonga believe that intermarriages have negative implications for the sustainability of cultural practices, such as *khomba* – girls' initiation ceremony – which the Tsonga believe sustains marriages through teaching adolescents how to treat their husbands when they marry. Relatives, especially parents, may refuse to recognise such a marriage as legitimate. Mbanyele emphasised that the Tsonga need to maintain their royal blood, and since a Tsonga couple would be related, such a marriage has the potential to strengthen the bond between two families. In Tsonga communities, people of the same totem, such as the Chauke and Baloyi, marry each other, since it is important for them to maintain their royal blood and it is believed that such a marriage provides little opportunity for divorce.

Marriage within the same cultural context is supported by the Tsonga idiomatic expression: '*Murhi ku dyiwa lowu u wutivaka*' (You feed on fruits from a tree that you know). When we asked culture experts Mbiza, Baloyi and Mbanyele whether their children still practise this convention, they stressed that a lot of their children now marry non-Tsonga people. Baloyi and Mbanyele emphasised that nowadays the rate of divorce is very high. They associated some of the divorces with conflicts that may arise because of cultural differences. For instance, if a Tsonga man marries a Zezuru woman, the Zezuru woman might not be aware of proper sexual practices, since they do not practise sacred rituals such as *khomba*. In *khomba*, Tsonga girls learn the proper sexual practices they should perform to satisfy their husbands' sexual needs and expectations. On the other hand, Tsonga men learn of various ways to satisfy women sexually. The culture experts also related the increase in divorce to the gradual decline of the performance of *xinombela*, which used to serve as a means of imparting indigenous knowledge to Tsonga boys and girls before marriage.

Our field studies and shared lived experiences revealed that if one marries a relative, the chances of divorce are expected to be low, since divorce is perceived as a breach of norms and values of the society. The Shangwe and the Tsonga believe that if problems arise in marriage, they are supposed to be resolved amicably in order to sustain the marriage. Divorce is viewed as a breach of the philosophy of ubuntu, which expects that couples should cherish the raising of their children together. In the Ndembu rituals studied by Victor Turner, social relations may be compromised by an infringement of the regulations that control human behaviours. Members sometimes break away from their social groupings, yet societies may be able to forgive them and reintegrate them (Turner 1987). In the world of politics, members of one political party sometimes get into conflicts, leading to crises that may reach alarming levels. Consequently, some members break away from the party. It is vital to note that the party sometimes accepts the return of such members and they reintegrate them after conflict resolution. In brief, this kind of conflict resolution is a symbolic interpretation of Turner's performance theory.

Xinombela mirrors idiomatic expressions, which are employed by the Shangwe and the Tsonga to encourage marriages between people within their own group; in Tsonga: '*Ku tekana tekanani va rixaka*' (Marry in the neighbourhood). A similar cultural practice used to exist among the Karanga, Korekore, Manyika, Ndau, Shangwe and Zezuru, which are Shona groupings with corresponding dialects. In Shangwe, they use the idiom '*Kuroorana rooranai vamatongo*', which also means 'Marry in the neighbourhood'. Shona philosophy is embedded in these idiomatic expressions. The Shangwe and the Tsonga believe that a person is expected to marry into a family famed for being hardworking – for instance, in farming. In the past, parents expected and even still expect their sons marry a girl whose mother has never been accused of witchcraft. Our study of Shangwe and Tsonga use of idioms seeks to augment the literature by further discussing Turner's (1987) performance theory, which highlights social groupings that may disintegrate because of their failure to resolve conflicts. While problems are a natural phenomenon and exist in every society, conflict resolution creates social harmony and those who would have broken away from the social bond, as a result of their breach of social regulations, can be reintegrated once the crisis is redressed.

'Let me pass it to you' is a symbolic expression that views marriage as something that should circulate and be passed on between people of blood ties. Marrying a non-Tsonga woman traditionally would be perceived as allowing an outsider to penetrate a 'closed society'. Closed societies have sacred rites of passage that are reserved for them only – for instance, the Tsonga *khomba*, an initiation of girls into womanhood. It should be emphasised that Tsonga sacred rites are intimate rites in which indigenous knowledge lore and heritage are preserved and the knowledge is perceived as their property and enshrined in ethical issues, which is why it is reserved for members of Tsonga culture.

Communities therefore attempt to safeguard their cultural heritages from external encroachment as a way of sustaining their values. In Zambia, the Bemba also protect their indigenous knowledge rights that are embedded in the *chisungu*, a girl's initiation rite that graduates Bemba adolescent girls into womanhood (Richards 1956). We would say therefore that the Bemba and Shona rites act as indigenous archives in which intangible heritage is preserved and passed on from one generation to another.

The decline in the practice of *xinombela* has rendered songs and texts less significant to Tsonga boys and girls and they no longer adhere to the expected cultural practices. Tsonga men were known for recalling their daughters who married non-Tsonga men. Their belief was that the daughters could disclose their sacred indigenous practices. With time, however, Tsonga men started marrying non-Tsonga women. Intermarriage is a result of migration and the interactions of people of different cultures in search of good farming land and employment in urban areas. Intermarriages are now common within the Shangwe and Tsonga communities and the rate of divorce is escalating. A concerned culture owner pointed out that the high rate of divorce was a result of the inability of families to resolve social conflicts because of their cultural differences. Different societies have social norms and values meant to regulate acceptable behaviours. Some of the problems confronting young marriages could therefore also be attributed to a society's failure to impart indigenous knowledge to adolescents. An English expression warns that you cannot teach an old dog new tricks. In this context, the idea is that one should be exposed to one's tradition when growing up, since it will be too late when one is older.

In *xinombela* the society attempts to reduce conflicts that may be encountered by teenagers when they eventually get married. The song titled 'Xibabela' is a metaphoric expression of this:

Xibabela xitatsemeka
Khomisani xibabeloo
Xi ta tsemeka khomisani
Xibabeloo xitatsemeka
Khomisani xibabela xitatsemeka.

> The *xibabela* will tear apart
> Hold the *xibabela* tightly
> It will tear apart, hold it tightly
> The *xibabela* will tear apart
> Hold the *xibabela* tightly, it will tear apart.

It seems from the lyrics that the song is warning girls that the skirt, *xibabela*, will tear during the *xinombela* dance. According to Mbiza, the idiomatic expression: '*Khomisani xibabela xitatsemeka*' (hold the *xibabela* tightly, it will tear apart) is richly embedded in symbols. *Xibabela* does not simply mean the actual skirt worn by Tsonga girls during the *xinombela* dance. In the ritual context, *xibabela* symbolises virginity. Baloyi and Mbanyele interpreted the expression 'It will tear apart' as a means of informing Tsonga girls that they should preserve their virginity until they marry. If a skirt is not tightly wrapped around the waist, it may fall off and the girl would be left naked. Similarly, if a girl loses her virginity before marriage, it would bring shame on her and her family. In the past, the Shangwe used to make a hole on the head of a *mupinyi*, a hoe stick, which was an expression that the girl had lost her virginity before marriage. The preservation of virginity among Tsonga girls is analogous to the Shangwe idiomatic expression: '*Humhandara idamba kamwe*', which literally means 'Virginity is lost once and forever'. In Tsonga they say: '*Tolo a nga ha vuyi, loko vukhomba byi hundza byi hundzile*' (Once virginity is lost, it is lost).

We conclude from our interviews that the Shangwe and the Tsonga use certain idiomatic expressions to pass on indigenous knowledge to encourage proper marriage practices among the youth. Aware that conflicts are inevitable in marriage, the Shangwe and Tsonga attempt to forewarn adolescents of such challenges. The elderly people expect their children to recall the teachings embedded in the *xinombela* rituals in order to address challenges. Turner's (1987) theory on Ndembu rituals is one means of understanding how passing on knowledge with regard to social problems and conflict resolution can create a harmonious society. Taking Turner's ritual conceptions of breach, crisis, redress and reintegration, we infer that indigenous knowledge systems are embedded in rituals and are models that societies should adopt and apply, if they appreciate the African philosophy of humanity.

The same concept of the preservation of virginity is further expressed by another Tsonga song:

Gangala le vanhu gangala
Mingadyi gangala le vanhu
Gangala le vanhu lihelile
Gangala le vanhu gangala
Mingadyi gangala le vanhu.

The red millet of the people, the red millet
Don't eat red millet of the people
The people's red millet will be finished
The red millet of people, the red millet
Don't eat people's red millet.

Mbiza and Mbanyele interpreted *gangala* to mean virginity. In the words '*Mingadyi gangala*' (Don't eat the red millet), the Tsonga are advising boys not to engage in sexual activities, so that girls' virginity is preserved. Tsonga boys are expected to value the significance of virginity among girls until marriage. Interviews revealed that boys are also being informed that since they are the ones who expect to marry virgins, they also should safeguard their virginity. Mbiza highlighted that this song had a great impact since it discouraged boys from fondling girls. It is meant to denounce bad habits of Tsonga men in the community, who might indulge in sexual practices before marriage. It was traditionally mandatory for Tsonga teenagers to abstain from sexual practices before they got married. As a result, there were limited cases of unwanted pregnancies among adolescents in the past when *xinombela* still had firm symbolic significance. If a pregnancy occurred, it was an embarrassment to the family concerned and the community at large. In Tsonga culture, boys who married virgins owed them a lot of trust and regarded such women as not capable of infidelity.

The symbolic handling of problems and finding resolutions as portrayed by the Ndembu ritual (Turner 1987) imply that despite the intensity and extent of the conflicts and crises, there are always possible solutions. Conflicts and crises are part and parcel of everyday life and societies should regard them as opportunities for innovation and creativity.

Reconceptualising 'cultural conditional gender equality'
When we asked culture experts if there was a possibility of marriage between *xinombela* dance partners, they indicated that it still is possible in the Tsonga

community. They acknowledged that in their community, there are still certain marriages attributed to the *xinombela* dance. They explained that the selection of a male dance partner by a girl signalled intentions for courtship. This was also noted in the study of the *jichi* dance, which 'is a spiritual procreation and rainmaking dance' of the Shangwe *mukwerera* ceremony in Gokwe District of Zimbabwe (Ngara 2014: 127). *Mukwerera*, just like *xinombela*, is a fertility ceremony that is performed in the context of rainmaking. The deeper meaning is that performers symbolically engage in the process of fertilisation, since they believe that rainfall is meant to sustain families through reproduction and food production. In *mukwerera*, the spiritual realm views *jichi* dance participants as humans who are symbolically engaged in the process of creating babies. In a real-life setting, however, for a couple to enjoy sexual activities, they need to create a friendly and happy environment through fondling and sexual arousal. During the *jichi* procreation dance, a favourable atmosphere is also necessary for the symbolic reproduction to happen. Contrary to Turner (1987), who argues that during a ritual performance crises and conflicts are rife, we infer that during *mukwerera*, this is not so. It could be that Turner's social conflicts were a result of a failure to honour the expected norms and values.

As in the *xinombela* dance, in which Tsonga girls are given the ritual freedom to identify their desired male dance partner, when performing the *jichi* dance ceremony, women are also the ones who choose their dance partners. However, perhaps influenced by Western culture, in a real-life scenario in Zimbabwe, it is the boys who are expected to court the girls. It can be argued that the equality in choosing a partner is conditional since both Tsonga girls' and boys' indigenous knowledge informs them that since they are engaging in a fertility dance, it must be performed along gender lines. Its conditionality is apparent in the notion that

> the biological studies on fertilisation inform that: a) A man and a woman have intercourse. b) Since one sperm fuses with one ovum, the couple's input to fertilisation and/or pregnancy to take place is equivalent. In offspring, the equal contributions of a mother and a father can be proved through the use of the Deoxyribonucleic Acid (DNA) tests (Ngara 2014: 131).

The equal opportunity is cultural since the Tsonga community expects girls and boys to dance as opposite-sex partners throughout the ceremonial rite for them to acquire indigenous knowledge on the symbolic significance of marriage practices.

Its cultural nature is further implied by the community's use of the *xinombela* dance as an ideal occasion to convey social values to the adolescents before they marry. When the dance is complete, Tsonga girls and boys resume their gender and sexuality roles, as do Shangwe women and men at the end of the *jichi* dance.

Turner's (1987) performance theory can further be employed along gender lines. The symbolic expression of social relations, crisis, resolution and reintegration of members in the Ndembu rituals are a good example of the challenges that are encountered in that community. The participants are able to resolve conflicts through rituals and also expect the Ndembu community to be able to settle issues that may lead to disharmony and disintegration. The idea of reintegrating members into the society during the ritual performance could be comparable with a practical application of the African philosophy of forgiving one another. When an African community adopts the concept of forgiving each other, they are fulfilling the philosophy of ubuntu. Ubuntu is a human ethos that expects African communities to live as one family, having respect for and loving one another in order to maintain social order. The Ndembu rituals studied by Turner could also be interpreted as replicas of the inequality that prevails in certain societies. The need for equal treatment between men and women could be a move towards the reduction of gender imbalances. In the *xinombela* dance, the creation of an equal opportunity could also be interpreted to mean women's aim to reduce male dominance over them in the day-to-day setting.

Xinombela songs may be viewed as indigenous modes of communication, through which social values are inculcated among the youth. Songs and idiomatic expressions are regarded and interpreted as indigenous models that prepare and equip Shangwe and Tsonga adolescents with skills to resolve conflicts and problems that may arise in their marriages.

Teenage and marriage challenges
As gathered from interviews and our lived experiences, the Shangwe and Tsonga communities are no longer closed societies and intermarriages are now dominant. For instance, the Ndebele now live among the Shangwe in Gokwe District, making intermarriages unavoidable. Intermarriages are regarded as possible factors that fuel divorce because of cultural differences. In Pittsburgh, Pennsylvania, Amy Slagle (2010: 234) cites the 'stories of intermarriage converts' of an orthodox church who fail to sustain their marriages because of cultural diversities. However, as Lynn White (1991) argues, divorce is a multifaceted phenomenon, which may

be perceived and interpreted from multiple perspectives. For instance, marriage breakdown can be associated with structural and life-course predictors, such as race, social class and age. Women seem to monitor their marital lives quite closely and are able to identify problems earlier than men (Thompson and Walker 1991). In contrast, men tend to avoid and withdraw from discussing marriage problems (Gottman 1994) and this could be another reason for marriage breakdowns (Kitson 1992).

Departing from a sociological perspective, *xinombela* is a reflection of masculine and feminine expectations for marriage. Joseph Kwabena Nketia (1974: 36), writing about black Africans in general, notes: 'There are songs performed by women during ceremonies and rituals that are a concern to them, puberty rites for girls, expectations of motherhood, mothercraft, certain healing rituals, and funeral music.' Isabel Phiri (1997: 40) concurs with regard to Chewa women in Malawi: 'It was during group pounding of maize that the women sang songs that expressed their feelings about life. Women used pounding sessions (*pamtondo*) to discuss issues that pertain to women in life. This provided an outlet for negative emotions that women had.'

In Malawi women employ specific songs as a means of expressing their deep-seated emotions. Kings Phiri (1983: 257–74) notes that women in the Chewa matrilineal community of Malawi show high degrees of 'respect and social freedoms', but 'socially and economically' depend on 'the uncles (*nkhoswe*)', especially in rural communities.

Conclusion

Turner's performance theory has shaped this chapter through an analysis of the *xinombela* dance model, a theory that further challenges scholars to interpret dance expressions. *Xinombela* dance is a personification of gendered politics, as is the Shangwe *jichi* dance, which creates an equal opportunity between females and males, a kind of equality that Ngara (2014) refers to as 'cultural conditional gender equality'. The Shangwe and Tsonga are concerned with the future welfare of their children, especially with regard to premarital and marital issues. They advocate for the respect of humanity by both genders and therefore attempt to pass on valuable local knowledge to adolescents in order to reduce and/or curtail destructive life challenges.

References

Gottman, J.M. 1994. *What Predicts Divorce?* NJ: Lawrence Erlbaum.

Kitson, G.C. with W.M. Holmes. 1992. *Portrait of Divorce: Adjustment to Marital Breakdown*. New York: Guilford.

Kwabena Nketia, J.H. 1974. *The Music of Africa*. New York: W.W. Norton.

Munthali, A.C. and E.M. Zulu. 2007. 'The Timing and Role of Initiation Rites in Preparing Young People for Adolescence and Responsible Sexual and Reproductive Behaviour in Malawi'. *African Journal of Reproductive Health* 11(3): 150–67.

Ngara, R. 2014. '*Jichi* Dance Structure, Gender and Sexuality'. *Studies of Tribes and Tribals* 12(1): 125–34.

Phiri, I.A. 1997. *Women, Presbyterianism and Patriarchy: Religious Experience of Chewa Women in Central Malawi*. Blantyre: Kachere/CLAIM.

Phiri, K.M. 1983. 'Some Changes in the Matrilineal Family System among the Chewa of Malawi since the Nineteenth Century'. *Journal of African History* 24(2): 257–74.

Richards, A.I. 1956. *Chisungu: A Girl's Initiation Ceremony among the Bemba of Northern Rhodesia*. London: Faber and Faber.

Slagle, Amy. 2010. 'In the Eye of the Beholder: Perspectives on Intermarriage Conversion in Orthodox Christian Parishes in Pittsburgh, Pennsylvania'. *Religion and American Culture* 20(2): 233–57.

Thompson, L. and A.J. Walker. 1991. 'Gender in Families: Women and Men in Marriage, Work, and Parenthood'. In *Contemporary Families: Looking Forward, Looking Back*, edited by A. Booth, 76–102. Minneapolis: National Council on Family Relations.

Turner, V. 1987. *Anthropology of Performance*. New York: PAJ Publications.

White, L. 1991. 'Determinants of Divorce: A Review of Research in the Eighties'. In *Contemporary Families: Looking Forward, Looking Back*, edited by A. Booth, 141–9. Minneapolis: National Council on Family Relations.

CHAPTER 3

Performing Subversion
Negotiating Social and Political Space in Zimbabwe through *Chinyambera* Traditional Dance

Innocent Tinashe Mutero

This chapter examines the effectiveness of *chinyambera* dance performances as a tool for social change in repressive environments. It focuses on the performances of the Tavirima traditional dance group in Gweru, Zimbabwe. Through the metaphors of *chinyambera* traditional dance and songs, Tavirima manages to articulate issues affecting society in contemporary Zimbabwe.

Tavirima was established in 2007 by Gilbert Zhou to support and promote the interests of Gweru's young musicians, dancers, actors and poets. However, the group has since outgrown its founding mission of giving space to and imparting technical skills to young artists. The performances of Tavirima, today, challenge the dominant master narratives, the gerontocratic and hegemonic realities in Zimbabwe. Often, in their performances, Tavirima uses traditional dance to speak out about communities' social and political fears and aspirations, offering alternative voices that envision a democratic, free and autonomous environment.

The fieldwork for this study was conducted for a period of six months. However, I was born in Gweru and my knowledge of Tavirima and its context therefore dates back to before the formal commencement of this project. I am also involved in community arts in the small but progressive city of Gweru. Tavirima was deliberately chosen for this study because their practice of *chinyambera* has been considered as subversive performance (Muwonwa 2012). Additionally, Tavirima was at the time of the study one of the two traditional dance groups consistently practising dance outside educational institutions and prisons in Gweru.

Subversion or coping mechanism?
Music performances by Tavirima draw mixed feelings and contestations. Their performances can either be viewed as subversion or as a coping mechanism,

depending on the political perspective of the viewer. Music, by its very nature, is ambivalent, in that it can mean different things to different people and it can evoke differing reactions. According to Tia DeNora (2016: xii):

> Music has the great advantage of affording ambiguity while simultaneously stirring up . . . to borrow a term from the Science and Technology studies, music can function as a 'boundary object,' meaning different things to different people and yet for all practical purposes being talked about as if those meanings are unified and shared.

This chapter refers to Tavirima's performances as subversive – not because the performances are riotous in nature, but rather because the Zimbabwe African National Union – Patriotic Front (ZANU–PF) government incorrectly views them in this way (Siziba 2009; Muwonwa 2012). The government views any person with divergent political views as treasonous and a sell-out (Human Rights Watch 2017: 683) and hence subversive. Nonetheless, the government of Zimbabwe cannot be entirely blamed for its stance on alternative music because in some instances music is used to stir disorder. Michael Shank and Lisa Schirch (2008: 11) posit that 'the arts, like any other tool, can be used for destructive purposes, such as inspiring hatred and division yet they are also powerful tools to be used wisely, non-violently, and strategically'.

It is in the best interests of ZANU–PF to view Tavirima and other related performances as subversive so as to protect its political status quo and interests. In Zimbabwe subversive performances can be categorised as those whose scope is outside the confines of the laws governing the parameters within which they create and conduct performances. In this regard performances by Tavirima in Gweru are referred to as subversive as they usually contravene section 16, subsection 1 of the Censorship and Control Act (2001), which stipulates that 'no person shall perform or permit any public performance unless it has been approved by the Censorship Board' and section 25, subsection 1 of the Public Order and Security Act (2002), which regulates the holding of public meetings, processions and demonstrations. In addition, the Zimbabwean government, which is often vilified in Tavirima's practices, is bound to take their performances as an attempt at discrediting it.

This chapter observes that most dictators have a penchant for conservatism and so they usually exalt traditional music. For instance, Adolf Hitler used the power of music to shape the ideas of the Hitler Youth.[1] The late former Tanzanian president Julius Nyerere, an often-praised pan-Africanist, is also spoken of as the most Islamophobic leader in postcolonial Africa (Abdullah 1999). He was not only intolerant of dissent, he also used music to propagate his political ideology (Otiso 2013: 193).

On the other hand, there is a possibility that these performances are misconstrued as acts of insurrection by ZANU–PF because some sections of society see Tavirima's performances as an important criticism of the government. However, labelling Tavirima's performances as subversion condemns and misrepresents the conceptually intended role of the musical arts as positive, applied, intangible agency and stable government practice in indigenous cultures, which remains effective for people-oriented contemporary societies. Karin Barber (1987: 11) argues that popular arts 'are free to operate within established cultural systems without conforming to their conventions' and they are determined to bring social change. Hence an insensitive and corrupt government resents and intimidates the overseeing, corrective role of the arts. It is regarded normal to have such divergent views on an art form, especially if its performance and the subject matter it tackles are marred with contestation and condemnation, as is the case in Zimbabwe's political milieu.

Rebecca Dirksen (2013: 50) suggests that music as a cultural object can 'enable positive discourse and provide a clear direction, as well as musical enjoyment'. Revered African music scholar Professor Meki Nzewi insists that the performance itself is not subversion, but rather a sanction of unruly behaviour and a direction to sublime societal living.[2] However, this chapter uses the term 'subversion' for the value it has in drawing attention to how musicians are using music as a coping mechanism. Later on in the chapter, the analysis and discussion of Tavirima's performances and music works towards advancing the argument on music as a coping mechanism, but it is important to first understand the context.

Brief on the economy, politics in Gweru
The city of Gweru has always had much potential for industrial growth because of its diversified industrial base, which includes mining, shoe manufacturing, tourism and cattle ranching. The economic instability in Zimbabwe, however, has taken its

---

1. http://holocaustmusic.ort.org/politics-and-propaganda/third-reich/music-hitler-youth/.
2. Personal conversation.

toll on most of the industries, with some ceasing operations altogether. Gweru has also faced major political challenges at different times in independent Zimbabwe. The city witnessed the Gukurahundi disturbances of 1983–7, which targeted people of the Matabeleland and Midlands provinces.[3] Gweru also experienced the worst violence perpetuated against opposition political parties in the 1990 elections. According to Masipula Sithole and John Makumbe (1997: 135): 'The violence perpetrated against the opposition during the 1990 election was the worst in an election year since independence, culminating in the shooting of Patrick Kombayi who dared to challenge Vice-President, Simon Muzenda in the Midlands city of Gweru.' There were also politically oriented violations of human rights in the city when the government embarked on Operation Murambatsvina.[4] Lyndsay Hilker and Erika Fraser (2009: 41) argue: 'Many people harboured feelings of hatred and revenge due to past violence and persecution of certain groups, in particular Operation Restore Order (Murambatsvina) in 2005 when the homes and livelihoods of some 700,000 people were destroyed and the massacre of some 2000 people during the *Gukurahundi* massacres.'

The political preference of Gweru's people rests with the Movement for Democratic Change (MDC), as revealed by election results and trends. The party's candidate, Amos Chibaya, has won the Mkoba constituency parliamentary seat ever since the first time he participated in a parliamentary by-election in 2005, after the death of Bethel Makwembere, who was also a member of MDC. The reign of the MDC in Gweru has opened up spaces for residents to openly raise their concerns and seek redress and to address the challenges they are facing through different platforms.

It is important to note within this discussion of Gweru that independent Zimbabwe has been entangled in internal and often violent political conflict from as far back as 1983, when the Gukurahundi disturbances erupted until they were settled in 1987, after the deaths of more than 20 000 civilians. General elections

---

3. Gukurahundi is a term referring to civil war, which broke in Zimbabwe after the notorious North Korean-trained Fifth Brigade murdered thousands of people in Zimbabwe's Matabeleland Province and parts of the Midlands Province. The war is largely seen as an effort by Robert Mugabe to exterminate the Ndebele people.
4. Operation Murambatsvina was an ill-conceived exercise meant to destabilise the Movement for Democratic Change in cities and towns under the guise of restoring order in Zimbabwe's cities.

in Zimbabwe have also been violent, resulting in brutal attacks on leading political figures and ordinary civilians. In recent years violence has often broken out betweeen ZANU–PF and MDC youths.

Music, power and liberty in Zimbabwe
Communities use music for communication and unavoidably some of the messages speak against bad leadership. Therefore, performances that include criticism have always been part of the Zimbabwean culture. In the communal areas of Zimbabwe people use *bembera* (public ridicule), either in the form of poetry or song to speak out on the subjugation of people. Tavirima and by extension most Shona artists in Zimbabwe relate to and use *bembera* in their performances. *Bembera* is aptly defined by Murenga Joseph Chikowero (2006: 47) as follows:

> Among the Shona, *bembera* is a recognised mode of correcting a wayward member of society by denouncing his/her aberrations or shortcomings at a public platform without naming their precise identities. Usually, this person's discomforted response gives him/her away during this public shaming. A *bembera* could be delivered in the form of a work song by a wife frustrated by a husband's uncaring attitude or by villagers against a thief at communal work parties. *Bembera* thus serves as a mode of dispensing shotgun justice but with corrective intent. The target is expected to reform.

In this light it is quite apparent that protest songs and music for social change have always been part of Zimbabwean culture. Similar to the Tavirima's *chinyambera* performances, *bembera* is a form of protest music usually used by the subaltern or any disadvantaged individual to challenge master narratives or to chide the authorities they cannot confront directly or to make suggestions about how sensitive issues can be solved. Such performances ensure that despite acrimony and tensions, which naturally exist in society, people are in a position to be outspoken about any crisis without attracting physical confrontations.

The Zimbabwean government has been subject to scrutiny by artists in their work. The legendary singer Thomas Mapfumo has always been consistent in using music to expose unruly conduct by the political elite through songs such as 'Corruption', a 1989 release. In the colonial period, indigenous musicians used *chimurenga* music to extend their disapproval of the white settlers' regime in the same way they sang against unjust indigenous majority rule in early postcolonial

Zimbabwe. Maurice Vambe (2004: 167) observes: 'Some critics of *chimurenga* music think that there is only one version of *chimurenga*, and have mistakenly reported its demise in 1980. After Zimbabwean independence, *chimurenga* continued as a vehicle for criticizing corruption, poor governance by new leaders, and delays in redistributing land to the African masses.'

The *chimurenga* musicians created music that spoke against the newly established indigenous government. Tavirima's performances of *chinyambera* are thus a continuation of *chimurenga* music, speaking out against a black government that is widely seen as subverting the people's will during elections.

Tavirima's strategies of evading arrest

Zimbabwean artists who sing against state oppression, disregarding threats from security agents working under instruction of the ZANU–PF government, have had to use a plethora of creative and innovative ways to avoid being arrested. I describe the different ways of evading arrest Tavirima uses as follows: (a) upholding cultural legacy; (b) the metaphorical meaning of the songs; (c) use of axioms; and (d) political prostitution. This section contributes to a better understanding of the concept of African popular culture (Barber 1987), as applied to the different forms of subversive performances by Tavirima.

The Zimbabwean Constitution affords citizens various rights, including freedom of expression and freedom of association. However, freedom after exercising some of the rights is not always guaranteed. This is regardless of the fact that the Constitution of Zimbabwe reigns supreme over Acts of Parliament. Tavirima therefore finds themselves in a difficult context where they must be tactful in speaking out against the ruling party.

The Zimbabwe Republic Police (ZRP) continues to unlawfully arrest people whose political views differ from ZANU–PF ideologies. As David Makwerere, Tafadzwa Chinzete and Collen Musorowegomo (2012: 134) point out: 'The ZRP has gained notoriety over the hounding of opposition politicians and other people or organizations with divergent ideas from those of government.' The ZRP is susceptible to manipulation by the ZANU–PF government in violating human rights because the Lancaster House Constitution, which was used in Zimbabwe until May 2013, did not provide for separation of powers. Makwerere, Chinzete and Musorowegomo (130) are of the opinion that:

> The complicity of the ZRP in the violation of human rights in Zimbabwe is not accidental. One of the most important axioms of government rule

in a democracy is that of separation of powers. Government must not only make and interpret laws but also have the ability to enforce them. The police make up part of the executive branch of the government, operate as part of the criminal justice system and operate at all levels of the government.

The relationship between ZANU–PF and the ZRP has blurred the ability of the police force to professionally execute its duties, as it works as an extension of ZANU–PF.

Evading arrest through upholding cultural legacy
Despite continued arrests of other performing artists across Zimbabwe, Tavirima has adopted measures to dodge arrests and continue with their work. Tavirima has benefited from using traditional dance styles in their performances since their acts are viewed as efforts to uphold and preserve Zimbabwean traditional cultures, which are being threatened by globalisation. In reference to how they have evaded arrest through the guise of preserving culture, Faith Matongo, a member of Tavirima, points out:

> The nature of your production can put you at a safe place when you are faced with the wrath of the law. We stage cultural performances, therefore in a way we uphold our values and morals. There are some lame cases, for example, when one records their music or run an unapproved modelling agency and expect not to get nabbed by the Censorship Board. We are a different case because our performance also upholds our culture. Therefore we believe we will always find a soft landing when faced with the law.[5]

Almon Moyo, a community artist from Mkoba, also reasons that it is practically impossible for the police to arrest Tavirima because of the musical style they use in their performance. Moyo says:

> Since *chinyambera* is our cultural dance, where we really know that this is our culture, so when they approach the police and they say we want to do traditional dance, they are just taken as traditional dances. *Chinyambera*

---
5. Faith Matongo, interview, 28 August 2013, Mkoba 20.

is a cultural dance, so by arresting us, not to use *chinyambera* they will be saying do not practise your culture. At the moment, given the prevailing situation, there is the Censorship Board and the National Arts Council, which gives clearances to almost every group and the police forces. I think these three groups believe that when a person is playing *chinyambera* it's just cultural. What matters most to these three organisations are the organisations attached to the performance – for example, NGOs [non-governmental organisations] are scrutinised.[6]

Tavirima also uses folk songs, which belong to the public domain, to avoid having open confrontation with the police. According to the Copyright and Neighbouring Rights Act (Chapter 26: 05, section 80), no one in particular has rights to the folk songs and therefore the Censorship Board cannot censor the songs and anyone who is Zimbabwean can use these songs. However, section 81 reserves special rights for the president of Zimbabwe to restrict the use of the songs, although this has never happened. The ultimate effect of the restriction that the president can impose is enshrined in section 82 of the same law, which reads:

Effect of reservation (I) Subject to this Part – (a) no person who is not a public institution or a citizen of Zimbabwe shall do anything or cause anything to be done in Zimbabwe in relation to a reserved work of folklore, where the right to do that thing has been reserved to the President; (b) no person who is not a public institution or a member of the community concerned shall do anything or cause anything to be done in Zimbabwe in relation to a reserved work of folklore, where the right to do that thing has been reserved to an appropriate local authority.

In addition, Tavirima's position as custodians of culture is amplified by the fact that they are currently the only community-based group in Mkoba, Gweru, which has not attempted to venture into contemporary dance performance. Some community arts groups, such as Kumuzi, Umzabalazo and Snipers, with the exception of Perfect Works, are now strictly contemporary dance performers. Perfect Works occasionally includes traditional dance in their theatre performances, for which

---

6. Almon Moyo, interview, 29 August 2013, Mkoba 16.

they always turn to Tavirima to hire Mitchel Matingwina for her expertise. The participation of Matingwina in Perfect Works' productions maintains Tavirima's visibility in the traditional dance arena in Mkoba. Therefore, the group is firmly positioned to get support from the community for their loyalty and sterling effort in preserving traditional dance, which is now almost exclusively the preserve of learning institutions such as Midlands State University, Mkoba 3 High School and Chikumbiro Primary School, as well as Hwahwa Prison, which all get funding from the government.

Research has established that Zimbabwean youth shun traditional dance performances (McLaren 2001: 13–14). Tavirima's performances are viewed as an effort to uphold Zimbabwean traditional culture and thus they are held in high esteem by the authorities. The status and importance they are accorded by the community shields them from being arrested. The group deliberately addresses youth behaviour in their performances, resonating with the older generation's vision of community. One of the popular folk songs in their repertoire is 'Vana Venyuvakura' (Your Children Have Grown), also widely known as 'Kurauone', sung in lead and response as shown below:

Lead: *Kurauone*
Response: *Mwana wenyu akura*
Lead: *Akurauone*
Response: *Kurera haizi nyore*
Lead: *Haizi nyore*
Response: *Mwana wenyu akura.*
Get old and you will realise
Your child is all grown
You've grown and you will realise
It is not easy to take care of a child
It is not easy, you will see, when you are old
Your child is all grown.

The metaphorical meaning of songs

My analysis of the contextual meaning of the song text above follows the lead and response provided for by the song structure. In analysing 'Kurauone' I treat the lead and response as a conversation, thereby bringing out the intention of the lead, as well as the meaning of the response. Where the songs refer to a subject whose name is not given, I take the gender of the person to be male, just for discussion purposes.

The lead voice belongs to a parent or guardian who went through a torrid time raising a child, but is not happy with the child's bad behaviour. The parent is telling the child that now that he is grown and will become a parent, he will see for himself that it is not easy to raise a child. The response is affirming that indeed the child is grown and he will realise how hard it is to take care of a child.

I noticed that the way that the young Tavirima performers carry themselves is one good reason why they are held in high esteem, and possibly another reason that their performances are rarely scrutinised. The group members of Tavirima respect each other and their actions are always cognisant of the fact that they do not exist in a vacuum, as enunciated by the values of ubuntu. 'Ubuntu is not only a dialogical African moral theory; it is also a way of life. This means that *hunhu/ ubuntu* does not only evaluate and justify moral acts in African settings, but it is also a world view for the Africans' (Mangena 2012: 11). Music in Africa is also a way of life, enshrining ubuntu values of peaceful coexistence and respect and proscribing moral transgressions.

Use of axioms as a strategy to evade arrest
Tavirima also taps into idioms from the rich Shona language as a way of protecting themselves from prosecution, even for impersonating the president and other crimes associated with criticism or subversive performances in Zimbabwe, through taking advantage of the ambiguity of meaning inherent in Shona idioms. Tavirima argues that they use idioms when criticising a political party, cultural activity or leaders, because the idioms cushion them from harassment by whoever is subject of the criticism or their supporters. For instance, they speak about 'the cork' in their songs, fully knowing that 'the cork' refers to a person, but when they are confronted about it, they argue based on the literal meaning of the song. In addition, these axioms help them to avoid embarrassing the leaders at public forums. They also add lighter moments to their criticism of the leadership through dance, thus bringing an entertaining aspect to their act.

Political prostitution as a strategy to evade arrest
'Political prostitution' loosely means showing support for more than one of rival political parties. The fieldwork for this chapter was conducted during a period when

Zimbabweans were preparing for their seventh general election, which eventually took place on 31 July 2013. The political field was abuzz with activity and, as I had anticipated, Tavirima was staging their politically toned performances. I was, however, surprised to note that Tavirima performed at both ZANU–PF and MDC rallies. On 21 September 2013, the group performed at Morgan Tsvangirai's star rally at Mkoba Stadium in Gweru and a week later on 27 September 2013 they were performing at Robert Mugabe's star rally at an open space located opposite Midlands AIDS Services Organisation. I managed to film their performance at the MDC rally, but unfortunately I could not film the proceedings at the ZANU–PF rally because of the high security presence. Even though the group lacked motivation and their usual high energy during the ZANU–PF rally, they were brave enough to voice out their worries to a ZANU–PF audience.

However, when I later interviewed some members of the Tavirima group, they refuted the allegation that they are political 'flip floppers', who wander from party to party, preferring to say that they are an objective watchdog that scrutinises the activities of both the MDC and ZANU–PF. When I asked them to explain their relationship with the two rival parties, Razor, one of the members, said:

> The packaging of messages for our shows is dependent on the party we will be performing for. Our performance whether we are performing at a ZANU or MDC rally will be speaking about our challenges and the torment we go through. The message in our performance will be a plea to the political parties to fulfil the promises they make. For instance, if MDC promises us jobs, we will ask for those jobs when we perform at their meetings, in the same vein if ZANU–PF promises us jobs will ask for that at their rallies.[7]

Commenting on their performance at both ZANU–PF and MDC rallies, Faith Matongo had this to say:

> Music in general and traditional dance in particular is helpful in addressing challenges posed by Zimbabwe's politics. Our country has two rival parties, the MDC and ZANU–PF. However, as a group, we are not affiliated to any

---

7. Joe Razor, interview, 28 August 2013, Mkoba 16.

political party. Our duty is to teach Zimbabweans through our cultural dances. We perform at all functions regardless of the hosting political party. What we intend to get there is remuneration and satisfaction that we have managed to get an audience with Zimbabweans.[8]

Even though both Matongo and Razor assert that they are politically neutral, facts point to them aligning with the MDC. I understand their participation at the ZANU–PF rally as one of the strategies they use to avoid prosecution. At the MDC star rally the group sang 'Tavaona', openly exalting Morgan Tsvangirai. The song was adapted from a Mhande song of the same title.

> Lead: *Tsvangirai ndiye baba*
> Response: *Tavaona havo ndibaba vedu tavaona*
> Lead: *Tavaona nekuguta*
> Response: *Tavaona havo ndibaba vedu tavaona*
> Lead: *Tavaona nehembe tsvuku*
> Response: *Tavaona havo ndibaba vedu tavaona*
> Lead: *Amos ndiye baba*
> Response: *Tavaona havo ndibaba vedu tavaona.*
> Tsvangirai is the father
> We acknowledge he is our father
> We appreciate he brings wealth
> We acknowledge he is our father
> We distinguished him by his red clothes
> We have noticed he is our father
> Amos is the father
> We acknowledge he is our father

The lead singer begins by calling, '*Tsvangirai ndiye baba*', literally meaning Tsvangirai is the father. Zimbabwe is a patriarchal society, so the father is the head of the house. Therefore, in the song Tavirima depicts Tsvangirai as the leader of Zimbabwe. The response answers, '*Tavaona havo ndibaba vedu tavaona*', loosely

---

8. Matongo, interview.

translated as 'we have seen him, he is our father'. In the context of campaigning this is not simply an affirmation that indeed people have seen that Tsvangirai is a leader, the response drums up support for Morgan Tsvangirai. The vociferous response, which was amplified by the audience who joined in the singing, intensified the deeper meaning that Tsvangirai is a leader through popular consent.

The lead singer has the liberty to change lyrics of the song, as where the message in his call is the anticipated happiness that Tsvangirai's ascendance to president of Zimbabwe will bring. He also reminds people of the MDC's symbols, a case in point being '*Tavaona nehembe tsvuku*', meaning we have identified him with his red regalia. During the 2013 election it was critically important that the MDC distinguished itself from the other splinter group of the MDC led by Professor Welshman Ncube, which used green as its party colour. Towards the end of the song, they substitute Tsvangirai's name with Amos Chibaya's – he was the MDC Member of Parliament for the Mkoba constituency.

Why did the group choose *chinyambera*?

In the course of my research I constantly asked myself why Tavirima had chosen *chinyambera*. While I do not intend to pre-empt my findings, I hasten to say that every indigenous dance has the potential to be used to speak out against any social or political ill. How that can be done is the subject of the ensuing discussion on why Tavirima used *chinyambera*.

Gweru is the provincial capital of the Midlands Province, which is a confluence of Ndebele and Shona culture. As a result, the city's residents witness a number of dances, including *mbakumba, jerusarema, shangara, amabhiza, amantshomane and isitshikitsha*. However, Tavirima only practises the *chinyambera* traditional dance in their subversive performances. Their choice is informed by three factors: *chinyambera* identifies with the culture of the majority, it is expressive and and it is energetic.

Chinyambera identifies with the culture of the majority

Even though the Midlands Province has a significant mix of Ndebele and Shona people, the Shona people of the Karanga dialect make up the majority of Gweru residents. These Karanga people came to Gweru from nearby rural areas, including but not limited to Shurugwi, Chirumhanzu and Chiundura. Ndebele people are more popularly resident in the lower Gweru area. Tavirima members agree that their choice of *chinyambera* was motivated by the need to use a medium that most of their audience identified with, so that they can easily engage with the medium. They argue that since they are residents of the Midlands Province, they observed that most of the Karanga people, including those who come from as far as Masvingo, always migrate to Gweru. Therefore, they use *chinyambera* because it is originally Karanga and a lot people identify with it, more than they would identify with any other dance.

Tapping into a people's culture increases their sense of responsibility and ownership of Tavirima's *chinyambera* interventions. Patience Munsahu (2003: 45) argues that the use of local languages and culture makes a performance more acceptable and effective. In addition, the group argues that the use of *chinyambera*, indigenous to most of Tavirima's audiences, ensures that the audience is engaged and joins in the performances, even without even a cue, since the performances are part of their culture. Tavirima's performances take an endogenous approach to development, which is essential in achieving community ownership and responsibility in influencing about social change. As Kennedy Chinyowa (2002: 47) makes clear:

> The endogenous approach realises that the processes of transformation are internal to the mechanisms of social systems and cannot necessarily be determined by external agents. In so far as it constitutes an internal process of action, reflection and praxis, the endogenous model has come to be characterised by a strong tendency to make use of people's own local resources.

To this end, Tavirima's use of indigenous dance to speak out against social and political injustice is meant to bring closer the realities of the subject matter addressed by the dance performances through the people's culture.

Chinyambera *as an expressive dance*

Tavirima's choice of *chinyambera* is also influenced by the possibility of dramatising events through the medium of *chinyambera* dance. The dramatisation of texts effectively relays the message to the people as it adds visuals to the song texts. The mimetic action in the performance is just as important as the song text because both carry the same messages. Mime amplifies and ingrains the song messages as it emphasises other aspects of the performance. Mshengu Kavanagh argues that 'mime is deep rooted in African Arts' (in Ravengai 2013: 394). Over and above being spectacular and able to draw audience attention, the fact that mime is indigenous to Zimbabweans makes Tavirima's use of it more appealing, as locals identify with the mimetic arts.

Tavirima's use of *chinyambera* is influenced by the opportunity to enact the song text through dance. This makes it possible for audiences to identify themselves with the performances, leading to discussions on matters raised by the performances. The dances are similar to drama performances and are capable of offering solutions to the problems faced by people in the same way that drama does. Usually when one watches a drama performance, one is stimulated to think through the issues raised and the reason why some characters behaved in a particular way. Tavirima's performances elicit a similar response. For instance, they can have a performance in which a dancer puts on a baboon costume and the audience is provoked to ask questions, which often lead to discussions.

Through participant observation in some of Tavirima's activities, I found out there is definitely theatre influence in their work. Tavirima's decision to use *chinyambera* and its theatrical aspects is parallel to Nicholas Cull's (2006: 13) functions of theatre:

> Theatre operates within cultural diplomacy in four main ways, each with a varying expectation of interactivity with the target public. At its first and most basic level it can be a prestige gift; second, it can be a way of shaping perceptions and informing; third, it can be a mechanism for generating engagement between the originating and target populations.

Indeed, besides enacting song lyrics in their performances, Tavirima's performances are meant to shape people's perceptions of their political environment, with the intent of garnering a common agenda of bringing about social change through deposing Zimbabwe's authoritarian government. The performances are also engaging, as evidenced by audience participation in the singing and dancing when Tavirima performs.

Tapping into chinyambera's *energies*
The 'animal energy' in *chinyambera* is particularly advantageous to the well-being of the performers as it provides an avenue through which they can release their pent-up frustrations over the government's poor service delivery and authoritarian rule. Tsitsi Matingwina believes that Tavirima's energetic performances are a

platform through which they find peace, even in the face of adversities, as the dance provides for a release of emotions. In an interview he shared his feelings:

> If you look at *chinyambera* it is a highly energetic dance. When performing the dance all my energies are drawn to the performance, creating a vent through which I release all my frustrations, which emanate from the poor state of community. I cannot beat anyone to release my anger, what I can only do is dance off the frustration.[9]

During performances, the thudding sound of the *chinyambera* drums is coupled with similarly energetic performances. The energies that drummers put into beating the drums have a direct link with how the dancers perform. Angela Impey and Barbara Nussbaum (1996: 5) argue that 'drummers and dancers are dynamically interlocked in performance and, should a dancer lack energy; the drum ensemble will similarly lose impetus. Conversely, if the drummers are highly motivated, the dancer will reflect their spirited momentum.' The audience is also inevitably drawn closer into the performances by this combined energy.

Chinyambera offers a platform to be aggressive. When a warrior goes to war or to hunt, he is not a soft person. So it is only reasonable to say that the very reason that Tavirima chose *chinyambera* is expressed in the way they dance.

Tavirima's performances draw attention to the Shona proverb '*Mutambigwi gwinyawo kuti vanotamba vamer ezenze*', meaning the host should be merry so that guests can be free on the dancefloor. The proverb is a command to whoever is working on something to put in more effort, so that those who are helping will do the same. In the context of Tavirima's performances, the proverb implies that the performers have to give it their all, if they are to get the desired outcome from the audience.

The importance of audience engagement cannot be overemphasised. Energy is critical for performances, which are meant to bring social change, as it is a sign that the audience is getting the message and some will possibly take action. Alan Brown and Rebecca Ratzkin (2011: 68) postulate: 'When audiences become an essential part of the process their investment of time and energy yields stronger connections with the individual artist(s), the work, and the organisation, some of

---

9. Tsitsi Matingwina, interview, 7 September 2013, Mkoba 16.

which may last a lifetime.' Implied is that the connection between the performer and the audience, which is brought about by an energetic performance, works towards sustainability of the performance outcome and its subsequently having a lasting impact.

The effectiveness of Tavirima's *chinyambera* performances

Through engaging in subversive or critical performances of *chinyambera* Tavirima seeks to contribute towards social change in Zimbabwe. Since their contribution is targeted at the political front, an evaluation of the effectiveness of their performances should look at the political environment and the results of the elections that were held during the time under review. Having said that, of course the election results and the prevailing political situation are not a product of Tavirima's performances only. There are a number of other crucial factors that also come into play for or against social change.

The incumbent Member of Parliament for Mkoba Constituency, Amos Chibaya, believes that Tavirima's performances have been instrumental not only in bringing about social change, but in helping him to retain his seat in Parliament. Responding to whether Tavirima has helped his cause as a Member of Parliament, Chibaya said:

> There are so many ways of killing a cat and Tavirima is another way. Information can be disseminated through the news chapters, radio, and the television. Information can also be spread through singing and traditional dance. Their singing is not just singing, it's well-managed singing. Let's take, for example, they can sing 'Chibaya Wenyu Wakura' [Your Chibaya Has Grown up] to show that their Member of Parliament is a mature leader. They can also sing some songs which include some activities that I have actually implemented in my constituency. Tavirima are experts in what they do, so they definitely get the message to the people.[10]

Tavirima's performances also work as a measure of restraint for the members of the group. According to Matingwina, their performance has given them 'purpose', unlike many other young people who do not have anything to do. As mentioned

---

10. Amos Chibaya, interview, 8 September 2013, Mkoba 13.

earlier, Matingwina also believes that the dance provides a platform to peacefully release anger. In this regard, the performances of *chinyambera* have aided in the reduction of incidences of politically motivated violence.

Conclusion
From my observation of Tavirima's rehearsals and the performances at both ZANU–PF and MDC rallies, I conclude that the group also uses the strategy of feigning support so that they evade arrest and can continue to perform with little or no interference from the police. During the rehearsals leading to, and on the day of the actual MDC rally they performed with gaiety, whereas at the ZANU–PF rally their rehearsals and the subsequent performance were rather more subdued. But Gilbert Zhou insists that they are an apolitical entity and serve Zimbabweans equally, irrespective of their political affiliation. Zimbabwe has a history of violent elections and people have learnt to be extra careful when showing their political affiliation. Most Zimbabweans have realised that they live in a politically insecure environment where citizens are often terrorised for having divergent political views from ZANU–PF. Therefore, one of the strategies that Zimbabweans employ to avoid violence is to attend political rallies for both parties. There are reports that people attend ZANU–PF rallies to get free T-shirts and to avoid the repossession of benefits that they would have accrued by showing support for the party.

Though traditional dance performance in Gweru is certainly not a widespread cultural activity, especially among young people, Tavirima has successfully managed to use their culture to speak out against the prevailing social and political environment. Through a functional metamorphosis of traditional music and dance, they manage to stand up against the totalitarian government in Zimbabwe. Their performances add currency to the use of indigenous arts in speaking to and solving contemporary issues and challenges. It is critical, however, to understand that no matter how important traditional music and dance are, as part of the African culture, their relevance and posterity is hinged upon their usefulness in the prevailing context. Therefore, the music and dance should be allowed to mutate, along with other aspects of culture – not necessarily as a reflection of globalisation, but as an advancement of indigenous African lore, useful to Africans and in resisting pillage in the global village.

References

Abdullah, M. 1999. 'Julius Nyerere: The West's Ultimate Anti-Islamic Warrior in Post-colonial Africa'. https://crescent.icit-digital.org/articles/julius-nyerere-the-west-s-ultimate-anti-islamic-warrior-in-post-colonial-africa.

Barber, K. 1987. 'Popular Arts in Africa'. *African Studies Review* 30(3): 1–72.

Brown, A.S and R. Ratzkin. 2011. *Making Sense of Audience Engagement, Vol. 1: A Critical Assessment of Efforts by Nonprofit Arts Organizations to Engage Audiences and Visitors in Deeper and More Impactful Arts Experiences*. San Francisco: San Francisco Foundation.

Chikowero, M.J. 2006. 'Singing the Contemporary: Leadership and Governance in the Musical Discourse of Oliver Mtukudzi'. *Muziki* 3(1): 36–47.

Chinyowa, K. 2002. 'The Liminal Function of Orality in Development Communication'. *Alternation* 9(1): 46–56.

Cull, N.J. 2006. *Theatre as Cultural Diplomacy: The National Theatre of Scotland's Black Watch*. http://uscpublicdiplomacy.org/sites/uscpublicdiplomacy.org/files/legacy/media/Black_Watch_Publication_010808.pdf.

DeNora, T. 2016. 'Foreword'. In *Music, Power, and Liberty: Sound, Song and Melody as Instruments of Change*, edited by O. Urbain and C. Robertson, i–xiii. New York: IB Tauris.

Dirksen, R. 2013. 'Surviving Material Poverty by Employing Cultural Wealth: Putting Music in the Service of Community in Haiti'. *Yearbook for Traditional Music* 45(3): 43–57.

Hilker, L.M. and E. Fraser. 2009. *Youth Exclusion, Violence, Conflict and Fragile States*. London: Social Development Direct.

Human Rights Watch. 2017. *World Report: Zimbabwe*. https://www.hrw.org/world-report/2017/country-chapters/zimbabwe.

Impey, A. and B. Nussbaum. 1996. 'Music and Dance in Southern Africa: Positive Forces in the Workplace'. In *Sawubona Africa: Embracing Four Worlds in South African Management*, edited by R. Lessem and B. Nussbaum, 63–79. Cape Town: Zebra Press.

Makwerere, D., T. Chinzete and C. Musorowegomo. 2012. 'Human Rights and Policing: A Case Study of Zimbabwe'. *International Journal of Humanities and Social Science* 2(17): 129–38.

Mangena, F. 2012. 'Towards a *Hunhu*/Ubuntu Dialogical Moral Theory'. *Phronimon* 13(2): 1–17.

McLaren R. 2001. 'Case Study: Teaching Dance in Zimbabwe, the Chipawo Experience'. Paper prepared for the Regional Conference in Primary and Secondary Schools as well as in Non-formal Systems, 26 June–1 July.

Munsahu, P. 2003. *Women's Voices and African Theatre: Case Studies from Kenya, Mali, the Democratic Republic of Congo and Zimbabwe*. https://www.article19.org/data/files/pdfs/publications/gender-women-s-voices.pdf.

Muwonwa, N. 2012. 'Performing Subversion: Youths and Active Citizenship in Zimbabwean Protest Theatre'. *Postamble* 8(1): 1–15.

Otiso, K.M. 2013. *Cultures and Customs of Tanzania*. Santa Barbara: Greenwood.

Ravengai, S. 2013. 'Reimagined Rural–Urban Landscapes and Zimbabwean Cultural Identities in Zimunya's *Country Dawns and City Lights*'. *African Identities* 11(4): 381–94.

Shank, M. and L. Schirch. 2008. 'Strategic Arts-Based Peace Building'. *Peace & Change* 33(2): 217–42.

Sithole, M. and J. Makumbe. 1997. 'Elections in Zimbabwe: The ZANU (PF) Hegemony and Its Incipient Decline'. *African Journal of Political Science* 2(1): 122–39.

Siziba, G. 2009. 'Redefining the Production and Reproduction of Culture in Zimbabwe's Urban Space: The Case of Urban Grooves'. *CODESRIA Bulletin* (3 & 4): 19–28.

Vambe, T.M. 2004. 'Versions and Sub-versions: Trends in Chimurenga Musical Discourses of Post-Independence Zimbabwe'. *African Study Monographs* 25(4): 167–93.

CHAPTER 4

Shangwe *Mukwerera*
Systems and Hierarchies of Communication in Gokwe, Zimbabwe

Renias Ngara

Gokwe District, which lies in the northern part of the Midlands Province of Zimbabwe, is subdivided into two sub-districts, Gokwe South and Gokwe North. Each of these two sub-districts is still larger than any one of the five other districts in the province: Mberengwa, Zvishavane, Shurugwi, Gweru and Kwekwe. The Gokwe South administrative offices are in Gokwe Town while those of Gokwe North are at Nembudziya Growth Point. Gokwe South District is administered by five chiefs; namely, Njelele, Nemangwe, Sai, Jiri and Mukoka and Gokwe North by Chief Chireya and Chief Jahani. Chireya's chiefdom is much larger and therefore Chief Chireya has three *masadunhu* (sub-chiefs): Makore, Nembudziya and Madzivazvido. These sub-chiefs perform administrative duties on behalf of Chief Chireya and the local people depend on them for the settlement of social problems. The jurisdiction of local people lies in the hands of the *masabhuku* (village heads). This social structure of the Gokwe community is a model of their indigenous communication system and all groups within it understand it and are aware of the protocols to be followed.

Chiefs are regarded as custodians of culture and have a semiotic pattern of interaction with people in their communities. A similar model of interaction is reflected in the *mukwerera* rain prayers that occur between the world of the living and the spiritual realm. *Mukwerera* is a Shangwe rainmaking ceremony, during which the Gokwe community prays for rain to Mwari (God) through local rain spirits. As discussed later in this chapter, the observation of social hierarchies in communication systems by Shangwe social groupings is comparable with the observation of *mukwerera* indigenous hierarchies of rain prayers to Mwari. Aware of the hierarchy of communication, community members do not present social problems to the chiefs directly, but via their *masabhuku*. In turn, the *masabhuku* present communal requests to the chiefs through the *jinda ramambo* (the chief's associate).

Gokwe is a dry region and normally receives poor rainfall, culminating in severe drought conditions. The farmers are aware of this problem and produce cotton, which is a drought-resistant cash crop. The community also grows maize, groundnuts, roundnuts, sorghum and finger millet, mainly for subsistence purposes. The farmers are also pastoralists who rear cattle, sheep and goats. However, during dry weather spells, animals are strongly affected by drought and many die. Local farmers believe *mukwerera* rain prayers provide a possible solution to drought if rain rituals are performed as expected by rain spirits. The chiefs, as custodians of culture, are annually involved in rainmaking ceremonies that are performed at Nevana, a village that was named after the primary rainmaking spirit called Nevana. In brief, Shangwe chiefs, who are living beings, present communal rain/food pleas following an indigenous model of communication to Mwari, through secondary spirits; namely Chikono, Chinamakwati, Musemwa, Newore, Nehowa and Nyamunda and one primary rain spirit, Nevana.

Communication systems are, among other things, mechanisms designed for the prosperity and continuity of organisations in the field of commerce (Barnett 2001; Maury and Kleiner 2002; Colangelo 2010). In addition, visual communications are evident in rituals such as baby welcomes, weddings, appeasing of gods and rainmaking ceremonies. In Ugandan communities, three 'talking' drums, *saagala agalamadde*, *mujaguzo* and *milaba*, are extensively used to convey indigenous messages (Mushengyezi 2003: 110). These drums are used as follows:

a) *Saagala agalamadde* is used for summoning the community to work, such as clearing roads, planting trees and removing siltation from village wells;

b) *mujaguzo*, when played in a particular rhythmic pattern and sound, heralds the ascendance of a *kabaka* (king) to the throne, as well as signalling the arrival of the king at a social function; and

c) *milaba* may either be played for anthems of various clans or for entertainment purposes.

Gisa Jahnichen (2013: 132) in Alak, Laos, argues that Alak ritual utilises a 'single gong' for its 'mutual communication with the spirits'. The 'master drummer' plays multiple layers of contrasting rhythms, recognisable to 'other drummers and dancers', thereby promoting 'dialogue' between the drummers, the dancers and the audience (Bokor 2014: 175). These drumming 'techniques' are orally learnt and passed on from one generation to another, 'as captured in the drum language and demonstration' (178). Apollinaire Anakesa and Marc Jeannin (2008: 75) deliberate on a small drum called *ikookole*, of the Mongo ethnic group found in the northern part of the Democratic Republic of Congo, which is used 'to communicate code messages or announce change of texts'.

This chapter is not concerned with visual communication portrayed in African contexts. Its focus is on the hierarchy of communication prevalent in *mukwerera* rainmaking rituals. This work further explicates how the Shangwe community perceives their rain spirits after offering them *mukwerera* traditional brewed beer and rain does not fall, leading to community starvation. From the community's perspective, the best way to register their food pleas is through their indigenous knowledge systems of communication. An 'indigenous knowledge system' refers to the local knowledge that is exclusive to a particular culture or society (Fonjong 2008; Mapara 2009). It is 'indigenous' since it is a precolonial way of presenting food grievances within the Shangwe culture. Consequently, Shangwe chiefs, rainmaking spirits and the Nevana spirit, in particular, participate in the hierarchy of *mukwerera* rainmaking prayers.

Preceding the onset of the rainy season, the Shangwe chiefs annually collect grains from Nevana village. These grains are eventually distributed among subordinates to combine with their various grains prior to planting. The local belief is that the grains shield their crops from devourers such as marauding elephants and swarms of locusts. In addition, it is the chiefs' responsibility to participate annually in *mukwerera* rainmaking ceremonies, which are centrally organised at the Nevana shrine, called *dumba*. The *dumba* is referred to as Nevana's hut in which this spirit is believed to dwell. After harvest, chiefs then request the village heads to gather small basketfuls (*zvitswanda*) of grains from the village members. My research revealed that it is the Shangwe custom for chiefs to hand over these gifts to Nevana as thanksgiving for rain. The culture owners stressed that they offer gifts to maintain a positive rapport with the *mhondoro* (rain priest), although he does not force them to do so. In the field of commerce, social reciprocity sustains business growth (Buell and Norton 2011; Gao and Bansal 2013). In African cultures, appreciating a gift with another gift is a common practice because all the participants want to celebrate achievements (Mauss 2000; Landau and Fargion 2012). This philosophy is captured in the Shona proverb: *Kandiro kanopfumba kunobva kamwe*, which literally translates as: One good turn deserves another.

Role delineation is a significant feature of the sacred Shangwe *mukwerera* beer brewing process in which different groups of people take part, such as *chembere* (elderly women), *zvipamba/zvipotera* (young girls), men and boys. My research was conducted among culture experts such as Evina Marariromba, Silindeni Makunga, Zondiwe Makunga, Gaison Gasura, Kwuti Takavadii, Phineas Maenzani and Obert Marariromba. Evina Marariromba, Silindeni Makunga and Zondiwe Makunga are *chembere*, solely responsible for brewing the *mukwerera* ritual beer. The concept of purity is highly associated with this beer. As such, these women who brew the beer are regarded in Shangwe language as *vakagura nhovo* (having cut the mat). Sexual symbolism is embedded in this figurative expression. This means that these women no longer engage in sexual practices because of their advanced age. Culture experts also expressed that today sexually active women may brew the beer. The society expects them to abstain from sexual activities as a way of purifying themselves. During their menstrual periods, women are not supposed to participate in the beer brewing process. The rain spirits associate menstrual blood with impurity. It is believed among the Shangwe that rain spirits would not accept the beer. *Zvipamba/zvipotera*, who have not yet reached puberty, are responsible for fetching water from the rivers Ume and Mapu, located in the villages Nevana and Kufahazvinei, respectively. The Shangwe believe that since these *zvipamba/zvipotera* are not yet sexually active, they are considered pure in the eyes of the rainmaking spirits. Men and boys fetch firewood and no issue of sacredness is attached to this role. The concept of sacredness associated with certain African rituals may be viewed as spiritually set conditions for societies to keep on venerating these spirits, if they still want to receive spiritual blessings.

The information obtained from Nevana village, a village named after the Nevana rainmaking spirit, reveals that the rain priest passed on in 2000. Since the death of the Nevana spirit medium, Tevasiira Samson Marariromba, the father of Obert Marariromba, is now the *sarapavana*, which literally means 'the one who stays with children'. In the *mukwerera* ritual context, the noun 'children' does not refer to biological children, but to all the Shangwe. Thus, the rain priest communicates food/rain pleas to Nevana on behalf of the Shangwe community. One of the culture experts, Gaison Gasura, is locally known as the *munyai* (the mediator). The term '*munyai*' is symbolic. In the Shona culture, a *munyai* is a person who conducts marriage negotiations between the son-in-law and the father-in-law. In the *mukwerera* context, the *munyai* communicates communal food and/ or rainfall requests between the chiefs and the rain priest. It is noted that the role delineations in rituals are intentionally designed to complement each other's effort for the success of the ceremony.

Theoretical framework: *Mukwerera* Indigenous Hierarchical Ethnomusicological Communication Model

Traditional power is concerned with the customs, traditions and habits designed to regulate human conduct (Weber 1962). Traditional society believes that a person bestowed with traditional authority has sanctified powers. Based on interviews, it seems the local people are aware of the chiefs' supreme powers and they follow the indigenous hierarchical ethnomusicological mode of conveying food/rain grievances. Max Weber's traditional authority theory guided me in formulating the *Mukwerera* Indigenous Hierarchical Ethnomusicological Communication Model (MIHECM).

Food/rain requisition to Mwari among the Shangwe follows an indigenous model of communication, a model I refer to as the MIHECM. The *mukwerera* rainmaking prayers are not mere hierarchies of communication, but hierarchies occupied by the living indigenes as well as spirits. The communication is an ethnomusicological hierarchy of communication: this local communication system is based on five hierarchies occupied by living beings as well as rain spirits. The first hierarchy is that of community members/locals. These locals do not directly present their food pleas to the spirit of Mwari, who occupies the highest position in the *mukwerera* model of communication. In the *mukwerera* prayers, locals register their food/rain grievances to *madzimambo* (chiefs), who are second in the hierarchy. The chiefs do not provide immediate responses to the general populace. They, in turn, express rain dilemmas by singing special songs directed to the *mhondoro diki* (minor/secondary rainmaking spirits), who occupy the third position in the *mukwerera* hierarchy. The secondary spirits also sing particular songs to the *mhondoro huru* (big rainmaking spirits), such as Nevana, occupying the fourth position in the Shangwe *mukwerera* hierarchy. Nevana, who is close to Mwari, would mediate these drought problems to Him. Mwari occupies the fifth position. Once the Shangwe receive rain from Mwari, the ritual communication is deemed complete.

The practice of culturally following this hierarchy of communication is portrayed in the Shona proverb *Kukwira gomo hupoterera*, which loosely translates as 'when you want to climb a mountain, you do not go straight. The African ethos, *unhu* (morals), is embedded in this expression. The word '*gomo*', mountain, denotes

Mwari. The Shona would be referring to Mwari when they pray for rain in their mother language saying: '*Mutisvitsireo kuna avo vari kumusoro-soro*' (Convey this on our behalf to the highest one). Ritual communication systems clearly delineate roles in the world of the living and the spirit realm. The spirits, who were once living beings, are seen as the intermediaries between these two worlds. The *mukwerera* theory of communication is used to analyse selected songs in order to understand how the Shangwe present their food/rain pleas to Mwari during the ritual.

The *Mukwerera* Indigenous Hierarchical Ethnomusicological Communication Model: Its application

The subjects
Mambo tipe tiravire?
Mambo tipe tiravirewo, hondende?
Tabvira nhambwe kwaNevana, hondende.
Mapudzi-pudzi tiravirewo hondende?
Tabvira nhambwe kwaNevana, hondende.
Chief give us to taste?
Chief give us to taste, *hondende*?[1]
We came as far as Nevana's, *hondende*.
Give us squashes squash to taste *hondende*?
We came as far as Nevana's, *hondende*.

From my research with culture experts, this song portrays the Shangwe, who are presenting their rain petitions to their various chiefs because of famine. In their singing, the community members seem to be castigating one chief for the failure of rain. Symbolically, they are referring to all the chiefs. The culture experts informed me that they would be worried about chiefs who collect various gifts in the form of grains and money in order to give them to Nevana, yet they continue experiencing drought. The culture owners emphasised that it was and still is their cultural

---

1. '*Hondende*' is a word that puts pressure on chiefs, so that perform their roles as expected by society.

practice that they should reciprocate Nevana's supernatural power to supply the rain by sending him gifts annually after harvesting their crops.

Mapudzi-pudzi tiravirewo, literally meaning 'Give us squashes to taste', is a figurative expression. In its daily use in Shangwe culture, it is the practice of wanting to taste whether there is enough salt in the relish. The expression 'Give us squashes to taste' has a deeper meaning. It does not only reflect a sign of desperation for rain, but mirrors a stern anger that results from a hungry community. One of the Shangwe culture owners said that they would be seriously complaining about why the chiefs are keeping on soliciting gifts, yet it is Nevana who provides the rain. My Shangwe informants told me that *mapudzi* were immediate food crops during hunger, but the song is not referring to *mapudzi* per se. I learnt that *mapudzi* stands for pumpkins, butternuts, watermelons and other foods.

Mapudzi symbolises all kinds of vegetables and grains that the Shangwe grow in their fields. *Mapudzi* is applied in the same manner in which Christians in reciting the 'Lord's Prayer' employ 'daily bread' to mean all provisions. These agricultural products are a sign of their instant relief from hunger, which they eat while waiting for the grains that are used in making *sadza* (thick porridge or pap), such as finger millet, maize, sorghum and wheat, to be ready for harvest. The Shangwe are simply echoing their sentiments that they are tired of asking for rain from Nevana, whom they have never seen taking their gifts, as is clear in the line '*Tabvira nhambwe kwaNevana*' (We came as far as Nevana's). According to the culture experts, they are wondering whether the chiefs still carry out their cultural roles of taking gifts to Nevana. The Shangwe have reached the point of considering giving up the practice of soliciting rain blessings from Nevana and they now doubt the *mhondoro* and the chiefs' credibility in rain supplication.

Community members do not tire in presenting their requests for rain to the chiefs. They also sing the song titled 'Nhai Ishe!' (Oh Chief!):

Nhai ishe!
Pasi pamera madhonantuna
Iwe she!
Pfumo rinobva mudziva, ishe.
Oh, Chief
Thorns have sprouted on the earth
You chief!
The spear comes from the pond, chief.

This song is referring to an intense and widespread famine. The culture experts provided more than two symbolic interpretations of the word *dziva* (pond). In their daily usage, *dziva* refers to a large pool of water, usually in a river. Also, the Shangwe talk of another *dziva*, which they normally see surrounding the moon at night during the rainy season. Throughout the rainy season, the community interprets the pool as an indication that there will be plenty of rain in that particular season. Accordingly, the Shangwe do not only conceive of the *dziva* as a source of food and life, but also as a source of joy since it implies an abundance of rain. The term '*dziva*' is also a metaphor for a mother since it directly or indirectly provides food to every creature on earth, but if the mother fails to supply food, then her children begin to worry. Children's presentation of food requests may further be interpreted as their ability to apply indigenous systems of communication they are exposed to from a tender age. Implicitly, Shangwe children are informally taught and exposed to theories of communication.

The Shangwe interpret the absence of the pool around the moon in certain rainy seasons as denoting hunger since a clear sky is a sign of no rain and rain epitomises food. Given the contextual explanation of the word *dziva*, it implies that the spear (*pfumo*) does not refer to the spear, a weapon, which is used to stab or kill animals in the Shangwe context. In rain rituals, the spear is said to emerge from the *dziva* and it has destructive effects, although the *dziva* is customarily known by the Shangwe as the real source of rain and life. The word 'spear' is symbolically used to describe not only the sun's harsh heat, which destroys the crops, but it is also an emblem of no rain; hence the community will be experiencing severe hunger. In the Shangwe interpretation, hunger, thunder and lightning, wind, floods and destructive swarms of locusts are signs that the *mhondoro*, and equally their Mwari, are angry. These calamities are further perceived by the community as a form of punishment for their misdeeds. The Shangwe believe that their social problems may be resolved if the community effectively applies the *mukwerera* theory of communication. They should perform rain prayers, as expected by the spirit realm, otherwise Mwari will not bring rainfall.

The expression '*Pasi pamera madhonantuna*' (there are thorns sprouting all over the earth) is also embedded in symbols. It is painful for someone to walk on a thorn-infested ground with their bare feet. The Shangwe culture owners noted that *madhonantuna*, thorns, do not refer to ordinary thorns. Thorns signify more than a sign of restlessness, which is a feature of a severe drought. The Shangwe's interpretation of the idiomatic expression (there are thorns all over the earth) goes beyond their widespread movement in the Gokwe community. The society's restlessness gives a picture of social disturbance, chaos, communal outcry and an intensive and extensive search for food to feed family members. Thorns depict extreme anxiety and desperation. The Shangwe imagine a human being who is set to destroy the entire Gokwe district. They turn their hopes to the chiefs, who used to petition for rain from the *mhondoro*. The song is a reminder to chiefs that they should not forget their customary duties. They should follow their established local model of conveying rain prayers to rain spirits or gods on behalf of their people, which is an application of the *mukwerera* hierarchical theory of communication. Songs that are sung by chiefs reflect their request for rainfall on behalf of the community. Two of these songs, 'VaChibanya' (Mr Chibanya) and 'Tondogare Kupiko?' (Where Are We Going to Live?) are discussed below.

> *VaChibanya!*
> *Mireniko.*
> *VaChibanya!*
> *Gore rino tozobaiwa, mireniko.*
> *VaNewore!*
> *Mireniko.*
> *VaNewore!*
> *Gore rino tozobaiwa, mireniko.*
> Mr Chibanya!
> Stand there.
> Mr Chibanya!
> This year we are going to be stabbed, stand there.
> Mr Newore!
> Stand there.
> Mr Newore!
> This year we are going to be stabbed, stand there.

As explained by two culture experts, the song portrays the prospect of a severe drought if the rain spirits do not intervene as soon as possible. In the figurative expression '*Gore rino tozobaiwa, mireniko*' (This year we are going to be stabbed, stand there), the Shangwe chiefs are echoing their sentiments that the community members are going to face serious food challenges if the drought persists. The expression includes all sorts of problems that the Gokwe community is going to face in times of famine, such as severe shortage of water, scarcity of food, dying of cattle, social unrest and all sorts of nauseating words that will be used by the Shangwe to despise the chiefs. 'Being stabbed' is an image of communal uprising against the chiefs. The chiefs are aware of their vulnerability in the society. In their indigenous mode of thinking, they envision a ruthless community that is about to descend upon them. They ultimately foresee death. Rain symbolises a shield the chiefs use in order to protect themselves from their community members. This song reminds the secondary spirits of their social role in the MIHECM.

According to the culture bearers, the names in the song designate Shangwe male rain priests who go to Nevana and request rain. The term 'priest' is symbolic and should be understood to denote any person who is possessed by any spirit, be it a healing or a divining spirit. In the context of the *mukwerera*, a priest is also a person who is possessed by a rain spirit and in Shangwe folklore, there are big and small spirits. The culture experts noted that the big (*guru*) spirit is called regional spirit (*mhondoro*), such as Nevana. Small spirits (Chikono, Chinamakwati, Musemwa, Nehowa and Nyamunda) ask for rain from Nevana, who in turn communes with Mwari on their behalf. This confirms the existence of a spiritual hierarchy of communication prevalent in the Shangwe community and embedded in the MIHECM. The participation of rain spirits in inducing rain during dry weather could be viewed as a practice that cuts across cultural divides and includes all who are actively involved in farming activities.

Speaking from the chiefs' perspective, secondary spirits such as VaChibanya and VaNewore would plead with Nevana to mediate in the chiefs' rain appeal as implied by the word '*mireniko*' (stand there). In other words: The chiefs are pleading with VaChibanya and VaNewore to lobby for rain/food to the rain spirit, Nevana. The immediate provision of rain is a deterrent against social disintegration. The Shangwe chiefs want to promote social harmony and cohesion. Rain failure is a great challenge to the community's agricultural and pastoral way of life, which the chiefs are custodians of. Drought negatively affects crops as well as pastures on which the livestock depend. The chiefs are clearly aware of the communal perception that the failure of rain can be interpreted as a sign that the spiritual world is not pleased with the community's actions and, by extension, the chiefs' leadership. Rain failure can thus be read as a symbol of the decline of their power and also creates an environment conducive to social disorder, strife and potential political uprising. Since chiefs serve as community mobilisers, collectors and conveyors of tributary gifts from the community to the spirits, when Nevana or the spirits do not send rain, the community might interpret this to mean that the chiefs have appropriated the gifts meant for the gods for personal gain and aggrandisement. Such a reading of the drought undermines the chiefs' authority over the community. Once more, their communications are hierarchical and they are also gender blind. A man or a woman can serve as a *svikiro*, spirit medium, and the spirits themselves can either be patriarchal or matriarchal. Indigenous hierarchies of communication systems existing in the spirit realm are a reflection of hierarchies of communication prevalent in societies and these hierarchies may further be interpreted as an application of the *mukwerera* hierarchical theory of communication.

Chiefs in the Shangwe community are burdened if rainfall fails, as reflected in the song titled 'Tondogare Kupiko?' (Where Are We Going to Live?):

Hiye iye
He-e hiye
Tondogare kupiko?
He-e hiye
Hiye iye
Yava hondo
He-e hiye
Hiye iye
He-e hiye
Where do we go to live?
He-e hiye
Hiye iye
It's now war
He-e hiye[2]

The *svikiros* are regional spirits and if people move from one area to another, the abandonment of a region is a sign of the breakdown of the socio-spiritual bond.

---

2. These songs often use exclamations, such as 'He-e hiye' to surprise a rain god or spirit and to get their attention.

The song above signifies contemplation of migration. People come from the soil and when children are born, they are made to symbolically step on the soil and, in some cases, they eat a small amount of soil to establish the bond.

In the precolonial period, the father was the owner of the land and hence the provider of *sadza*, whereas the mother provided relish. In the *mukwerera* rainmaking ceremony, such roles are clearly delineated in the spirit realm, just as they are in the real-life setting. In the song 'Ndatadza Kurima' (I Have Failed to Plough/Grow Crops) the names Chibanya and Chikono feature. In their singing, the Shangwe will be reminding Chibanya and Chikono to present their rain requests, since it is these spirits' responsibility in the *mukwerera* hierarchical model of communication. Apart from these two spirits, the name Chinamakwati also features in this song. Chinamakwati is comparable with a Karanga *ngano* (folktale), which is about a boy also called Chinamakwati. A certain boy would be able to call rain by singing: '*Vakuru vava muno vasina mano, voti Chamatowo pfudza mombe. Ndondodzipfudzirepi wuhwa kwangu? Ndera ndera hoye*' (Elderly people who are here do not have wisdom. They ask Chamatowo to herd cattle. Where am I going to herd them? *Ndera ndera hoye*) (Ngara 2013: 129). 'African folktales of this nature' reflect the kind of 'communication systems that exist between the world of the living and the spiritual realm'.

Culture experts such as Evina Marariromba, Gaison Gasura and Obert Marariromba note that the song 'Musemwa Wee!' below conveys a sad message of famine:

Musemwa, wee!
Wanyara wee nhumbu yaoma.
Musemwa, wee!
Wanyara wee ndatadza kuenda
Oh, Musemwa!
You are ashamed the stomach is dry.
Oh, Musemwa!
You are ashamed I failed to go.

Musemwa is one of the minor rain spirits who is in command of a medium at a rain ceremony. One culture expert said that the song is sung by another rain spirit in a trance, or someone possessed by the spirits. The same spirit would be questioning why Musemwa decided to possess his medium when he saw that it was now raining and yet he was initially shy during the time when the weather was dry. The spirit in question would be openly telling Musemwa that he was incapable of providing rain. The name Musemwa is symbolic – it is a noun derived from the verb *kusemwa*, which literally means not having the attributes of being liked or admired by other people/the despised and dishonourable/the loathed one. For instance, if one has such a feeling of *kusemwa* towards food, one feels nauseous the moment one sees it. I understand that Musemwa symbolises a person who is not admirable and that could be the reason why other rain spirits do not believe that this spirit has the capacity to provide rain.

The rain spirit that opposed Musemwa desired to be recognised by the Shangwe as the one who saved them from hunger, which shows that the spirit was superior. Therefore, the song refers to a power struggle in the spirit realm, which could also be a reflection of the power struggles often experienced in communities. Rain spirits demonstrate their power struggle through the MIHECM. Power wrangles that occur in the spirit realm put pressure on spirits that they should not tire of asking for rain if the spirits expect the community to venerate them. The spiritual venerations prevalent in ritual theories of communication are ethnologically designed to raise the self-esteem of the spirits, such that their will to provide is sustained. In the metaphoric expression, '*ndatadza kuenda*' (I failed to go) the rain spirit in question wanted to make sure that Musemwa should leave before him. This particular rain spirit did not want Musemwa to have an opportunity to interact with the Shangwe since he suspected that Musemwa was possibly going to tell them that he was the one who had just brought rain and hence would be credited for the provision. The Shangwe believe that spiritual powers are not of the same strength. Furthermore, they visualise the spirit world as a place of disharmony, power struggle and turmoil, just as societies tend to be. In this scenario, spirits fight for adoration and gifts that the living people bestow on them. The MIHECM applies in the song. If the spirit had left, it could be interpreted as a gesture of surrender in participating in the *mukwerera* hierarchical theory of conveying the people's prayers for rain and food. To the Shangwe, limited participation in the rainmaking prayers is not only perceived as negligence of duty, but as a sign of insincerity.

The expression '*nhumbu yaoma*' (the stomach is dry) means that the rain spirit is signalling hunger. I suggest this is a challenge to Musemwa to demonstrate that he is also able to provide rain. Musemwa views the song not only as a mockery and an insult, but also as a symbol designed by other rain spirits to isolate him from the Shangwe community. The other inference is that Musemwa perceives that the community now doubts his ability to bring rain. The belief is that the spirits were once living human beings and they can take criticism, even when it is disrespectful. Another example is the song 'Ndiro Diro' (It Is a Baboon), which was sung with a *hera mbira* at dawn, when it is still dark and the spirit has refused to come at the *bira* (a soul-bringing rite).[3] The song refers to the spirit as a baboon! The people are not afraid to use such language, as it may draw the spirit's attention and shame it into action. Essentially, provocative communication systems that are rampant in between the spirit realm and traditional communities are vital tools that are purposely manipulated towards attainment of the intended goal.

Major rainmaking spirit(s): **Mhondoro *as the spiritual lion that protects people***

In this section, I examine the last phase of the MIHECM by analysing one song that is sung for Nevana.

> *Hoye, hoye!*
> *Hiye, hiye!*
> *Hoya, ahonde!*
> *Waita murudzii pana ambuya?*
> *Hoye, hoye!*
> *Hiye, hiye!*
> *Hoya, ahonde!*
> What humanity/behaviour do you show in the presence of the mother-in-law?

The culture experts explained that this song conveys an embarrassing message. According to them, it is sung soon after the Shangwe have presented the *mukwerera* traditional brew offering at the Nevana graveyard, which is another shrine for performing *mukwerera* rain prayers. Among the Shangwe and even the Karanga, a mother-in-law (*mbuyawasha*) and a son-in-law (*mukwasha*) owe each other great

---

3. The *hera mbira* is also known as *mbira dzaVaHera*. As the second name suggests, this type of *mbira* was named after the Hera people who are of the Shava totem. The *hera mbira* is used at ritual ceremonies such as a *bira* (soul-bringing rite) to invite the spirits.

respect and the society expects the two to keep a social distance. *Mbuyawasha* and *mukwasha* are customarily not expected to shake hands, but simply to greet one another by kneeling down and clapping their hands. According to the Shangwe, the question 'What humanity/behaviour do you show in the presence of mother-in-law?' does not address a real human being. It denotes the Nevana rain spirit, which will be moving in the form of a harsh wind, even though it has been offered *mukwerera* ritual brew. The 'mother-in-law' refers to the Shangwe *mukwerera* performers and participants. The Shangwe culturally expect a son-in-law who would have been offered food by his mother-in-law to show gratitude and appreciation. They believe the same in the *mhondoro*, Nevana, who would have been offered *mukwerera* traditional brew. This is a sign of social reciprocity and yet the *mhondoro* has not provided rain in exchange. Social reciprocity is a principle that states that a human being is traditionally expected to show gratitude by giving a gift after they have received a gift. By reciprocating gifts, a good rapport is sustained between the giver and the recipient (Mauss 2000). Reciprocity evokes obligations toward one another on the basis of past behaviour (Diekmann 2004) and it reveals that once one has been given something, one feels driven to give back something in order to maintain a positive relationship. John Deckop, Carol Cirka and Lynne Anderson (2003) note that it is also a Middle Eastern cultural construct that human beings should reward a gift by another gift. In Christian societies, this is formulated in the biblical 'Do to others as you want them to do to you' (Luke 6:31). In Western culture, it is expressed in the idiom 'One good turn deserves another', in Shona translation, '*Kandiro kanopfumba kunobva kamwe*'. These expressions all underscore the concept of social reciprocity. They also emphasise the Shona morals ethos (*unhu*). The lack of such a gesture of appreciation is viewed by the community as a lack of humanity. The concept of social reciprocity is prevalent in the *mukwerera* indigenous theory of communication. In the *mukwerera* rainmaking context, the Shangwe offer Nevana ritual brew. According to Shangwe social expectations, the *mhondoro* is expected to bring rains in order to maintain the social principle of acknowledging one's giving. Linda Molm, David Schaefer and Jessica Collett (2007: 211) point out that 'cultural variation in the strength of communal relationships imply that reciprocal exchange assumes a more prominent role in close relationships than what has been previously observed in the communal/exchange tradition'. The provision of rainfall by rain spirits in return for the ritual beer offerings is interpreted by the Shangwe as a practical application of the *mukwerera* theory of communication. Rainfall supplication is further perceived by the community as a means of not only strengthening the social bond between the spirit world and the living, but is also viewed as a symbol of acknowledging the symbiotic relationship that exists between these two worlds.

The above song is thus meant to evoke the Nevana spirit to possess his medium. The song's question seeks to find out what prompted the *mhondoro* to show this lack of social reciprocity in response to the beer offerings. In the Shangwe world view, Nevana is perceived as a human being who has lost humanity. Here, the Shangwe are concerned as to why signs of hunger should still prevail. The community is simply informing the *mhondoro* that he should address their rain petitions otherwise there are possibilities for him to lose his popularity and customary veneration. The Shangwe are also expressing their deepest anger at the rain spirit since they believe that he is holding back the rains. The community intentionally provokes Nevana to communicate their prayers for rain and food to Mwari because this spirit is close to Him in their spiritual hierarchy of communication.

In essence, certain songs are mechanisms manipulated by communities to remind people and spirits that occupy influential positions to act as expected. Once Mwari receives the community's prayers, the MIHECM is deemed complete and the entire community anticipates rain as a reciprocal reward for the brewed beer. It is Mwari who completes the hierarchy of communication by ultimately providing rain. Similarly, Breck Parkman (1993) argues that the Indian god Indra brings rain during dry periods and Donald MacKenzie (1985) notes that in southern Europe it was believed that Zeus Pater wielded a thunderbolt for breaking rocks.

Conclusion

The MIHECM is a theory in practice by the Shangwe during times of drought. The *mukwerera* rainmaking prayers are presented to Mwari through five established hierarchies of communication. The community members utilise rainmaking songs as a way to remind the spirits and Mwari that hunger is now deeply rooted in the society and that chiefs should provide food or social uprising will occur. Similarly, chiefs manipulate the local model in presenting their subordinates' prayers to rain spirits. In this scenario, the Shangwe seek protection from the spirits by requesting rain through songs that are meant to provoke them to possess mediums in order for the community to have an opportunity to speak with them. The Nevana spirit is traditionally expected to communicate the food shortages to Mwari and it is only when the rain falls that the local communication model will be completed and the community can then continue to relate as a family.

References

Anakesa, A. and M. Jeannin. 2008. 'The Rhythmic and Melodic Variations in Traditional African Music and Dance: Mongo's Bongolo Culture'. *The World of Music* 50(1): 73–88.

Barnett, R.E. 2001. 'The Original Meaning of the Commerce Clause'. *University of Chicago Law Review* 68(1): 101–47.

Bokor, M.J.K. 2014. 'When the Drum Speaks: The Rhetoric of Motion, Emotion, and Action in African Societies'. *Rhetorica* 32(2): 165–94.

Buell, R.W. and M.I. Norton. 2011. 'The Labor Illusion: How Operational Transparency Increases Perceived Value'. *Management Science* 57(1): 40–56.

Colangelo, A.J. 2010. 'The Foreign Commerce Clause'. *Virginia Law Review* 96(5): 949–1041.

Deckop, J.R., C.A. Cirka and L.M. Anderson. 2003. 'Doing unto Others: The Reciprocity of Helping Behavior in Organizations'. *Journal of Business Ethics* 47(2): 101–13.

Diekmann, A. 2004. 'The Power of Reciprocity: Fairness, Reciprocity, and Stakes in Variants of the Dictator Game'. *Journal of Conflict Resolution* 48(4): 487–505.

Fonjong, L.N. 2008. 'Gender Roles and Practices in Natural Resource Management in the North West Province of Cameroon: Local Environment'. *International Forest Review* 13(5): 461–75.

Gao, J. and P. Bansal. 2013. 'Instrumental and Integrative Logics in Business Sustainability'. *Journal of Business Ethics* 112(2): 241–55.

Jähnichen, G. 2013. 'Field Note: Musical Instruments Used in Rituals of the Alak in Laos'. *Asian Ethnology* 72(1): 119–42.

Landau, C. and J.T. Fargion. 2012. 'We're All Archivists Now: Towards a More Equitable Ethnomusicology'. *Ethnomusicology Forum* 21(2): 125–40.

MacKenzie, D.A. 1985. *Indian Myth and Legend*. New York: Avenal Books.

Mapara, J. 2009. 'Indigenous Knowledge Systems in Zimbabwe: Juxtaposing Postcolonial Theory'. *Journal of Pan African Studies* 3(1): 139–55.

Maury, M.D. and D.S. Kleiner. 2002. 'E-Commerce, Ethical Commerce'. *Journal of Business Ethics* 36(1/2): 21–31.

Mauss, M. 2000. *The Gift: Forms and Functions of Exchange in Archaic Societies*. New York: W.W. Norton.

Molm, L.D., D.R. Schaefer and J.L Collett. 2007. 'The Value of Reciprocity'. *Social Psychology Quarterly* 70(2): 199–217.

Mushengyezi, A. 2003. 'Rethinking Indigenous Media: Rituals, "Talking" Drums, and Orality as Forms of Public Communication in Uganda'. *Journal of African Cultural Studies* (16)1: 107–17.

Ngara, R. 2013. 'Shangwe Music for Spiritual Rituals: A Symbolic Enactment'. *Studies of Tribes and Tribals* 11(2): 127–33.

Parkman, E.B. 1993. 'Creating Thunder: The Western Rain-Making Process'. *Journal of California and Great Basin Anthropology* 15(1): 90–110.

Weber, M. 1962. *Basic Concepts in Sociology*. New York: The Citadel Press.

CHAPTER 5

If Vagina Had Teeth
Song, Film and the Reshaping of Female Identities through Rituals of Rainmaking Ceremonies among the Shona People of Western Mozambique

Maurice T. Vambe

The aim of this chapter is to explore orality as expressed through the mediums of songs and films. Theoretically, Walter Ong (1988) postulates that when popular songs exist within the intestines of secondary forms, such as film, then they must be explored as subversive in the sense that there is no guarantee that the meanings will favour the primary instance of enunciation or the multiple meanings that manifest from secondary interpretation of the film mode. This chapter explores the fecund power of the vagina in the symbologies of the rituals of the rainmaking ceremonies of the Shona people of western Mozambique, as depicted in the film *If Vagina Had Teeth*. Geographically, colonialism enforced physical boundaries that did not correspond to the spiritual imagination of the African people. Shona people live largely in Zimbabwe,[1] although there are fairly significant groups of Shona-speaking people in Mozambique. They are not necessarily Ndau or Manyika, but Shona-speaking Mozambican citizens and the Shona-speakers in Zimbabwe understand one another. Mozambican Shona women seem to control the spiritual symbols of the imagined community of the Mozambican/Zimbabwean nation, thus rendering the Zimbabwean/Mozambican physical boundary not only arbitrary, but also clearly revealing it as a colonial artifice. Although Mozambican men command the physical symbols of political power, it is in fact the women's songs that ensure that power is reshaped and infused with female-centred identities that provide regenerated layers of syncretic identities for the Shona women of Mozambique. Through the performance of songs and films, women configure new identities,

---

1. The Shona people of Zimbabwe are made up of Karanga, Zezuru, Korekore, Manyika and Ndau.

through which they influence or manipulate the power of patriarchy and, in the process, create their own identities, which are sometimes considered dangerous to men. This link between danger and gender is associated with the power of women's rituals of rainmaking, which are perceived as sustaining community stability.

Theorising ritual song in film

Since Ruth Finnegan's path-breaking *Oral Literature in Africa* (1970), the academic field of oral studies has grown steadily and dynamically. Particularly, the song genre has been analysed in different contexts, emphasising its transforming forms, styles and content. The general trend in the 1970s was to view song as a vehicle of cultural expression for themes such as celebrations of African nationalism and the concomitant expectation that songs were the carriers of anti-colonial values. Alec Pongweni's *Songs That Won the Liberation War* (1982) focuses on how the Zimbabwe African National Liberation Army (ZANLA) liberation forces deployed songs to mobilise the masses against colonialism. The link between songs and visible organised forms of African nationalism reveals how elite and patriarchal authorities manipulated the cultural form to give some stability to their anti-colonial narrative. While agreeing on the potency of songs in representing national aspirations, Leroy Vail and Landeg White's (1986: 194) study on forms of resistance in songs in colonial Mozambique questions the nationalist tendency to narrow the genre of songs' 'cultural potential to representing resistance and collaboration'. Their contention is that songs reveal multiple forms of human behaviour when we free interpretation from the binary of resistance and collaboration. African people are at all times resisting something or collaborating with forces viewed as negative. To think in these inflexible ways would deprive the songwriters and the songs themselves of alternative values. Furthermore, each song is ultimately singular, although its degree of communal acceptability is linked to what individual creators share with the community.

The capacity of the song genre to be stretched in different directions has allowed songwriters to invent new song styles, combining African traditional and Christian narratives (Rafapa 2009). In the case of women's songs of West Africa, a variety of themes and emotions – ranging from initiation, funeral, praise performance, lamentation and sex education – occurs (Hale and Sidikou 2014). Most studies on song still prefer to analyse a song as a stand-alone form occurring outside other genres. This tendency has in some cases yielded in-depth analyses of the songs and the variety of themes and diverse styles. For example, song advances noble causes, such as the fight against HIV and AIDS, and deftly handles critical debates on matters such as representing female identities (Mdluli 2009).

A shift in thinking about the dynamism of song is signalled when songs are viewed not as texts in writing, but as oral performances. Thabazi Ntshinga (2000) notes that this shift introduces ambiguities, one of which is how audiences are drawn to participating in reshaping a new song from the old one. The new conditions of performance flexibly accommodate the multiple but contradictory interests of a heterogeneous audience that can respond in a variety of unexpected ways. Linking song to performance further enhances the communicative capacity of a song, as accompanying dance and mime utilise the body as their medium of expression. Samuel Ravengai (2013: 3) views the 'shift from the dominance of dramatic dialogue to the body [as] an insurgent act' and, according to Liz Gunner (1994: 118):

> Through their expressive art [women] could reshape and control in a way that was otherwise not possible. This notion of power relates to the acceptance in many African societies of licence, in some situations, within song and poetry – that singers may tell terrible things in song and poetry, set out what it is not usually heard and survive with impunity

In Gunner's view, female performers are perceived as dangerous, in that they might influence other women to follow their lifestyle, as they are often single or divorced. The sense of danger from women who perform is linked to the power dynamics of the stage as a liminal space where new identities can be recreated during performance. Furthermore, the power of women singers is also connected with women's ability to revision their lives. In other words, portraying women's power in their expressive art could reshape and control audiences in ways unanticipated or otherwise not possible in formal and everyday interactions between men and women.

While women push boundaries of meanings in song and performance, this is further enhanced when song is used in the narrative interstices of other forms, such as the novel and film. Within any novel, songs embrace the aesthetics of non-closure in order to provide space for shadow narratives that would complicate any attempt by the songs to settle select meanings as natural and sealed with closure against interpretive negation. When songs appear in film, they are not mere soundtracks filling in, for instance, when dialogue is absent or standing in for transitions from one shot to another. This view makes songs in film narrative appear as ancillary as Nyasha Mboti (2012: 728) argues unfairly about the presence of Yvonne Chaka Chaka's pop song 'Umqombothi' in *Hotel Rwanda*: 'The promise of song and of genocide are made to attract, comingle and become synonymous within the same sinister register and memory that cause others to be killed'. It must be pointed out that 'Umqombothi' was not written for the 1994 genocide. The song also could not have caused 'others to be killed' because it was used in a film made ten years after the genocide. It can be argued that song in film is provided with a wider context in which the verbal, the aural and the visual form narratives that 'are not merely coterminous with others but centrally constitutive of each other' (Vambe 2012: 19). Conventional wisdom suggests further that the life of an artistic form as secondary orality encourages what Urther Rwafa (2008: 189) describes as 'dynamism, poly-valence and heterogeneity in meaning within lyrics [which] lend credibility to the view that musical lyrics in film can construct, mediate and interrogate taken for granted socio-cultural realities'.

In fact, listening to lyrics in film is a practice of listening otherwise. Not only words but sounds, how they are made, when they are made and by whom they are uttered are all the elements that secrete surplus meanings to the visual, musical and verbal signifiers in the film. An encounter with words, rhetoric and voice in film means paying attention to words that appear to give songs an independent source of semantic meaning; to rhetoric in which words are used in a special musical way, which draws attention to features and problems of speech and with voice made up of words being spoken or sung in human tones, which are themselves meaningful signs of persons and personality. Approaching a musical film in a way that considers the simultaneous combining and uncoupling of these genres promotes a spirit of disarticulating authoritarian emotions of reverence to the words uttered in song. Thus, song in film cannot be reduced to the role of 'covering up the noisy clanking of clumsy contraptions, or for cuing characters or functioning as film score and the soundtrack' (Mboti 2012: 734).

Other critics have also fallen into this conceptual mistake that song in film is an add-on and not a constitutive narrative without which ritual in film has no significance. Innocent Uwah (2011: 93), for instance, writes that song in film serves merely to 'introduce the next sequence by using thematic issues in the film to highlight actions and reactions of characters'. This view can provide a shortcut to understanding the agency of song, especially when it must be remembered that from the point of view of the audience, song, visuals and verbal signifiers appear in the virtual interstices of film narrative simultaneously as complementary and competing narratives, where sometimes neither is allowed the privilege to project itself as more important than the other. Each of these genres – song, pictures, voice and verbal languages – are for a critical audience a journey into the narrative-ness or constructedness of the content of form and meanings that depends on a 'knowingness, a collusion between performer and (implied) audience, between audience and (implied) performer, which is both inclusive and exclusive, worrying and reassuring' (Bailey 1994: 144). Rey Chow (1993: 396) indicates that comprehending the fluid narratives within the technology of film requires watching or listening otherwise to musical films, which for him changes the meaning of music from its traditional association with a plenitude that escapes concrete articulation on account of its infinity, to that of a part object whose field is elsewhere. At the same time, this part object is surplus; it is not reducible or graspable in the form of an externalised image. It therefore requires a different kind of theorising.

If song admits sophisticated interpretation, the expansive nature of sanctioning and disputing metaphors inherent in ritual songs enacted in a highly visualised film text and fertility rites of women demand a different theorisation. Uwah has attempted this reconceptualisation, taking the Nollywood film industry as point of focus. He reveals that in Nollywood film, African traditional religion and ritual song perform two functions. First, the ritual songs reshape notions of African time and identities and may in visibly performed experience emphasise stability. Secondly, ritual song in film may allow one to enter 'into a symbolical experience of community which is deeply emotional and pleasurable and then returning to the context of structure with a sense of social values' (Uwah 2011: 86).

The rituals performed through song in film also function as sites of memory, invoking the presence of the departed ancestors for their validation as 'living-dead'. Sites of memory, according to Pierre Nora (1989: 7), are cultural spaces where

> memory crystallises and secretes itself . . . at a particular historical moment, a turning point where consciousness of a break with the past is bound up with the sense that memory has been torn – but torn in such a way as to pose the problem of the embodiment of memory in certain sites where a sense of historical continuity persists.

The rituals of rainmaking ceremonies performed by the Shona women of western Mozambique manifest the conscious and the unconscious elements of the culture of a people who have been visited by communal traumas induced by natural processes that result in drought, which threatens the very existence of the people and their physical and spiritual cosmology. In describing performances of rituals of rainmaking as acts of bearing witness to a communal trauma, as represented in the film *If Vagina Had Teeth*, I use Dori Laub's formulation of bearing witness as a form of vicissitude to performers, listeners and watchers who are transformed into witnesses of the trauma. The significance of this paradox is elaborated by Laub, who states that in the process of bearing witness to a catastrophe and its possible communal resolutions, the emergence of the narrative which is being listened to – and heard – is therefore the process and the place wherein the cognisance, the 'knowing' of the event is given birth to. The listener therefore, is a party to the creation of knowledge *de novo* (Laub 1992: 25).

In the section below, I describe the physical sequence of the movement of the community in *If Vagina Had Teeth* from Chief Chassuka's village into the forest and back to the village in a performance that mimics rainmaking rituals.

Sequence of rainmaking ceremony in *If Vagina Had Teeth*

It is important to state at the outset that the ritual of rainmaking captured in *If Vagina Had Teeth* is an artistic fragment and does not represent the entirety of the actual rainmaking ceremony. Thus the film is a representation of a ritual and the complexity of this subjective depiction is only apparent after identifying the different sequences captured in this short film. It begins at the village of Chief Chassuka in the Manica Province of Mozambique. The early shots of the film depict a group of men and women sitting down and as is usual the men are the ones talking. The subject of the men's talk is the importance of informing the ancestors of the community's aim to supplicate for rain. In this shot, drought is declared a community trauma and reasons are given for the cause of the drought: people have committed taboo acts, such as burning the forest.

Some inhabitants of Chassuka's village have not followed natural land uses and have cut down trees and this is said to have disrupted the natural cycle of rain. When drought occurs, it affects everyone, but the community registers it as a tragedy caused by the wrong actions of people. In these early shots of the film, the women are either merely listening to, or agreeing with the men, and pointing out that some of the violators are women, who sell wood to people across the border in Zimbabwe. This first sequence reveals that social problems are dissected by the community and that in Shona cosmology communication assumes talking to the living, the unborn and the 'present' who are departed. Furthermore, the male-centred scene affirms patriarchy's mostly uncontested role in naming the source of the problem and then indicating what the possible solution might be. Thus, in this initial 'ritual' of identifying causes of social pressure and communal destabilisation, the dialogue led by men mainly reassures male authority that it is in control during the rainmaking ceremony. The second sequence of the community ritual is the movement from the village into a part of the forest where the rainmaking dance, song and fertility rituals take place. The third movement is signalled by the community of women and men returning to Chief Chassuka's village, where the people share food and beer in a gesture that suggests that the ancestors have accepted the community's ritual offerings.

The passage from the 'real' world of the mundane village life into the exalted and symbolic world of myth and ritual in the forest suggest a sense of a threshold crossed. Ato Quayson (1997: 46) suggests that in traditional African stories and imaginaries, the 'bush is the antithesis of settled communities and is conceived of as the problematic "Other", harboring all sorts of supernatural forces'. The forest is seen as potentially a place of cruelty and imprisonment and, together with the spirit world, embodies the chaotic and anxiety-generating forces of nature. Quayson qualifies his observation by adding that the forest is also a space not beyond human or supernatural habitation. Northrop Frye (1976) argues that the forest is a physical space where hunters can derive heroism from the processes of adventure and confrontation of challenges to which the hero is exposed. Thus, for Frye, the ascent from the lower world of the forest signals spiritual readjustments from momentary imprisonment to higher levels of 'freedom', signalled by protagonists' 'escape, remembrance, the discovery of one's real identity, growing freedom and the breaking of enchantment' (129).

The significance attached to forests and African sacred groves is further underscored by Michael Sheridan and Celia Nyamweru (2008: 2), who argue that African forests relate to land tenure systems, communal processes of environmental management and reveal 'how these key symbols relate to both group identities and Africans' experiences of colonization'. The vocabulary of the women's bodily movements during the dance and performance for rain in the forests introduces meanings associated with women's capacity to reconfigure the forests into entities that engender fertility, which is associated with bringing rain. This perspective emphasises human sexual fecundity in the ritual of rainmaking and charges women's performances with a variety of meanings. According to David Lan's research in Dande, northern Zimbabwe, among the Korekore fertility rites and performances provide the energy for rainmaking and, most significantly, 'amongst the Shona the right of land ownership is demonstrated and proved by the ability of a particular set of ancestors to control its fertility. The people whose ancestors bring the rain own the land' (Lan 1985: 98). However, unlike in *If Vagina Had Teeth*, where women's sexual/fertility dances are centralised in rainmaking, Lan believes that in Dande there is a consensus that only men possessed by the spirit of *mhondoro* (lion) have the power to conjure rainfall.[2] In Lesibana Rafapa's (2009) view, in the rainmaking ceremonies of the Mamaala people in South Africa, they use rituals to temper the malignant forces of globalisation. One could argue that rainmaking ceremonies show that Africans can construct alternative contexts where their agency is felt outside the dichotomy of tradition versus modernity. In other words, rainmaking rituals pre-date Western colonisation and demonstrate African people's understanding of their physical and spiritual environment. To suggest that these rituals are performed to prevent the effacement of subaltern forces is to deny Africa any other context within which human agency can be realised in restoring their communities.

What is further important, however, to underscore about the bodies of women during the ritual dances and songs in the liminal zone of the forest is the focus on the meanings generated by the women performers. The body is itself a site of performance and presents or refracts different meanings to the audience. Ravengai (2013: 16) correctly observes that in ritual theatre or songs in films, the songs continue to carry the freight of the theme of the occasion, but are not the only source of meanings:

> When parataxis takes place it dissolves the dominance of the word and assigns dominance to other modes of performance of a visual dramaturgical nature. Since action on stage ceases to be an imitation of action, but the action itself, it forces the audience to wonder whether they are watching the event as fiction or as reality. This occasional irruption of the real on the stage compels audiences to react to the event as real and more often than not join in the performance with performers at appropriate times.

---

2. According to Lan, the *mhondoro* possessed chiefs and some members of royalty. The spirits were the guardians of the people. Since the spirits were said to possess the power to make rain fall, by virtue of that power they claimed ownership of land in Zimbabwe (Lan 1985).

By 'dissolves' I understand Ravengai not to mean that the words are totally occluded. When we watch or listen to music, we listen to words, pay attention to rhetoric and also consider the voice and tones through which a performance is produced (Vambe and Vambe 2006). In *If Vagina Had Teeth*, the space of the forest enables women to enact performances that would not normally be acceptable in the politics of the everyday life. During the songs women transform themselves into 'men', holding sticks between their legs, running after men in gestures that imitate aggressive sexual encounters. Some men try to trip and fall and the women dive on top of these men, imitating sexual gyrations. Most of the men take to their heels in different directions in the forest, away from the women who have become men by virtue of wielding stick symbols of the penis. Women also act out their own fantasies of satisfactory sex that is procreative and lifegiving. Some men feign shame, others are encircled by women aggressively contorting their lower bodies in all sorts of sexually provocative ways. This up-ended world continues with singing songs that would be considered profanity in the world outside the ritual of rainmaking. The symbolism is that women are wet (Lan 1985) and that men are dry and need the powers of women's fecundity and fertility to regenerate the community. The presence of the departed is acknowledged and the intimation that the unborn shall see the light of day is also underlined in the visual dances. Shona women thus command authority in the forest – their powers arise when they are outside of the village. As outsiders, in the sense that women are brought into a man's lineage to bear children, the value of women as sources of rain and of procreation is thus affirmed.

Analysis of the women's songs in *If Vagina Had Teeth* manifests three archetypal metaphors of renewal contained in the performance: (1) satirical images, (2) celebration of metaphors of genital power, and (3) reconstruction of women's identities as possibly the true bearers of a communal – and, by extension, a national – consciousness among the Shona people of Mozambique.

Complaint songs of rainmaking ceremony in *If Vagina Had Teeth*
The ritual songs in *If Vagina Had Teeth* are straightforward fragments of three or four lines each. This means that the power of the songs stems from the context in which they are uttered, the purpose the songs are perceived to fulfil and most importantly the attitudes exuding from tonal inflections of the words. For example, the first fragment rhetorically protests against sexual enslavement of women by men:

Herere, ndaneta kubata mboro nejende
Herere, ndaneta kubata mboro nejende.
Whew, I am tired of holding the penis and testicles
Whew, I am tired of holding the penis and testicles.

It is from 'holding' the male sexual organs that the biological identity of maleness is politicised and associated in the minds of the community with power. Thus patriarchy bases its authority over women using socially constructed narratives in which it is made to seem as if not having penis and testicles should make women feel less human, if not subhuman. The women in the song complain that they are tired of being enslaved; made keepers of instruments that oppress them. 'Penis' and 'testicles' are straightforward words, which in the literal sense do not evoke perceptions other than that they are biological appendages. However, because it is the women who mention these organs during the rainmaking ceremony, complaining to men who are present to endure the mockery, the words mean something else. The song undermines male authority and reveals that actually it is men who are dependent on women. Without women with vaginas in whom men can exercise their sexual power, men are deprived of authority. This means that although men ejaculate into women, it is the bodily fluids of women and fecundity of their ovaries that ultimately create new life.

The subversive element of the song is that the reference to men's genitalia can be uttered without fear of reprisal in the context of rainmaking ceremony. Nancy Glazener (1989: 113), who reflects on the power of language in affirming and denying men's power, notes that women mock men by 'em-bawdying' the men's organs. In the Shona poetic genres of *mavingu* (protest poetry) and *jikinyira* (complaining poetry), women can tell off a wayward husband in a song without attracting punishment. Vail and White (1986) observe that in protest songs in Mozambique and other southern African cultures, women can swear at men and insult the source of power/respectability (penis and testicles), but to attack the men outside the song would not be tolerated. That the focus of women's complaint and derision is on men's sex organs connects with the very core theme of rainmaking ceremonies that celebrate fertility and fecundity.

In *If Vagina Had Teeth* the visuals show women faking being drunk and exhausted and posing as wanting reprieve from men's insatiable sexual appetites. Other women pretend to remove their underclothes and seek out weak men and then run away. One woman retorts that the problem is that the men's 'penises are heavy because [they] are full of soil and [also because] their testicles have been cut off and hung on the trees'. The upended world is created by the very fact that women can utter sex-related words that they would not do in 'normal' situations. Women feel empowered to challenge male ancestors and patriarchy on both physical and spiritual grounds. In the song women have created an alternative centre of power whose authority rests on their capacity for inducing rain to fall. Thus, the world of the ritual creates multiple worlds that allow for 'dialogical leakage which can be exploited for the ends of resistance both within fiction and beyond' (Pechey 1989: 55).

Derisive songs of the rainmaking ceremony in *If Vagina Had Teeth*
In some songs in the film men are depicted as incapable of bearing children or even laying claim to any child because in the absence of modern technology for paternity tests, women emerge as the uncontested owners of children. Women grow babies for nine months in their wombs and that also entitles them to be significant to other rituals of birth and human renewal, such as bringing rain to the community. In the song 'Nyamboro', any man with a penis is an owner or possesses '*mboro*', but is depicted as having to use it to satisfy women as well as to create new life through procreation. Such men are mocked and they are metaphorically dry. In fact, they spend their time defecating and women have to almost seek enjoyment from themselves:

> *Nyamboro waenda kunhengeni.*
> *Gunguo rineyi? Gunguo rine mboro.*
> *Watorerwa uripi?*
> *Waenda kundo mama.*
> Nyamboro has gone to gather fruits.
> What does a crow have? It has a penis.
> So how has Nyamboro lost his wife?
> Nyamboro had gone to defecate.

The failure of men to bring rain by themselves is considered in the piece above as akin to sexual abdication. This, once again, leaves women starved of sex – as one of the female singers in the film says: 'We are putting our vaginas away because there are no men to use them.' Men are supposed to feel embarrassed, again, women empower themselves as bringers of rain.

In the film's long shots, the women move towards the men and some women sit on men's laps to provoke them. One woman shouts, 'There it is, it is coming, it's waiting by the trees, come, come.' A woman gyrates towards a man who enacts sexual penetration on the woman, but the man quickly withdraws, runs away and sits down and this leaves the sexually hungry woman livid and she derides the man: 'It's as if he is stealing. It's not fair when he comes too quickly.' This might suggest selfish men who ejaculate too early during the sexual encounter. Women desire 'long' play during the sex act and in the language of rainmaking this would symbolically represent prolonged downpours of much-needed rain. Again, the women's freedom to complain and deride the men is tolerated in the context of the ritual ceremony, but would be considered deeply offensive outside the popular festive world created by ritual rainmaking. Although in *If Vagina Had Teeth* most men are drummers for the women's taunting songs, some men take the women's challenges in their stride. One of the men pushes away a woman about to sit on him and sings about what he thinks of women in language that diminishes women's sexual power:

Mheche inonhuwa vakuruwe
Hamusati maona mukati mayo.
The vagina stinks
You have not seen its inside.

No woman in a normal wife-husband relationship would listen happily if the man was to insult and refer to her vagina as smelly, but because these lines are uttered in the context of the ritual, the women can tolerate how they are mocked. The women's response throws further aspersions on the manhood of patriarchy, further diminishing its role in procreation and renewal of humanity:

Mboro inonhuwa wakurure
Hamusa timaona mukati mayo.
The penis stinks
You should see its inside.

In these lines the women mock the male organ and depict it as debased. Among the Shona people of western Mozambique, female power carries authority. How this female voice carnivalises the sources of patriarchy's authority clears ground to install the female principle as significant in the ritual of rainmaking. Commenting on the role of the genitalia in rituals, Mikhail Bakhtin (1984: 372) states that debasement is the fundamental artistic and ritualistic principle in that in the language of the marketplace all that is sacred and exalted is rethought on the level of the material body, resulting in the momentary 'uncrowning' of men from their traditional positions of power.

It is important to say that from the perspective of the ritual of rainmaking where new life is announced through images of negation, the reciprocal insults of male and female organs by men and women are not taken seriously because they are not meant to offend the physical human form, but to provoke spiritual ancestors to unleash the rains. Thus, in the spiritual world reconstructed in the ritual, mockery is accepted and undertaken by men and women. This ensures that both men and women are expected to be responsible in resolving the physical and spiritual trauma brought about by the drought that has necessitated the rainmaking ritual in the first place.

Triumphalist women's songs in the rainmaking ceremony in *If Vagina Had Teeth*

The triumphant moment of the female principle over male authority in *If Vagina Had Teeth* is registered through visual narratives of women who openly partake in the merriment of drinking beer with men. The focus of the film shots on the big, round beer pots frosted with beer resembles not only the women's wombs from which human life begins to develop, but also points to the fact that ritual of 'wetness' should invoke rain to fall. In the visual narrative, women break into freestyle dancing, holding their private parts, clustering around Chief Chassuka as a symbol of 'arresting' him for the moment of the ritual, thus claiming to render his earthly power weak. The women sing:

Ndashaya musungo, ndisunge mboro.
I cannot find a rope to tie the penis.

The ribald language does not offend the ancestors, whose presence is acknowledged by both men and women appealing to them to intercede to make rain fall. Because it is the female principle that must be prominent, women sing this song, indicating that male organs depend on women's lifegiving principle for creating new life. Women run around the physical space where ritual enactment takes place in the cleared portion surrounded by foliage, big green trees announcing that all men succumb to the influence of labial authority. The women sing of their sexual organs in positive terms, thus 'crowning' the female organs while male organs are described as effete as shown in the song where even Chief Chassuka, for all his earthly and socially ascribed authority, had to marry a woman to fertilise the fecund womb of women without which there is no life and rain:

Gongondiye mambo
Gongondiyeishe
Chassukka aibvisa mombe
Kutengagongo.
Vagina lips are king
Vagina lips are king
Chief Chassuka paid cattle
To buy the vagina lips of his wives.

'*Gongo*' or vagina lips provide comfort to men and accept what the penis offers and vagina lips are wet as rain. The shift in viewing female sexual parts is that they are not the ones viewed by men as debased; female sexual organs acquire a new role and symbolise regenerated life. Writing about the representation of genital power and female sexuality in West African literature and film, Naminata Diabate (2011: 3) complains that in male writing: '[W]hen questions about female sexuality in the West African context emerge, they tend to be bound up in issues of ethics, the paradigm of victimization, and/or an uncritical celebration'.

However, in *If Vagina Had Teeth*, the meanings of women's genital powers are resignified and ascribed positive virtues. Women have acquired this new status of authority over life through negating and then expropriating men's spiritual authority. In the film, Shona women mock men and sit on men's laps as symbols of demeaning the sexual powers of men. Women's songs celebrate women's bodies. The women partially bare their nether parts and suspend the everyday social roles that would normally limit them to minors, together with children. This view somehow modifies Lan's observation that among the Korekore (a branch of Shona) of Zimbabwe that 'women participate only as singers and as dancers but never individually, only as members of a group, never creatively, always repeating what has been repeated time after time in the past' (1985: 95).

In *If Vagina Had Teeth*, instead, the women even enact same-sex erotic acts and gyrate in front of coy men and in this way can be said to be resisting the tacit cultural taboos around questions of sexuality and images of female sexuality. According to Diabate (2011: viii), this phenomenon in which women usurp the sexual powers of men should properly be called 'genital power', meaning that women can shake off and deny authority to male narratives that mainly image women's bodies as 'an exclusive site of female subjugation'. In the film it is immaterial that at the end of the ritual ceremony, Shona women return to their age-old and socially sanctioned roles of serving men. When the women 'become' ordinary people again after the ritual, it is women who dutifully serve food and beer to men before they themselves eat or drink. What is significant is that within the world constructed by ritual, a world that disturbs an ideal male society where women are only powerful when they are 'least like women and most like men' (Lan 1985: 94) women's 'genital power' is manifested. The main oral text with which women begin and end the film is contained in the song 'Beche', which insists:

Beche dai riine mazino, beche
Mboro dzose dzingapera.
If the vagina had teeth
All penises would be finished.

The revealed contempt, voiced sexual insults and curses by women warn that there is nothing that men can do to extend their male lineage without women. This statement might sound contradictory and Diabate (2011) cautions against romanticising women's power. In spite of this observation, the audience of *If Vagina Had Teeth* emerges from the experience with the knowledge that the symbolism of the women's dances and songs depicted in the film visuals has already asserted women's agency. In other words, the context in which women exercise power to influence and even control the natural rhythms of their communities does not always have to be in situations of overt struggle with men, colonialism or neo-colonialism. This argument is important because it modifies Diabate's (2011) exploration of women's agentive powers of performance in contexts overdetermined by men and their male-driven economic systems. The other view that rainmaking ceremonies perform the function of tempering the excesses of Western modernity (Rafapa 2009) is potentially patronising because of the assumptions that everything that Africans carry out in their backyards must be responding to Western modernity. It is an argument that credits Western modernity with dynamising African traditions, conceived in this argument is as static. Another view, advanced in this chapter, is that African people have agency, can create their own contexts of actions where they struggle to change their physical and spiritual environments in the best ways that they have evolved and know. Therefore, if rituals of rainmaking ceremonies are viewed as another way of organising rural/community economies, it must be said that in these contexts both ordinary men and women attempt to harness their indigenous knowledge systems, so that they do not have to be seen as relying on the so-called Western-inspired modernity. In one sense, it is immaterial whether rain falls or does not fall just after the ritual; what is significant are the meanings of the symbolism of women's participation in rainmaking ceremonies. A community harnesses its subterranean cultural and spiritual resources when confronted by large-scale natural traumatic events, such as drought, that threaten the very existence of the community. Ritual overcomes the community stress and ritual energies are charged with a plethora of meanings for those who perform the ceremonies.

Conclusion

This chapter shows that the Shona women of western Mozambique command significant sexual/spiritual powers when a community is faced with a life-threatening phenomenon such as drought. The community searches for solutions from within itself. The songs used in the ritual of rainmaking are not stylistic embellishments of the film narrative of *If Vagina Had Teeth*. The verbal signifiers in the songs create independent interpretive social frames through whose meanings the role of women in Shona communities is repositioned positively. The visual signifiers that the film medium provides bring the experience of women close to the audience, showing how listening to songs and watching the actual physical performance by women generated meanings beyond the instance of the ritual. In the film women curse, mock and laugh at men's genitalia and these forms of carnivalising patriarchy suspend the traditional power relations in which women are always slotted into the victim paradigm. The ritual and its songs momentarily change roles and emphasise not only the procreative powers of women, but also their capacity to spiritually intervene in society in order to effect desired change for the community's good.

By their very symbolic nature, rituals and particularly rituals of rainmaking ceremonies in *If Vagina Had Teeth* generate and transport surplus meanings beyond the literal word in the song. This observation is important because it allows one to explore the songs in film from other perspectives. One such crucial interpretation of the rituals analysed in this chapter emphasises the fecund power of the Shona women's genital powers whose symbologies transcend the geographically and colonially enforced physical boundaries, which did not correspond to the spiritual imagination of African people. Ritual is important not only in reinterpreting space, but also in understanding time, as the rainmaking ritual layers time, allowing the performers to remember how they have in the past succeeded over natural and human adversities. Ritual also tells the Shona community that something more than the past strategies are needed to confront new challenges.

References

Bailey, P. 1994. 'Conspiracies of Meaning: Music Hall and the Knowingness of Popular Culture'. *Past and Present* 144.

Bakhtin, M. 1984. *Rabelais and His World*. Boston: Massachusetts Institute of Technology.

Chow, R. 1993. 'Listening Otherwise, Music Miniaturized: A Different Type of Question about Revolution'. In *The Cultural Studies Reader*, edited by S. During, 385–6. London: Routledge.

Diabate N. 2011. 'Genital Power: Female Sexuality in West African Literature and Film'. PhD diss., University of Texas, Austin.

Finnegan, R. 1970. *Oral Literature in Africa*. Nairobi: Oxford University Press.

Frye, N. 1976. *The Secular Scripture: A Study of Romance*. Boston: Harvard University Press.

Glazener, N. 1989. 'Dialogic Subversion: Bakhtin, the Novel and Getrude Stein'. In *Bakhtin and Cultural Theory*, edited by K. Hirschkop and D. Shepherd, 109–29. Manchester: Manchester University Press.

Gunner, L. (ed.). 1994. *Politics and Performance: Theatre, Poetry and Song in Southern Africa*. Johannesburg: Witwatersrand University Press.

Hale, T.A. and A.G. Sidikou (eds). 2014. *Women's Songs from West Africa*. Bloomington: Indiana University Press.

Lan, D. 1985. *Guns and Rain: Guerrillas and Spirit Mediums in Zimbabwe*. Harare: Zimbabwe Publishing House.

Laub, D. 1992. 'Bearing Witness or the Vicissitudes of Listening'. In *Testimony: Crises of Witnessing in Literature, Psychoanalysis, and History*, edited by S. Felman and D. Laub, 25–30. New York: Routledge.

Mboti, N. 2012. 'Song and Genocide: Investigating the Function of Yvonne Chaka Chaka's "Umqombothi" in *Hotel Rwanda*'. *Critical Arts* 26(5): 728–44.

Mdluli, S. 2009. 'Swazi Women, Song and the Constructions of Social Awareness in Swazi Culture'. *Muziki* 6(1): 58–78.

Niglas, L. and F. Storaas (directors). 2009. *If Vagina Had Teeth: The Shona Rainmaking Ceremony in Western Mozambique*.

Nora, P. 1989. 'Memory and Counter-Memory'. *Representations* 26: 7–24.

Ntshinga, T. 2009. 'Song Texts and the Ambiguities of Oral Performance'. *Muziki* 6(1): 36–48.

Ong, W.J. 1988. *Orality and Literacy: The Technologizing of the Word*. London: Routledge.

Pechey, G. 1989. 'On the Borders of Bakhtin: Dialogisation, Decolonisation'. In *Bakhtin and Cultural Theory*, edited by K. Hirschkop and D. Shepherd, 39–67. Manchester: Manchester University Press.

Pongweni, A. 1982. *Songs That Won the Liberation War*. Harare: The College Press.

Quayson, A. 1997. *Strategic Transformations in Nigerian Writing*. Bloomington: Indiana University Press.

Rafapa, L. 2009. 'The Use of Oral Hymns in African Traditional Religion and the Judeo-Christian Religion'. *Southern African Journal for Folklore Studies* 19(2): 76–84.

Ravengai, S. 2013. 'The Political-Aesthetic Function of Song and Dance in Zimbabwean Theatre 1980–1996'. *Muziki* 10(1): 1–18.

Rwafa, U. 2008. 'Lyrical Film: The Case of *Tanyaradzwa*'. *Muziki* 5(2): 188–95.

Sheridan, J. and C. Nyamweru. 2008. *African Sacred Groves: Ecological Dynamics and Social Change*. Oxford: James Currey.

Uwah, I.E. 2011. 'The Representation of African Traditional Religion and Cultures in Nigerian Popular Films'. *Catholic Institute of West Africa* 23(2): 81–102.

Vail, L. and L. White. 1986. 'Forms of Resistance: Songs and Perceptions of Power in Colonial Mozambique'. In *Banditry, Rebellion and Social Protest in Africa*, edited by D. Crummey, 193–227. London: James Currey.

Vambe M.T. 2012. 'Songs of Biafra: Contrasting Perspectives on the Igbo Genocide in Chukwuemeka Ike's *Sunset at Dawn: A Novel of the Biafran War* (1993) and Chimamanda Ngozi Adichie's *Half of a Yellow Sun* (2007)'. *Muziki* 9(2): 15–40.

Vambe M.T. and B. Vambe. 2006. 'Musical Rhetoric and the Limits of Official Censorship in Zimbabwe'. *Muziki* 3(1): 48–78.

CHAPTER 6

Doing the 'Serious Business of Older People' Correctly
Zimbabwean *Mbira* Popular Adaptations

Vimbai Chamisa

The aim of this chapter is to examine various strategies adopted by popular musicians to reconstruct Shona indigenous *mbira* sources in the Zimbabwean music industry. Through analysing certain popular songs and conducting interviews with musicians Oliver Mtukudzi, Chiwoniso Maraire and Thomas Mapfumo, who sometimes borrow from Shona traditional sources, I seek to understand Zimbabwean popular musicians' understanding of accuracy with reference to the adaptation of *mbira* traditional music and what they regard as unchanging in (re)presenting this genre, regardless of the differences from one adaptation to another. Through focusing on selected songs by Mapfumo, Mtukudzi, Maraire and Andy Brown, this chapter also interrogates in detail why the musicians adopt certain strategies when adapting *mbira* traditional sources. Having identified three adaptation strategies mainly used by the musicians, I explain that although the adapted *mbira*-based pieces have been 're-orchestrated' for a contemporary audience, the traditional beliefs behind the sound's potential and the meanings traditionally associated with particular indigenous songs have transcended time and space. In precolonial Zimbabwe, Shona traditional music was always performed in a dynamic environment, as Ezra Chitando (2002: 22) notes: 'There was considerable movement of people and ideas or the invention of the concept of globalization' in the Shona community. The country was colonised by the British in around 1890 and the cultural life of many indigenous people of what became Southern Rhodesia was profoundly affected. This caused the transformation of performance contexts for traditional music, as people migrated into urban centres, especially Salisbury (now Harare). This meant that the contexts of traditional music became increasingly urban in the late nineteenth and early twentieth centuries.

Several factors reshaped the performance of indigenous music in urban centres in the 1930s. Firstly, the increasing rate of unemployment in Bulawayo and Harare and the cultural dislocation during this period saw indigenous music and dance becoming the 'mainstay' of townships such as Mbare (Dube 1996: 104). This context gave birth to greater musical professionalism and the 1950s saw the emergence of popular indigenous-based music and guitar bands. These bands were, in Thomas Turino's words, 'modernizing village music by arranging it for electric instruments, recording it for mass media diffusion and performing it for cosmopolitan settings quite distinct from its original contexts, functions and meanings' (2000: 275).

Secondly, the Second Chimurenga (1964–79), which was a result of the steady imposition of white minority rule and the proclamation of the Unilateral Declaration of Independence (UDI), also became significant in the performance and transformation of indigenous music in Zimbabwe. This is the period that marked what Alec Pongweni (1982: i) describes as the 'earth-shaking revival of ethnic music' in his work on the songs that won the liberation struggle. The Zimbabwe African National Union – Patriotic Front (ZANU–PF) recognised the importance of mobilising the masses through the use of song and dance. Most songs appropriated styles from Shona musical genres, especially *mbira* music (Vambe 2004: 175). *Mbira* traditional music, for example, became an ideological statement of protest (Kwaramba 1997: 18).[1]

Thirdly, Zimbabwe's post-liberation history also offered moments that redefined the performance of traditional music in the popular music industry. Therefore, encounters with various experiences and challenges in Zimbabwe have in precolonial, colonial and postcolonial times had an impact on the production and performance of Shona traditional music. Of particular interest to this chapter is the adaptation of *mbira* traditional music in the popular music context. Certain popular musicians claim to have approached *mbira* indigenous sources with caution during the adaptation process, 'so as to reproduce [them] correctly' (Turino 2000: 296). Oliver Mtukudzi, for instance, clearly states:

---

1. Popular musicians have always adapted Shona traditional music to express political sentiments in Zimbabwe. The reasons for this, as explained by Pongweni (1982), are that indigenous music promotes feelings of solidarity and often contains subtle meanings that are implicitly political.

> You have to stick to the *mbira*, and if you're doing *mbira* songs your guideline is how the *mbira* is played you can't go beyond that. If you go beyond that [you] are not doing it right. I mean, if you try and improve from there, you can only add a guitar or something, so you have to play it like that [because] *mbira* is the serious business of older people, and it has to be done correctly (in Turino 2000: 296).

Other popular musicians have expressed similar sentiments. Thomas Mapfumo believes that *mbira* music was invented by the ancestors, 'that's something original and you cannot change that' (Guma 2013). Chiwoniso Maraire also raised the idea that 'changing traditional *mbira* songs becomes disrespect to the elders who have created them'.[2]

Despite these claims of the importance of remaining true to the ancestors, many *mbira* popular adaptations show that *mbira* indigenous sources can be reproduced in different ways. The question of how these musicians consider their *mbira* adaptations to have been respectful of the traditional sources when they have actually conceived of different pieces using traditional elements in different ways is thus central in this chapter. Adaptation of tradition and the notion of invention are not the same processes or necessarily done for the same reason. However, Eric Hobsbawm and Terence Ranger (1983: 2) remind us that these processes are 'the contrast between the constant change and innovation of the modern world and the attempt to structure at least some parts of social life within it as unchanging and invariant'. Veit Erlmann (1991: 10) also writes in relation to South African music that 'changing musical systems display a remarkable persistence of fundamental procedures of stylistic patterning beneath the more obvious changes in the surface structure'.

My personal background as a Shona triggered my interest in embarking on this research. I naturally had exposure to the cultural performances of Shona traditional music at an early age. I grew up in a rural area in the district of Shurugwi in the Midlands Province of Zimbabwe. I remember very vividly the childhood game songs that we sang in the village, the work songs and the music of *mapira* ceremonies – for example, the annual *mutoro* rainmaking ceremony.[3] Traditional

---

2. Chiwoniso Maraire, interview, 29 January 2013, Harare.
3. The Shona word *mapira* is plural for *bira*. According to Berliner (1993) *bira* is a ritual,

music was performed in almost all activities of everyday life, from social to ritual events, and this environment enabled me to internalise many rhythms and melodies, as well as the texts of various traditional songs. I later learnt how to play some of the traditional Shona songs from my cultural repertoire on *mbira* and marimba at the Midlands State University, Zimbabwe, where I did my undergraduate studies in music and musicology (2005–9). This experience of the performance of Shona folk music as an insider and as a performer has made me appreciate the inherent aesthetic worth of Shona traditional music and informed my aim to comprehend the performance of Shona music in the Zimbabwean popular music industry.

Historical background to the performance of *mbira* indigenous music

Whether or not the musicians strategically or subconsciously draw from the *mbira* indigenous sources, 'the basic tendencies for decision making are grounded in the cultural formation in which one was originally socialized' (Turino 2008: 127). Thus to understand these musicians' positions with regard to the utilisation of traditional *mbira* sources, it is first necessary to give some historical background to the traditional performance of the *mbira* in Shona society.

Shona society believes that *mbira* music was conceived by the ancestors. This largely shapes the beliefs and values ingrained in traditional musical performances – for example, that it is associated with spirituality and strongly believed to induce spirit possession (see, for example, Tracey 1963, Kauffman 1969 and Berliner 1993). At a Shona *bira* ceremony, for instance, the *mbira dzavadzimu* (songs of the ancestors) are considered to have the 'power to project its sound into the heavens, bridging the world of the spirits and the world of the living, attracting attention of the spirits' (Berliner 1981: 132). Through mediums, Shona ancestral spirits are believed to 'offer moral insights into the human conditions . . . moderating social relations ethically, mediating disputes and curing illness' (Scherzinger 1999: 110). They are identified as culture heroes and they exert a protective influence over all society. They withdraw their protection in reaction to moral transgressions (Dewey 1991: 26). It follows therefore that *mbira* indigenous music is treated with respect; in the face of problems beyond human control, *mbira* music is believed to

---

celebrated by Shona people calling for guidance and intercession from ancestral spirits (*midzimu*). The word *mutoro* is a name of a Shona rainmaking ritual ceremony. It is during such a ceremony that *mapira* are held.

create a context conducive for the ancestors to intervene. Though many people in Zimbabwe today have become Christians and no longer depend on such traditions for life, the beliefs associated with *mbira* have remained.[4] In 1999 Mapfumo explained in an interview with the Canadian journalist Minister Faust, in relation to his song 'Shumba' (Lion) (1995), 'That song is for the medium, the spirits. This *shumba* is not just a wild animal. It's the spirit lion. Whenever there is a gathering of this sort they always expect that the spirit lions are outside looking after them.'[5]

Thus the value of *mbira* music performances in the Zimbabwean popular music context lies in its ability to evoke ancestral beings.[6] There have always been expectations that must be met in the performance of *mbira* music for it to be accepted by the people and the ancestors. As a result, traditional *mbira* performances are judged good or bad. Paul Berliner (1993: 202), for instance, notes a scenario where a possessed woman stopped some musicians from performing at a ceremony; she took their instruments and threw them away because they were playing poorly. *Mbira* traditional music has also become widely associated with war and resistance in Zimbabwe. Zimbabwean historian Moses Chikowero (2013) explains:

> The *mbira* is one instrument that really was a metaphor in the suppression of the indigenous, not just music, but cultures, ways of knowing, ways of doing things, indigenous knowledge. So it is not surprising that this is an instrument that had been at the forefront of defining how Africans conceptualize music prior to and during the colonial decades.

Alice Kwaramba (1997: 18) also asserts that *mbira* traditional music became an ideological statement of protest during and after the liberation struggle in Zimbabwe. The majority of the arranged popular *mbira* songs I have chosen for this chapter are pre- and post-*chimurenga* songs – for instance, Mapfumo's songs

---

4. For more information on the influence of Christianity on traditional cultural practices in Zimbabwe, see Turino (2000: 35) and Chitando (2002: 25).
5. Thomas Mapfumo, interview by Minister Faust, May 1999, Edmonton, Canada.
6. In the Shona culture it believed that after death people can go on to protect their families as spiritual beings. It is during the spirit possession ceremony called *bira* that the spirits communicate with people and *mbira* music plays an important role to facilitate possession. See Berliner (1993) for more detail. These spirits are classified differently depending on their relationship with the living. There are family spirits, clan spirits, territorial spirits and alien spirits. See Matiure (2007) for more information on Shona cosmology.

'Hondo' (War), 'Pasi Paenda' (The World Is Coming to an End), 'Zimbabwe Yakauya Nehondo' (Zimbabwe's Independence Was Achieved through Liberation Struggle), 'Zvichapera' (It Shall Come to Pass), 'Waurayiwa' (Killed), 'Chamunorwa' (Why Fighting) and 'Muchadura' (You Shall Confess).[7] It is clear that *mbira* music was adapted to contemporary music partly because of its strong association with suppressed Zimbabwean traditions (Kwaramba 1997: 18). This is because *mbira* music has been appropriate and adaptable to the ongoing political injustices and economic crisis that has characterised Zimbabwe since the pre-independence era and musicians found ways to protest through this music. In this context, the reconstruction of *mbira* traditional music in certain ways should be interpreted as an attempt to carve Shona people's space within the history of colonial and postcolonial Zimbabwe.

Strategies for adapting *mbira* traditional music

In considering structural analysis as a methodology for analysing the repertoire of adapted Shona popular songs to develop a set of criteria for categorising the songs as versions of Shona traditional music, my work mirrors Jim Chapman's approach. He has constructed a set of frameworks to analyse and understand the processes involved in cross-cultural composition (Chapman 2007).[8] Chapman's approach shows how various musical structures composed of material from across cultures can be analysed in order to reach particular decisions. In my work, however, I focus on musical works that have been arranged by musicians from within the same culture, but whose styles and approaches to Zimbabwean popular music performance vary. Studying the patterns involved in the adaptation of Shona traditional elements, I examine the impact that certain Shona indigenous sources and elements have on Zimbabwean popular music composition and the effect that has on representing the Shona concept of tradition. I believe that there is some 'inner consistency' that makes it possible for some of these songs to be valued as Shona traditional pieces, despite the various popular genre labels into which

---

7. *Chimurenga* songs are songs that capture the sentiment of war and the longing for freedom in Zimbabwe. *Mbira* music is now associated with the *chimurenga* musical genre (Vambe 2004: 167).
8. Chapman is a Western jazz and popular music composer, but his compositions are greatly influenced by his strong interest in traditional contemporary African musical styles (Chapman 2007: 1).

they are categorised. I also think that the relationship between musical works cannot only be understood through focusing on the consistencies or similarities between various musical structures; reflecting on why certain inconsistencies occur in the presentation of particular elements in different works may also be useful to interpret connections between them.

Adopting terms such as 'sampling', 'imitation' and 'abstract appropriation' from Chapman (2007: 84–9), I wish to examine various approaches to the adaptation of indigenous Shona musical elements, as reflected in the distinct Zimbabwean musical styles. Several musicological and ethnomusicological scholars have discussed these three terms. Kelvin Holm-Hudson, for example, writes in relation to the sampling technique that it is the repetition and recontextualisation of music that musicians have heard before (in Chapman 2007: 82): the 'creator of a sampled sound piece is merely an arranger, pasting together fragments of a musical history in such a way that the total exceeds the sum of the quotes'. Examples of sampling include Deep Forest's 'Sweet Lullaby' (1992) and Peter Gabriel's 'Last Temptation of Christ' (1989). Citing Herbie Hancock's 'Watermelon Man' as an example of imitation, Steven Feld describes it as a direct quotation from the original piece (in Keil and Feld 1994: 280). And abstract appropriation is when a musician such as Ligeti 'uses abstract rather than surface details' (Taylor 1997: 21).

Expanding on these ideas, Chapman (2007: 88) defines imitation as 'the quotation of riffs and rhythms and other musical devices into a new setting . . . direct quotation, modification and improvement of the original'. While using the term 'direct quotation' both Feld (in Keil and Feld 1994) and Chapman (2007) explain that in the imitation process the borrowed material should be clearly transparent such that the reproduced piece is almost identical to the imitated piece. The modifications to the original work enable it to simply fit within a new performance context without necessarily making it different from the original piece. Similarly, in the context of this chapter, I use the term 'imitation' to refer to the reproduction of a certain traditional Shona *mbira* piece in its entirety. I categorise these as 'entire *mbira* adaptations'. Chapman (2007: 88) goes on to define sampling as the 'direct incorporation of a sound, or recording without alteration'. However, sampling is a technique in popular electronic music/disco that takes only part of the material from another source (Hesmondhalgh 2006); yet Chapman uses the term to mean wholesale verbatim 'quotation'. How does this differ really, from imitation? The two frames (imitation and sampling) are used by Chapman in way that they seem to overlap and the difference between them needs to be critically analysed. In the context of this chapter, popular songs that fall within the sampling category only adapt the basic *mbira* part of a particular traditional *mbira* song, which is core material to any Shona *mbira* traditional piece and any other elements are optionally used. In the imitation technique a musician quotes certain material from a traditional *mbira* source. However, limited material is borrowed; the bulk of the material is newly composed. Therefore these songs are not obviously identified with traditional *mbira* sources. This is discussed in more detail later in the chapter.

Chapman (2007: 88) defines abstract adaptation as the 'use of ideas from another culture's music in a conceptual way . . . and then application of the ideas in a different context to the original'. This suggests that the new piece is further removed from the original, and yet the original is still recognisable, so how abstract can it be said to be? The category of abstract *mbira* adaptations in this chapter refers to the idea that they solely utilised indigenous Shona *kudeketera mbira* tunes and text, excluding the core part of Shona *mbira* music.

Chapman's frames as explained here are not only necessary to critically determine the elements that acknowledge which Zimbabwean popular songs have commodified indigenous Shona *mbira* music, but also to establish relationships between various musical elements in the composition and performance of *mbira* music. Through identifying the structural elements that continue to define traditional Shona music within the Zimbabwean popular music industry, my work shares the goal of Shona musicians, namely, facilitating the continued history of traditional Shona *mbira* musical culture and identity. I therefore argue that popular musicians generally adopt three different strategies for the adaptation of traditional m*bira* songs. Firstly, some of the songs have been adapted entirely from identified traditional *mbira* sources, others adapt the 'standard basic *mbira* part' only and some adapt the '*kudeketera*' tunes and text only, or just the text.

Characteristics of traditional Shona *mbira* music and the relationship between its various components have been well documented (Berliner 1993; Maraire 1990; Titon 2009). All Shona *mbira* pieces are composed of at least two 'standard basic parts' on which they are based. The first one is called the *kushaura* part, meaning to lead or call. It consists of two lines, namely *kushaura kwepamusoro* (high tone lead) and *kushaura kwepasi* (low tone lead) and these provide much of the melodic essence of a piece. The second is called the *kutsinhira*, meaning to exchange parts of a song or to interweave a second interlocking *mbira* part. It also consists of two lines and these are *kutsinhira kwepamusoro* (high tone response) and *kutsinhira kwepasi* (low tone response). *Kutsinhira* lines are performed in response to the *kushaura* part.[9] Most indigenous *mbira* pieces consist of a 48-beat pattern divided into four major phrases of 12 beats each, performed cyclically in a call and response pattern (Berliner 1993: 75).[10] However, some of the songs have two phrases (binary form) also performed in a call and response pattern (Maraire 1990: 42). In terms of *mbira* vocal content, there are three distinct styles: *kudeketera*, *huro* and *mahon'era*. Since *huro* and *mahon'era* are generally characterised with vocables and yodelling (Berliner 1993: 117), I mainly focus on *kudeketera*. This is a verbal style that draws from Shona poetry and is considered a form of singing.[11]

Imitation: Entire mbira *adaptations*

Mbira adaptations in this subcategory utilise all the elements – melodic lines, rhythm and lyrics – from their indigenous *mbira* sources, hence here I call them 'entire adaptations'.[12] They also usually maintain the names or titles of the original versions. Examples include, among many others, 'Mutavara' (Beat the Drum Harder) by Mtukudzi; Maraire's 'Nhemamusasa' (Temporary Shelter), 'Zvichapera' (It Will Come to Pass) and 'Chembere Dzemusango' (Evil People); as well as Mapfumo's 'Nyama Yekugocha' (Meat to Roast), 'Butsu Mutandarika'

---

9. The *kushaura* and *kutsinhira* standard basic *mbira* parts are performed simultaneously by at least two people and they always have a call and response or question and answer relationship to each other.
10. Andrew Tracey (1963) refers to beats as 'pulses' and devised pulse notation paper to notate *mbira* (and other types of African) music, to free it from association with staff notation's concept of bars and beats. In my analysis of Shona traditional music in this chapter, I use Berliner's concept of beats and bars because I used Sibelius for transcribing certain musical examples.
11. The term '*kudeketera*' can be defined in different ways in the Shona language. See footnote (d) in Berliner (1993: 162). In this context, I use it to refer to a form of singing known as '*kuimba*' in Shona.
12. The *Hosho* rhythmic pattern, which is an essential part of traditional Shona *mbira* performances, is retained in these examples. Harmony is also an important aspect of *mbira* music (see Scherzinger 2001). Analysing the *mbira* piece 'Nyamaropa', Scherzinger explains that harmony in traditional *mbira* songs can be used to distinguish one *mbira* piece from another. In this chapter, the focus is on other aspects of *mbira* music that are not analysed in Scherzinger's work.

(Long, Oversized Shoe), 'Chemutengure' (Wagon Wheels) and 'Taireva' (We Used to Warn You). A song such as 'Hanzvadzi'(Sister), arranged entirely from 'Nhemamusasa' by Mapfumo, may be exceptional, but this new name seems to have been derived from the poetry traditionally sung to the original 'Nhemamusasa'. This type of adaptation of *mbira* traditional music can be referred to as imitation, which according to Chapman (2007: 88) is a direct quotation of the original.

It is possible in some situations that in adapting the 'same' traditional *mbira* song, popular songs are composed of different material in some sections. For instance, 'Hanzvadzi' and 'Nhemamusasa' by Mapfumo and Maraire respectively have both been arranged from the traditional war song 'Nhemamusasa', but their lyrical content is not necessarily the same throughout. While the *chimurenga* musician Mapfumo borrows the lyrics, which emphasise the idea of war in his popular version – for instance, the phrase 'Roverera museve' (Stab with an arrow) – Maraire eliminates such phrases in her version. Therefore, depending on context and individual creative skills, entire *mbira* adaptations may not sound exactly the same in every respect. This makes the songs sound different even though they have the same traditional source. These subtle differences around entire *mbira* adaptations (imitation) means that after directly quoting the main framework of the musical pieces and their associated texts, musicians can modify them by adding their own material and 'other foreign styles' or they may decide to exclude variations.[13]

Most of the *mbira* songs in this subcategory were traditionally performed in ritual and spiritual contexts. Such songs are believed to be 'songs of the ancestral spirits' (Locke 2009: 95). These songs include 'Nyama Musango' (Meat in the Forest), 'Nhemamusasa' (Temporary Shelter) and 'Chembere Dzemusango' (Old Women of the Forest). I believe this influences how different popular musicians consider using the individual aspects of these *mbira* traditional songs in their own versions. Maraire, for example, explained to me that Adam Chisvo (a former member of her band Vibe Cultures, who played the *mbira* on this song) would 'go under the water, he would go places with the sound of "Nhemamusasa"'.[14]

---

13. Each traditional *mbira* piece has variations that can be played alongside its basic standard material. As these variations are optional for performance, they impact on the way a particular tune is interpreted by different musicians.
14. Chiwoniso Maraire, interview, 19 January 2013, Harare.

This explains a deeply spiritual situation where during performance, certain musical sounds facilitate spiritual connection for the performer and as a result s/he experiences or does things that s/he cannot do under normal circumstances. So when Chiwoniso and her band arranged their version of 'Nhemamusasa', 'every aspect of the original song was relevant' in this particular case.[15] Therefore, what popular musicians believe in relation to traditional Shona *mbira* songs determines in some cases how the indigenous elements of *mbira* songs may be presented in popular versions.

This brings to mind Carol Muller's insights on 'inalienable possessions' in her work on the Nazarite religion of South Africa, where she explains that inalienable possessions 'are artifacts of emotion and experience given form through expressive culture and circulated among members in systems of ritualized exchange' (1999: 59). Things such as spirituality and power are identified as inalienable possessions in the Nazarite religion and songs and dances are also seen in this way. Outside ritualised and localised contexts, some Zimbabwean popular musicians have made sure the reproduction of such inalienable treasure (*mbira dzavadzimu*) takes place without alteration. Chiwoniso explained that such an approach to the adaptation of traditional Shona *mbira* music has enabled traditional spirituality to continue to be experienced in contemporary 'urban' settings. This contemporary setting represents the current postmodern musical environment, which is a significantly different context from the rural setting where the music traditionally used to be performed. Thus, 'in changing times and different places, traditional *mbira* music becomes the centre for traditional spirituality to negotiate the boundaries of identity' (Preston 2007: 24).

However, other musicians, such as Mtukudzi and Brown, have been very flexible and incorporated within *mbira* music adaptations of their own material, as well as foreign styles. 'Mutavara' by Mtukudzi and 'Kutapira' (Sweet) by Brown are good examples. In 'Kutapira', arranged from 'Manhanga Kutapira' (Sweet Pumpkins), for instance, Brown added his own lyrics to the pre-existing poetry – '*Huya uone kutapira kunoita manhanga*' (Come and taste the sweetness of our pumpkins), traditionally performed in a call and response style to 'Manhanga kutapira'. Below is some of Brown's modified text for his version:

---

15. Maraire, interview, 19 January 2013.

> *Huya uone kutapira*
> *Kunoita manhanga iwe muZimbabwe*
> *Aha kutapira*
> *South Africa uchakamirirei kurima mumunda wako*
> *Mozambique usambofa wakatengesa ivhu rako*
> *Namibia kutapira kunoita manhanga*
> *Aha kutapira*
> *Zambia kutapira kunoita manhanga*
> *Africa usafa wakanyengerwa*
> Come and taste
> The sweetness of pumpkins in Zimbabwe
> Oh sweet
> South Africa enjoy your land
> Mozambique never sell your land
> Namibia pumpkins are sweet
> Oh sweet
> Zambia pumpkins are sweet
> Africa beware not to be deceived

'Kutapira' was completely adapted from its indigenous *mbira* source and appeared on the album *More Fire: Third Chimurenga Series* by Brown and Keith Farquharson in 2002. In the traditional context, this song was performed for secular reasons; after a successful and fruitful farming season, a proud farmer would tell neighbours of his achievements. Presented partly in the call and response pattern and partly in a rap singing style from about two to two-and-a-half minutes into the recording, the song presents to Africa what was termed the 'Hondo Yeminda' (War for Land) in Zimbabwe, promoting farming and the land redistribution programme of 2000. Without omitting any of the indigenous elements of the original song and in order to present 'cultural-ethnographic accuracy' for the global music market, Brown invokes the traditional song's meaning by simply adding his choice of text (Taylor 1997: 26).

Entire *mbira* popular adaptations present a way in which all elements of the indigenous source are significantly utilised to determine the overall meaning of a particular popular song. According to the information that I obtained from the Zimbabwe Music Rights Association (ZIMURA), entire *mbira* adaptations are registered as traditional arrangements and musicians get partial royalty payments. Chiwoniso, for instance, is given 50 per cent royalties on both performance and mechanical rights on her song 'Nhemamusasa' – the other 50 per cent is accredited to the originating community.[16]

Sampling: Adapting the standard basic mbira part

Songs in this subcategory utilise material from the standard *kushaura* and *kutsinhira* basic parts of the indigenous *mbira* sources, largely eliminating the traditional *kudeketera* tunes and text. The *hosho* rhythmic pattern is usually included, but the addition of contemporary instruments – for example, when the *hosho* rhythmic pattern is played on hi-hats – makes the rhythmic idiom sound more contemporary. This is the approach used mostly by Zimbabwean popular musicians to arrange traditional *mbira* songs. The ethnomusicologist Dumisani Maraire (1990: 42) describes this standard basic material as 'direct' or 'present and obvious' lines in traditional *mbira* music. Since popular musicians adapt this material into a new musical context, composing new lyrics and messages for their songs, this approach to the adaptation of *mbira* musical sources can be called sampling.

Sampling, as explained previously, involves 'direct incorporation of a sound, or recording' (Chapman 2007: 88). It differs from imitation in the sense that imitation is quotation of the whole piece while sampling only quotes part of the original source and incorporates it into a new composition. The records from ZIMURA indicate that popular songs in this subcategory are regarded as original compositions and the musicians are allocated 100 per cent royalties on both performance and mechanical rights.

The song 'Chamunorwa' (Why the Fighting) on the album *Chamunorwa* (1989) by Mapfumo adapts both the standard *kushaura kwepamusoro* and *kutsinhira*

---

16. Zimbabwean copyright law stipulates how the partial royalties are supposed to be paid to the originating community. However, whether the originating communities are receiving these benefits is quite a fraught topic (see McConnachie 2008). McConnachie examines how certain South African communities have received royalty payments from the use of their traditional music archived at the International Library of African Music. Further research on precisely how ZIMURA's royalty policy works would be worth pursuing.

kwepasi parts of the indigenous Shona mbira *song* 'Taireva'. Figure 6.1 shows the transcription of the original 'Taireva', as performed by Fradreck Mujuru.[17]

Figure 6.1 'Taireva' standard *kushaura* and *kutsinhira* parts, as performed by Fradreck Mujuru. Transcription by Vimbai Chamisa

Note: I have used a 6/8 time signature in this transcription because the song has a 24 beat pattern divided into four phrases and each of the phrases consist of 6 beats.

In Figure 6.2, the *mbira* 1, *mbira* 2 and the bass played on 'Chamunorwa' directly quote the right and left hand *kushaura* as well as the *kutsinhira kwepasi* lines from 'Taireva'.

---

17. Fradreck Mujuru is a widely recognised Shona traditional *mbira* performer in Zimbabwe. He was born in 1955 in Rusape and he is a grandson of the late Muchateta Mujuru, a respected Shona spirit medium. See http://mbira.org/index.html and Zindi (2003: 84) for more detail on his *mbira* musical life and the contribution of the Mujuru family to traditional *mbira* music.

Chamunorwa

Figure 6.2 'Taireva' standard *mbira* lines in 'Chamunorwa', 0:29–0:36. Transcription by Vimbai Chamisa.

On the hi-hats, he also retains the rhythmic time line often played on *hosho* in *mbira* traditional performances. Mapfumo combines these well-known lines with his own material produced on guitars; the vocal lines and text are also completely different from those traditionally performed. The parts that Mapfumo borrows from the original source are cyclically repeated throughout the song, with the bass dominating. Thus, despite the change of text and the tune traditionally associated with 'Taireva', anyone familiar with this indigenous source would immediately recognise it in 'Chamunorwa'.

Similar to Mapfumo's 'Chamunorwa', the song 'Amai' (Mother) on Maraire's *Ancient Voices* (1998) was arranged from the traditional Shona *mbira* song 'Chipindura' (Answer) and is based on the melodic and rhythmic material of both the standard *kushaura* and *kutsinhira* basic parts of its indigenous source. Clearly heard in the recording, the first *mbira* in Maraire's song imitates the *kushaura* line of 'Chipindura', while the second *mbira* and the bass reproduce the traditional *kutsinhira* line. In contrast to 'Chamunorwa', 'Amai' imitates all the standard parts of its traditional source without altering or eliminating anything, but the music played on the guitars throughout is Maraire's own composition. Singing in Shona and English, Maraire composes her own vocal lines with new lyrical content. Because it identically reproduces the standard basic parts of its traditional source, 'Amai' can also be immediately identified with the indigenous source. This is intensified by the fact that Chiwoniso maintains the timbral and rhythmic patterns similar to those traditionally played by *hosho* and *ngoma* in Shona *mbira* performances.

Comparing these two popular songs in relation to the original songs, both resemble their traditional *mbira* sources by drawing on the melodic and rhythmic material of the standard basic *mbira* part. How the musician will then conceive text depends on his/her compositional goal and performance context. In my interview with Maraire, for instance, she explained how she conceptualised 'Amai'. After the death of her mother, Linda Nemarundwe Maraire in 1997, she found herself singing the traditional *mbira* song 'Chipindura': 'I would find myself humming "Chipindura" and then play it on my *nyunganyunga*.[18] I really had to sing for my mother at this particular moment and so I composed the lyrics'.[19] Below is an excerpt from the song's lyrics:

Sometimes I imagine I hear your voice in the trees whispering
Mai fambai zvakanaka [Mother, have a safe journey]
Mai tichazomuona [Mother, we shall see you]
Forever I remember your loving smile
Sunshine to my eyes

---

18. The *nyunganyunga* is one of the types of *mbira* instruments played in Zimbabwe, but it is important to note here that when Maraire recorded 'Amai' she used the *mbira dzavadzimu* instead.
19. Maraire, interview, 19 January 2013.

You had a spirit so full of joy
The sweet surprise
I find myself searching for your face
Though I know you are gone
It's so hard to say goodbye.

The way Maraire presented her song explains how she believes that by using the entire standard part of 'Chipindura' (which belongs to the *mbira dzavadzimu* repertoire) as a medium, she could express her feelings directly to her late mother, whom she is assuming to be listening to the music.[20] Explaining her adaptation approach for this song, Maraire revealed: 'I don't go my way changing the base of these [*mbira dzavadzimu*] songs, to me it becomes disrespect to the elders who have created them'.[21] Undeniably, almost all of Maraire's *mbira dzavadzimu* adaptations – including 'Mukaranga Ane Shanje', 'Hupenyu kutenderera' and 'Handimbozorora' – retain unaltered basic standard parts. Maraire's position explains that sometimes the shape of ritual *mbira* songs for Zimbabwean popular music is determined and negotiated through the Shona concept of *hunhu* or respect, 'a discourse that is deeply personal and moral' (Kyker 2011: 2).

'Chamunorwa' has a clear and very sharp message of resistance, with Mapfumo protesting against disunity and injustice almost a decade after independence:

Chamunorwa
Kunyangwe mungandituka
Inga munonditya
Nyangwe mukandozonda
Inga munonditya
Mapepa kudondinyora
Inga munondiziva
Zvamunondiita handizvide.

---

20. Maraire's mother was also a musician. Despite the fact that Maraire was born and spent almost fifteen years of her life in Olympia, Washington, in the United States (Chitando and Mateveke 2012: 46), most of her songs, especially on *Timeless* and *Ancient Voices*, show how she strongly believed that ancestral spirits have the power to control people's lives today. Maraire died on 24 July 2013 in Zimbabwe, at the age of 37.
21. Maraire, interview, 19 January 2013.

> Why do you fight me?
> Even if you insult me
> You are afraid of me
> Even if you don't like me
> You are afraid of me
> Even if you say bad things about me
> You know me
> I don't like your attitude towards me.

One could argue that since the song this is based on, 'Taireva', is a traditional war song, Mapfumo's choice of text for 'Chamunorwa' was influenced by the original source. Important to note in this regard is that in this song Mapfumo borrowed the phrase '*Baya Wabaya*' (To Spear, to Spear) commonly associated with the traditional war song 'Nyama Yekugocha' and incorporated it into his new lyrics, reinforcing his classification of this song as a *chimurenga* song and placing it in the postcolonial discourses of *chimurenga* in Zimbabwe (Vambe 2004).[22] Mapfumo also complies with international audiences' expectations of Zimbabwean popular musicians 'to speak directly to current political realities' (Kyker 2011: 138). Therefore, how popular musicians compose lyrics for their sampled *mbira* pieces is largely determined by their own goals and the contexts of performance locally and internationally. The way 'Chamunorwa' and 'Amai' were arranged typify how other popular songs in this subcategory have been adapted – that is, borrowing the basic part of the traditional tune and superimposing new sung tunes and lyrics over it. A few examples mainly by Mapfumo, however, show how the basic parts of more than one traditional *mbira* song are combined. These include 'Chitima Nditakure', where Mapfumo used a *kutsinhira* part of the *mbira* piece 'Nyamaropa' as his *kushaura*; then 'double-tracked that same part a beat behind as his *kutsinhira* and triple-tracked a variant of "Karigamombe" as a second *kutsinhira* part' (Turino 2000: 279).

---

22. In a conversation with Tinashe Mandityira about how Mapfumo uses the phrase '*Baya wabaya*' in this song, he suggested to me that 'sometimes traditional *mbira* songs are similar; they belong to the same mode. For example, "Taireva", "Baya Undidye" and "Zeve-zeve Rinamambo" or "Karimugomba", "Hore Mudenga" and "Mugariro Wakanaka" or "Nhemamusasa", "Ndofa Ndichibaiwa" and "Baba Munyaradzi" and so forth. Therefore lyrics may be interchanged or presented as a medley' (Tinashe Mandityira, interview, 7 February 2013, Harare).

The two examples of 'Chamunorwa' and 'Amai' show how popular musicians borrow the standard basic *mbira* parts and compose their own tunes and text. The lyrics, according to Maraire, can be performed in English without compromising the original traditional source. Stephen Chifunyise (2013) agrees, saying that Maraire

> demonstrate[s] how a singing voice that is well grounded in uniquely indigenous vocal texture and potency can be innovatively utilized to render songs in English or other foreign languages and musical instruments to produce a clearly identifiable Zimbabwean sound that remains authentic even when handled with a creativity that benefitted from wide contacts with other music of the world.

Chifunyise's view that it is possible to produce an authentic and identifiable Zimbabwean sound in the singing voice itself raises a very important issue with regard to adaptation and authenticity. Vocal qualities such as texture can define a certain musical culture and musicians can adapt these for their lyrics composed in any language to represent that particular culture. The fact that vocal quality can be articulated differently from one musician to the other and can also define a certain culture reinforces the point that authenticity should be viewed in a fluid rather than fixed way.

Mapfumo, however, has a contrasting opinion regarding the use of English when performing *mbira* traditional music. He explained in an interview with journalist Lance Guma that 'we got *mbira* music that we play, you cannot sing that in English, yah, that's something original and you cannot change that' (Guma 2013). Such differences between Maraire's and Mapfumo's perceptions with regard to the use of English in *mbira* music can be attributed a number of things, such as the musicians' personal history. Maraire's flexibility in using English may have been influenced by the fact that she was born in the United States, spent her childhood and acquired part of her education there.[23] Mapfumo, who is 31 years older than Maraire, has strong connections with his rural home in Guruve (Chikowero 2013). Mapfumo lived a rural Shona life until around the age ten before moving to Mbare Township in Harare with his parents. It was in Harare where he was exposed to Shona traditional music. Mapfumo's age and place of

---

23. Maraire, interview, 19 January 2013.

origin might also have played a significant role in shaping his position that lyrics for *mbira* music should only be composed using Shona.

Additionally, while many of Mapfumo's *mbira* adaptations – such as 'Amai Vemwana', 'Ngoma', 'Marima Nechisi' and 'Marehwarehwa' – also directly quote the standard *mbira* part and only change the vocal lines and lyrics as Maraire does, the song 'Chamunorwa' shows that the *kushaura* and *kutsinhira* parts can be used separately and their melodic rhythms can be altered. According to my second category on *mbira* adapations, sampling techniques adapt material that constitutes the standard basic *mbira* part, but the melodic and rhythmic material of this basic part can be altered. The majority of *mbira*-based popular songs identified in this chapter use this approach. The standard *mbira* part can be considered the core of traditional *mbira* music during the process of adaptation. The core constitutes the basic *kushaura* and or *kutsinhira* traditional *mbira* lines.

The purpose of the new rhythms and melodies that popular musicians compose outside the standard basic parts in their arranged versions needs to be explained. In many of the songs in this subcategory, this new material is played over the repeated progression produced by the basic parts and, as a result, it functions more as a variation. As a Shona *mbira* player, I have experienced that a traditional *mbira* mode can be performed differently because of the possibility of adding variations and this sometimes depends on how good the performers are. While *mbira* players have the freedom to improvise during performances, they always have to ensure that they 'return from time to time to the basic patterns of the piece such that its identity will not be obscured by improvisations' (Berliner 1978: 97). Although indigenous *mbira* pieces have well-known standard variations, the majority of the songs in this subcategory do not adapt these variations, except for a few, such as Mapfumo's 'Dangurangu', 'Chamunorwa' and 'Zimbabwe'. In the song 'Zimbabwe', for instance, Mapfumo borrows both the *kutsinhira kwepamusoro* and *kutsinhira kwepasi* standard variations from the traditional *mbira* song 'Chemutengure' and adapts them for dance-drumming rhythm as accompaniment. Therefore, indigenous *mbira* variations cannot independently, from the standard parts, represent the identity of their sources and can be adapted for other Shona traditional genres without changing their distinctiveness.

Abstract adaptation: Adapting sung mbira melodies

There are popular songs that have solely utilised indigenous Shona *kudeketera mbira* tunes and text and in some cases either text or melody only. Eliminating the basic parts well known to these tunes and texts, the musicians mainly compose their own accompanying instrumental lines. The major difference between songs in this category with those in the two categories explained above is that here the core (the standard *mbira* part) is not included. In this section, I examine the effect of using sung tunes and texts in the absence of the standard basic material of particular indigenous *mbira* songs in popular music composition and also determine whether such songs can be considered arranged versions of those traditional songs. The popular song 'Ancient Voices' on the album *Ancient Voices* (1998) by Maraire only adapts the *kudeketera mbira* text of the traditional *mbira* song 'Chaminuka Ndimambo' (Chaminuka Is King). Traditionally, this song was performed for Chaminuka, 'the 19th century spirit medium of the Shona people' (Pfukwa 2007: 99).[24] Similar to the majority of traditional Shona *mbira* songs, 'Chaminuka Ndimambo' consists of a standard basic part composed of vocal lines different from those performed in the basic part. Adopting the compositional technique employed in *mbira* traditional songs, in 'Ancient Voices' Maraire composes her own *kushaura* and *kubvumira* basic parts and these are performed using a cyclic pattern throughout. Distinct from 'Chaminuka Ndimambo', however, Maraire's version eliminates the well-known *hosho* percussive rhythmic timeline usually found in traditional *mbira* performances. This makes the rhythm of 'Ancient Voices' sound more contemporary and suitable for dancing. The lyrics in Maraire's version are for the most part in English and presented in a verse and chorus style, in contrast to the call and response pattern in which 'Chaminuka Ndimambo' is traditionally performed:

> Pasipamire was just another young man in the village. Leading a simple life
> Of peace and harmony. No troubles on his mind for he was a simple man
> And then Chaminuka came and Pasipamire was changed.
> And then the spirit came, Chaminuka was his name,
> And everywhere there was jubilation.
> A leader had been found,
> Chosen by the ancestors.
> And people came from afar to see him for themselves
> And he said children beware.

---

24. Chaminuka was one of the earliest elders possessed by a spirit that guided Shona people during times of war, hunger and disease outbreaks. See Pfukwa (2007: 127) for more detail on Chaminuka.

Strangers want this life. Soon they shall arrive
From the west across the ocean.
And will have to fight, children, fight to survive
You must be brave. You must be strong.

It is only after three-and-a-half minutes (in the closing part of the song) that Maraire integrates the text of 'Chaminuka Ndimambo', changing its well-known vocal tune. Compare Figure 6.3 with Figure 6.4:

Chaminuka

Figure 6.3 *Kudeketera* tune and text traditionally sung for 'Chaminuka Ndimambo'. Transcription by Vimbai Chamisa

Ancient Voices

Chiwoniso Maraire

Figure 6.4 *Kudeketera* text from 'Chaminuka Ndimambo' performed on 'Ancient Voices', from 3:36–3:51. Transcription by Vimbai Chamisa

In the entire song, only two phrases, '*Chaminuka ndimambo*' and '*Shumba inogara yega musango*', were adapted from the indigenous source. Each of the four phrases in both songs has 12 beats and each cycle in both songs has 48 beats, but what happens on each beat in Maraire's version is sometimes quite different. In 'Chaminuka Ndimambo', the same rhythmic idea that consists of quaver beats only is repeated from one phrase to another in lines 1 and 2 throughout the piece. Maraire introduces other note values – semiquavers, crotchets and dotted crotchets – thus changing the rhythmic pattern significantly. Another thing that differentiates Maraire's version is that she introduces responding vocals and these reinforce the message on lead vocals. Such a way of combining voices is typical of the call and response pattern in African music.

Despite the fact that Maraire composes her own lyrics in addition to the pre-existing ones, she maintains the meaning of the song. The historical novel *Chaminuka: Prophet of Zimbabwe* (1983), written by Solomon Mutsvairo, is the inspiration behind the composition of 'Ancient Voices'.[25] As in the novel, the song praises and narrates the roles played by spirit mediums such as Chaminuka and the ancestors during the war of liberation. Forward Kwenda explained to me that the traditional lyrics Maraire borrows in her song were composed anonymously during the First Chimurenga as an accompaniment to *mbira* music performed in praise and recognition of Chaminuka's power.[26] Even though Maraire altered the *kudeketera* traditional rhythm of the tune and also eliminated the traditional standard basic *mbira* part, she combines the traditional poetry with her own lyrics, which means that Maraire's song is more of a modified version of 'Chaminuka Ndimambo', with the story about Chaminuka presented in more detail. In my interview with her, Maraire told me that 'Ancient Voices' is a combination of two songs, her own composition and 'Chaminuka Ndimambo'. Therefore, while *mbira* vocal content largely functions as accompaniment in *mbira* performances and is usually not considered the basis for the identification of particular indigenous *mbira* songs, as explained in previous studies (Berliner 1993), the combination of indigenous lyrics in subsequent versions successfully establishes a relationship

---

25. Maraire, interview, 19 January 2013.
26. Forward Kwenda is a renowned Shona *mbira* player from Zimbabwe. He was born in 1963 in the Buhera rural area and started playing *mbira* and other traditional music at a young age. He has made a number of *mbira* recordings, including *Svikiro: Meditations of an Mbira Master* (1997).

between popular songs and recognisable indigenous *mbira* pieces. This approach to the adaptation of indigenous *mbira* music encourages a type of popular *mbira* music composition that is not necessarily identical to the traditional *mbira* songs while enabling the interpretation of important historical events within Zimbabwean popular *mbira* music.

Another example of a popular song that utilises indigenous *mbira kudeketera* texts alone, without the vocal melodies traditionally associated with them, is Mapfumo's 'Kusarima'. He uses certain phrases traditionally associated with the indigenous *mbira* song by the same name. Such phrases include:

Kusarima woye
Torai mapadza tirime
Not ploughing
Take hoes and let's plough

However, the musician performs these lyrics to a *katekwe* Shona traditional dance rhythm. In relation to how indigenous *kudeketera mbira* texts are used, Tinashe Mandityira explained to me:

> Sometimes it becomes difficult to assign certain lyrics to only one song in particular, seeing that some *kudeketera* texts are common to several songs – for example, phrases such as *meso murima dzinenge nyimo*; *nzara dzapera nekuridza mbira*; *baba maamai mandiregerera: mati ndife zvangu ndisina kuwana* and *mune mvana ndinopinda runa: kashanu ndinobudawo neyangu* can be sung to many *mbira* traditional songs.[27]

In this case, since the traditional dance is performed for the purpose of 'thanksgiving for a successful harvest' in Shona society (Kyker 2011: 53) and lyrics associated with the traditional *mbira* song 'Kusarima' are also traditionally performed during *nhimbe* (a harvest ceremony), it is possible that the lyrics in Mapfumo's song were performed in both contexts. Additionally, Shona *kudeketera mbira* text can be drawn from commonly used proverbs and idioms. Therefore, it is difficult to classify a song as an arranged version of an indigenous song solely on the basis of

---

27. Mandityira, interview.

its text, especially if it lacks the melodic essence of the traditional vocal material. An exception may occur in cases where the text has been adapted in its entirety. In this case I believe that Mapfumo's 'Kusarima' cannot be classified as a popular version of the original indigenous *mbira* song, even if they share the same name, but should rather be seen as a dance-drumming popular version of *katekwe*.

Certain songs in this subcategory only adapt the vocal melody from particular traditional Shona *mbira* songs. In 'Titambire' (Dance for Us) by Mapfumo, for instance, the keyboard and the bass imitate the traditional vocal lines well known to the indigenous *mbira* song 'Manhanga Kutapira' (Sweet Pumpkins). What Mapfumo does in this piece is to omit the familiar lyrics of the original, but slightly modifies and maintains the vocal tune on which the traditional text was sung and then composes his own lyrics. However, all this material is performed around the musician's own standard basic timeline played on the *mbira*. Though Mapfumo omits the traditional poetry of 'Manhanga Kutapira' in his popular version, his utilisation of its melodic lines played on the keyboard may be interpreted as an indirect presentation of the traditional poetry. 'Titambire' was released as a *chimurenga* song in 1999, a few months before the 2000 parliamentary elections in Zimbabwe. Contrary to most of Mapfumo's *chimurenga* songs, however, the lyrical content of 'Titambire' cannot be literally interpreted as political protest:

Titambire ngoma iwe titambire
Titambire mutambirwo wekwedu titambire
Kurira kwengoma
Titsikire ngoma iwe titsikire
Ngoma yekwedu yarira
Inga yekwedu yarira
Dance to the music for us, dance
Dance the way we usually do
The drum is playing
Dance to the music for us, dance
Our music is playing
Ours is playing.

Yet the statement '*Huya unone kutapira kunoita manhanga*' (Come and test the sweetness of our pumpkins) traditionally sung in 'Manhanga Kutapira', is sometimes interpreted as 'a brag, a boisterous assertion' and was used by Nathaniel

Manheru (2013) in a Zimbabwean *Herald* article to describe the political situation between ZANU–PF and the Movement for Democratic Change (MDC) a few months before the elections scheduled for July 2013. This suggests that text well known to a particular melody will always resurface and be experienced when that melody is performed, even if it is not verbalised. I therefore believe that the traditional vocal melody of 'Manhanga Kutapira', presented as instrumental music in Mapfumo's 'Titambire', connects the listener familiar with its traditional source to the original lyrics, even if it is not a version verbalised in the adapted version.[28]

The example of 'Titambire' explains the importance of pre-existing vocal melodies; their use within various forms of popular music styles determines their overall meaning and interpretation. How 'Titambire' has been composed explains that *mbira* players can play tunes that have political connotations, without the original lyrics, as a way of signifying their feelings through the music alone. This echoes Pongweni's observation that 'Shona people often express their feelings about personal, political or social matters through allusion rather than direct statements' (1982: ii). This could have been true of *mbira*'s history from precolonial times through to the postcolonial period and might be one of the major reasons for its enduring social significance.

Popular songs, since they eliminate the basic *mbira* part, cannot be immediately identified with certain *mbira* songs. Following Chapman (2007: 88), I describe this type of adaptation as 'abstract adaptation', which is 'the use of ideas in a conceptual way such that they are largely only revealed in analysis'. However, given the non-verbal significance of *mbira* music explained above and how pervasive and well known *mbira* tunes are in the Shona communities, I do not agree with Chapman that abstract adaptation is only discernible through music analysis by musicologists. Composers purposefully combine their music with certain traditional aspects in a subtle way in order to present their intended ideas in specific contexts. On the other hand, audiences familiar with the music also interpret song meanings in connection with the abstractly adapted material. Despite the effects of traditional

---

28. In her study of music of the coloured community of the Kroonvale of South Africa, Marie Jorritsma observes something similar. She examines how the use of the melody of 'Senzeni na', performed to Christian text in this community, 'subtly and non-verbally' expressed anti-apartheid gestures in South Africa, stating that 'the performance of this tune created a powerful sense of shared experience during apartheid' (2011: 67). See also Ray Pratt (1990) for more detail about the way tunes alone, without text can refer to political situations.

tunes and texts in abstract adaptations, data I obtained from ZIMURA largely shows that songs in this subcategory are registered as original compositions and the musicians are entitled to full royalty payments. Thus, similar to the songs in the sampling category, ZIMURA considers abstract adaptations as creatively and respectively enhanced, that is, re-composed.

Conclusion

The belief that some traditional *mbira* songs facilitate connections with ancestors has influenced the production of entire *mbira* adaptations by musicians such as Chiwoniso Maraire. Upon performing or listening to such popular songs, some people become spiritually connected to the ancestors. Musicians such as Andy Brown have been flexible in incorporating their own material within the adapted songs. There are two things that distinguish basic *mbira* part adaptations (sampling) from entire adaptations (imitation): the absence of indigenous *mbira* texts and the inconsistent use of *kushaura* and *kutsinhira* parts and the material that constitute the main *mbira* parts. However, while the lead and response parts can be adapted separately and while their melodic rhythm can be altered, the melodic essence of at least one of the *kushaura* and the *kutsinhira* standard *mbira* parts has always been retained.

Abstract adaptation is the smallest subcategory of *mbira*-based pieces. In contrast to songs that use sampling, songs that use abstract adaptation completely eliminate the standard basic material of their sources. What relates them to the entire adaptations (imitation) is their utilisation of some indigenous *mbira* vocal material, but this has also been inconsistently applied. I have noted the significance of indigenous *mbira* vocal melodies in representing particular *mbira* pieces in the absence of the traditionally sung poetry and also in the absence of its well-known *mbira* basic melody. It can be concluded from these strategies that borrowing the standard *mbira* parts and/or the vocal melodies affects whether the music can be labelled as commodified Shona songs.

Evidence from ZIMURA shows, however, that only entire *mbira* popular adaptations are regarded as arrangements – adopting the other two strategies allows musicians to be credited with original compositions. It is clear that what renders *mbira* popular adaptations as correct and unchanging in relation to their traditional sources is their utilisation of pre-existing material that constitutes the standard *kushaura* and *kutsinhira mbira* parts or the indigenous sung melodies and/or the associated text. Musicians sometimes maintain indigenous lyrics, but in some cases they compose new ones. Despite the changes in lyrics as traditional *mbira* songs are adapted for various popular music contexts, the popular texts maintain themes and symbols rooted in the musical history and culture, such as Shona spiritual figures – for example, Chaminuka. These inconsistences in the presentation of *mbira* lyrics from one adaptation to another thus suggest that the choice for the majority of popular *mbira* lyrics is largely determined by indigenous *mbira* sources. How musicians shape their lyrics differs from one performance to another and this depends on the musicians' compositional goals. The repertoire of *mbira* popular adaptations shows how indigenous *mbira* elements can be intertwined within various Zimbabwean popular styles to form a Zimbabwean popular music aesthetic that has characteristics and an identity strongly grounded in Shona musical tradition.

References

Berliner, P.F. 1978. *The Soul of Mbira*. Berkeley: University of California Press.
——. 1981. *The Soul of Mbira: Music and Traditions of the Shona People of Zimbabwe*. Chicago: Chicago University Press.
——. 1993. *The Soul of Mbira: Music and Traditions of the Shona People of Zimbabwe*. Berkeley: University of California Press.
Chapman, J. 2007. 'Composing Syncretic African/Western Music: Eleven Compositions and the Frameworks for their Systematic Analysis'. PhD diss., Queensland University of Technology, Brisbane.
Chifunyise, S. 2013. 'Zimbabwe's Cultural Heritage Gift: Chiwoniso Maraire'. 29 July. http://samuelravengai.blogspot.com.
Chikowero, M. 2013. 'A Historian's Take on Thomas Mapfumo and Robert Mugabe'. http://afropop.org/articles/mhoze-chikowero-a-historians-take-on-thomas-mapfumo-and-robert-mugabe.
Chitando, E. 2002. *Singing Culture: A Study of Gospel Music in Zimbabwe*. Stockholm: Nordic Africa.
Chitando, E. and P. Mataveke. 2012. 'Challenging Patriarchy and Exercising Women's Agency in Zimbabwean Music: Analysis of the Careers of Chiwoniso Maraire and Olivia Charamba'. *Muziki* 9(2): 41–52.
Dewey, W.J. 1991. 'Pleasing the Ancestors: The Traditional Art of the Shona People of Zimbabwe'. PhD diss., Indiana University, Bloomington.
Dube, C. 1996. 'The Changing Context of African Music Performance in Zimbabwe'. *Zambezia* 23(2): 99–120.
Erlmann, V. 1991. *African Stars: Studies in Black South African Performance*. Chicago: University of Chicago Press.
Guma, L. 2013. 'Thomas Mapfumo on Mugabe, Chiyangwa and Winky D'. Interview, Nehanda TV, April. http://nehandaradio.com/2013/04/11/transcript-thomas-mapfumo-on-mugabe-chiyangwa-and-winky-d/.

Hesmondhalgh, D. 2006. 'Digital Sampling and Cultural Inequality'. *Social & Legal Studies* 15(1): 53–75.

Hobsbawm, E. and T.O. Ranger. 1983. *The Invention of Tradition*. Cambridge: Cambridge University Press.

Jorritsma, M. 2011. *Sonic Spaces of the Karoo: The Sacred Music of a South African Coloured Community*. Philadelphia: Temple University Press.

Kauffman, R. 1969. 'Some Aspects of Aesthetics in the Shona Music of Rhodesia'. *Ethnomusicology* 13(3): 507–11.

Keil, C. and S. Feld (eds). 1994. *Essays and Dialogues: Music Grooves*. Chicago: University of Chicago Press.

Kwaramba, A.D. 1997. *Popular Music and Society: The Language of Protest in Chimurenga Music – The Case of Thomas Mapfumo in Zimbabwe*. Oslo: University of Oslo.

Kyker, J.W. 2011. 'A Person among Others: Music, Morality and Postcolonial Politics in the Songs of Oliver Mtukudzi'. PhD diss., University of Pennsylvania, Philadelphia.

Locke, D. 2009. 'Africa/Ewe, Mande, Dagbamba, Shona, BaAka'. In *Worlds of Music: An Introduction to the Music of the World's Peoples*, edited by J.T. Titon, 67–106. Belmont, CA: Schirmer Cengage Learning.

Manheru, N. 2013. 'F.O.Z Breakthrough or Birdliming Zimbabwe?' *The Herald*, 5 April.

Maraire, D.A. 1990. 'The Position of Music in Shona "Midzimu" (Ancestral Spirits) Possession'. PhD diss., University of Washington, Seattle.

Matiure, P. 2007. *The Zezuru Mbira Dzavadzimu Legacy and Spirit Possession: The Spiritual Efficacy of Mbira Dzavadzimu within the Zezuru Cosmology*. Lausanne: Unique Publishing.

McConnachie, B. 2008. 'Legal Access to Our Musical History: An Investigation into the Copyright Implications of Archived Musical Recordings Held at the International Library of African Music (ILAM) in South Africa'. MMus thesis, Rhodes University, Grahamstown.

Muller, C. 1999. *Rituals of Fertility and the Sacrifice of Desire: Nazarite Women's Performance in South Africa*. Chicago: University of Chicago Press.

Mutsvairo, S. 1983. *Chaminuka: The Prophet of Zimbabwe*. Washington, DC: Three Continents Press.

Pfukwa, C. 2007. 'The Function and Significance of War Names in the Zimbabwean Armed Conflict (1966–1979)'. PhD diss., University of South Africa, Pretoria.

Pongweni, A. 1982. *Songs That Won the Liberation War*. Harare: College Press.

Pratt, R. 1990. *Rhythm and Resistance: Explorations in the Political Uses of Popular Music*. New York: Praeger.

Preston, T.M. 2007. 'Spiritual Continuity amongst Musical Change'. In *Zimbabwean Mbira Music on an International Stage: Chartwell Dutiro's Life in Music*, edited by C. Dutiro and K. Howard, 17–26. Burlington: Ashgate.

Scherzinger, M. 1999. 'Music, Spirit Possession and the Copyright Law: Cross-cultural Comparisons and Strategic Speculations'. *Yearbook for Traditional Music* 31: 102–25.

———. 2001. 'Negotiating the Music-Theory/African-Music Nexus: A Political Critique of Ethnomusicological Anti-formalism and a Strategic Analysis of the Harmonic Patterning of the Shona Mbira Song *Nyamaropa*'. *Perspectives of New Music* 39(1): 5–117.

Taylor, T. 1997. *Global Pop: World Music, World Markets*. New York: Routledge.

Titon, J.T. (ed.). 2009. *Worlds of Music: An Introduction to the Music of the World's Peoples*. 5th edition. Belmont, CA: Schirmer Cengage Learning.
Tracey, A. 1963. 'Three Tunes for "Mbira Dza Vadzimu"'. *African Music Society Journal* 3(2): 23–6.
Turino, T. 2000. *Nationalists, Cosmopolitans and Popular Music in Zimbabwe*. Chicago: University of Chicago Press.
———. 2008. *Music as Social Life: The Politics of Participation*. Chicago: University of Chicago.
Vambe, M.T. 2004. 'Versions and Sub-versions: Trends in *Chimurenga* Musical Discourses of Post-Independence Zimbabwe'. *African Study Monographs* 25(4): 167–93.
Zindi, F. 2003. *Music Workbook: Zimbabwe versus the World*. Harare: Zindisc Publications.

Part II

Zimbabwean Urban Popular Music across Time

CHAPTER 7

The Middle Class and the Popularisation of Musical Concerts in Harare Township, Salisbury, from the 1940s to 1970

Barbara Mahamba and Azon Twala

This chapter examines the role of the Zimbabwean middle class in popularising musical concerts as a form of leisure in the colonial township (now Mbare) in the country's capital, what was then Salisbury (now Harare). The main focus is not on music per se, but on the social history of the Africans in Harare Township, from the 1940s to 1970 through the lenses of musical concerts. Scholars have emphasised bands, musicians and the development of music itself, paying little attention to the audience as a lens through which the social history of leisure and entertainment can be analysed. The chapter investigates the musical concert tradition as an aspect of leisure and entertainment in the African middle class or elite in the African township during the colonial period. It shows how this emerging African class popularised musical performances as an expression of transformation, not only from rural to urban dwellers, but also from 'uncivilised' to 'civilised' and how the concerts provided space to express their assimilation of 'civilisation'. The chapter uses Thomas Turino's characterisation of concerts as a form of urban popular music that 'grew out of, and flourished in parallel to, the urban based choirs' (2003: 329) and Michael West's definition of the middle class as also being the elite or the *évolué* – an evolved or developed class (2012: 46).

The middle class of Harare Township
Established in 1907 outside the boundary of Salisbury, Harare Township was the first black residential area in the city. The Native Urban Location Ordinance in 1906 provided the legal framework for the establishment and administration of a black residential area, outlining that black people live within the designated location. It was referred to as the Salisbury Native Location until 1946, when it was renamed Harare African Township, a name it retained till 1982, when it was

renamed Mbare. The 1930s and 1940s saw rapid growth of Harare Township, stimulated by the need for African labour, which in turn was necessitated by a boom in the manufacturing industry in Salisbury (Vambe 2007: 355). When, in 1958, the Federation of Rhodesia and Nyasaland came into being, there was a new wave of immigrants (Vambe 1976: 142). All Africans from within and outside Southern Rhodesia who migrated to seek employment opportunities in Salisbury lived in the native location. According to Mahmood Mamdani (2001: 654), the colonial state divided the population into races and ethnicities. Europeans fell under 'races' and were governed by civil law while all black people fell under 'ethnicities' and were governed by customary law. The native location was separated from the settlers spatially and conceptually. Spatially, all black people were supposed to live in Harare Township, where they could be easily monitored. Conceptually, unlike the settler, who was defined by history, the black person was defined by geography and, unlike the settler who inhabited the modern dynamic world of civilisation, the black person was constructed as the function of a fixed and unchanging culture (Mamdani 2012: 6). Attending concerts was an expression of the opposition of the middle class in Harare Township to the settlers' misconception of African culture as fixed and unchanging.

The settler administration and the policymakers regarded all African residents in Harare Township as a classless race and thus lumped them all together as 'natives'. However, according to Lawrence Vambe (1976), who resided in the township during this period, the Africans were conscious of the existence of differences among themselves and desired that these differences be visible. He acknowledges that the term 'class' in Harare Township could only be used in a broad sense and that the existence of a working class, a middle class and an elite class was only recognised among the Africans. The *matanyera*, the lavatory cleaners, street-sweepers and garbage collectors were the lowest class in the community. They were mostly from outside the colony and were unschooled, ate the cheapest and least nutritious food and lived in 'prison-like' hostels, which were crowded. Their form of leisure was mainly the consumption of the poisonous *skokiaan* – home-brewed alcohol. In terms of production, they were inefficient and an economic liability to employers. The Europeans used this class as a yardstick to categorise all Africans, much to the annoyance of people who regarded themselves as the more evolved middle class (Vambe 1976: 195–7). The middle class began to dissociate themselves from the lower class by projecting the ethos of hard work and reliability taught at mission schools such as Chishawasha.

THE MIDDLE CLASS AND THE POPULARISATION OF MUSICAL CONCERTS

Instead of drinking *skokiaan*, they desired to drink bottled alcoholic drinks, which were illegal for Africans to consume till 1962 (Vambe 1976: 216). Coloured people were exempt from this law and so they supplied these drinks to the *shebeens* in the township, some of which were run by respectable people. Middle-class people would be entertained in such *shebeens*, while listening to dance music, mostly by African musicians. Above the lowest class of people were 'various strata ranging from middle class to elite', which included 'politicians, teachers, journalists, court interpreters and radio announcers' (197). The distinction between the middle class and 'elite' class was not clear, which is probably why for West (2012: 46), as mentioned earlier, the term 'middle class' is synonymous with elite or *évolué*. Africans who, through education or business enterprises, challenged the social barriers imposed by colonialism were also considered middle class. According to West (2002: 3), education was a mechanism for the creation of the African middle class. African education, though inadequate, controlled and aimed at producing obedient Africans, produced articulate African men who were able to challenge colonial policies (Vambe 1976: 118). Education was regarded by Africans as an avenue through which one could become a special member of society. However, the colonial administration did not respect the African middle class and did not respond to their call for respectability. Armed with education, some Africans were employed as journalists, clerks, nurses, teachers, doctors and lawyers, messengers and boss boys, and regarded themselves as the African middle class (Mlambo 2014: 130). Among them also may have been those who were underemployed despite having received a good education by African standards at that time. The middle class in Harare Township were frustrated by racial barriers imposed by colonialism and agitated for political and social change. Therefore this interplay between the economic class and the attainment of Western education became the foundation upon which musical concert culture was popularised in Harare.

Harare Township housing, originally meant to be temporary, was characterised by insufficient houses, sanitation and recreational facilities. Vambe (1976: 144) describes Harare Township as an 'overcrowded, lively and noisy shanty town', 'a collection of shacks made of empty paraffin and petrol tins', with no proper sanitary facilities. He makes references to it being 'the most vital and explosive ghetto in Mashonaland, if not in all Zimbabwe', until 1945, when other townships were established. General poverty was widespread in the township and musicians began to produce songs that highlighted the living conditions endured by all Africans who lived in the township, regardless of class. Africans who had been to mission schools were not comfortable sharing the same living space with people who were socially below them. It was within this environment that the middle class strived to use concerts to domesticate the urban environment they found themselves in. They desired better living conditions, for the colonial administration to distinguish between Africans who were married and regarded themselves as 'responsible and educated' and those regarded as 'unstable and prone to *mapoto* relationships'.[1] Frustration arising from the fact that Rhodesian native policy and its supporting laws regarded Africans as a classless people, making no distinctions especially in the provision of living conditions in Harare Township, was partly responsible for the middle class being politically active.

Vambe notes that a person's job was not a reliable yardstick to measure their standing in society, as some of the most respectable people in Harare Township worked far below their academic qualifications because of limited opportunities. He gives an example of Mr Shoko, founder of the Salisbury African Waiters Association, who was a reputable leader among Africans in Harare Township, but worked in Pocket's Tea Room, where he served tea to white people. There was also Mr David, who arrived in the 1920s from Malawi. He never attended any mission school and did not earn much as a chef at one of the leading Salisbury hotels. An impeccably well-dressed man, his lifestyle earned him respect in Harare Township, for he later became a successful entertainer in the township, forming his own band (Vambe 1976: 197–8). He also owned a grocery shop, which was run by his wife Magumede.

Musical concerts became an agent of transition for rural to urban dwellers, from the lower class to the middle class, and a space in the ghetto where the middle class could express their assimilation of 'civilisation' as well as their difference from the lower class. The concerts in Harare Township rose in popularity as a result of the need by an emerging African middle class to live a dignified lifestyle and offered forms of leisure that the colonial authorities were reluctant to provide. Concert attendance was a way of appropriating colonial leisure and respectability. The fact that the settlers were oblivious to distinctions within the African residents of Harare induced a need by those who regarded themselves as middle class to be recognised

---

1. *Mapoto* literally translates to pots. Schmidt (1992: 93) describes a *mapoto* relationship as 'informal and often temporary liason with a male worker, providing him with domestic labour and sexual services in exchange for shelter'.

as a distinct class. While the African middle class used conferences, tea parties, the adoption of refined English accents, wearing suits and attending meetings as symbols of respect, upward mobility and 'civilisation' (Turino 2003: 328), this was also an important way of negotiating cultural space (Vambe 2007: 362) and expressing their cultural agency. The middle class wanted to separate themselves from other less respected forms of leisure, such as the *shebeens* and *mahobo* parties (Jenje-Makwenda 2005: 25). *Mahobo* parties were social leisure gatherings of the poor black workers and migrants who occupied marginal spaces, from which they experienced urbanity. These parties were popularised by, and perhaps derived their name from, the song lyrics '*Aya mahobo andakakuchengetera*' (here are the big breasts and big buttocks that I am keeping for you) (Vambe 2007: 364). It is the association between *mahobo* parties and noise and uncontrolled sexuality that the middle class wished to dissociate itself from. While the concerts became a cultural space for the middle class of that time, the *mahobo* parties became a subculture for the poorer residents of Harare Township who could not afford to attend concerts.

Emmanuel Akyeampong and Charles Ambler (2002: 3–5) point out that leisure is a social construct whose meanings differ along the boundaries of race, ethnicity, gender, class and age. In the context of colonial Africa, leisure was as 'an important sphere of activity and reflexivity', where people affirmed what was socially valuable'. Akyeampong and Ambler characterise leisure time as including community activities that confirm one's membership in a social group, activities considered fun or pleasurable, rest and renewal from the demands and routine of work and a relatively autonomous sphere, where individuals can flesh out their own social identities (3). In Harare Township, Africans in general tried to create an environment that was free from the constant harassment of colonial control. Concerts, as a form of leisure, were appropriated by the African middle class in specific ways that reflect how this class responded to the limits imposed by colonial administration. For the middle class, concerts became a means of asserting their presence, which is why their desire was to present concerts as distinct from leisure activities associated with lower-class Africans.

Writing on leisure in colonial Brazzaville, Phyllis Martin (1995: 3) argues that 'leisure time and space were arenas of contest and mediation within European and African sub-communities as well as between them'. Leisure activities fostered the development of networks and the emergence of particular identities in the African population. In constructing their ideas on leisure, Africans in the growing urban centres of colonial Africa, particularly the emerging middle class, drew from European cultural values. Although the music concerts in Harare Township borrowed from the English middle-class values of leisure, they retained a degree of Africanness, confirming John Kelly's view that the definition of leisure should also be defined from the point of view of the participants (2003: 50).

Musical concerts in Harare Township were events at which musicians performed to an African audience, who had transformed from rural to urban dwellers. The African middle class was responsible for the popularisation of the music concerts and, for them, attending the concerts not only popularised this dimension of leisure, but also became an enactment of the middle class as a social category. The concerts became arenas where the African middle class showed the extent to which they had retained African forms of entertainment they valued, while also showing the Western values they had adopted.

The middle class and promotion of concerts

The middle class popularised music concerts by being musicians and bandleaders and by attending the concerts. Prior to 1935, performances were held in open spaces and it was difficult to charge fees and those in attendance would throw money as a sign of appreciation (Jenje-Makwenda 2005: 17). Musical concerts in Harare Township started as early as 1935, but they were few and not very popular. The musical concerts were influenced by traditional forms of leisure, borrowing from the various rural areas from which the residents of of the township originated. These were mainly dances that were performed in the open market area, drawing large crowds. They included the *Muchongoyo* (Ndau), *Mbakumba* (Karanga) and *Dinhi* (Korekore) and the Zezuru became associated with *mbira* music and *Jerusarema* dance (Turino 2000: 143). The *Nyawu* dances were very popular. Although traditional performances continued to take place outdoors, they were sometimes adapted to indoor concerts and performed mainly in the Methodist Church Hall at the Kaufman Centre. For instance, the *Jerusarema* dance, which made inroads into Harare Township in the 1940s and 1950s, would be performed by groups such as De Black Evening Follies, who were also known for using Western musical instruments (Turino 2003: 330) The dance is linked to the beginning of nationalism and through the dance, performers were able to express coded messages and critique and ridicule the colonial system. The dance was later performed at political rallies. Everyday experiences, such as dance, were thus deployed as 'weapons of the weak' (Scott 1985).

Concerts began with singing in choirs (*makwaya*), which involved the adaptation of performance practices learned in mission schools or from people who had some education. This is why they became associated with the middle class. Kenneth Mattaka's Bantu Actors, which emerged in 1937, was the first important concert ensemble in Harare Township and its performances were refined, progressive and sophisticated, traits the African middle class wished to be identified with. Graduates from mission schools often led the concerts. The mission-educated youth emulated black American choirs and synchronised singing. The early 1940s saw the rise of the Salisbury African Male Voice Choir, an all-male vocal group founded by Ezekiah Chihota, which staged and popularised what Vambe (1976: 213) describes as 'stage concert music'. Having been born in the well-known and influential family of Chief Chihota, Ezekiah fitted into Harare Township's middle class. He composed his own songs, which 'brought indigenous Shona music into the twentieth century' (212). The Salisbury African Male Voice Choir became very popular and a central feature of Harare's cultural life, performing at all sporting and official events. When the government built its own schools, music was an important aspect of the education curriculum and graduates from these schools also influenced musical concerts. Kenneth Mattaka, 'the grandfather of township music and entertainment' (Jenje-Makwenda 2010) and leader of one of Harare Township's first 'concert' ensembles, the Bantu Actors, went to Musami Mission and later trained in singing at the Domboshawa government training school (Turino 2003: 330). Mattaka and his mates – Remington Mazabane, Josaya Hadebe and John White – formed the group, which was initially called the Expensive Bantus, while at the training school in 1936. They were joined in 1939 by Samuel Gotora, Elisha Kassim and Ernest Gwaze (Jenje-Makwenda 2010). As concerts became popular, they introduced instruments such as pianos, guitars, bass, traps and winds. In the 1940s concerts began to factor in South African and American influences and the circle of performers widened to include De Black Evening Follies, the Salisbury African Male Voice choir, the All Mills Brothers, and the Ink Spots (Turino 2003: 330).

One of the earliest links between the middle class leaders in Harare Township in the 1930s and music bands was Mr David, mentioned earlier in this chapter. Besides his job as a head chef, Mr David's deep interest in music prompted him to form his own band, which attracted huge crowds. Among his band members was Charles Mzingeli, a talented violinist who turned to music performance for a living after the demise of the Industrial and Commercial Workers Union in the 1930s (Vambe 1976: 198). Charles Mzingeli was born at Embakwe Roman Catholic mission, where he attended school until the age of fourteen. He probably learnt to play musical instruments while at Embakwe because Empandeni, a neighbouring mission school, had a brass band similar to the one at Chishawasha (94).

Social clubs such as the Bantu Social and Cultural Centre organised recreational activities for the better-educated residents of the township. Under the chairmanship of Enoch Dumbutshena, a Bachelor of Arts and Bachelor in Education graduate (Chikowero 2008), the club popularised musical groups such as the City Quads and De Black Evening Follies. Moses Mphahlo, leader of the 'concert' ensemble De Black Evening Follies (sometimes referred to as De Pitch Black Evening Follies), described their performances as 'variety programmes which juxtaposed many different kinds of music and arrangements' (in Turino 2003: 330).

The musical concerts in Harare Township reveal how the black middle class approached African artistic products during the colonial period (Turino 2000: 154). The popularisation of the musical concerts was an indication that the African elite had adopted aspects of the European concept of leisure. While the middle class adopted European styles of music, they did not only imitate everything Western, but infused ideas from local, regional and international music styles to come up with something new they could call their own. This redefinition of the concert tradition involved abandoning some traditional instruments and replacing them with Western instruments, such as guitars, banjos, trumpets, French horns, harmonicas and accordions (Zindi 2010: 40), which were expensive and could only be afforded by those with high income. Kenneth Mattaka's passion for music was kindled when he received a mouth organ as a Christmas present from his father's employer, a farm owner (Jenje-Makwenda 2010) and by the time he went to Domboshawa School, where he met future members of the Bantu Actors, he had already developed an interest in music. Thus, those who had the economic means became most influential in the concert tradition, both as sponsors and as fee-paying audiences.

Graduates from Chishawasha mission school, renowned for its brass band, which entertained people in popular marches, also became musicians. Emmanuel Murwira, who could play all instruments, and Guido Chitengo, a 'drummer par excellence', joined the police band (Vambe 1976: 39). Some members of the police band became what Turino (2000: 143) refers to as 'moonlighting musicians', who joined bands such as the Harare Hot Shots and the City Slickers. The Harare

Township middle class also desired to keep up with modern times through listening to popular European ballroom dance music. This led to the formation of music groups that performed at concerts, bringing in European instruments such as saxophones, violins and drums. Benedict Mazura, educated and trained in music at Chishawasha mission, who later played for the police band, became a reputable performer and played a big role in popularising concerts in Harare Township in the 1940s. At this time the Epworth Singers, whose music was distinguished by the use of the piano, were the first group to perform in the Recreational Hall that was later named after Mai Musodzi (for more on Mai Musodzi, see Yoshikuni 2008). They adapted worldwide sounds and styles to indigenous need. However, while the African elite were at the centre of concerts, they were not the only class who attended the concerts. Everyone was free to attend, provided they could pay the entrance fee. Developments within Harare Township, which were not spearheaded by the middle class, also contributed to the popularity of concerts. The building of the Harare Township's Recreational Hall in 1935 stimulated both the popularisation and professionalisation of indoor performances, which were preferred by the middle class because they were perceived as more dignified. The indoor venue also made it possible for promoters to charge and efficiently collect entrance fees. Among African promoters were Jack Sadza, J.J. Chavhunduka and Musekiwa Kumbula. Hosting indoor performances, coupled with the gradual introduction of Western instruments thereafter, they enhanced the popularity of musical concerts. The new sound introduced by the combination of pianos, bass, traps and other modern instruments attracted bigger audiences than when traditional instruments were being used in the 1940s (Turino 2000: 126).

Apart from the traditional dances, another form of entertainment before the popularisation of music concerts was the *mahobo* dance. However, the colonial administrators associated these dances with the consumption of *skokiaan*. In addition to this link with *skokiaan* and romantic affairs that were deemed immoral (Demissie 2012), *mahobo* gatherings were also associated with fights, which sometimes took the form of organised boxing matches (Chikowero 2008). Nonetheless, Vambe (1976: 215) asserts that the parties were a healthy form of recreation, adding that the Rhodesian administrators vilified them as sex orgies only after negative reports had been written in African newspapers by reporters such as Nathan Shamhuyarira. The *mahobo* parties were therefore not popular with Africans who regarded themselves as respectable. They drew their audiences from the lower working class and for the so-called elite, being viewed as 'civilised' was a form of distinction from the less refined peasants and working class (Turino 2003: 328).

Municipal authorities encouraged concerts at recreational centres as a way of introducing their notion of order and discipline in the township.[2] Colonial authorities perceived Africans as people who needed constant monitoring. The municipal authorities regarded the *mahobo* gatherings as hostile to their rule and were constantly disrupting them. This, coupled with the consumption of illicit beer, was a crime and regarded as a rejection of the municipal beer halls, which were a fundraiser for the municipality. The beer halls were part of the control system. In 1920 the colonial administration passed the Kaffir Beer Amendment Ordinance (No. 21), which covered the whole of Salisbury town and Harare Township, as an instrument of control (Yoshikuni 2007: 48). Native Commissioner Sir Herbert Taylor expressed that it would be a disappointment not to stop kaffir beer and activities associated with it.[3] Although he acknowledged that the restrictive legislation often proved ineffective, Taylor was of the opinion that if the missionaries joined the crusade against beer consumption by preaching the gospel of moderation, the harmful effects of excessive beer consumption would be curbed.

The link between *skokiaan* and African entertainment is reflected in an article published in 1936 in the *Bantu Mirror*, which also condemned excessive beer drinking. The article, titled 'Don't Brew Beer', described how a woman called Emma Magumede and ten African men were arrested by the police for possessing *skokiaan* at an occasion that resembled a musical concert. Against such a background of close monitoring and interference from the municipal officials, the growth and development of concerts in Harare Township was disrupted. To the middle class, shunning *mahobo* parties was not a way of collaborating with colonial rule, but a way of negotiating and projecting a middle-class identity.

Technology, mainly in the form of radios, aided the rapid popularisation of music concerts. As the middle-class residents of Harare Township began to procure more radios, they became exposed to more music, especially from outside the colony, including jazz, which became central in their concerts. They became

---

2. National Archives of Zimbabwe, NAZ DHCS, C/27/MB /L, Mai Musodzi Community Hall, p.180.
3. National Archives of Zimbabwe, NAZ, S235/493. Conference of Natives and Native Commissioners of Colony of Southern Rhodesia. Held in Salisbury, 12 December, 1927.

familiar with different genres, which they adopted alongside their traditional music and dance. Moreover, in the early days, traditional music was not broadcast on the radio and only began being broadcast after the mid-1950s (Turino 2008: 143). The African middle class appreciated the Western music they heard on the radio and began to associate themselves with it. Bands began to play the music for concerts suitable for people in regular employment, such as teachers, clerks, nurses, drivers and policemen. By their attendance, these people promoted the rising popularity of concerts. Another aspect of technology that significantly contributed to the popularity of musical concerts was the availability of loudspeakers and the cinema in the municipal halls. These were put in place not only for concerts, but also to enable news broadcasts to reach the majority of Africans residing in Harare. After the news bulletins, foreign Western music would be played (Stapleton 2011: 95). This also contributed to the familiarity and popularity of Western music in the African middle class.

Marabi and *omasganda* music that were popular in African township concerts began to appear in South Africa in the 1920s and achieved considerable popularity, particularly in the 1930s and 1940s. *Marabi* is a South African jazz style that originated in the 1920s and had strong inspiration from American jazz. This genre came into existence in the ghettos and the *shebeens* of Johannesburg and it is rooted in traditional South African music.[4] Having assimilated the South African sounds, musicians, workers and traders from South Africa introduced them to Harare upon their return. The new sounds became instantly popular. Since there were no recording facilities in Southern Rhodesia during that time, music could only be transmitted through live performances.[5] Some singers, such as Moses Mphahlo, shunned recording because they felt it distorted the originality of their songs (Jenje-Makwenda 2010). South African jazz influence was also evident in August Musarurwa's tune 'Skokiaan' (Turino 2003: 328). Other musicians, such as Dorothy Masuka, who had spent part of her childhood in Harare Township and is credited as having been one of the pioneering female voices in music (Vambe 2007: 367), later relocated to South Africa, but continued to positively influence local artists, especially female ones. Influential also were world-renowned artists Frank Sinatra and Elvis Presley (Turino 2003: 330).

---

4. http://www.southafrica.info/about/arts/922563.htm#.Vmv4zb8UhZ0.
5. http://www.southafrica.info/about/arts/922563.htm#.Vmv4zb8UhZ0.

Although the local musicians imitated outside influences, they also internalised them, infused them with their own language, local ideas and locally relevant messages to produce a product that could be described as their own. This infusion of local and outside influences made concerts popular because the music was diverse and highly entertaining.

Foreign music and bands that became popular among the African middle class in Harare Township included South African groups such as the Manhattan Brothers and North American groups such as the Mills Brothers. Local bands such as the Black & White Band, the Golden City Dixies, the Coloured Arcadia Rhythm Lads and De Black Evening Follies began to model their music along the lines of the bands they listened to on the radio (Zindi 2010: 42). The local bands began by producing foreign-influenced music firstly for radio commercials, then later began to play such music for entertainment at the music concerts (Koskoff 2008). Popular with the local bands were Western artists such as Jimmy Rogers, whose music was played at concerts in the local entertainment hall in Harare.[6]

However, though inspired by Western music, African township music was able to capture local and regional elements in order to produce music that was unique and responsive to local needs and the transformations that were taking place in the colony. Since African urban musicians appropriated music from other parts of Africa, their music can be viewed as a compromise between Western and African music traditions. South African jazz and kwela influence was particularly strong in the growth and popularity of concerts in Harare Township. Apart from the fact that South African music was played on the radio, people who went to work in South African mines returned home with a taste for not only South African music, but also American jazz music. They also brought home gramophones and records. According to Joyce Jenje-Makwenda, a certain area in Harare that became known as Majubheki or Jo'burg lines was named after people who would have gone to work or trade in South Africa and returned.[7] However, Vambe (1976: 149) is of the opinion that the area was called Majubheki because the people who resided there had criminal tendencies similar to residents of Johannesburg. Some musicians, such as Robert Muzengeri, would go to South Africa to record, giving them exposure to South African music, which they appropriated. Muzengeri started his

---

6. Professor George Kahari, interview, Harare, 5 May 2015.
7. Joyce Jenje-Makwenda, interview, Harare, 31 December 2014.

musical career in the 1930s, the time during which he became popular through his songs 'Vaigara Mumakomo' (They Stayed in Mountains) and 'Nhamo Yaive Nava Agrippa' (The Trials and Tribulations of Mr Agrippa) (Zindi 2003: 7). The name 'Agrippa' referred to a man who faced unemployment and poverty while residing in Harare Township. This reflects the poverty that most residents of the township experienced. 'Vaigara Mumakomo' is a nostalgic song about the way African people lived before colonialism.

Muzengeri's later brand of music that became popular in the 1940s and 1950s was *tsava-tsava*. Most musicians played *tsava-tsava* because during that time 'almost everyone played the same rhythm' (Zindi 2011). The name '*tsava-tsava*' was derived from the *tsaba-tsaba* dance. Other prominent players of *tsava-tsava* were De Black Evening Follies, the Black & White Band, the Golden City Dixies, Kandido Sabau and Elijah Muzanga. *Tsava* style became associated with the working class in Zimbabwe, although it was played across southern Africa. In Harare Township, *tsava-tsava* was associated with 'tea parties', a euphemism for weekend dance parties (Turino 2000: 142). Tea parties were not always respectable occasions. Sometimes music groups would perform at undignified venues, which did not attract the middle-class audience. Mura Nyakura, for instance, upon his return from Zaire, played at the Gwaku hotel and composed a jingle called 'Hotera yaGwaku', which made the restaurant popular. However, it was closed after being suspected of trading in the illicit *skokiaan* beer, which the 'middle class did not want to be associated with. His recording, "Ndiye Gwaku Akatangisa Matapi" was an instant hit'. Turino notes that local groups also appropriated music trends from outside the colony through musicians who came into the country to perform. Some of them, notably the OK Success band, which originated from the Congo, later permanently stayed in the country, producing music that infused Congolese and Shona lyrics (Makombe 2013: 163). In 1948, Nyakura returned to Zimbabwe, bringing with him Zairean influences, including the *kanindo-rhumba* beat, which later developed into what is today known as the *sungura* beat (Tembo 2013: 145).

The economic recession, which was experienced the world over, also enhanced the chances of the middle class in influencing the spread of music concerts. The colony was not spared the effects of the recession, which mainly manifested in high unemployment levels. Unemployment made people want to explore the music industry. The need to address the unemployment problem also helps to explain the popularity of concerts in Harare Township. During this period the African middle class assisted in the formation of new bands as a way of alleviating unemployment problems in the Township.[8] The middle class also helped bands to secure municipal contracts, which lasted between six months and a year, depending on the demand of the concert audience. Businessmen such as 'Rambanai, Samuriwo and Vito' also offered their assistance, especially in getting municipal contracts.[9] These contracts enabled music bands to operate without restriction from municipal authorities, which controlled entertainment in the African township. The artists were also able to earn concert royalties, which resulted in the rise of popular musicians and bands for paid performances, such as De Black Evening Follies, the Black & White Band, the Golden City Dixies, Isaac Musarurwa, Oliver Musvarwe, and the Zimunya Danger Group, among others (Zindi 2010: 42).

The formation of the Federation, which drew together Northern Rhodesia (Zambia) and Nyasaland (Malawi) into administrative, commercial and primary commodity circuits of capital centred in Salisbury (Bond 1993) also had an impact on the rise of music concerts. The city was poised to attract large numbers of people, as it was opened for industrial production, which required a large labour force. This resulted in diversity, as well as an increase in the number of Africans living in Harare Township, which had a positive impact on the popularity of music concerts, with the increase of paying audiences (Zindi 2010: 41). Harare Township was able to capitalise on the increase in the numbers of people who needed entertainment because more venues for concerts were opened. These were the Kaufman Centre, close to Mbare marketplace, the Methodist Church in Magaba, Mai Musodzi Hall (formally the Recreational Hall) and Stodart Hall. Stodart Hall was built in 1956 (Jenje-Makwenda 2005: 50).[10] Although other townships were established, Harare Township remained the hub of entertainment in Salisbury.

The role of De Black Evening Follies in making music concerts popular is worth emphasising. The group came into existence in 1943 when its founder and leader Moses Mphahlo Mafusire and Elisha Kassim broke away from the Bantu Actors. Their group became the second-most popular group in Harare Township (Jenje-Makwenda 2010), quickly rising to become one of the most well-known African singing groups in southern Africa (Stapleton 2011: 95). De Black Evening Follies was associated with the introduction of the Miss Harare Pageant in 1951.

---

8. Mr Makope, 74 years old, interview, Hatcliffe, 27 December 2014.
9. Mbuya Mashiri, 78 years old, interview, Hatcliffe, 27 December 2014.
10. Makope, interview.

The pageant was sponsored by a Miss B. Tredgold of St Michael's Mission (Falola and Fleming 2012: 228) and was held in conjunction with music concerts, thereby increasing their audience. Joyce Ndoro, one of the contestants in the pageant, became a singer and dancer (Saidi 2012). It is important to note that although concert performances were dominated by men, notable female musicians also made their mark on the music concert scene. De Black Evening Follies worked with female singers such as Lina Mattaka, Kenneth Mattaka's wife; Charlotte Phiri; Thandi Sheba and Rennie Jones (Jenje-Makwenda 2010). People's views towards concerts were broadened to accept that women could be entertainers as well.

The African Music Union, which supported concerts in Harare Township, also helped the concert tradition to become popular. Its mandate was to help African musicians in the Harare location with performance and with the conducting of concerts.[11] It also popularised concerts by inviting sponsors to support concerts by funding instruments and venue bookings. The Zebrons Band achieved immense popularity through the influence of the African Music Union. Associations such as British American Tobacco became major sponsors, providing musical instrumentals in 1956 (Zindi 1985: 4). Later, bands such as the Safe Brothers, Golden Brothers, City Rhythms and City Slickers received financial sponsorship from the Coca-Cola Bottling Company.[12] This was achieved through the efforts of the African Music Union, which also promoted the growth of concerts through effective advertising in the press, particularly the *African Daily News* and *Bantu Mirror*, which were widely read by African residents.[13] These newspapers not only informed readers about domestic and international news, but they also updated them on the social calendar, including schedules for concerts (Molefe 2010: 81). This publicity resulted in the growing popularity of the African bands that played in these concerts.

The Kwanongoma College of Music for Africans was also created under the African Music Union. It provided equipment and lessons for the performers.[14] They were instructed on voice, performance and instruments such as the piano, guitar and drums. The college catered for students from all over the country, so its

---

11. *African Daily News*, 21 February 1957.
12. *African Daily News*, 5 December 1956.
13. Josiah Mudadi, 72 years old, interview, Mbare, 19 January 2015. He was a Zebrons Band guitarist.
14. *African Daily News*, 15 February 1957.

influence was spread countrywide, including to Harare Township. The musicians were also taught to appreciate traditional music such as *mbira* and this enabled the fusion of *mbira* into the concert tradition.[15] The college worked closely with the city council beer hall administration in promoting concerts.

The availability of decent venues enabled the middle class to successfully promote the concert tradition. Harare Township had several venues where musical concerts could be held, but not all the venues were suitable for night concerts. For instance, Kaufman Centre's close proximity to the marketplace made it an unsuitable venue as far as the audience was concerned because of rampant theft and prostitution.[16] The Methodist Church was a potential venue for holding concerts since it could accommodate a large number of people. It also had seats, which allowed the audience to be seated comfortably for the performance. However, the Methodist Church authorities were not keen on the idea of holding musical concerts in their place of worship.[17] Stodart Hall was the largest hall in the Harare location.[18] It was well designed and staged in such a way that all the audience could sit. However, this venue was expensive to hire, thereby restricting attendance to the more affluent residents of Harare (Jenje-Makwenda 2005: 50). This left Mai Musodzi Hall as the most popular venue for musical concerts in Harare Township. The hall was named after a pioneer female social welfare worker known for her humanitarian work among the less privileged. Mai Musodzi Hall had a lower hiring fee than Stodart Hall, so music concerts there were almost always well attended.[19]

Since concerts were meant for Harare Township's middle class, most of whom had regular jobs, weekends were reserved for concerts when most people were not working and needed entertainment. The concerts would be combined at times, to offer a variety of performances at once, and venues would always be sold out. Special performances also drew large crowds.[20] The City Quads, De Black Evening Follies and the Mashonaland Melodians were popular bands that performed every Saturday night.[21] The concert performances were only for adults and they were

---

15. *African Daily News*, 15 February 1957.
16. Petros Musenga, 81 years old, interview, Mbare, 18 January 2015.
17. Gogo Monica Chinsamba, 76 years old, interview, Mbare, 18 January 2015.
18. Musenga, interview.
19. Makope, interview.
20. Mbuya Benza, 88 years old, interview, Mbare, 17 January 2015.
21. *African Daily News*, 22 December 1956.

hosted at night because during the day these venues were being used for other activities, such as teen clubs, which were held during the day for the protection of girls (Gelfand and Ritchken 1961: 182). William Saidi (2012), who, as part of Harare Township's middle class, contributed to the popularisation of concerts as a songwriter, as a reporter and as a singer with the Milton Brothers Band, reminisces that his early life as a child revolved around Mai Musodzi Hall, where his schooling began in 1945. Concerts usually started at 7:30 p.m. and ended at 11:00 p.m. (Radano and Bohlman 2000: 561), marked by the singing of 'Ishe Komborerai Africa' (God Bless Africa) by the audience.[22] In some instances, Friday night concerts would last till early morning.[23]

The middle class also popularised music concerts through linkages with fashion. Concerts became arenas where fashion could be showcased and where people could show how much of African forms of entertainment they still valued and how much of Western values they had adopted. Concerts in Harare Township were treated as special occasions and loyal concertgoers would dress up fashionably for the occasion. Middle-class women, such as nurses who were employed at the maternity wing of the municipal clinic (Vambe 1976: 150), would wear evening dresses that swirled on the floor as couples swayed round from corner to corner dancing to the music.[24] Long dresses that swept the floor were common among married women at the concerts, while men would wear suits as a mark of status.[25] Stiff dresses, *mastifi*, were commonly worn by single women. Women would also wear dresses with rounded shoulders, shapely bust lines, closely defined waistlines and long narrow skirts, which were quite popular. Performers would imitate world-renowned musicians such as the Beatles in their dress. In the 1960s they would wear 'jackets without collars, high-heeled shoes that became known as Beatles shoes' and audiences would, in turn, imitate the way local performers dressed.[26]

The participation of different audiences in the concerts had an impact on the popularity of concerts. The audience's responses to concert performances depended on the ability of the performers to offer amusing entertainment. Sometimes performances would be long and often involved the participation of the audience.

---

22. *African Daily News*, 7 May 1957.
23. *African Daily News*, 24 January 1962.
24. *African Daily News*, 23 May 1957.
25. Benza, interview.
26. Professor Fred Zindi, interview, Harare, 24 February 2016.

Both women and men would be invited to engage each other on the dancefloor and danced according to the command of the lead singer.[27] Concert audiences expected performers to deliver exciting performances in accordance with their payment. The audience would complain if they thought the performance was poor, as this made them feel they had been shortchanged. At one such incident at Mai Musodzi Hall, in 1956, the City Quads received a negative response from the audience after their failure to deliver a good performance, which was a result of the fact that they had performed without a microphone.[28] Lack of adequate equipment was frequently at the centre of poor performances, which would sometimes make the audience angry and trigger open fights.

While the colonial administration used laws to deal with issues of excessive beer drinking and illicit beer brewing, these did not always have the desired effect. The African elite took it upon themselves to discourage the *mahobo* parties, which the municipal authorities associated with the consumption of *skokiaan* and with immoral behaviour. Men were encouraged to be responsible to their families by discouraging irresponsible consumption of beer. On the other hand, concerts also sought to raise awareness of the social problems in Harare Township, such as theft, the rape of young girls and women, robbery, poor living conditions, unemployment and general poverty.[29] Young girls were at risk of being raped not only by African men, but European men as well (Vambe 1976: 137). The songs' lyrics also articulated solutions for these social problems, while conveying messages of social responsibility – for example, 'Kudzidza Kwakanaka' (Education Is Good), which was sung by the Epworth Theatrical Strutters, released in 1950 (Falola and Fleming 2012: 228). It implored African people to get a good education as a way of escaping the trap of poverty and earning the respect that the colonial government denied them. The songs spoke to the everyday experiences of the residents of Harare Township, which was very significant in popularising the concert tradition and instilling hope in the residents.

The concerts could not avoid the political issues faced by the people in the township. However, although the middle class is associated with political activism, Vambe (1976) notes that not all were active and some were reluctant to show

---

27. *African Daily News*, 22 December 1956.
28. *African Daily News*, 13 June 1957.
29. Benza, interview.

their support for national politics, while others supported white rule. Concerts became sites of political confrontation between the colonial administration and the elite, some of whom were also at the forefront of nationalist politics. The colonial administration sought to use concerts as platforms for moulding Africans and as a way of improving social and moral order among the African population (Falola and Fleming 2012: 240). Ironically, however, the concert phenomenon created spaces for addressing the oppression, poverty, suffering and domination that was being perpetrated by the colonial administration. Policies such as the Land Apportionment Act seemed bent on keeping Africans isolated and overcrowded in the township, racial policies that reserved good jobs for white people and kept African people in low-paid jobs, regardless of their educational skills and qualifications, as well as petty policies such as the pass laws that were meant to humiliate Africans were criticised through concerts. Songs sung against the abusive colonial government were also part of such concerts, which helped to form the political consciousness of the middle-class elite. Such songs include 'Nyika Dzapera Nevarungu' (The Europeans Have Taken Over the Countries), which became popular with choir concerts. Hymns of endurance, which were a response to the hardships of colonial rule and poverty in the township, such as Psalm 23, 'The Lord Is My Shepherd', were also popular at these concerts.[30] Music thus became a release and escape for the township residents, as they would yield to the entertaining aspect of the concerts, rather than dwelling on their bitterness and anger.

Although most concerts were sanctioned by the municipal council, the colonial administration was always suspicious that immoral activities, such as prostitution and beer drinking, were taking place at the concerts. In the Harare location, immorality was associated with premarital sex, cohabitation, theft and unscrupulous drinking of alcohol.[31] Violence was also part of the immoral behaviour during concerts and was triggered by issues to do with seating space, single men fighting over single women and also drunkenness. Some people would turn up at the concerts already drunk because the authorities forbade the consumption of beer in public spaces, preferring that Africans consume beer in beerhalls, where there was some form of control (West 1997: 651). Locals referred to the African police as *mabhurakwacha* (a derogatory name), who were always part of the

---

30. Kahari, interview.
31. Benza, interview.

audience in order to maintain peace and order.[32] Some residents lost interest in attending concerts, especially the Christians, because they believed that crooks and gangsters, prostitutes and drunkards coming from *skokiaan* and gambling dens and beerhalls would mix with them.

Colonial repression, the middle class and concert popularity

As a result of the real or imagined association of concerts with rowdy behaviour, the colonial administration put in place policies and regulations to regulate African conduct, even at concerts. Africans were persecuted under unclear laws, which regarded African concerts as unlawful meetings. Such laws accused Africans at concerts of disturbing law and order. Venues could be closed down if the regulatory authorities suspected that illicit beer was being consumed. The fact that the middle class were also the leaders of the nationalist movement, linked the three together, making concerts the target of colonial control. Through controlling concerts, the colonial administration was also hoping to control nationalist activities. The administration invoked the Municipal Areas Act of 1897, which empowered municipalities to control African activities in the cities. This Act was already in existence before both concerts and the liberation struggle started. The period before the official launch of the liberation struggle was characterised by labour protests by railway and industrial workers. This labour militancy and its quasi-political movements became a model for urban centres in Southern Rhodesia in the 1960s (West 2002). This was all projected in Harare Township's music concerts, which were blamed for stimulating strikes and riots in Salisbury townships. The state of emergency imposed in 1959 also affected concerts because some of the sponsors were detained. The colonial rulers aimed to suppress African nationalism and political activities. Nationalism in music had been noted in liberation songs, which were now being sung at concerts, thus triggering a need by the colonial government to deprive Africans of leisure through autonomous control measures. New Acts were constantly put in place, including the Hall Hiring Act, the Public Entertainment Act of 1965 and the Censorship and Entertainment Act of 1967, which were aimed at maintaining colonial dominance. This mistrust heightened when the armed struggle started and the concerts began to be regarded as *pungwes* (night political meetings) that were held in the rural areas during the Second

---

32. Makope, interview.

Chimurenga.³³ The genre of *chimurenga* music, which characterised the nationalist struggle, started to be recognised as a genre in the music concerts from the late 1960s to the early 1970s, especially with the rise of musicians such as Thomas Mapfumo. The colonial officials began to regard African leisure and entertainment as a threat to their rule (Akyeampong and Ambler 2002: 8). However, colonial repressive laws did not have the anticipated effect of stifling the concerts; rather, they strengthened their popularity and influence.

Thus, for the nationalists, musical concerts became arenas to influence the fight against colonial rule and to advocate for black independence. Residents of Harare Township used concerts as meeting points to express political opinions and to discuss issues of mutual interest. Nationalist politicians also used concerts as platforms to politicise people, as well as to get support in their struggle against the colonial regime. Political figures such as Stanislaus Mudenge sponsored musical concerts, hiring instruments and paying venue fees for concerts so that they would get the chance to make political statements.³⁴ Songs related to the liberation struggle would be sung at musical concerts, encouraging the spirit of nationalism,³⁵ while boosting the popularity of concerts in the process. The colonial authorities reacted by engaging the Special Force, referred to by Africans as *Mabhatimani* (Batmen) to monitor activities at the concerts.³⁶ On one occasion in 1966, tear gas was used to disperse a crowd at a concert by the Golden Brothers and the Safe Brothers, after the colonial authorities suspected that the concert had been turned political.³⁷ This concert was sponsored by a member of the African middle class, Bernard Vito, who was also engaged in African nationalism. The link between music concerts and nationalism was reflected by the form of lyrics in songs such as 'Mukatiende' (Get up and Let's Go) and 'Tondobayana' (We Will Fight), which had insinuations of political liberation and protest against colonial rule (Jones 2000: 33).

The colonial administration responded to this development by empowering the municipality as an instrument of social control (Akyeampong and Ambler 2002: 8). The Salisbury Municipality invoked various Acts to control African leisure

---

33. *Chimurenga* is a Shona word meaning 'war' or 'struggle'. Its appearance within the framework of colonial period makes clear the situation of the day.
34. Sekuru Benson Mungwada, 77 years old, interview, Mbare, 31 January 2015.
35. Makope, interview.
36. Mungwada, interview.
37. Mungwada, interview.

time. Some songs were banned because of their lyrics. The City Quad's first album was banned because of the song 'When Will the Day of Freedom Come' (Jenje-Makwenda 2015). The Milton Brothers were also prevented from recording one of their songs because the lyrics, '*Honai rudzi rwevatema, runongochema, nokuti tagara nevachena*' (See the Black race are always crying because we now live with the white men), were deemed too political (Saidi 2012). To exert control the municipality made it illegal for musical concerts to be held without authorisation from the city municipality and colonial officials. The Censorship and Entertainment Act No. 28 of 1967 stated that no person could use a theatre for entertainment unless a permit in respect of the theatre had been obtained. This Act also governed musical concerts, which were related to performance. The colonial administration made sure that concerts were only held with approval from the city's municipality and failure to conform would result in a fine or arrest. On several occasions concert organisers were arrested for breaching clearance regulations and a concert had to be cancelled abruptly whenever the organisers failed to produce paperwork authorising the event.

The Law and Order Maintenance Act of 1966 was also passed to deal with all suspected African political activists. This included Africans who were involved, or suspected of being involved, in supporting the liberation struggle. Some musicians, though not found guilty of a prosecutable crime, risked being detained for holding or supporting political opinions regarded as sabotaging the colonial administration. Detention was used as a way of deterring political activism and suppressing African opposition to Rhodesian colonial rule (Munochiveyi 2013: 287). This Act applied to every aspect of African life, including entertainment and leisure, and therefore musical concerts. The Act worked intimately with the Detention Order, which resulted in the isolation of African political activists to remote and inaccessible parts of the country, so as to render political activists and supporters of the struggle for liberation politically, intellectually and socially irrelevant.

Conclusion

This chapter has discussed the role of the colonial African elite in the rise and popularity of music concerts in Salisbury's Harare Township. The elite, consisting of businessmen and Africans who had received education mainly in mission schools, some with university degrees, who worked as teachers, doctors, nurses, messengers and court interpreters, desired ways of spending their leisure time. African musicians responded to this need by producing music that suited the needs of the elite. Apart from being the audience for rising musicians, the middle-class elite also assisted the musicians, for instance, by sponsoring them. The elite used the concerts as a platform to fight the colonial stereotype of Africans as uncivilised, excessive drinkers and rowdy, by promoting responsible drinking and respectability. Because the African elite became leaders of nationalist movements, concerts came to be associated with opposition to colonial rule, as concerts became platforms to mobilise against repressive colonial rule, resulting in tightening of rules regulating concerts. Nonetheless, the concert tradition continued to thrive in urban townships.

References

Akyeampong, E. and C. Ambler. 2002. 'Leisure in African History: An Introduction'. *International Journal of African Historical Studies* 35(1): 1–16.

Bond, P. 1993. 'Economic Origins of Black Townships in Zimbabwe, Contradictions of Industrial and Financial Capital in the 1950s and 1960s'. *Economic Geography* 69(1): 72–89.

Chikowero, M. 2008. 'Struggles over Culture: Zimbabwean Music and Power, 1930–2007'. PhD diss., Dalhousie University, Halifax.

Demissie, F. (ed.). 2012. *Colonial Architecture and Urbanism in Africa, Intertwined and Contested Histories*. Burlington: Ashgate Publishing Company.

Falola, T. and T. Fleming. 2012. *Music, Performance and African Identities*. New York: Routledge.

Gelfand, M. and J. Ritchken. 1961. 'Life at Harare'. *Central African Journal of Medicine*, 7 May.

Jenje-Makwenda, J. 2005. *Zimbabwe Township Music*. Harare: Storytime Promotions.

———. 2010. 'The Grandfather of Township Music and Entertainment Is No More'. *The Herald*, 8 September.

———. 2015. 'Zimbabwe Township Music 1930s–1960'. *The Herald*, 18 November.

Jones, C. 2000. *Making Music, Musical Instruments of Zimbabwe Past and Present*. Harare: Academic Books Zimbabwe.

Kelly, J. 2003. 'Leisure as life: Outline of a Postculturalist Reconstruction'. In *Leisure in Urban Africa*, edited by P.T. Zeleza and C.R. Veney, 39–56. Asmara: Africa World Press.

Koskoff, E. 2008. *The Concise Garland Encyclopedia of World Music*. Volume 1. New York: Routledge.

Makombe, E.K. 2013. 'A Social History of Town and Country Interactions: A Study on the Changing Social Life and Practices of Rural-Urban Migrants in Colonial Harare and Goromonzi (1946–1979)'. PhD diss., University of Witwatersrand, Johannesburg.

Mamdani, M. 2001. 'Beyond Settler and Native as Political Identities: Overcoming the Political Legacy of Colonialism'. *Comparative Studies in Society and History* 43(4): 651–64.

———. 2012. *Define and Rule: Native as Political Identity*. Cambridge: Harvard University Press.

Martin, P. 1995. *Leisure and Society in Colonial Brazzaville*. Cambridge: Cambridge University Press.

Mlambo, A.S. 2014. *A History of Zimbabwe*. New York: University Press Publishers.

Molefe, S.C. 2010. 'Leisure and Making of KwaMashu, 1958–1989'. Master's thesis, University of Cape Town, Cape Town.

Munochiveyi, M.B. 2013. 'The Political Lives of Rhodesian Detainees during Zimbabwe's Liberation Struggle'. *International Journal of African Historical Studies* 46(2): 283–305.

Radano, R.M. and P.V. Bohlman (eds). 2000. *Music and the Racial Imagination*. Chicago: University of Chicago Press.

Saidi, B. 2012. 'Life and the Recreation Hall'. *The Herald*, 20 January.

Schmidt, E. 1992. *Peasants, Traders, and Wives: Shona Women in the History of Zimbabwe, 1870–1939*. Portsmouth: Heinemann.

Scott, J. 1985. *Weapons of the Weak: Everyday Forms of Peasant Resistance*. New Haven: Yale University Press.

Stapleton, T. 2011. *African Police and Soldiers in Colonial Zimbabwe, 1923–80*. New York: University of Rochester Press.

Tembo, C. 2013. 'An Embodied Culture of Optimism and Struggle: The Sungura Music of Tongai Moyo'. *Journal of Pan African Studies* 6(5): 144–55.

Turino, T. 2000. *Nationalists, Cosmopolitans and Popular Music in Zimbabwe*. Chicago: University of Chicago Press.

———. 2003. 'The Middle Class, Cosmopolitanism and Popular Music in Harare, Zimbabwe'. In *Leisure in Urban Africa*, edited by P.T. Zeleza and C.R. Veney, 321–41. Asmara: Africa World Press.

———. 2008. *Music as a Social Life: The Politics of Participation*. Chicago: University of Chicago Press.

Vambe, L. 1976. *From Rhodesia to Zimbabwe*. London: Heinemann.

Vambe, M.T. 2007. '"Aya Mahobo": Migrant Labour and the Cultural Semiotics of Harare (Mbare) African Township, 1930–1970'. *African Identities* 5(3): 355–69.

West, M.O. 1997. 'Liquor and Libido: "Joint Drinking" and the Politics of Sexual Control in Colonial Zimbabwe, 1920s–1950s'. *Journal of Social History* 30(3): 645–67.

———. 2002. *The Rise of an African Middle Class: Colonial Zimbabwe 1898–1965*. Bloomington: Indiana University Press.

———. 2012. 'The African Middle Class in Zimbabwe: Historical and Contemporary Perspectives'. In *The Making of the Middle Class: Toward a Transnational History*, edited by A. Ricardo Lopez and B. Weinstein, 45–57. Durham: Duke University Press.

Yoshikuni, T. 2007. African *Urban Experience in Colonial Zimbabwe: A Social History of Harare before 1925*. Harare: Weaver Press.

———. 2008. *Elizabeth Mai Musodzi and the Birth of African Feminism in Early Colonial Zimbabwe*. Harare: Weaver Press.

Zindi, F. 1985. *Roots Rocking in Zimbabwe*. Gweru: Mambo Press.

———. 2003. *Music Workbook, Zimbabwe versus the World*. Harare: Zindisc Publications.

———. 2010. *Music Guide for Zimbabwe*. Harare: Zindisc Publications.

———. 2011. 'Who Are the Pioneers of Zim Music?' *The Herald*, 20 September. https://www.herald.co.zw/who-are-the-pioneers-of-zim-music/.

CHAPTER 8

The Promotion of Popular Music in the Major Cities of Zimbabwe
A Contested Terrain by Musicians and Promoters

Victoria Blessing Butete

Music promotion is central to the development of any music industry. This chapter examines the status quo of popular music promotion in Zimbabwe, particularly the relationships between musicians, the media and promoters, among other key stakeholders such as venue owners, music consumers, recording studios, censorship boards and distribution companies. The study primarily seeks to describe the opportunities and challenges existing between the musicians, who happen to be the principal stakeholders, and the promoters and other stakeholders in the industry. I describe in detail the social context of Zimbabwe and the current state of the music industry. Christopher Ballantine (1993: 3) argues that 'music can best be understood in relation to the context that gave birth to it'; in other words, there is a symbiotic relationship between music and the environment in which it is performed and produced. Context involves performance venues, funding, media and legislation, such as censorship and copyright law, among other factors, which impact on business transactions of key stakeholders. Hence, context has a significant bearing on the industry's overall performance.

Current socio-economic conditions in Zimbabwe have had a significant impact on the music industry. The relationship between musicians and promoters attracted my attention because it is central to the success and development of the music industry. Also, the socio-economic context impacts on both the musicians and the promoters, making it necessary to describe their relationship. The musicians, as principal stakeholders, have suffered the consequences of this state of affairs mainly because their success depends on the operations of other stakeholders in the industry. It is therefore important to identify and discuss the challenges facing the musicians and promoters in order to find possible solutions to develop the industry. This is despite Antony Mhiripiri's (2012) contention that the music industry has been resilient in the face of a struggling economy. It could be argued that the industry remained functional, but there is no doubt that it felt the impact of the socio-economic and political context, as did other industries that unlike the music industry were forced to shut down. On the surface, it looked as if the music industry was flourishing, whereas in actual fact it was not.

To develop a full appreciation of the nature of popular music promotion in Zimbabwe, interviews and questionnaires were used to collect data from musicians, promoters, venue owners, media representatives, National Arts Council of Zimbabwe (NACZ) provincial managers and Zimbabwe Music Rights Association (ZIMURA) licensing provincial managers from Gweru, Harare, Bulawayo and Mutare. Purposive sampling was employed to select the above-mentioned research participants while qualitative analysis was utilised for data interpretation in order to establish the nature of popular music promotion in Zimbabwe. The data is eclectically presented and grouped into categories and/or themes. The findings demonstrate the paradox of music promotion in Zimbabwe.

Liz Hill, Catherine O'Sullivan and Terry O'Sullivan (2003: 192) suggest that there is a need to review the marketing mix offered by the arts to ensure relevance to the ever-changing external environment, the pattern of which is determined by precedent because of time, lack of imagination or insufficient experience. This chapter adopts the Socio-cultural, Technological, Economic and Political (STEP) model developed by Hill, O'Sullivan and O'Sullivan (2003), designed for the analysis of the arts marketing environment where promotion takes place. STEP factors impact on the context of popular music promotion in Zimbabwe, as depicted in the historical contextualisation. Since STEP factors influence the cultural field, determining the capital/gain the stakeholders realise from their operations, their views are largely based on these benefits. Pierre Bourdieu defines capital as that which constitutes gain for the musicians; any type of resource, both tangibles and intangibles, such as money, expertise, social networks or prestige (in Webb, Schirato and Danaher 2002: 178). He differentiates between capital as cultural, social or economic, arguing that it shapes social relations and enables participants to exercise power, determining their movement in the cultural field. Capital includes goods that are material and symbolic and exist as social, economic or cultural capital. Since popular music in Zimbabwe is a profitable market for the musicians and their promoters, capital in its diverse forms has a huge impact on the musicians' success or lack of it.

The findings of this chapter reveal the contested perceptions that key stakeholders hold regarding popular music promotion in Zimbabwe. The complex nature of the relationship between stakeholders, particularly the promoters and the musicians, show an imbalance of power tilted in favour of the former and hence detrimental to the latter, in terms of profitability of their core business. There is a lot of blame shifting, which implies that until the concerned parties choose to reflect and compromise for the benefit of both, the industry will continue to struggle. The prevailing tensions are not conducive to the development of the industry at large and there is need to educate especially the musicians on how to conduct their business professionally, since the majority of them are not formally trained. As I have observed in earlier research, there is need for proper management of musicians to facilitate informed, formal business transactions between musicians and the promoters (Butete 2014). The fact that musicians are dependent on promoters for exposure means that local musicians' negotiating power is compromised because their relationship with the promoters is projected as that of 'he who pays the piper calls the tune'. Consequently, given the prevailing socio-economic conditions, the musicians are forced to settle for less than they deserve in order to earn a living.

Historical contextualisation of popular music promotion in Zimbabwe

Paul Berliner (1993) was one of the first Western writers to study Zimbabwean popular music. He discusses *mbira* music performance in the context of Shona traditional music. His focus on music functions is reminiscent of its general roles in African society, such as ritual, work, lullabies, ceremonies and festivals, storytelling, dancing, communication and ethnic or group identity. Joseph Kwabena Nketia (1974) and Francis Bebey (1975) share the same view of the centrality of music to social activities in the African context. The advent of popular music did not change the functionality of music because the themes of the songs are based on the socio-economic and political issues that impact on the audience's lives. In this regard, popular music becomes a social commentary, reflecting the experiences, needs and aspirations not only of the musicians themselves, but also of the audience and society at large. This is reflected through the audience's patronage, which is an important factor in the success of musicians.

Additionally, several writers attribute the development of popular music to the advent of colonialism. Paul Berliner (1993), Caleb Dube (1996), Thomas Turino (2000) and Antony Mhiripiri (2011) agree that colonialism marked the development of popular music in Zimbabwe. The growth of urbanisation and mass communication fuelled rural to urban migration by employment seekers. Dube (1996) argues that colonialism imposed Western cultural values on African cultural ideologies, forcing lifestyle changes, and hence impacted on Zimbabwean popular music as it diluted indigenous culture. He also suggests that the presence in urban areas of regional migrant workers from Zambia, Malawi and Mozambique also contributed to the development of local popular music. Consequently, local traditional music styles were combined with both regional and Western music styles, as observed by Joyce Jenje-Makwenda (2005). She discusses the role of municipalities in the development of popular music in the 1930s. The British colonial system promoted popular music and created performance spaces in the form of community halls. Municipalities promoted musical activities, as these spaces were open to musicians and other community members involved in other art forms, such as theatre. Fred Zindi (1985) observes that at this time hotels and most entertainment venues had resident bands, which enabled musicians to earn a living. This shows that the hospitality industry was used as promotional space for popular music. However, from independence in 1980 to date, municipal facilities have deteriorated and have become inaccessible to musicians. Consequently, Muchadeyi Masunda, mayor of Harare, speaking at the Harare International Festival of the Arts (HIFA) Symposium observed that cultural infrastructure in the city is in a state of disrepair. He added that a coherent cultural policy on arts and culture is lacking (HIFA Symposium 2012). This implies that the government is not as involved in promoting music as in earlier times – hence the many challenges the industry is facing.

However, during British colonial rule, as is the case in post-independent Zimbabwe, only musicians who supported the ruling government benefited from state patronage. Musicians such as Thomas Mapfumo and Comrade Chinx Chingaira, who championed the cause of the struggle for independence, were ostracised by the Rhodesian regime and their music was only played in allied countries, such as Zambia and Mozambique (Pongweni 1982). Dianne Thram (2006) depicts the Zimbabwean nationalist government as restricting freedom of expression in the same manner as the British colonial government and the South African apartheid government. She focuses on Oliver Mtukudzi, Thomas Mapfumo and Leonard Zhakata to demonstrate the government's gatekeeping role, which, she argues, impedes the development of the industry, rather than promotes it. Although Mapfumo played a critical role during the struggle for independence, he has since fallen out of favour with the nationalist government for being critical of its corrupt tendencies (Eyre 2001, 2015). In South Africa, musicians of colour could not perform songs the apartheid regime considered inappropriate; neither could some whites who were critical of the regime (Baines 2002). These are some examples of the government's role in censoring music; its ownership, control, and use of the state-owned media to perpetuate its agenda by both the former Rhodesian Broadcasting Corporation and Zimbabwe Broadcasting Holdings.

Colonialism brought about industrialisation, which led to technological developments, such as mass communication systems, particularly radio and television, which became important in popular music promotion. Consequently, in a bid to promote music recorded by indigenous musicians, the Rhodesian Broadcasting Corporation paid for its airplay (Zindi 1985). This endeavour by the colonial government marked the beginning of the commercialisation of African music in Zimbabwe. According to Hill, O'Sullivan and O'Sullivan (2003: 190), 'promotion is the element of the marketing mix that communicates the benefits of what is on offer to the target audience'. The colonial government used radio and television to bring music to the masses. This was important in the commercialisation of music because it led to the formation of many bands (Sibanda 2004). Also, the radio played an important role in championing the cause of the struggle for independence, although this was with the help of Zambia and Mozambique since freedom fighters had no access to the Rhodesian Broadcasting Corporation (Pongweni 1982). The struggle for independence became a platform that popularised the works of indigenous musicians, such as Mapfumo's *chimurenga* music.

Turino (2000) examines the history of urban popular music in Harare, Zimbabwe's capital city, from the 1930s to the mid-1990s. Zimbabwe's sociopolitical history has had a profound impact on the development of popular music, which makes Turino's work a significant contribution to literature on local popular music. He discusses the interactions between the 'global' and the 'local', concerning himself with their dynamics in the context of urban popular music production in Harare. He clarifies the continuities and parallel cultural effects of colonialism, nationalism and cosmopolitanism on popular music. He depicts Zimbabweans as people who experience and embody globalising processes at the level of their own 'lifeways', cultural values and sense of identity, expressed through popular music.

Mhiripiri (2012) observes that in recent years the once-applauded radio and television stations, which used to promote musicians, are riddled with corruption. Not that corruption has stopped airplay; rather, it has encouraged bribes and payola. This has eroded the quality of music that gets airplay because the DJs play anything they are bribed to play and that music is not a true reflection of Zimbabwean talent. This has had adverse effects on the local industry at large because internationally it is not seen as competent and not highly rated, except for a few outstanding musicians who have largely made it on their own efforts (Mhiripiri 2012).

Fred Zindi (1985) and other writers, such as Ezra Chitando (2002), Caleb Dube (1996) and Silindiwe Sibanda (2004), discuss the role of government in popular music implicitly when they address music industry dynamics. They raise issues to do with musicians' experiences, especially the challenges they face and their relationships with promoters. Mhiripiri (2012) discusses the government's attempt to promote musicians through the galas that characterised music performance spaces during the economic downturn. However, the galas were short-lived because self-serving organisers eventually manipulated these activities to their own advantage. Also, the short lifespan of the galas was because of the fact that the government ran out of funds as the country's economic crisis deepened. This, according to the STEP theory, is a 'cross over' between the political and economic categories where government policy has a close bearing on the economic conditions. Hence, in the Zimbabwean situation, Leonard Sachikonye (2012: 97) contends that 'a crisis of stagnation and decline in living standards, unemployment and lack of growth and transformation during the second half of the 1990s came as a result of the economic plans and programmes the government of Zimbabwe adopted'. The music industry has been affected because audiences, the primary consumers, did not have money to spend on music.

Mhiripiri (2012: 2) argues that 'marketing techniques are crucial in ascertaining the survival of the music industry'. Thus, the sole purpose of music promotion should be to develop musicians. Given this historical glimpse into popular music promotion in Zimbabwe, below is a presentation of the current contesting stakeholder views, presented through the lens of STEP theory to examine the peculiarities of the arts marketing environment.

The following ideas about promotion were drawn from Hill, O'Sullivan and O'Sullivan (2003: 190) who define promotion as 'the element of the marketing mix that communicates the benefits of what is on offer to the target audience ... the most visible aspect of marketing activity'. In other words, promotion is concerned with taking the music products to the target audience. It also arouses 'interest of new audience' and therefore the product should be reasonably priced, attractive, relevant and accessible. For the product to reach many of the intended consumers, there is need for careful planning and execution and this requires 'flair and imagination . . . clear thinking and a highly disciplined approach' (191). Theorists divide promotion into four main areas: advertising, public relations, sales promotion and personal selling. Direct marketing is sometimes added as a fifth element because it is crucial for the development of long-term relationships with customers.

The arts industry has 'historically adopted a typical industry mix of promotional activity, tending to rely heavily on public relations and a wide distribution of printed material, including direct mail, supplemented by low-cost advertising and an element of sales promotion' (Hill, O'Sullivan and O'Sullivan 2003: 191). The intrinsic news interest of the arts makes public relations an important element of promotion and the media enjoys novelty in arts events and activities involving 'firsts' of different sorts. Musicians are also people in the public eye and make for good copy. In this regard, media critics are important influencers over a wide potential audience. Advertising is expensive and consequently is used minimally for information purposes. Print and poster advertising are the most popular forms in the various media where advertising takes place. Email, the Internet, cellphone technology, digital media, flyers and CD sampling are suggested as promotional techniques that musicians can use to their advantage. However, most local musicians are not trained and do not make maximum use of these methods of information dissemination. Different media, existing and new should be considered in order to reach the audience in an impactful and effective way. Since promotion is a cost, limits are imposed by the promotional budget, which can be stretched through negotiation, co-operation and/or collaboration. According to the STEP theory, limits are also imposed on the promotional budget by the socio-cultural, technological, economic and political context. It is therefore imperative to discuss the relationship between musicians and promoters against the backdrop of this theory.

Findings: Stakeholders' contesting perceptions on the promotion of popular music

Data revealed that popular music promotion in Zimbabwe is a contested terrain, characterised by diverse views among the stakeholders. I first consider the musicians' views, as they are the principal stakeholders, followed by the promoters, the media and finally other stakeholders interviewed for the purposes of this study. However, in so doing, I collate the different stakeholders' views. There is no intention to create tension among the stakeholders because their work is mutually dependent, so they are anonymous because of the controversial and sensitive nature of the subject under discussion. The participants' identities are hidden because they know each other and some have clashed to the extent that revealing their identities might fuel already existing rivalry. Given the power imbalance between the different stakeholders, using actual names might potentially destroy the musicians' careers because of their limited negotiating power in the promotional mix.

Musicians' perspectives: 'We are robbed in broad daylight'
The data gathered from the musicians from the four major cities of Gweru, Bulawayo, Mutare and Harare revealed that they perceive music promotion in more or less the same way. Below is a summary of their thoughts and views regarding local music promotion in relation to the STEP theory, which is employed because promotion is central to arts marketing.

The data revealed that musicians' general perceptions of local music promotion are as follows:
- profiteering at the expense of musicians;
- focus on established musicians;
- underpayment of musicians;
- lack of transparency;
- closed door policy – shunning of upcoming musicians;
- exploitative contracts;
- preferential treatment of international musicians;
- preferential treatment of famous local musicians;
- self-serving and self-enriching.

The majority of local musicians believe that most Zimbabwean music promoters are chancers who prefer to come into the picture and ride on musicians' fame only after the musician has built a name. One Harare musician observed that the promoters take advantage of musicians whose works are popular at the time:

Chandakaona Zimbabwean promoters' vanofokasa nezvinhu zvavari kuona kuti zvitori pahiti 'that time'. Zviri kudiwa nevanhu vanobva vangoziva kuti 'already' patori nemari 'open cheque'. Kuti vatarise vanhu vari pasi havakwanisi kudaro ku identifaya kuti ava tika dai dai vanosimuka. Izvozvo havazvikwanisi.

What I have noticed about Zimbabwean promoters is that they focus on the music that is popular at that particular time. They know that what the fans want is an open cheque for them. They do not look at upcoming musicians to uplift and nurture them from the grassroots.

Another musician from Mutare said:

The problem with most promoters is that they get into the business, but do not have music at heart. Their only focus is making money and they are the ones abusing musicians. A real promoter identifies, nurtures and exposes talent, not having favourite musicians. What we have are commercial promoters who are after money and not because they want to promote music or our culture. No. They promote where they see a chance to dip into the 'honey'.

According to these musicians, local promoters do not take the initiative to identify and nurture talent. This implies two issues: either the promoters are just greedy and do not want to invest in the process of identifying and growing the talent or they do not have the know-how. The latter issue resonates with Gweru and Harare NACZ officials' observations that most local music industry players lack education and training in their areas of interest. The NACZ is responsible for monitoring the arts and culture sector, of which the music industry is a subsector. The two officials I interviewed argued that most promoters are not genuine and hence try to evade registering with the NACZ to avoid accountability. Such behaviour by promoters is a clear indication of unethical behaviour and misconduct, which in most cases is characteristic of non-professionals. Promoters' avoidance of accountability also testifies to their lack of commitment in developing the art, the musician and the industry at large. It is for this reason that the musicians characterise local promoters as self-serving and self-enriching and say that their actions show no respect for either the art or the musicians.

Audience members who responded to questionnaires observed that the music industry operates informally, which results in the rampant lack of professionalism exhibited during music promotion. The implication is that the promoters lack education and training and hence do not understand the essence of music promotion. The NACZ officials confirmed that there are promoters, whom they dubbed 'fly-by-night', who hold once-off festivals and then disappear for good.

Such occurrences are a clear indication of these promoters' manipulative tendencies and lack of commitment and explain why they do not want to identify and groom talent from the grassroots level.

Additionally, the issue of music genres impacts on the musicians differently. Musicians who perform traditional music suffer the worst as they feel that they are sidelined. One Harare musician who performs traditional music lamented that most promoters

> ... *vanotarisa futi like isusu tinoita* traditional music *and kazhinji apa pese paipisa mamusicians eSungura, saka unoona kuti mapromoters ese anopromota sungura* artists. So *imi kana muri vari* kuita traditional music *mozoona kuti hapana. Kana mukada kuva approacher vanenge vachitoita zvimwe zviye zviye hamukwanisi kutaura navo.*

They are also selective and when *sungura* was popular they preferred it to traditional music, which some of us perform.[1] As a traditional music performer, you realise that there is nothing in it for you. Whenever we try to talk to them, they avoid us.

The scenario painted above depicts local promoters as unstable because they all scramble to promote one particular genre that is popular at any given time, without making an effort to promote less popular ones. In so doing, the promoters project themselves as chancers who are not only unselective, but also lack focus in terms of genre preference. Their non-selective tendency proves that they are only after making money, as they embrace whatever is popular so long they get money. Additionally, the promoters' lack of knowledge in the field is projected through their failure to sustain the fame of the preferred musicians whose work's lifespan is relatively short. However, the short lifespan can also be explained by the fact that popular music is an element of popular culture (Butete 2013).

It also emerged that local promoters are exploitative. Not only do they make musicians sign self-serving contracts, given a chance they also make musicians perform for free. One prominent Harare musician-cum-producer observed: 'There

---

1. *Sungura* is a local fusion of East African *kanindo* and Democratic Republic of Congo rhythms, which are usually sung in indigenous languages, primarily Shona. It is a mass-selling music genre. It has a fast-paced beat and its roots are associated with rural people and the lower working class (Mhiripiri 2012).

are a lot of complaints, especially from upcoming artists, that at times they are told that they are performing to expose themselves to the fans. Then they are abused in the name of exposure because they are not paid for those performances.' Concerning the issue of contracts, another musician from Harare pointed out:

> Musicians also have a problem of rushing into signing certain contracts without understanding what is going on, especially for international tours. Most local musicians are excited by being on the plane, but then *ndege haidyiwe manje. Saka panenge pachida kuti munhu utange wanzwisisa kuti kwauri kuenda uri kunogara mazuva mangani, uri kunotambiriswa marii. Saka umwe anoenda asingatombozivi* even huwandu *hweemari kuti ari kutambira marii. Saka hukama hwema* musicians *nema* promoters *hwanga hwakazara kuhwandirana.*
> ... but you do not eat the plane. So one needs to understand the logistics of where they are going, how long they will be there and how much they will be paid. But some go without even knowing how much they will be paid. So there is lack of transparency in the relationship between musicians and promoters.

As much as these views explain the situation on the ground regarding music promotion, the bottom line is that the majority of musicians lack knowledge and understanding of contractual agreements because of a lack of education and training in relevant areas, a point observed by the NACZ officials I interviewed. The musicians do not even realise the importance of negotiating payment before signing contracts. The fact that musicians get excited by the prospect of going on international tours and do not consider remuneration demonstrates misplaced priorities because as one Gweru musician observed, they end up with 'fame without fortune'. Additionally, it also demonstrates a lack of proper structures and the informal way in which musicians conduct their business – under normal circumstances, music managers and lawyers should preside over these contracts. In the absence of lawyers, one would expect the musicians to consult the collecting society (ZIMURA in this case) before signing the contracts. The musicians I interviewed alleged that ZIMURA lacks transparency in its dealings with them. Although the collecting society in turn alleged that musicians display serious unprofessionalism, this disparity to some extent reflects its ineffectiveness in terms of its role in educating the musicians and the unbalanced relationship between the two. This scenario, according to the STEP theory, shows how general economic conditions affect the way the collecting society and the music industry at large function, thereby disadvantaging the musicians (Hill, O'Sullivan and O'Sullivan 2003). Hill, O'Sullivan and O'Sullivan add that most political administrations value the arts as something worth promoting, but this does not seem to be the case in the government of Zimbabwe.

Another issue that emerged is preferential treatment of international musicians. One musician based in Harare pointed out:

> Then there are also cases where there are international shows that artists from outside Zimbabwe are treated better than local artists. The problem with most promoters is that they are into the business, but do not have music at heart. Their only focus is making money and they are the ones abusing musicians.

Arguably, the promoters' attitude towards international musicians is not based on genuine interest, but rather the musicians' potential to draw huge crowds, which results in their receiving substantial amounts of money. Knowing that they will partake of the proceeds from international musicians' shows, the promoters allegedly treat them better than local musicians.

Elsewhere, I published my findings of the same preferential treatment of international musicians in Port Elizabeth, South Africa (Butete 2012). The late Shirley Lebakeng, a female jazz vocalist, described an incident in which she and the late Nomzamo Mkuzo (another well-known female jazz vocalist), were 'curtain raising' for a female musician from outside their locale. Lebakeng said that they used the ladies' restroom to change for the performance, while the guest musician had a changing room all to herself, which had refreshments and all kinds of comforts.[2] Stan Mosia, who was master of ceremonies at this occasion, confirmed Lebakeng's point, as he also had to change in the men's restroom (Interview, 13 November 2009).[3] In the context of this study, the South African musicians' experiences serve to show that preferential treatment of international and popular local musicians is not unique to Zimbabwe and the gravity of such cases is context specific. It also

---

2. Shirley Lebakeng, interview, 24 September 2009, Port Elizabeth.
3. Stan Mosia, interview, 13 November 2009, Port Elizabeth.

shows that generally promoters in these two locales prioritise profiteering over developing and nurturing musicians.

Musicians expressed concern that opportunities for international tours are not based on merit because the best performers were always left behind. They argued that there is a lack of transparency in the selection of musicians who represent Zimbabwe in the international arena because mostly it is only the musicians who support the ruling party and/or those who have relatives who hold important positions in the government and the corporate world. One musician from Gweru stressed that selection of musicians for international tours was not based on proficiency:

> What is crowd pulling when crowd pulling is all a matter of Hararian capitalism? It has nothing to do with proficiency and art. It has nothing to do with the goodness of the music. It is something to do with how well do you get along with [so and so] . . . for God's sake why would I want to get along with people whose intelligence is so limited?

Generally, musicians from Bulawayo, Gweru and Mutare believe that promoters from their own cities and Harare prefer famous musicians from Harare. They allege that they are sidelined to the extent that musicians are hired from Harare for shows in their hometowns, while they are left out and are even denied the chance to open such shows. Rarely, if at all, do they find themselves being hired for shows in Harare. The majority of musicians from outside Harare concurred that the capital-based musicians monopolise the Zimbabwean music industry. However, some musicians from Harare also expressed discontent regarding the selection of musicians for international tours. They argued that to succeed they have to conform to the demands of the sponsors. If not, they will not even be considered, which obviously has financial implications and complicates their situations even more, as they cannot sustain their careers.

Promoters are thus accused of perpetrating self-serving agendas and practising favouritism, and in the process leaving behind talented musicians. This projects a wrong impression of the quality of Zimbabwean music because what is exposed to the world is substandard, compared to the sidelined works of accomplished musicians. Some musicians from Bulawayo believe that there are no promoters to talk about in the first place. Rather, the musicians must see to it that they source performance opportunities and organise the shows themselves. Three Bulawayo musicians said:

> And promoters here . . . I won't talk about promoters in this region because I haven't seen any. We are the managers of our talents. We manage our talents. We promote our own music. That's how we work this side. That is what I can say. I haven't seen any musician who says I have a promoter so and so in this region . . . It's up to you to go and organise that show.
>
> I think with music and every other trade you have to be at the right place at the right time. If you meet up with the right people, then you make it. It's all about connections, knowing the right people. For example, Jah Prayzah and Sol Jah Love have good sponsorship; that is why they are making it. With us here, the musician is not 'someone' – people even budget for what they need first and think about him afterwards.
>
> We have been in the industry for so long we have even forgotten when we started, but we are still not known . . . There must be somebody who says, 'Let me take this guy to the next level' after they have heard you play. You do not take yourself. It's very difficult . . . The musician cannot do it alone.

The second musician quoted above alludes to what Colleen Mills (2011) calls relational social capital where sociability plays an important role in creating profitable connections for the parties involved. It is unfortunate that not a single promoter from Bulawayo was there to respond to the allegations the musicians levelled against them. The fact that there are no forthcoming promoters from Bulawayo serves to authenticate the musicians' views and explains why it is difficult for them to develop their talent. Also compared to the sentiments of musicians from the other three cities, their complaints depict the City of Kings as a very difficult context for musicians to grow their talent. The worst-case scenario is the Bulawayo musicians' alleged exclusion from major events, such as galas, in which the majority of musicians from all over Zimbabwe participate. They generally feel that they are sidelined regarding many music industry-related issues, making them conclude that musicians in Harare are better off.

Explaining the STEP theory, Hill, O'Sullivan and O'Sullivan (2003: 16) contend that the political environment exists at three different levels: the local, regional and international. They add that at local level, local authorities are an important source of support for the subsidised arts, as they provide the principal source of income and have significant representation on management boards. The

Bulawayo musicians' sentiments do not reflect any of the three contributions local authorities are expected to be making towards developing the music industry. Their views go back in time to the historical period where the popular sentiment among the Ndebele people, who happen to be the majority in Matabeleland province, was that at governmental level Bulawayo is neglected on tribal grounds. This viewpoint is, however, debatable because the local city council is responsible for running the day-to-day activities of the city and the community is responsible for voting office-bearers into power. Zimbabwe has several tribes, but the Shona and Ndebele are the majority; the former outnumbering the latter.

These two dominant tribes gave rise to the two most active political parties during the liberation struggle: Zimbabwe African National Union – Patriotic Front (ZANU–PF) and Zimbabwe African People's Union (ZAPU). The Movement for Democratic Change (MDC) is the first opposition party to challenge the nationalist government since independence. MDC is a rainbow party with members from different tribes who are bona fide Zimbabweans. Hill, O'Sullivan and O'Sullivan (2003) argue that the priorities and perspectives of the local authority may differ from those of the national government and its funding agenda places civic amenity and local identity first. Drawing from the views of the Bulawayo musicians, the local authority is accessible, but lacks the resources because it is funded by the national government. UNESCO (1980: 3) advocates: 'It is necessary and appropriate for governments to help create and sustain not only a climate encouraging freedom of artistic expression but also the material conditions facilitating the release of this creative talent.' However, this is not forthcoming in Zimbabwe, given the country's current financial position. Funding the arts could be the least of the government's current priorities, although the arts have the potential to contribute to the economy if managed well (OAU 1976). Hence Mhiripiri (2012: 2) observes that 'socio- economic and political dynamics and marketing techniques are crucial in ascertaining the survival and growth of the Zimbabwean music industry'.

The situation described above has caused a massive influx of musicians from Bulawayo and every other part of Zimbabwe to Harare, intensifying the competition for limited performance opportunities in the capital. The musicians say, 'Harare *ndoine yese*' (Harare has everything). It is what has prompted the promoters to focus on Harare-based musicians at the expense of other cities. Port Elizabeth experiences the same thing, as musicians relocate to central and vibrant urban music culture spaces such as Johannesburg, Cape Town and Durban, the hub of South African music (Butete 2012). The phenomenon is therefore not unique to Zimbabwe, but rather serves to underscore the importance of the performance context to musicians' success, as argued by Mhiripiri (2012) and Ballantine (1993). Ballantine argues that context determines and influences the conditions under which music is made, the means by which it is made, the reasons for which it is made and, by extension, its quality. Mhiripiri argues that the socio-economic and political context in the period beginning in 2000 has forced musicians to adapt to their circumstances so as to survive the odds against them.

A Gweru NACZ official observed that a lack of unity among musicians gives promoters leeway to manipulate them. The official gave evidence of this by saying that if one musician refuses to perform for 'peanuts', another will readily accept the meagre offer. A musician from Bulawayo corroborated this viewpoint, saying, 'The promoter will ask you how much you want and you say $600 and he will say you are crazy. He will even tell you that he can even call Jays Marabini and he will do the same show for $300.'

It could be argued that the musicians are exploited out of desperation, but such behaviour sets the wrong precedent for the promoters. Additionally, this particular modus operandi of the musicians justifies and determines to a large extent the promoters' attitude and conduct towards them. Hence, local promoters view musicians as 'money-making machines', to be manipulated at will. One musician from Gweru who seems to know his worth as a performer had this to say about poor remuneration:

> I told them I am not a *sadza* musician and they hated me for that. You can't pay me with *sadza*, I make my own. Pay me with money. My music is of value, pay me with money. I need to live in a beautiful house. I need to make millions so my government can tax me and people can survive.[4]

The preceding two quotations show lack of consensus regarding payment, demonstrating that musicians do not speak with one voice. The Gweru musician has the liberty to speak his mind and has chosen to sever his relationship with the said promoters because he knows he deserves better. Some of his Bulawayo

---

4. *Sadza* (*pap* or mealie meal) is a stiff porridge, the principal staple food in Zimbabwe. It is mainly made from maize, rapoko, sorghum and millet. Sometimes wheat is also used.

counterparts cannot do the same. Nevertheless, given the situation of Bulawayo musicians, highlighted earlier in this chapter, it is not surprising that they opt to perform for meagre payments. The Gweru NACZ official stressed that in order to have their concerns addressed properly, musicians should unite because 'there is power in numbers', instead of fighting lone battles. But because of this exploitation, the majority of musicians survives on a 'hand-to-mouth' basis and have second jobs outside the industry. Their South African counterparts in Port Elizabeth experience the same (Butete 2012). Since the musicians do music on a part-time basis, the odds are that its quality is compromised, creating more problems for them. One musician from Mutare said that some of them end up abandoning music completely to look for alternative sources of income to sustain their families.

However, it is interesting to note that views regarding music promotion vary, even among the musicians from Bulawayo. One musician in the group interview commented:

> Of course, we can blame the newspapers, we can blame the radio stations and we can blame the promoters, but like I am saying there are different factors. But then even if your song is played once a week or a month, you hardly find people from Matabeleland calling in to try and request for your song in these request programmes. So it's a complicated situation really because the promoters find it hard to hire you when they hardly hear your song being requested on radio. The only community remaining here does not listen to FM. They are not interested.

According to this musician, the audience's lack of interest in local music is responsible for the promoters' lack of motivation in promoting Bulawayo-based musicians. Another musician from Bulawayo added: 'It's all about the attitudes of our target audience', the majority of whom have relocated to South Africa to escape economic hardships.

However, the fact remains that the duty of the promoter is to identify and nurture talent – something the few available local promoters shy away from. In addition, the audience is autonomous in terms of their music preferences and how they choose to spend their money. The onus is on musicians to produce quality work to draw the attention of the audience, particularly under the prevailing socio-economic hardships where spending on music is a luxury many cannot afford.

A musician from Harare said, 'The economy has not been performing well . . . so music is taken as a luxury. It is the first to be affected by bad economy.' Two Bulawayo musicians observed:

> When the economy is not doing well, consumers find it difficult to consume the arts, so fans have no money to buy music.

> The meltdown came and the problem was that music was something you would think about after you have done everything else. Like you have bought your groceries, you have paid school fees and rent and only then can you think about buying a CD. But a lot of people stopped buying music because it was like a luxury. For most of the artists it was a difficult time indeed because as long as the consumers of the product don't have that disposable income to buy the music, to attend the shows, then it means musicians don't have any business to talk about.

This argument was borne out by the fact that 100 per cent of the audience members who responded to a questionnaire said that they focused on basic needs rather than music, which impacted negatively on live show attendance and record sales. According to Hill, O'Sullivan and O'Sullivan (2003: 2), creative arts marketing 'focuses on the customer because their needs define relevance of the musicians' work and their resources empower it'. It is therefore, in the socio-economic context of contemporary Zimbabwe, difficult for musicians to succeed, particularly those whose work is still developing and those whose work does not conform to the norms and values of Zimbabwean society. For this reason, not many urban grooves, hip-hop or Zimdancehall musicians attract as many adult audiences as *sungura* does, arguably as a result of the content of their music. Most parents among the audience I interviewed do not want their children to be associated with urban grooves music, arguing that it perpetuates and perpetuates moral decadence, which they said has destroyed our youth. Most urban grooves lyrics are frowned upon because of the somewhat conservative nature of Zimbabwean society. Many adults do not attend the shows of such musicians and therefore the musician is disempowered as he loses his income source. Again, musicians' behaviour in this regard reflects the need for education and training for them to remain relevant in the marketplace or their careers will remain stagnant, which in most cases forces them to quit.

Exonerating the audience, one musician based in Mutare rather blamed the quality of the music and the use of vulgar/bad language for the audience's lack of interest. He further argued that it is for the same reason that the music cannot be aired on national radio and/or television. Not wanting to play the blame game, another musician from Mutare appealed to the promoters saying: 'As upcoming musicians we appeal to promoters to uplift us. They must desist from focusing on musicians who have already made their names. At times we can just be curtain raisers, we won't be asking for a lot of money. We just need something to take home at least.'

If musicians are lowering their standards, it is because they do not have much choice and will settle for whatever the promoters are prepared to pay them, just so that they can make a living. Both Welekazi Mosia and Vuyelwa Qwesha of Port Elizabeth also claimed that they were more concerned about getting performance opportunities than about how much they took home.[5] Both cases serve to show that the musicians do not have the upper hand when it comes to negotiating payment. Limited performance opportunities compromise their bargaining power as the stiff competition erodes remuneration.

Other stakeholders' perceptions of music promotion: Zimbabwe Music Rights Association, National Arts Council of Zimbabwe, promoters, the media, recording studios and the audience

There are varying perspectives regarding music promotion in Zimbabwe. My research revealed a dire shortage of promoters in comparison to the multitude of musicians who require their services. I was unable to interview any promoters in Bulawayo and Gweru since those I contacted were not forthcoming. There are two possible reasons for this. The first is that there could be no authentic promoters in these cities. The second is that promoters could be there, but were unwilling to come forward because they were not registered with the NACZ, which is mandated to monitor the operations of arts and culture stakeholders. This means that some promoters are operating illegally and therefore do not want the authorities to know about their existence. This implies that such promoters manipulate the musicians: why else would they have a problem being identified as promoters?

---

5. Welekazi Mosia, interview, 6 February 2010, Port Elizabeth; Vuyelwa Qwesha, interview, 26 September 2009, Port Elizabeth.

Only three promoters were interviewed in Harare and they showed determination to identify, nurture and develop talent, despite the adverse socio-economic conditions. Nevertheless, three is too small a number to cater for the musicians who are resident in the capital and beyond. In Mutare only one upcoming promoter was interviewed while the so-called seasoned ones seemed busy all the time. Consequently, the conclusions drawn from my research are limited because there are so few promoters, relative to the size of the local music industry. The shortage of promoters is a strong pointer to the difficulties musicians face in developing their careers and explains why the local music industry is somewhat moribund. The lack of promoters gives rise to the emergence of 'fly-by-night' promoters who exploit the musicians to enrich themselves and it explains why most promoters would rather not register with NACZ to avoid accountability. This state of affairs allows the promoters free reign to take advantage of the musicians' desperation to earn a living. This scenario portrays how the environment determines the nature and course of events in the Zimbabwean music industry, as the STEP theory contends (Hill, O'Sullivan and O'Sullivan 2003). The Zimbabwean political environment is seen impacting the socio-cultural, technological and economic environments, thereby facilitating the exploitation of the musicians by promoters, which further undermines the industry.

While so far in this chapter most local promoters have been depicted as exploitative and self-serving, it is interesting to note that there are still some who are committed to music promotion. According to Patson Chimbodza of Chipaz Promotions in Harare:

> The company popularised Tongai Moyo before he was even known. And I must say he also promoted the name of the company through his performances, which attracted huge crowds over the years. We also nurtured Fred Manjalima (Kapfupi) and Mukudzei Mukombe (Jah Prayzah). We are currently mentoring Boss Lee from Glenview and Pringo who hails from Bindura.[6]

A Mutare-based upcoming promoter-cum-manager of the once popular Assegai Crew Band views promotion as follows:

---

6. Patson Chimbodza, interview, 22 July 2014, Harare.

> *Ndoda kutarisana nevanhu vachiri kusimuka, maband achiri kusimuka. Kana maband mamwe aya aya asingachakwanisi kuzvimiririra. Ndendichida kuvabatsira kuti kana vaine mashows avanenge vachida kuita ndogona kuvaprovider nezvinhu zvavanenge vachileka like ma instruments mostly ndo anonyanyo kuita kuti maband akawanda astiragule akundikane. Dai kuri kunzi iri mari chaiyo yakawanda ndogona kuvaoganizira kana kuti venue yekuti gentlemen tinoita entertainment panzvimbo yakati ndichafanda zvese and everybody anenge aripo ndichabhadhara. Ndopane vision yangu.*
>
> I want to focus on upcoming bands and those that cannot sustain themselves yet. I would like to help them hold shows by providing instruments because most bands struggle to access them – hence they fail to make it. If I had a lot of money, I would love a situation where I can organise a performance venue for them and say, 'Gentlemen, let's go entertain at such and such a place' and provide them with everything they need, as well as paying them. That is my vision.

Although the upcoming promoter displays a commendable approach to promotion, it remains to be seen whether he will stand the test of time, given the dicey nature of the music industry.

The role of both print and electronic media is to disseminate information to society. However, both have come under siege in all four cities where the musicians and audience agreed that payola (Mhiripiri 2012) has killed the essence of music promotion. Musicians and audience members appealed to both electronic and print media to give equal opportunities to all musicians regardless of race, colour, creed or gender, as this will help to expose their talent to the target audience. A producer based in Gweru lamented:

> Even if I take the music that I produce to the radio and television stations they don't play it until I buy them a drink . . . It's mostly the musicians who pay the DJs whose music gets played. Instead of the rest of Zimbabwean musicians being played on air, they are playing 'Hararians' . . . but that doesn't mean people from Harare are the only ones doing music. We are also doing music. You can find one or two artists from outside being played.

The producer's views were buttressed by one Bulawayo musician who said:

> I think it is lack of publicity. Basically the problem is in the media itself. Artists from this side are not being recognised much as compared to the artists from the other regions. Hence the press can write about a local artist once a month, but the artists from other regions they will be written about daily. And on the radio stations nothing is being played. They will say we don't have your music, but we give them our music ourselves. We always have meetings with them and they say we are working on that, every time, we are working on that. The local newspapers are writing about musicians from other regions.

Allegations of character assassination were also levelled against print journalists who publish confidential information about musicians' lives, which destroys their careers. The journalists who were interviewed denied claims that there have always been strained relations between them and the musicians. One journalist from Harare stressed that musicians must lead by example because they are role models in society. He emphasised that at times they are forced to put the musicians' dirty laundry in public as a deterrent, particularly after they had shunned the journalists' advice to conduct themselves well.

Different stakeholders view music promotion in different ways. A ZIMURA official based in Harare accused musicians of a lack of professionalism, arguing that this is the reason they have problems with the promoters:

> Attitude is the same challenge that the promoters and venue owners have with musicians. They sometimes do not come to perform or they are not on time. They sign a contract with the promoter that they should perform from say 8:00 p.m. for four hours and the artists do not show up. Or they only show up an hour or two later and fans are already shouting.

The ZIMURA and NACZ officials from the four provinces confirmed this view. However, it can be argued that ZIMURA and NACZ are shortchanging the musicians because it is their duty to facilitate workshops to educate musicians about professionalism. It can thus be argued that the government, through the responsible ministries and other stakeholders, owe it to the nation to educate musicians and to develop the industry, given its potential to contribute to both household and the national economy (Culture Fund of Zimbabwe Trust 2009; OAU 1976).

Interestingly, there are some musicians who are critical of their fellow musicians' conduct. They argued that unbecoming behaviour impacts negatively on their relations with other stakeholders and society at large and so they are not considered to be serious about their work. They stressed the need for introspection and commitment to improving their conduct for the sake of developing the industry.

Other musicians shift the blame to the audience whom they accuse of lacking interest in local music. But this does not take into account the prevailing socio-economic conditions. Although audience members were aware of the impact it had on musicians, they stressed that they could not prioritise music over their families. One long-serving band member of Assegai Crew said that the quality of music products is responsible for consumers' negative attitudes: 'The presence of cheap quality home studios is killing our music. These backyard studios record just about anything as long as they are paid, but then the music cannot meet the standards required on national radio. Our band has not yet experienced this problem.' According to this musician, their music has been receiving airplay because it measures up to the standards required on radio. This shows that the quality of the music is crucial in determining how the media and the audience receive the music. Therefore, it would benefit musicians if they could invest in the production of good quality music, which is bound to attract the attention of the audiences.

The cash-upfront mode of payment adopted by established recording studios has prompted the emergence of numerous underequipped recording studios manned by underqualified personnel. A producer based in Harare observed:

> In the absence of piracy, it's more profitable to record an artist for free, then get your money from music sales. That's when auditions are held and you choose talented musicians whom you record and then share the money after selling the music. But due to piracy now the artists pay the studio and as it is said the one with the money calls the shots. This is affecting the quality of music . . . It's not about talent anymore, it's about money. There are producers who are serious and those who are not serious so even if you refuse to record an unpolished musician, you lose out to the next producer.

Furthermore, unorthodox lyrical content is another factor that has damaged musicians' relationships with the media. Another Assegai Crew band member said that 'dirty' lyrical content in some compositions drives away the audience, promoters and the media because our society is conservative:

> With the music we are playing . . . some of the words sung are not fit to be played on national radio. You hear one saying, '*Kanzuru ndoda kuiita kafira mberi. Handitye mupurisa wekanzuro ini*' [I want to destroy the council. I am not afraid of the council police]. That type of music does not promote our relationship with the consumers because we are scaring them with the violence of beating up council police.

Another musician from a different band in Mutare said:

> Sure, the newspapers cannot publish bad things. That is why we are not succeeding in our work. We can make it through very small things, which do not require money or fame, but just the message. Bad language brings us down, but some of us are using it to seek fame, for example, the song 'Munotidako' by Joseph Moyana.[7] He is trying to get popular by using bad language . . . That cannot be played on radio.

The use of obscene language goes against the policies governing the airwaves, such as the Censorship Act of Zimbabwe, among others. The Broadcasting Services Act, Chapter 12.06, Part V, 2 (a) and 5 (c) of the Code of Conduct and Programme Standards, advocates that broadcast service providers must broadcast 'programmes that are in accordance with community values and standards' and avoid the 'use in programmes of offensive language, including hate speech'. According to this Act, the musicians shoot themselves in the foot by using inappropriate language because the media and the promoters cannot publicise their music if it contravenes the law. The code of conduct is premised on the norms and values of the Zimbabwean society and audiences do not accept musicians whose works are unorthodox. Drawing on the STEP theory, the musicians' modus operandi of using unorthodox means to gain popularity can be viewed as a reaction to the harsh socio-economic conditions; unfortunately, it

---

7. The word 'munotidako' has a double meaning. It can either be translated as 'You need us there' or 'You are saying "bum"', meaning the part of the body one sits on.

brings them no returns as it causes the audience to shun such work. This depicts the vicious circle of the Zimbabwe music industry, a situation that can only be salvaged if the socio-cultural, technological, economic and political environment improves.

The 75 per cent local content policy introduced by Professor Jonathan Moyo during his tenure as minister of information and publicity was a noble attempt to promote local musicians, but it fuelled payola (Mhiripiri 2012) as musicians paid DJs, competing for the limited number of radio and television stations. In response to my quesionnaire, 90 per cent of the audience applauded the policy for introducing them to new talent, but bemoaned the resultant poor quality products, which eventually made them lose interest in local music. This demonstrates how, according to the STEP theory, the socio-cultural, technological, economic and political factors impact on the arts environment. The existing political developments have resulted in adverse economic conditions, which have had a negative effect on the nation as a whole. Consequently, the working relationships of the music industry stakeholders have been severed and the musicians are affected the most.

Conclusion

The current state of music promotion in Zimbabwe has a serious negative impact on the development of the industry at large. This is largely attributed to the prevailing socio-cultural, technological, economic and political factors. The musicians, who are the principal stakeholders, are the worst affected by this status quo. The economic meltdown, which has stretched beyond a decade, has worsened the working relations among most music industry stakeholders, fostering unprofessional conduct, which has led to exploitation, blackmail, backbiting, crudeness, jealousy, corruption and a lack of transparency. The resultant poor quality of music products and services have distanced the local industry from the international arena, as both local and foreign music promoters are not keen to promote the music to the multitudes of Zimbabweans in the diaspora and the rest of the world. Also, my findings show that there is general lack of consensus among musicians and other stakeholders. To a great extent there is a lot of blame-shifting, especially among key stakeholders, which is unproductive. The working relationships between the musicians and promoters are complicated; however, this scenario is not unique to Zimbabwe, as proved by the parallels drawn from Port Elizabeth music scene. The state of affairs calls for a unity of purpose and dialogue between the parties involved to pave the way for open communication and to promote co-ordination. There is therefore a need for profound education and training of Zimbabwe music industry stakeholders to build capacity and relationships and to improve music promotion for the development of the industry. In so doing, the different stakeholders' views need to be taken into consideration to map the way forward for the industry as a whole.

References

Baines, G.F. 2002. *A History of New Brighton, Port Elizabeth, South Africa, 1903–1953: The Detroit of the Union*. New York: Edwin Mellen Press.

Ballantine, C. 1993. *Marabi Nights: Early South African Jazz and Vaudeville*. Johannesburg: Ravan Press.

Bebey, F. 1975. *African Music: A People's Art*. Westport: Lawrence Hill.

Berliner, P.F. 1993. *The Soul of Mbira: The Music and Traditions of the Shona People of Zimbabwe*. Chicago: University of Chicago Press.

Butete, V.B. 2012. 'The Jazz Divas: An Analysis of the Musical Careers of Six New Brighton Vocalists'. MMus thesis, Rhodes University, Grahamstown.

———. 2013. 'Audience Reception: An Interpretation of Gospel Music in the Everyday Life of Midlands State University Students, Gweru'. BA Special Honours thesis, Zimbabwe Open University, Harare.

———. 2014. 'The Challenges Facing the Music Industry in Zimbabwe: A Case of the National Arts Council of Zimbabwe'. *The Dyke* 8(3): 163–83.

Chitando, E. 2002. *Singing Culture: A Study of Gospel Music in Zimbabwe*. Uppsala: Nordic Africa Institute.

Culture Fund of Zimbabwe Trust. 2009. *Baseline Study on the Culture Sector in Zimbabwe*. Harare: Culture Fund of Zimbabwe Trust.

Dube, C. 1996. 'The Changing Context of African Music Performance in Zimbabwe'. *Zambezia* 23(2): 99–120.

Eyre, B. 2001. *Playing with Fire: Fear and Self-censorship in Zimbabwean Music*. Copenhagen: Freemuse.

———. 2015. *Lion Songs: Thomas Mapfumo and the Music that Made Zimbabwe*. Durham: Duke University Press.

HIFA (Harare International Festival of the Arts) Symposium. 2012. *'Giving Voice to the Artist': The Impact of Current Cultural Policy Discourse on Zimbabwean Arts*. Harare: Zimbabwe Creative Civil Society's Plan of Action for Arts and Culture (NPAAC).

Hill, L., C. O'Sullivan and T. O'Sullivan. 2003. *Creative Arts Marketing*. Oxford: Butterworth-Heinemann.

Jenje-Makwenda, J. 2005. *Zimbabwe Township Music*. Harare: Storytime Promotions.

Kwabena Nketia, J.H. 1974. *The Music of Africa*. New York: W.W. Norton.

Mhiripiri, A.N. 2011. '"Welcoming the *Sungura* Queens": Cultural Studies and the Promotion of Female Musicians in the Zimbabwean Male-Dominated Music Genre'. *Muziki* 8(1): 103–19.

———. 2012. 'Dancing through the Crisis: Survival Dynamics and Zimbabwe Music Industry'. In *Contemporary African Cultural Productions*, edited by V-Y. Mudimbe. Dakar: CODESRIA. https://www.researchgate.net/publication/318532199_Dancing_through_the_crisis_Survival_Dynamics_and_Zimbabwe_Music_Industry_in.

Mills, C. 2011. 'Coping with the Cutting Edge: Enterprise Orientations and the Creative Challenges of Start-up in the Fashion Design Sector in New Zealand'. In *Entrepreneurship and the Creative Economy: Process, Practice and Policy*, edited by C. Henry and A. de Bruin, 169–200. Cheltenham: Edward Elgar Publishing.

OAU (Organisation of African Unity). 1976. *African Cultural Charter*. Port Louis, Mauritius: OAU.

Pongweni, A. 1982. *Songs That Won the Liberation War*. Harare: College Press.

Sachikonye, L.M. 2012. *Zimbabwe's Lost Decade: Politics, Development and Society*. Harare: Weaver Press.

Sibanda, S. 2004. '"You Don't Get to Sing a Song When You Have Nothing to Say": Oliver Mtukudzi's Music as a Vehicle for Socio-political Commentary'. Master's thesis, University of the Witwatersrand, Johannesburg.

Thram, D. 2006. '*Zvakwana*! Enough! Media Control and Unofficial Censorship of Music in Zimbabwe'. In *Popular Music Censorship in Africa*, edited by M. Drewett and M. Cloonan, 72–91. Aldershot: Ashgate.

Turino, T. 2000. *Nationalists, Cosmopolitans and Popular Music in Zimbabwe*. Chicago: University of Chicago Press.

UNESCO (United Nations Educational, Scientific and Cultural Organization). 1980. *Records of the General Conference Twenty-first Session, Belgrade*. Paris: University of France Press.

Webb, J., T. Schirato and G. Danaher. 2002. *Understanding Bourdieu*. London: Sage.

Zindi, F. 1985. *Roots Rocking in Zimbabwe*. Gweru: Mambo Press.

CHAPTER 9

Chimurenga Music and Narratives of Zimbabwe's Liberation Struggle[s]
Rethinking Simon Chimbetu's 'Zimbabwe Iyoyi', 'Ndarangarira Gamba' and 'Pane Vasipo'

Urther Rwafa

There has been extensive literature written about Zimbabwe's liberation struggle, but not much about the narratives of comrades who actually participated. In a classic text titled *Songs That Won the Liberation War* (1982), Alec Pongweni, a non-combatant, produced an anthology of songs that were sung during Zimbabwe's liberation struggle to inspire comrades, as well as to garner support from the masses. The aim of this chapter is to explore music by Simon Chimbetu, a guerrilla who fought during Zimbabwe's liberation struggle. Firstly, Chimbetu stands out as the most popular and successful musician, with more than 36 albums to his name, compared to other musicians who also fought during Zimbabwe's liberation struggle. Secondly, an exploration of Chimbetu's music offers an insight into his vision regarding the struggle – its aims, challenges and anticipated benefits from the point of view of the combatants. Thirdly, Chimbetu is well known for singing about 'other' struggles in post-independent Zimbabwe and how these struggles should be viewed as a continuation of black people's efforts to fight residual elements of [post]colonialism in Zimbabwe and Africa. Given that Zimbabwe's nationalist leaders seem to have deviated from the ideals that shaped the liberation struggle, Chimbetu's music traces the roots of 'epistemic disobedience' (Mignolo 2009: 1) in post-independent musical narratives that confront official arrogance, as well as interrogate the legitimacy of political leadership. Chimbetu's seemingly patriotic lyrics are not as blameless as they seem – they are loaded with satire and metaphors that can pester and annoy nationalist leaders who seem to have forgotten how independence in Zimbabwe was gained after much bloodshed.

(Re)engaging the revolutionary dimensions of *chimurenga* music

The historical origins of *chimurenga* music can be traced to before the 1890s, but the genre was later appropriated and revived by the Shona and Ndebele warriors to produce protest music that pointed out, contradicted and confronted the presence of colonial oppressive policies in Southern Rhodesia (now Zimbabwe). The term '*chimurenga*' comes from a legendary Shona ancestor, Murenga Sorore Nzou, who was believed to possess extraordinary features, such as a huge head (*soro*), the size of the head of an elephant (*renzou*). Maurice Vambe (2004: 167) writes: 'Murenga was known for his fighting prowess, and legend has it that he composed war songs to encourage his soldiers to continue to fight against their enemies in pre-colonial Zimbabwe.' The revolutionary zeal of *chimurenga* music, embedded in its nature as a polysemous and liminal space, (Turner 1992: 66) invests the genre with the capacity to resist the reification and reductive symmetries of a (single) grand cultural narrative (Titlestad 2004) promoted by the Rhodesian government. Anne Gibbs (2009: 1) elaborates on the rebelliousness in *chimurenga* music:

> When formal means of political representation are closed to a group of people, music can provide an outlet for their anguish and bitterness about the system. Resistance to oppressive rule becomes covert. A new artistic genre emerges, dedicated to articulating the people's experience under a new system, partly as a way of coping with the new challenges and also as a way to express their protest against it.

Certainly, *chimurenga* music emerged as a genre of political protest, which crystallised in the mid-1960s after the Unilateral Declaration of Independence (UDI) by Ian Smith, after which he intensified the government's military offensive to stamp out political activism. While the songs in Pongweni's (1982) masterpiece captured the mood, challenges and aesthetics of the liberation struggle, the book recognised the Zimbabwe African National Union – Patriotic Front (ZANU–PF) party, led by Robert Mugabe, as the originator of the armed struggle, ahead of the Zimbabwe African People's Union (ZAPU), led by Joshua Nkomo (Ndlovu-Gatsheni 2011). In the same way, ZANU–PF was presented as the carrier of the 'burden of history', enjoying the prophetic visions and oracular blessings of Nehanda and Kaguvi – the heroes of the First Chimurenga and revered ancestors of the Shona people (Mugabe 1978; Chitando 2002; Chitando 2005).[1] For its blind celebration of nationalist historiography, *Songs That Won the Liberation War* earned itself a place in the house of the historical canon shaped by Terence Ranger (1985), David Lan (1985) and David Martin and Phyllis Johnson (1981) – some of whom became uncritical scribes of a celebratory African history that profoundly shaped official accounts of Zimbabwe's liberation struggle (Robins 1996: 73). Shani Robins (1996) goes further to single out Martin and Johnson's *The Struggle for Zimbabwe: The Chimurenga War* (1981) as a book that provided an unambiguously heroic narrative, which was later incorporated into school textbooks.

In the same manner that the history about national triumphalism is narrated without contradictions, most of the songs that were composed during the liberation struggle in the 1960s and 1970s helped to construct a *chimurenga* monologue bereft of alternative articulation of the nation (Ndlovu-Gatsheni 2011), what Paul Gilroy (1993: 23) calls 'counter-cultures'. While most songs that were sung in the 1960s and 1970s, especially during *pungwes* (night vigils), or by popular musicians such as Thomas Mapfumo, Oliver Mtukudzi and Tinei Chikupo, articulated memories of *chimurenga* through metaphors popularised by ZANU–PF, memories of ZAPU were disarticulated. In a way, the disarticulation of the memories of ZAPU helped to erect a toxic myth that overshadowed or undermined the contribution of ZAPU towards Zimbabwe's liberation struggle. The violent contest for winning political legitimacy between the Zimbabwe African National Union (ZANU) and ZAPU demonstrated at Mgagao training camp in Tanzania was also to find expression in and about songs that won the liberation war (Pongweni 1982).

When Zimbabwe attained independence in 1980, musicians celebrated through songs that heaped praises on ZANU–PF and its leader Robert Mugabe. Again, the *chimurenga* monologue (Ndlovu-Gatsheni 2011) started in the 1960s and 1970s resurfaced and was projected through some of the songs sung by musicians such as Simon Chimbetu, Ketai Muchawaya and Marko Sibanda – all of whom were

---

1. The first *chimurenga* was an armed struggle fought by the Shona and Ndebele in 1896–7 against encroaching British colonialism in Zimbabwe (formerly Rhodesia). The second *chimurenga* was the armed struggle of black Africans against Ian Smith's regime in Rhodesia, led by nationalist leaders such as the late Ndabaningi Sithole, the late Joshua Nkomo and Robert Mugabe. The third *chimurenga* is the name given to the economic struggle in post-independent Zimbabwe.

guerrilla soldiers who participated in the liberation struggle. However, the pain and terror that was caused by the state in Matabeleland and parts of the Midlands between 1982 and 1987; the corruption scandals of 1985; the Economic Structural Adjustment Programme and its marauding effects on the economy and general mismanagement by the political leadership in post-independent Zimbabwe caused a paradigm shift in the context and content of *chimurenga* music. There were many songs that criticised the government's failure to deliver on its promises and deal decisively with the cancer of corruption that was slowly eating into the lives of Zimbabweans in all walks of life. Interestingly, songs such as Mapfumo's 'Maiti Kurima Hamubviri' (You Said You Were Good Farmers) and 'Corruption' and Leonard Zhakata's 'Mugove' (Reward), 'Hupenyu Mutoro' (Life Is a Burden) and 'Bhora Rembabvu' (A Dangerous Soccer Match) became new voices of protest that fractured the 'myth' of national triumphalism (Robins 1996: 74) embedded in the revolutionary songs of the 1960s and 1970s. A new view of things looked beyond the telos of official historiography and the assumed insularity of the war narrative. A counter-history and history from the fringes or the subalterns (Spivak 1994: 102) is being constructed, which provide a wake-up call to those barren histories that uncritically elevate discourses of *chimurenga* war narratives. Dumiso Dabengwa, a former intelligence officer in Zimbabwe People's Revolutionary Army (ZIPRA) – ZANU's military wing – makes an eloquent call to address the 'aporias', 'silences' and 'points of undecidability' (Derrida 1976: 45) in popular discourses built on conformist historical narratives. He proclaims:

> For too long historians have failed our people because of their timidity, sectarianism and outright opportunism. Conditions should be created in Zimbabwe wherein a new breed of social scientist ... can emerge. This class of scholars should be capable of withstanding threats and intimidation and will rise above those racial, ethnic and tribal considerations [and] oppose the suppression of any information ... A complete history of the struggle for national liberation is a long way from being produced and will only be achieved when the chroniclers of the struggle are no longer afraid to confront the truth head-on and openly, and have rid themselves of biases resulting from our recent political past – a past which saw the brutal killings of innocent people in the name of unity, peace, stability and progress ... Anything short of a tradition of selfless inquiry and exposure of truth will certainly lead to a nation of sycophants and robots who do

not possess the power of independent thought which we should all cherish (Dabengwa 1995: 24).

Dabengwa could be calling for the construction of new kinds of historical narratives that interrogate praise texts (Robins 1996: 77) of the 1980s that ignore guerrilla violence and the authoritarian culture of state terror in post-independent Zimbabwe. The new song of protest has been used as an instrument to expose the 'precarity and precariousness' (Butler 2010: 3) of the ruling ZANU–PF party, which received vitriolic attacks from ordinary people who felt betrayed by the political leadership for its failure to provide a redemptive economic programme. Even a musician such as Chimbetu – who acted as an official mouthpiece, especially in his celebratory songs of the 1980s, began to show signs of 'epistemic disobedience' (Mignolo 2009: 1) in songs such as 'Pane Vasipo' (There Are Others Who Are Absent). The concept of *chimurenga* music could no longer be confined to 'narrow and exeptionalised' (Rwafa 2011: 57) discourses of national triumphalism or grand narratives of the ruling elite class, but were being extended to include to other sites of struggle, such as gender and culture and the social and economic life of ordinary Zimbabweans. It is the intention of this chapter to trace the revolutionary consciousness of Chimbetu embedded in his brand of *chimurenga* music, with the aim of explicating the change of tone and mood in his protest songs that could simply be dismissed as pro-ZANU–PF.

This chapter purposively samples 'Zimbabwe Iyoyi', 'Ndarangarira Gamba' and 'Pane Vasipo' composed and sung by Simon Chimbetu. Purposive sampling was chosen as a non-random selection technique to explore Zimbabwe's liberation struggle from the point of view of a war veteran who turned singer in post-independent Zimbabwe. A point to note is that Chimbetu composed and sang many songs before his death on 14 August 2005, but for the purpose of this chapter, I have only sampled three songs that specifically address the aims and objectives of the Second Chimurenga, its challenges and anticipated benefits in post-independent Zimbabwe. Songs sung by Chimbetu were selected for the specific reason that he stands out as the most popular and successful musician, compared to other musicians, such as Marko Sibanda and Ketai Muchawaya who also fought during the liberation struggle. Chimbetu was also well known for singing about other struggles, such as gender inequalities, the challenges of national reconciliation, the imperatives of the Third Chimurenga and political struggles in post-independent Zimbabwe.

'Zimbabwe Iyoyi' and the articulation of the 'nationalist agenda' during Zimbabwe's liberation struggle

The song 'Zimbabwe Iyoyi' traces the journey of an individual comrade to the war front. When black Zimbabweans joined the liberation struggle, they were motivated by different grievances – which, if summed up together, projected the totality of versions and sub/versions (Vambe 2004: 167) that constituted the nationalist agenda of fighting for freedom. Most blacks that joined the liberation struggle did so in the spirit of wanting to eliminate an oppressive and suppressive system engendered by the Smith regime. For the protagonist of 'Zimbabwe Iyoyi', it was inevitable to join the liberation struggle because the urge for a free Zimbabwe, ruled by black people, was irresistible. The intensity of the feeling for freedom is encapsulated in the expression *'yanga yanditora moyo'* (it had taken my mind). Jacques Derrida's iteration and iterability (in Lucy 2004: 4) of this phrase reveal the reality that it was not easy for an individual to simply join the liberation war without a deep conviction to seek individual freedom while at the same time projecting the desire of the majority of people who struggled desperately under the yoke of British colonialism.

What is energising in Chimbetu's phrase is its linguistic doubleness (Bakhtin 1981: 45) or its doublespeak that cannot allow the song to settle on a singular interpretation of the motivations that drove blacks to join the liberation struggle. While the self-conscious historiography (Mirmotahari 2011: 374) offered in 'Zimbabwe Iyoyi' is specifically deployed to push forward a nationalist agenda about a free Zimbabwe, the unconscious capacity of the self finds itself creating dissident narratives (El Saadawi 2007), which bring into crisis the narrative discourse offered by the dominant ideological powers. *'Yanga yanditora moyo'*, ironically, is a powerful counter-narrative with the capacity to undercut the song's official rhetoric about collective vision. *'Yanga'* is a Shona word used to show the causative agent, which, in this case, is love for a free Zimbabwe. Yet in *'yanga'* there is an aura of resistance against the reification and reductive symmetries of a (single) grand cultural narrative (Titlestad 2004), which implicitly shows that Zimbabwe had the potential of attracting blacks who yearned for independence, but that the sentiment must have been dampened by nationalist leaders who hijacked the revolution for self-serving interests. Hence *'yanga'* is also registering a yearning for hopes and aspirations that were fractured by the culture of greed and corruption in post-independent Zimbabwe. If reconfigured further to reflect the status quo in post-independent Zimbabwe, *'yanga'* can constitute part of the epistemic discourses of protest (Mignolo 2009) that seek to destabilise the stable narratives constructed by the nationalist leaders in describing the nation (Bhabha 1990) of Zimbabwe through narrow ideological teachings. The lyrical instability in *'yanga'* inheres in its projection of a populist discourse that did not materialise about a free and democratic Zimbabwe where people are not forced to support a single political party.

The lyrics of 'Zimbabwe Iyoyi' are as follows:

Zimbabwe iyoyi yanga yanditora moyo × 2
Taide kusvika Gairezi, ndokuudza vabereki Zvikanzi fambaso, fambaso
Ukwire gomo Uyambuke ramba uchifamba
Pakakomo ako kamunoona ako, ndipo pane vana vaNikodhimasi
Famba zvakanaka mwanangu ndimi munaoka masango
Zimbabwe iyoyi yanga yanditora moyo × 2
Taide kusvika Mudorowa ndokuudzwa namasvikiro.
Zvikanzifambaso, Mwanangu Fambaso.
Ukwire gomo, uyambuke ramba uchifamba. Musanete kusvika tatore ivhu
Nesu hatineti kusvika tatora dunhu redu, famba zvakanaka mwanangu,
    ndimi munawoka masango
Zimbabwe iyoyi yangaa yanga yanditora moyo × 2
Zimbabwe iyoyi yanga yandipedza Taide kusvika kuDorowa ndokubvunza
Mujambejecha zvikanzi fambaso Vakomana fambaso.
Mukwire gomo muyambuke rambai muchifamba.
Musanete Kusvika matatore ivhu, nesu hatinete kusvika tatora dunhuredu,
Fambai zvakanaka vakoma tarirai munawoka masango, tarirai munawoka
    masango.
This Zimbabwe had actually taken my heart. × 2
We had reached a place called Gairezi, and then we were told by the parents.
Then they said go this way, go this way and climb that mountain. Go round
    it and continue walking.
See that hill, that is where the children of Nikodhimasi were buried.
Go well, my son, you are the ones pushing the liberation cause in these
    forests.
This Zimbabwe had actually taken my heart × 2
We wanted to reach Dorowa, then we were told how to reach there,
We were told how to reach there. This is the way to go.

Climb that mountain, turn around and continue to walk.
Don't get tired until we take back our land.
We are not also to get tired until we have taken back our locality.
Go well, my son, you are the ones leading the struggle.
This Zimbabwe had actually taken my heart. × 2
This, Zimbabwe had actually drained me.
We wanted to reach Dorowa, and then we asked Mujambajecha,
We were told to go this way. Boys, go this way.
Climb that mountain and continue to walk.
Don't get tired until we take back our land.
We are also not going to get tired until were have taken back our locality.
Go well, my son, you are the ones leading the struggle.

When the liberation war broke out in the 1960s, many young black men and women from all over the country opted to join the struggle. They had to slip through the porous borders of Zambia and Mozambique to receive military training. The journeys were dangerous and life threatening because Rhodesian soldiers and intelligence units were fully aware that young blacks were being recruited and receiving training abroad (Ranger 1985). Getting to Zambia or Mozambique also meant crossing crocodile-infested rivers and traversing thick African forests infested with dangerous snakes and wild animals. Michael Sheridan (2008: 17) emphasises the shift from viewing African forests as simply physical entities towards projecting forests as symbolic spaces, introducing ambiguities in the meanings that African forests and their ancillary environs can engender:

> These new associations of forests with symbols and metaphors describe ecosystems as ongoing mosaics of processes (rather than endpoints) within the new paradigm [which] includes resistance (the degree to which an ecosystem absorbs disturbance without change), resilience (the rate of recovery to a former state), persistence (the period over which a given state exists), variability (the degree of change over time), sensitivity (the relative vulnerability of particular variables to change), and surprise (unexpected, stochastic, and nonlinear causation).

The capacity of African forests to symbolise something else other than their natural self has been seized upon by music and literary artists. In African music and musicology, environments that include forests are imbued with meanings that become a commentary on the dynamics of power struggles and identity (re)formations and constructions in African communities during colonialism and the postcolonial period. For Chimbetu, getting to Mozambique for training as a guerrilla soldier implied passing through the Gairezi district of Nyanga found in the eastern part of Zimbabwe. Nyanga is known for high mountain ranges covered with thick forests and these provided much-needed cover for young men and women during their escape to Mozambique for military training. When Chimbetu sings '*Taide kusvika Gairezi, ndokuudza vabereki Zvikanzi fambaso, fambaso / Ukwire gomo Uyambuke ramba uchifamba*' (We had reached a place called Gairezi, and then we were told by the parents. / Then they said go this way, go this way and climb that mountain. Go round it and continue walking), he is acknowledging the contribution of ordinary people towards the liberation cause. This 'decolonial episteme' (Grosfoguel 2011: 2) unmasks the hypocrisy behind the politics of exclusion (Rwafa 2012) sometimes practised by the ruling elite in Zimbabwe to dismiss the contributions of ordinary people to the liberation cause if they suspect that their powers are being threatened through opposition politics.

In 'Zimbabwe Iyoyi' Chimbetu makes reference to the land question as part of the critical discourse that forced blacks to take up arms against the Smith regime. His vision of a free Zimbabwe is clear when he sings:

. . . *fambaso.*
Mukwire gomo muyambuke rambai muchifamba.
Musanete kusvika matatore ivhu, nesu hatinete kusvika tatora dunhuredu,
Fambai zvakanaka vakoma tarirai munawoka masango, tarirai munawoka masango.
We were told to go this way. Boys, go this way.
Climb that mountain and continue to walk.
Don't get tired until we take back our land.
We are also not going to get tired until were have taken back our locality.
Go well, my son, you are the ones leading the struggle.

Historically, the minority settler regimes headed by Cecil Rhodes and Ian Smith usurped African land and formalised its exploitation through a plethora of laws, such as the Land Apportionment Act (1931), the Land Husbandry Act (1951) and the Land Tenure Act (1969). All the liberation struggles in Zimbabwe or *zvimurenga* were fought by black people with the express aim of freeing blacks from the shackles of colonialism and that implied regaining land that had been expropriated from blacks through Rhodesian separatist land policies. Jocelyn Alexander (2006: 1) underscores the politics of land expropriation when she writes:

> In the territory that was to become Southern Rhodesia, the violence of military subjugation was followed by the displacements of territorial segregation. Africans faced eviction, sometimes several times over, from their homes and farms. Half of the agricultural land, and much of the most fertile, was designated for European occupation, while Africans were forced into reserves . . . In the 1950s, many were denied land in the reserves altogether, a measure that vastly expanded the burgeoning ranks of African nationalism. Land was central once again in provoking the brutal conflict of the liberation war, and in ultimately bringing about the demise of the settler state.

Land was therefore central to the liberation struggle and its significance is clearly spelt out in 'Zimbabwe Iyoyi'. While the song views the land question as one of the critical areas that defined the nationalist agenda (Rwafa, Viriri and Vambe 2013: 26), the land question remained contested terrain in post-independent Zimbabwe. For instance, the land reform also dubbed the 'Third Chimurenga' (Mugabe 2001: 23) that started in 2000 triggered a wave of violent occupations of white commercial farms by veterans of Zimbabwe's armed struggle, security forces and youth militia, backed by leaders of the ZANU–PF.

When Chimbetu sings about getting land back, he is inspired by popular discourses (Sibanda 1989: 31) in Zimbabwe started by heroes of the First Chimurenga, which continued to define the contours of nationalist struggles for Second and Third Chimurengas. However, surplus meanings from Chimbetu's song could be taken as a direct affront to: (1) the methods adopted by blacks in acquiring land; (2) the nature of beneficiaries of land reform; and (3) the lack of productivity and the slow pace of economic development in commercial farms by blacks. These interpretations are not far-fetched because a work of art, such as music, is tied to ideology not so much by what it says, but by what it does not say (Eagleton 1985). The duty of the cultural critic, therefore, is to locate the tonal and lyrical spillages (Attali 1985: 50) in Chimbetu's song that point towards alternative discourses about the myths and realities on the land question in Zimbabwe. In fact, the aporias or silences in national discourses about the realities of land reform in Zimbabwe are bound to invite the ire of critics such as Lloyd Sachikonye (2004) who view the land reform process as reflective of a competitive scramble for commercial farms by members of the ruling elites and their sycophants. In the same vein, Alexander (2006: 181) argues that, in practice, it was not the landless but the indigenous elites who dominated land redistribution in Zimbabwe. Although this view seems to have overlooked the reality that thousands of black families that used to lead a precarious existence in rural areas benefited immensely through land reform, it does hold some truth. In Chimbetu's song, the repetition of the phrase '*Zimbabwe iyoyo*' is an irritation, a stubborn reminder to the present leaders that their orgies and spectacles of excessive consumerism (Russell 1993: 174) in disregard of *chimurenga* protocols are at the expense of the blood that was shed during the liberation war. Thus, a seemingly innocent song can be potentially subversive and destabilising if read against the grain of grand cultural and historical narratives constructed by the state.

While 'Zimbabwe Iyoyo' sets the protagonist on a journey in search of strategies and methods to execute the liberation struggle, 'Ndarangarira Gamba' memorialises war experiences, as well as presenting the harrowing experiences symbolised by the image of a guerrilla in the throes of death.

History, memory and the construction of *chimurenga* identities in 'Ndarangarira Gamba'

Heroic accounts of guerrillas fighting the liberation war of Zimbabwe have been captured variously in historical textbooks such as Martin and Johnson's *The Struggle for Zimbabwe: The Chimurenga War* (1981), Ranger's *Peasant Consciousness and the Guerrilla War in Zimbabwe* (1985) and Lan's *Guns and Rain: Guerrillas and Spirit Mediums in Zimbabwe* (1985). Equally significant are literary works such as Edmund Chipamaunga's *A Fighter for Freedom* (1985). Music has also been a valuable source of remembering heroic acts of comrades who died on the front. The song 'Ndarangarira Gamba' falls within the genre of *chimurenga* music that proffers a glimpse into personal experiences of comrades such as Chimbetu who fought during the liberation struggle. Chimbetu's 'authority of presence' (Chennells 2009: 98) is etched in mournful tones in the song. Music, like written history, 'relates, reflects, comments on or critiques' (Rosenstone 2008: 39) already existing memories about Zimbabwe's liberation struggle. Chimbetu uses the power of song to recollect memories of a dying comrade when he sings:

> *Ndarangararira musi watisiya gamba*
> *Mwana wenyu amai, amire panguva yakaoma*
> *Handikanganwe comrade* × 2
> I remember the day when the hero was killed
> Your son, mother, during the difficult times of his last moments
> I will never forget the comrade × 2

Memorialising the pain of others, especially during their last moments, was a way in which surviving guerrillas during Zimbabwe's liberation struggle created and authenticated their identities as the sole liberators of the country. As Hayden White (1987: 4) writes:

> Historiography is an especially good ground on which to consider the nature of narration and narrativity because it is here that our desire for the imaginary, the possible, must contest with the imperatives of the real, the actual. If we view narration and narrativity as the instrument with which the conflicting claims of the imaginary and the real are mediated, arbitrated, or resolved in a discourse, we begin to comprehend both the appeal of narrative and the grounds for refusing it.

For listeners of 'Ndarangarira Gamba', the appeal of its *chimurenga* narrative is manifested in the symbolic depiction of a dying comrade. Through Chimbetu's eyes, we see a vision of pain, a convulsive body of a dying comrade, helpless in the throes of death, but brave enough to shout out these last revolutionary words:

> *Akasheedzera ndokusheedzera. Katanurai zvikasha zvangu zvose*
>   *muendereremberi*
> *Nehondo fambai makashinga comrade muchiti ZANU, ZANU ...*
> He called out, and called out Remove all the war equipment on me,
> And go ahead with the war. Go well, comrade, saying ZANU, ZANU ...

Through this extract from Chimbetu's song, narration and narrativity (White 1987) of the history of the liberation is based upon the imperatives of the real and actual events that happened during the Zimbabwe's war of liberation. While the reality of the deaths of comrades is constructed here to authenticate the ZANU–PF political party as the true liberator of Zimbabwe, the same discourses are used to disremember or erase the history of ZAPU as a political party that also played a significant role in liberating Zimbabwe. In other words, the imaginary world created by Chimbetu through his song becomes a 'regime of regimenting' (Hall 1997: 259) ordinary people's opinions towards preferred interpretations of the war narrative set by the nationalist leaders that ZANU is the only legitimate political party that people should continue to support in post-independent Zimbabwe. The repetition of 'ZANU, ZANU' reverberates the dominance of ZANU in as much as the words act as a harbinger of death to the political life of ZAPU in post-independent Zimbabwe. However, while the image of a dying comrade in Chimbetu's song evokes the issue of mimetic realism, the *chimurenga* voices in the same song evoke 'a realism of delegation and interlocution; a situated narrative of speaking from [individualised experiences] and speaking to' (Shohat and Stam 1994: 45) Zimbabwean audiences, some of whom had not yet been born when the liberation struggle took place. The exclusion of ZAPU war narratives complicates the historical memory encapsulated in the song in the sense that in its desire to destabilise other memories and other histories of the liberation struggle, the song necessitates a preliminary critique of its claims to be able to represent uncontested truths about the history of the liberation struggle (Vambe 2004). By extension, the exclusion of ZAPU narratives serves to point to the reality that

> every narrative, however seemingly "full", is constructed on the basis of a set of events that might have been included but were left out; this is as true of imaginary narratives as it is of realistic ones. And this consideration permits us to ask what kind of notion of reality authorizes construction of a narrative account of reality in which continuity rather that discontinuity governs the articulation of the discourse (White 1987: 10).

When the dying comrade shouts out in the extract from Chimbetu's song above, it is as if he is constructing narratives of continuity; narratives that immortalise ZANU–PF, on the one hand, and immobilise ZAPU, on the other. Ultimately, what counts is not to view personal experiences of Zimbabwean war veterans as guarantors of incontestable truth, but rather as a basis to interrogate the ontology and ideological construction of that truth. However, the seductive appeal of *chimurenga* narratives in 'Ndarangarira Gamba' can be difficult to resist:

Ndarangararira musi watisiya gamba
Mwana wenyu amai amire panguva yakaoma
Handikanwe comrade × 2
Akasheedzera ndokusheedzera chionaika comrade
Ini ndave neropa pachipfuva zvinotopesana muupenyu
Shinga comrade × 2
Akasheedzera ndokusheedzera katanurai zvikasha zvangu zvose muenderere mberi nehondo
Fambai makashinga comrade muchiti ZANU, ZANU...
I remember the day when the hero was killed, your son, mother, during the difficult times of his last moments
I will never forget the comrade × 2
He called out and called out. You see, comrade, my chest is now full of blood, now we're going to be separated by my death, be brave comrade × 2
He called out and called out remove all the war equipment on me and go ahead with the war. Go well comrade saying, ZANU, ZANU . . .

The repetition of '*Akasheedzera ndokusheedzera*' (He called out and called out) provides a poetic touch to the musicality of the song and yet its semantic dissonance becomes a pestering voice to the present leadership in Zimbabwe that seems to have deviated from the revolutionary ethics of *chimurenga* by permitting crass rottenness, corruption and gross mismanagement of economic resources. The same streak of resistance and vestiges of despair and antagonism that can be traced in this song are further amplified in the song 'Pane Vasipo'.

Epistemic disobedience: The roots of political protest in 'Pane Vasipo'
The song 'Pane Vasipo' gives the impression that its discourses are aimed at reforming national and leadership structures that seem to have lost memory of the critical role that late comrades played during the liberation struggle. In doing so, the song reveals a profound feeling of nostalgia that it uses to caution and criticise the extravagance and carelessness sometimes demonstrated by the leadership at rallies and national celebrations when millions of dollars are splashed about with little regard of how it took other people's lives for such luxuries to be enjoyed. The caution is clearly spelt out in the lyrics:

Gungano ramaita iri-i pane vasipo.
Mabiko ataita aya pane vamwe vasipo.
Kuguta kwataitauku
pane vamwe vasipo × 2
The gathering that we have done here
Remember there are others that are not present
The celebrations that we have done here
Remember there are others that are not present × 2

Since independence, the government of Zimbabwe has set aside public holidays, such as Independence Day, Heroes Day, Defence Forces Day and Unity Day, on which there are national celebrations for Zimbabwe's freedom and its capacity to run its own affairs as a sovereign nation. During the gatherings, which often take place around the country at designated points such as schools and stadiums, there are national speeches that are delivered by government representatives, music entertainment, song and dancing, drinking and partying till late. The song 'Pane Vasipo' cautions people that when they attend national gatherings, they should remember that there are some people that are not present because they were killed during the liberation struggle. Zimbabweans have a culture of remembering their heroes and this is a healthy exercise because collective memory is a repository of national identities; it reconfigures and realigns individual hopes and aspirations into common goals that any state can strive to achieve. Lawrence Taitz (1996: 8) writes that not only do we create and maintain the memories we need to survive and prevail, but those collective memories both shape and constrain us. While it is significant to remember those that are absent ('*pane vasipo*'), Zimbabweans need to forge ahead with their lives and, in the process, create new memories and realities about the need for freedom, thereby vindicating the deaths of thousands of black people during the liberation struggle.

However, in 'Pane Vasipo', the leadership crisis in Zimbabwe seems to be emanating from '*kuguta*' (having enough), which has made the leadership forget about the sacrifices that others have made. Yet, when Chembetu says, '*kuguta*', he seems to have ignored the reality that in Zimbabwe there is a condition of '*kugutisa*' (having excess) among the leadership, who dismiss others by labelling them as the '*povo*' (derogatory name for ordinary people) who did not participate fully during the liberation struggle. In their forgetfulness the leadership indulges in corrupt acts, abuses the rights of others through violence and is implicated in crimes against humanity and of economic mismanagement. All this does not constitute '*kuguta*' (having enough), but '*kugutisa*' or '*kugutisisa*' (having excess or excessive). In their arrogance and excessive waste of Zimbabwe's resources, the leadership seem have forgotten that it is the same arrogance and maltreatment of the majority of blacks by the Smith regime that triggered a nationalist revolution that put an end to white domination in Zimbabwe.

In theorising memory, history and historicity Rangarirai Musvoto (2011: 184) argues:

> It is not how the past is known to have happened that matters, but how memory is applied to present need that is significant. Thus, understanding social memory as products of cultural selections of elements of usable past disorders the assumed neatness of conventional history and tosses it back into the tangle of unordered approaches to the past to escape from.

This argument is significant in that it challenges narrow and essentalised notions of the conceptualisation of memory in which the political leadership in Zimbabwe fails to translate that very memory gained through years of colonial brutality into changing the social and economic situation of the ordinary people that they claim to have been fighting for. So, the 'assumed neatness of conventional history' is not after all neat and pristine; it is challenged by the inescapable reality that remembering and memory as sites of struggle are revealed as always in flux to the extent that there is not only potentially one memory, but also multiple memories constantly battling for attention within the cultural-scape of Chimbetu's song (Vambe 2004). The contestation of memory, deriving from statements such as '*Tatadza kukanganwa isu kukanganwa takoniwa*' (We have failed to forget, we have failed to forget) shows that while some comrades who participated in the liberation struggle still show an unquestionable degree of commitment towards fighting the temptation of forgetfulness, others have allowed forgetfulness to drown their memory and the history of suffering engendered by colonialism. However, what boggles one's mind is this question: If the liberation struggle was fought to enable blacks to have access to their own economic resources, why after 35 years of independence, are the majority of Zimbabweans still living in abject poverty and eking out a precarious existence? It is also heartbreaking to know that there are comrades who died in the war whose bones are still lying in shallow graves and the government has not been seriously committed to carrying out traditional rites and rituals to bring their souls back home. In this regard, Chimbetu sings:

Jojo akasarako kusango; Moli akasara ikoko. Lavhu akasarako kuhondo.
Jonah akasara ikoko. Mweya wadzungaira mweya; mweya wadzungaira
   × 2
Mavaudza amai vake here? Kuti mwana wenyu akashaika akafire
Kusango kurenyika isina neniwo-o × 2
Makumbira kunzinza rake here? Kuti tambirai mwana uyu kani
Mupei pekugara igamba rehondo × 2
Mweya wadzungaira mweya, mweya wadzungaira × 2
Mavaudza amai mavaudza, mavaudza amaivake here? × 3
Makumbira, makumbira, makumbira kudzidza rake here? × 3
Jojo was left in the forest; Moli was left in the forest. Lavhu was left killed during the war.
Jonah was also killed in the war. The soul is restless; the soul is restless × 2
Did you tell his/her mother that your child was killed? She/he was killed during the war × 2
Did you seek permission from his/her clan of ancestors that receive your child?
Give her/him a place to live because he/she is a war hero × 2
The soul is restless, the soul is restless, and the soul is restless × 2
Did you tell mother, did you tell mother? × 3
Did you seek permission? Did you ask for permission?
Did you seek permission from his/her clan ancestors? × 3

The above lyrics memorialise the heroes of the Second Chimurenga who were killed during Zimbabwe's armed struggle. Chimbetu's appeal is that the heroes should be given due respect by exhuming their bones and reburying them in their communities. Within the African cosmological belief system, a person does not die forever; s/he can communicate with the living. Souls of comrades that are not brought home through decent burial are believed to appear to the living demanding that they be buried in their communities, as well as receiving the full honour accorded to the heroes of the Chimurenga. When Rwanda embarked on the reconstruction programme following the 1994 genocide, in which Hutu extremists decimated the lives of more than 800 000 Tutsis and moderate Hutus, the government emphasised that victims of genocide should be exhumed and reburied in decent graves. The reburials and memorialising of bones in museums was a national project that involved Rwandans regardless of sex, gender, class or creed. However, despite the achievements yielded by such a national project, critics of the government of Paul Kagame accuse him of 'genocide credit' (Reyntjens 2005: 35), meaning that skulls and bones were being used to fix into permanency a Tutsi history in post-genocide Rwanda. Similarly, Obed Nkunzimana (2009) and Véronique Tadjo (2002) argue that while Tutsi bones mixed with other bones at memorial sites can articulate their pain through official narratives, the cries of Hutu bones are often silenced. In the case of Zimbabwe, the epistemic cry from Chimbetu is that some bones of common guerrillas were neglected by the government and their fellow Zimbabweans. Through the song, Chimbetu also wishes to gain '*chimurenga* credit', as well as to legitimise the comrade as the 'only' actor who should be given credit for victory in the Second Chimurenga. Ordinary men and women who also perished during the liberation struggle are erased by the song whose focalisation on the comrade is very clear:

> *Mweya wadzungaira mweya, mweya wadzungaira* × 2
> *Mavaudza amai mavaudza, mavaudza amaivake here?* × 3
> *Makumbira, makumbira, makumbira kudzidza rake here?* × 3
> The soul is restless, the soul is restless, and the soul is restless × 2
> Did you tell mother, did you tell mother? × 3
> Did you seek permission? Did you ask for permission?
> Did you seek permission from his/her clan ancestors? × 3

To say that the bones of dead comrades in Zimbabwe were completely neglected is to present a partial statement that fails to acknowledge some attempts by the government and communities to appease the spirits of dead comrades through a traditional ceremony known in Shona as *bira* that was held in different parts of the country. According to Arthur Makanda (2013: 105), an academic and former freedom fighter:

> Deceased freedom fighters create an alternative paradigm to archeological work and display the power of the African traditional beliefs and its philosophical importance as opposed to some non African Religion. In some cases they [spirits of deceased freedom fighters] also seek to be reconciled with persons who may have facilitated their demise, people such as those who sold them out to the colonial authorities, those who facilitated their death through the use of non-natural means or wizardry.

The contradictions raised here by Makanda about the workings of the spirits of a deceased freedom fighter bring about fresh readings of the realities of the liberation struggle. While earlier war narratives (Martin and Johnson 1981; Ranger 1985; Lan 1985; Chipamaunga 1985) constructed official history on the basis of national triumphalism, Makanda and 'Pane Vasipo' make the brave acknowledgement that comrades were not automatons – that they also died like anyone else exemplifies the existence of a 'decolonial episteme' (Grosfoguel 2011: 4) within the body politic of Zimbabwean war narratives, which are otherwise presented as incontestable or inviolable by scribes supported by the ruling ZANU–PF. Put differently, there is a need for a new *chimurenga* narrative in Zimbabwe whose epistemological and ontological truths confront war narratives constructed on what Godknows Chera (2015: 13) refers to as 'tattooed ideologies', which are etched into the epidermis of Zimbabwean history whose internal monologues can be used to suffocate the growth of versions and sub/versions (Vambe 2004: 167) in narratives of the liberation struggle.

An attempt to wean *chimurenga* music from its internal monologues brings us to the issue of how music in post-independent Zimbabwe has been used to tell stories of common men and women who suffer daily because of the failure by the government to craft and implement effective economic policies to eradicate poverty, unemployment and corruption, among other issues. This has resulted in the birth of a new brand of *chimurenga* music popularised by musicians such as Leonard Zhakata and Oliver Mtukudzi who use sarcasm, political satire and sly rebuke to attack the excesses of the ruling party and its leadership, uncouth ordinary men and women, the predatory ways of the corporate world and the government. Zhakata and Mtukudzi were, in a way, influenced by *chimurenga* maestro and self-exiled Thomas Mapfumo, who became unpopular with the state because of his songs that directly attacked the government for its failure to deliver on its promises.

Conclusion

This chapter has theorised the revolutionary dimensions of *chimurenga* music. It has reflected that this genre was historically started by heroes of the First Chimurenga to convey their grievances to the colonial administration instituted in 1890. The genre was appropriated by ZANLA and ZIPRA forces and used as an instrument of protest and rebellion against British colonialism. However, over time *chimurenga* music has been used by the ZANU–PF to consolidate its position as the only true liberator of Zimbabwe. In this way, the memories of ZAPU have been marginalised or even erased from the songs that won the liberation struggle. The domineering stance of ZANU–PF is encapsulated in the songs collected by Pongweni (1982), most of which espouse masculinist discourses that sideline the narratives of female guerrillas.

In all of Chimbetu's songs under scrutiny in this chapter, he seems to be espousing a nationalist triumphalism, yet a closer analysis reveals some cracks and fissures in discourses of nationalism otherwise presented as incontestable or inviolable. This epistemic disobedience is brought about by the reality that music can reveal more in what it is prevented from saying than in what it says. This implies that *chimurenga* discourses in 'Zimbabwe Iyoyi', 'Ndarangarira Gamba' and 'Pane Vasipo' can be read as an indirect attack on Zimbabwe's nationalist leaders, who seem to have forgotten that Zimbabwe is a product of the blood of fellow comrades who died in the liberation struggle. The political leadership in Zimbabwe has failed to eradicate oppression and exploitation, for it allows corruption, human rights abuses and the mismanagement of the economy to prevail, thereby constructing Zimbabwe as a country at war with itself. The songs by Chimbetu constantly pester and annoy the leadership because their vibrant tones and rhythms cannot be stopped; they are a constant reminder of sacrifices made by fallen comrades to bring peace in Zimbabwe. The lyrics penetrate right into one's conscience and stir up open rebellion, flamed by the biting political satire articulated in the songs by Thomas Mapfumo, Leonard Zhakata, Hosiah Chipanga and Oliver Mtukudzi.

References

Alexander, J. 2006. *The Unsettled Land: State-making and the Politics of Land in Zimbabwe 1893–2003*. Oxford: James Currey; Harare: Weaver Press; Athens: Ohio University Press.

Attali, J. 1985. *The Political Economy of Music*. Manchester: Manchester University Press.

Bakhtin, B. 1981. *The Dialogic Imagination: Four Essays*. Austin: Texas University Press.

Bhabha, H. (ed.). 1990. *Nation and Narration*. London: Routledge.

Butler, J. 2010. *Frames of War: When Is Life Grievable?* New York: Verso.

Chennells, A.J. 2009. 'The Authority of Presence: Reading Judith Todd's *Through the Darkness* as Diary'. *Journal of Literary Studies* 25(1): 98–114.

Chera, G. 2015. 'Manifestations of Power and Resistance through Film: An Exploration of the Films *12 Years a Slave* (2013) and *Django Unchained* (2012)'. BA Honours thesis, Midlands State University, Gweru.

Chipamaunga, E.A. 1985. *A Fighter for Freedom*. Gweru: Mambo Press.

Chitando, E. 2002. '"Down with the Devil, Forward with Christ!" A Study of the Interface between Religious and Political Discourses in Zimbabwe'. *African Sociological Review* 6(1): 1–16.

———. 2005. 'In the Beginning was Land: The Appropriation of Religious Themes in Political Discourse in Zimbabwe'. *Africa* 75(2): 220–39.

Dabengwa, D. 1995. 'ZIPRA in the Zimbabwe War of National Liberation'. In *Soldiers in Zimbabwe's Liberation War*, Vol. 1., edited by N. Bhebe and T. Ranger, 12–40. Harare: University of Zimbabwe Press.

Derrida, J. 1976. *Of Grammatology*. Baltimore: Johns Hopkins University Press.

Eagleton, T. 1985. *Marxism and Literary Criticism*. London: Methuen.

El Saadawi, N. 2007. 'Dissidence and Creativity'. In *African Literature: An Anthology of Criticism and Theory*, edited by T. Olaniyan and A. Quayson, 172–7. London: Blackwell.

Gibbs, A. 2009. '*Chimurenga* Music in Zimbabwe'. *Campbellsville Review* 1(1): 1–13.

Gilroy, P. 1993. *The Black Atlantic: Modernity and Double Consciousness*. London: Verso.

Grosfoguel, R. 2011. 'Decolonizing Post-colonial Studies and Paradigms of Political Economy: Transmodernity, Decolonial Thinking and Global Coloniality'. *Transmodernity* 1(1): 1–38.

Hall, S. 1997. 'The Spectacle of the "Other"'. In *Representation: Cultural and Signifying Practices*, edited by S. Hall, 258–63. London: Sage.

Lan, D. 1985. *Guns and Rain: Guerrillas and Spirit Mediums in Zimbabwe*. Harare: Zimbabwe Publishing House; London: James Currey.

Lucy, N. 2004. *A Derrida Dictionary*. Oxford: Blackwell.

Makanda, P.T. 2013. 'Ethical Challenges of Using Video Technologies in the Production of Narratives of Healing Voices of Deceased Freedom Fighters'. *Journal of African Cinemas* 1(1): 102–17.

Martin, D. and P. Johnson. 1981. *The Struggle for Zimbabwe: The Chimurenga War*. Harare: Zimbabwe Publishing House.

Mignolo, W.D. 2009. 'Epistemic Disobedience, Independent Thought and De-colonial Freedom'. *Theory, Culture & Society* 26(7–8): 1–23.

Mirmotahari, E. 2011. 'History as Project and Source in Achebe's *Things Fall Apart*'. *Postcolonial Studies* 14(14): 373–85.

Mugabe, R.G. 1978. 'ZANU Carries the Burden of History'. *Zimbabwe News* 10(2): 45–56.

———. 2001. *Inside the Third Chimurenga*. Harare: Department of Information and Publicity.

Musvoto, R.A. 2011. 'Rethinking History and Identity in Zimbabwe'. *Latin American Report* 27(1): 181–94.

Ndlovu-Gatsheni, S.J. 2011. 'The Construction and Decline of *Chimurenga* Monologue in Zimbabwe: A Study in Resilience of Ideology and Limits of Alternatives'. Paper presented under Panel 109: Contestations over Memory and Nationhood: Comparative Perspectives from East and Southern Africa at the 4th European Conference on African Studies, Nordic Africa Institute, Uppsala, 15–18 June.

Nkunzimana, O. 2009. 'Beyond Colonial Stereotypes: Reflections on Postcolonial Cinema in the African Great Lakes Region'. *Journal of African Cinemas* 1(1): 79–94.

Pongweni, A. 1982. *Songs That Won the Liberation War*. Harare: College Press.

Ranger, T. 1985. *Peasant Consciousness and Guerrilla War in Zimbabwe*. Harare: Zimbabwe Publishing House; London: James Currey.

Reyntjens, F. 2005. 'Rwanda, Ten Years On: From Genocide to Dictatorship'. In *The Political Economy of the Great Lakes Region in Africa: The Pitfalls of Enforced Democracy and Globalization*, edited by S. Marysse and F. Reyntjens, 15–47. New York: Palgrave MacMillan.

Robins, S. 1996. 'Heroes, Heretics and Historians of Zimbabwe Revolution: A Review Article of Norma Kriger's *Peasant Voices* (1992)'. *Zambezia* 23(1): 73–91.

Rosenstone, R.A. 2008. *History on Film/Film on History*. Harlow: Pearson.

Russell, C. 1993. 'Decadence, Violence and the Decay of History: Notes on the Spectacular Representation of Death in Narrative Film'. In *Crisis Cinema: The Apocalyptic Idea in Postmodern Narrative Film*, edited by C. Sharrett, 73–90. Washington, DC: Maisonneuve Press.

Rwafa, U. 2011. 'Song and the Zimbabwean Film, *Flame* (1996)'. *Muziki* 8(1): 47–58.

———. 2012. 'Language Censorship in Selected Zimbabwean films in Shona and English'. DLitt diss., Pretoria: University of South Africa.

Rwafa, U., A. Viriri and M.T. Vambe. 2013. 'Music, Land and Liberation Theology: Mai Charamba's "Africa" and Fungisai Zvakavapano-Mashavave's "Hamheno Anoramba?"'. *Muziki* 10(3): 24–32.

Sachikonye, L.M. 2004. 'The Promised Land: From Expropriation to Reconciliation and Jambanja'. In *Zimbabwe: Injustice and Political Reconciliation*, edited by B. Raftopoulos and S. Tyrone, 1–18. Cape Town: Institute of Justice and Reconciliation.

Sheridan, M.J. 2008. 'The Dynamics of African Sacred Groves'. In *African Sacred Groves: Ecological Dynamics & Social Change*, edited by M.J. Sheridan and C. Nyamweru, 9–41. Oxford: James Currey.

Shohat, E. and R. Stam. 1994. *Unthinking Eurocentrism*. London: Routledge.

Sibanda, M.J. 1989. 'Early Foundations of African Nationalism'. In *Turmoil and Tenacity: Zimbabwe 1890–1990*, edited by C.S. Banana, 25–49. Harare: College Press.

Spivak, G.C. 1994. 'Can the Subaltern Speak?' In *Colonial Discourse and Postcolonial Theory: A Reader*, edited by P. Williams and L. Chrisman, 66–111. New York: Columbia University Press.

Tadjo, V. 2002. *The Shadow of Imana: Travels in the Heart of Rwanda*. Portsmouth: Heinemann.

Taitz, L. 1996. 'Where Once Our Heroes Danced There Is Nothing but a Hideous Stain: Nationalism and Contemporary Zimbabwean Literature'. Master's thesis, University of the Witwatersrand, Johannesburg.

Titlestad, M. 2004. *Making the Changes: Jazz in South African Literature and Reportage*. Pretoria: University of South Africa Press.

Turner, V.W. 1992. *Blazing the Trails: Waymarks in the Exploration of Symbols*. Tucson: University of Arizona Press.

Vambe, M.T. 2004. 'Versions and Sub-versions: Trends in *Chimurenga* Musical Discourses of Post-independence Zimbabwe'. *African Study Monographs* 25(4): 167–93.

White, H. 1987. *The Content of the Form*. Baltimore: Johns Hopkins University Press.

CHAPTER 10

Music and Violence
Discordant Siblings? A Study of Political Music in the Land Reform Programme of Zimbabwe, 2000–10

Bridget Chinouriri and Munyaradzi Nyakudya

The colonisation of Zimbabwe was predicated on the search for minerals and, when this failed, the white settlers turned to agricultural production. Colonial rule was therefore characterised by extensive land expropriation from the indigenous African population, resulting in the prime land being parcelled out to the white settlers while the blacks were confined to unproductive sandy soils and dry regions. This threatened the natives' human security and, to be precise, destroyed their land rights by undermining their means of livelihood. Sabelo Ndlovu-Gatsheni (2009: 65) argues that this rampant land expropriation was part of the colonial grand strategy of creating propertyless natives, dependent on selling their labour.

With time, Zimbabwe's communal areas surpassed their ecologically safe carrying capacity (Moyo 1995). In 1980, when Zimbabwe attained its independence, the natives' agricultural economy had already been severely battered. The bulk of the choice land was in the hands of a mere 4 500 white commercial farmers while Africans were seriously overcrowded in the reserves. The new government thus set out to correct the land tenure imbalances. However, despite the enactment of the Land Acquisition Act (No. 3 of 1992), which allowed for compulsory land acquisition for resettlement by government, by the late 1990s very little progress had been made in terms of land acquisition and resettlement (Muzondidya 2009). This situation, combined with a number of other factors, led to the government condoning the forcible occupation of land by land-deprived peasants from 2000 onwards, thus heralding the commencement of what has come to be termed the 'fast track land reform programme' (FTLRP). Sam Moyo (2013) postulates that the FTLRP was meant to improve the equitable ownership of agricultural land in order to enhance food security through broad-based production and employment through self-employment, and to improve the wider livelihoods and incomes of the rural population. The programme led to the distribution of over 10 million hectares of land to about 150 000 families, including landless peasants, war veterans, middle-class urbanites and a few farmworkers.

Sabelo Ndlovu-Gatsheni and Wendy Willems (2009: 952) are cognisant that across Africa and beyond, failing regimes such as that of Mobutu Sese Seko in Zaire have often resorted to cultural nationalism as a way of managing society. In the midst of diminishing economic resources and a failure to deliver material goods, governments facing a crisis of legitimacy have fallen back on culture in an attempt to renew themselves. In a context in which the legitimacy of the Zimbabwe African National Union – Patriotic Front (ZANU–PF) government was increasingly contested, the nationalist struggle proved a valuable resource for the party in order to rejustify its rule, particularly in the face of an opposition party that drew large support from white Zimbabweans, civil society organisations and major world powers such as the United States and the United Kingdom. It was at this juncture that cultural nationalism became an important project for ZANU–PF and a means of reasserting its anti-colonial message in the face of what it saw, and increasingly represented, as a new imperial threat embodied by the Movement for Democratic Change (MDC).

It is within this context that this chapter examines the uses and abuses of music during the Zimbabwe land reform programme from 2000 to 2010. The ambiguity of music made it a powerful force and a necessary conduit in perpetrating cultural and structural violence that was inherent in the land reform. This chapter examines how the innocuousness of music was abused by political parties, musicians and consumers to unleash cultural and structural violence while in the process destroying what constitutes human security in Zimbabwe. This chapter employs an ethnographic approach. As Joseph Kwabena Nketia (1990: 79) suggests, descriptions of the ethnographic contexts of music enable one to convey part of the meaning and significance of a music event through a vivid portrayal of the circumstances under which it takes place and the identity of those who participate in it.

Music and violence as discordant siblings

During the land reform programme of 2000–10 in Zimbabwe music was used to culturally and politically manipulate people for egoistic ambitions – either defending one's view or attacking opponents. This chapter will use the term 'hate music' because most of the lyrics are quite personal and raise factual issues that may cause harm or hurt to the so-called victims mentioned in the songs. ZANU–PF and MDC both used propaganda and counter-propaganda in musical expressions to articulate, demean, conquer and outdo each other's political ideologies. Music was an integral part of the cultural and structural violence perpetrated by both the ruling party and the opposition parties, particularly at the time of the haphazard violent land occupations.

Music and violence typically exist on opposite ends of the interpretive spectrum within popular discourse, which holds music to be largely innocuous and violence to be universally destructive (Lynch 2012). This research authenticates the notion that music and violence are discordant siblings, but society has manipulated and abused the former for egoistic ambitions. There is an African maxim that says if a drum does not sound well enough, we dance to it all the same with a lot of aesthetic tolerance (Kwabena Nketia 2005). This reveals that in indigenous Africa there was aesthetic tolerance towards all musical performances in a society. If music was not aesthetically appealing, the society would listen to it anyway out of respect for whoever was playing. Bridget Chinouriri (2014: 74) notes that this also showed the listener's emotional ability and disposition towards a given musical environment. Such tolerance was also used as an index for evaluating whether a composition had achieved its musical intention or not. In the Zimbabwe land reform struggle, some music was not tolerated by the ruling party, as it was regarded as politically 'incorrect' because it did not advance their political ambitions.

One thing that clearly emerged during this period in Zimbabwe is that musicians and consumers were very vulnerable. The musicians could act strategically trying to advance their careers and as people with their individual fears, traumas and hopes. Conceptually, human security has, since the turn of the millennium, taken on a broader and more encompassing viewpoint that places human beings at the centre of security concerns in the quest for peace, security and sustainable development (Commission on Human Security 2003).[1] The new focus considers

---

1. 'This report's call for human security is a response to new opportunities for propelling development, for dealing with conflict, for blunting the many threats to human security. But it is also a response to the proliferation of menace in the 21st century – a response to the threats of development reversed, to the threats of violence inflicted. With so many dangers transmitted so rapidly in today's interlinked world, policies and institutions must respond in new ways to protect individuals and communities and to empower them to thrive. That response cannot be effective if it comes fragmented – from those dealing with

a whole range of security threats emanating from socio-political, economic and environmental causes, as opposed to the traditional concerns with state-centric security. These threats to broader human security include poverty, disease, human rights violations, crime, climate change and terrorism, among others.

Violence of any form propagated for any purpose by anyone is a serious threat to human security. Music activists who were against the land reform programme were at the forefront in producing a counter-narrative that fractured the state's idea of a massive land-centric national project, exposing it as parochial (Chikowero 2008). Musicians who were pro land reform pursued the land-acquisition project with vigour, laying emphasis on preserving the land as a birthright from the British imperialists. This close link between social and political life has been a catalyst in the political manipulation of music as a strategic force for advancing and negating political ideologies in Zimbabwe. There have been different types or versions of *chimurenga* (struggle) music promulgated by different artists who were affiliated to the contesting political groups in Zimbabwe or who considered themselves independent.

Hate music during the land reform process

Denigrating, insulting or hate music can be directed at an individual, party or government and it usually results in a form of violence. An example is the land reform song 'The Blair That I Know Is a Toilet' by Last Chiyangwa aka Tambaoga (a pun referring to a type of outdoor toilet developed by Blair laboratories) on the album *Sendekera Mwana Wevhu* (2005). The song sanctions the obligation

---

rights, those with security, those with humanitarian concerns and those with development. With human security the objective, there must be a stronger and more integrated response from communities and states around the globe. Security centered on people – not states. The international community urgently needs a new paradigm of security. Why? Because the security debate has changed dramatically since the inception of state security advocated in the 17th century. According to that traditional idea, the state would monopolize the rights and means to protect its citizens. State power and state security would be established and expanded to sustain order and peace. But in the 21st century, both the challenges to security and its protectors have become more complex. The state remains the fundamental purveyor of security. Yet it often fails to fulfil its security obligations – and at times has even become a source of threat to its own people. That is why attention must now shift from the security of the state to the security of the people – to human security. Human security complements state security, enhances human rights and strengthens human development' (Commission on Human Security 2003).

by the ruling party to take back land from the white farmers and return it to its rightful owners, as it captures the metaphors of land and nationalism of Zimbabwe. Tony Blair's name was punned, corrupted and degraded through linguistic semantic extensions to mean what the singer wanted to convey to his listeners. In the song, the British were sarcastically renamed the 'Brishit', equating them with human waste. Morgan Tsvangirai, the opposition leader who led the MDC party, had his name corrupted to 'Tsvangison', the 'son' added as a means of scornfully identifying him as 'kith and kin' of the British. Jairos Kangira (2005: 53) says the derogatory anglicised form of 'Tsvangison' gave the impression that Tsvangirai had already 'sold' his soul and would eventually auction Zimbabwean land to the British. Tsvangirai was also portrayed as a clown and a vulnerable political novice who lacked shrewdness and maturity, the prerequisite of an astute presidential candidate (Chitando 2005). Tsvangirai and Blair were being scoffed at because to the ruling party they represented British imperialism. In the late Simon Chimbetu's song 'kuState House Kure' (The Journey to State House Is Very Far) Tsvangirai was advised that the residence of the president was not for the political novice. Chimbetu was a war veteran whose song intimidated any political figure who dared to have ambitions of presidency of the country. Cde Chinx (Dickson Chingaira Makoni), a ZANU–PF eulogist, reconnected ZANU–PF's patriotic history in the First and Second Chimurengas to the land reform. The land issue had remained unresolved since the First and Second Chimurengas, so the so-called Third Chimurenga was seen as a continuation of the land struggle. Cde Chinx took the opportunity through song to teach those he called the born-frees (children born after independence) while deriding white people. In his song 'Hondo Yeminda' (War for Land), he equated imperialists and ordinary white people with the devil because of the deception of the historical land injustices in Zimbabwe. This was authenticating President Mugabe's blunt statement about whites in general that the only white man you can trust is a 'dead white man'.

Artists who refrained from composing music for the ruling party were perceived as *zvimbwasungata* (sell-outs). For instance, Tambaoga ridiculed Albert Nyathi, a poet and musician, by saying: '*Vana Nyathi vari kuramba kuimbira magamba vachinokwesha chembere ku* UK' (Nyathi is refusing to sing about our heroes yet he goes to United Kingdom to ill old women and gets paid).[2]

---

2. Albert Nyathi, interview, Harare, 11 October 2011.

On the other hand, hate music was also composed by the opposition party musicians (Madzore, Chikunguru, Chirikure and others) to scoff at the land reform as a flawed and disorganised exercise and also to offer scathing criticism of some members of the ruling party. This kind of music was used to make fun of the old age of President Mugabe as an 'expired man'. For instance, Madzore sings '*Dare renyu ndere chembere dzoga*' (Your party consists of very old leaders). The MDC party musicians used the age of President Mugabe to make Zimbabweans aware that they allowed an old man to rule over them. The theme of old age and wishing for the death of President Mugabe was popular in the song 'Saddam Waenda Sare Bob' (Saddam Has Died, Next Is Bob) by Happison Mabika – also known as Dread Reckless – and Patience Takaona – also known as Sister Fearless.

A female musician, using the pseudonym Viomak, rhetorically asks 'Uchaenda Riini Mugabe?' (When Are You Dying Mugabe?) and pleads with God to take him away. In indigenous ethics and sensibilities and particularly in Zimbabwean culture, it is not morally condoned for one to so openly wish for the death of a member of society, especially an elder who is in a position of authority. The Shona people value the respect of elderly people and the sacredness of death. Such cultural violence through hate music has been imprinted in the musical lyrics of the land reform era in Zimbabwe. In his song 'Tombana' (Toddler), Madzore sings that Bob (short for Robert) behaves as a child and chronicles instances when he thought that President Mugabe behaved like a toddler – for example, the Operation Murambatsvina debacle, which was alleged to be a punishment of urban dwellers who had resoundingly voted for the opposition party.[3]

Hosiah Chipanga claimed to be apolitical during the land reform programme. His song 'Ivhu Ramakafira Nderipi?' (Which Soil/Land Did You Die For?) mocked

---

3. Operation Murambatsvina, also officially known as Operation Restore Order, was a large-scale Zimbabwean government campaign to clear illegal structures that had mushroomed in urban areas. It started in 2005 and, according to United Nations' estimates, has affected at least 700 000 people directly through loss of their homes or livelihoods and thus could have indirectly affected around 2.4 million people. The campaign met with harsh condemnation from opposition parties, church groups, non-governmental organisations and the international community (http://en.wikipedia.org/wiki/Operation_Murambatsvina). There is some dispute over the figures and some analysts are of the view that the United Nations team that conducted the exercise used shoddy methodology, relying on the evidence of unaccountable civil society organisations, rather than more widespread sources and rigorous methods (Moyo and Yeros 2007: 115).

the sacrificial role the war veterans and all collaborators made in fighting for land in the liberation struggle. In this song, Chipanga rhetorically and ironically questions the land that the local people call their own land. He questions that if Zimbabweans fought in the liberation struggle in order to get land, why is it that the black government is selling urban land to the people? This has been painful and hurtful to the war veterans and the people who suffered during the colonial period in order to get their political freedom.

In 'Chauraya Nyika' (What Has Destroyed Our Nation?) Chikunguru, an MDC supporter, laments that ZANU–PF has given land to unproductive people who lack farming skills. He challenges President Mugabe's famous political statement 'Blair, keep your England and I keep my Zimbabwe' by singing that Zimbabwe is not a Mugabe private limited company. Chipanga and Chikunguru's stance seems contrary to the aspirations of the war veterans, who in their hunger for land acquisition, urged listeners through song to reminisce on the tribulations, pain and bloodshed experienced during the liberation struggle. But these musicians were very aware of the historical injustices of land dispossession suffered by landless Zimbabweans who were moved from low-lying flat land into rocky and marginal mountains during the colonial era. Chipanga and Chikunguru are, in fact, challenging Mugabe and his cohorts' expropriation of the country's wealth.

Structural violence during the land reform
During the FTLRP, the ruling ZANU–PF had total control of music production and dissemination, especially via electronic media. The reason for such control resonated with safeguarding sovereignty and hegemony from political opponents. The unwillingness to accommodate political differences from the MDC was evident in how they were labelled adversaries of the land revolution. Land played a central and complex role in the cultural and symbolic politics of the Third Chimurenga, as both material resource and cultural heritage. This was perhaps best expressed in ZANU–PF's campaign slogan, 'The land is the economy, the economy is the land' (Ndlovu-Gatsheni and Willems 2009). It is this intolerance of political plurality that bred hatred and violence, which inevitably led to the polarisation of Zimbabwean society.

The ruling party enacted legislation to protect law and order in 2002. These regulations infringed upon the freedom of expression and movement of opposition parties. The Public Order and Security Act is an extensive piece of legislation, which gives extraordinary powers to the police and includes provisions to control political gatherings, requiring individuals and groups to obtain police clearance before any gathering is held. This minimised the movements and gatherings of opposition parties and they were often denied police clearance for flimsy reasons. The Access to Information and Privacy Protection Act controlled the print and electronic media and thus anything contrary to the political hegemony of the ruling party was outlawed.[4] The musicians who did not support the ruling party's land and political aspirations – such as Madzore, Chikunguru, Thomas Mapfumo, Leonard Zhakata and others – were denied access to music airplay on the state-controlled media musicians.[5] In the song 'Sakunatsa' Zhakata questions the human rights violations in the name of law and order. Maurice Vambe and Beauty Vambe (2006: 65) acknowledge the 'miscarriage' of justice when they quote Zhakata's lyrics: '*Mitemo yepano yakanyangara, inosaidhira divi rimwe*' (the laws of this place are evil as they are only one sided). Zhakata narrates how some sections of the Public Order and Security Act and the Access to Information and Privacy Protection Act are oppressive and have been applied selectively and arbitrarily, depending on one's political affiliation. These laws were also in contravention of

---

4. The Access to Information and Privacy Protection Act was passed to provide members of the public with a right to access records and information held by public bodies, to make public bodies accountable by giving the public a right to request correction of misrepresented personal information, to prevent the unauthorised collection, use or disclosure of personal information by public bodies, and to protect personal privacy. The Broadcasting Services Act of 2001 empowered the designate minister to control programming on radio and television (http://www.sokwanele.com/pdfs/AIPPA.pdf).
5. The history of a state-controlled media dates back to the 1800s of Southern Rhodesia. Those who pioneered the media were not necessarily professional journalists, but adventurers motivated by the desire to expand their personal interests, as well as British colonial interests. The *African Daily News* was introduced in 1962 and sought to inform Africans. It was banned in 1964 by Ian Smith's regime, which accused it of supporting people who indulged in violence and intimidation. It was later unbanned, with Smith instituting government control of editorial policy. *Moto* magazine became the principal voice of African aspirations. Its circulation rose from 15 000 to 30 000 and this attracted the eye of the white minority regime censors. It was permanently banned in November 1974. The electronic media was officially opened in Rhodesia in 1958, but it was controlled by the colonial government. At independence in 1980, the people appointed to run the media were and are still largely drawn from ZANU–PF. The same strategy used by Cecil Rhodes and Ian Smith was also used at this point: rewarding friends for their support of military or political interests or both. Thus Mararike (1998: 213) concludes, 'There is always a relationship between the media and the ruling class. Owners of the media in most cases are interested in a political agenda.'

the Zimbabwean Constitution, which enshrined freedom of speech and of the press. The implications of these laws for musical arts in general were that the government showed intolerance of criticism by 'silencing' creative arts, thus threatening public interest, human security and human rights.

Music censorship and self-censorship
In Zimbabwean politics music that expresses criticism of the ruling party has generally been termed politically 'incorrect' music. Some songs composed during the land reform process were perceived as 'discordant voices' from either the opposition or from non-partisan musicians who sang non-political tunes. Musicians who sang messages contrary to the ruling party's political aspirations raised pertinent issues that negatively affected ordinary people. Other musicians censored their creative expression in order to humour the ruling and opposition parties at the expense of their own creativity and integrity and to their fans' loss. Some musicians suffered from both cultural and structural violence, their freedom of cultural expression was hindered and the liberty to perform was stifled through legislation formulated by the ruling party.

The non-censorship of some music or its political correctness did not mean that it was embraced, comprehended and accepted by every listener. Oliver Mtukudzi, one of Zimbabwe's most celebrated musicians, has been called derogatory names, such as 'the bugling lunatic of Dande' by his fans and by opposition print media (Dande is his home town), while others have called him a 'two-faced musician' because they could not figure out his political stance on land reform (Mano 2007). Mtukudzi denied allegations that he was aligned to any political party after he performed at the inauguration of Vice President Joyce Mujuru of the ZANU–PF party. When he composed 'Bvuma' (Admit), some of his fans were happy as they deduced that the song was satirically against President Mugabe's unwillingness to resign despite his old age. However, the meaning of music is not entirely a musician's dictate to his listeners (Chinouriri 2014). In the land reform era, musicians were assimilated into the politicking of society and were sometimes in a quandary as to how to satisfy the diverse listeners. In society such as this, there is a failure to appreciate a musician as having their own aspirations and creative imperatives.

Chikowero (2011: 295) notes that a new era of unprecedented music censorship emerged in which the government not only controlled the music played on the national public broadcaster, but also commissioned music production to bolster its ultra-nationalist propaganda crusade. Some songs that were deemed potentially 'dissident' or unpatriotic were gagged and disappeared from the airwaves, replaced by state-commissioned or -approved patriotic songs that celebrated the land reform. This resulted in the creation of people's own alternative music and means of communication. The national broadcaster, Zimbabwe Broadcasting Corporation, which held an increasing monopoly on the airwaves, played a central role in the state's propaganda machine (Ndlovu-Gatsheni and Willems 2009). Those who dared to sing their minds and reflect society took risks, exposing themselves to reprisals and recriminations. Such musicians include Mapfumo, Chipanga, Madzore, Zhakata and others. The ruling party used its privilege to access and disseminate its own ideologies while hindering the other parties from enjoying the same privilege. 'Dissident' musicians had to search for alternatives to record and disseminate their music to avoid the state surveillance systems. In an interview with Banning Eyre in 2000, Mtukudzi comments: 'If you restrict a song, people get curious, they want to know the song more. You are only promoting the song. Maybe they [government] don't understand how the media works' (in Eyre 2000).

The late Andy Brown, who was once a critic of the ruling party, suddenly and unexpectedly changed his political stance during the land reform programme. Interviewed by Eyre (2001) before his conversion to ZANU–PF ideologies, Brown once said: 'Zimbabwe doesn't respect its culture. So being censored when the song comes out is even a very minute situation. There's a bigger one: they have censored their own culture.' Later on, Brown extolled the ruling government's land reform policies through his music and was duly rewarded by the state's acceptance of his music.

Albert Nyathi, a dub poet, musician and secretary-general of the Musicians Union of Zimbabwe reported that he was one of the censored artists. Nyathi said that initially he thought his songs were being denied airplay because of his minority background (Ndebele), but later he realised that most musicians had experienced censorship in one way or another. Nyathi observed: 'Censorship is the restriction of the creative mind and an attempt to limit the limitless and it must be resisted.'[6] Eyre (2001) corroborates by saying that when music is banned the very soul of a culture is being strangled and if music is banned for a decade or more, a whole generation grows up without an essential cultural reference.

---

6. Nyathi, interview.

Conclusion

Music has been used as a potent force to reflect and influence non-musical events in Zimbabwe. The power of music has been used to instil violence in one way or another – against political parties, political personalities, music makers and the people in general. This has been detrimental to the general human security of Zimbabweans. During the land reform programme, music was at the centre of struggles, as the ruling party exerted tight regulations on the production and consumption of music and the opposition party to a lesser extent also manipulated music for its political ends. Music became a tool for inciting hate and for deriding political opponents. In the period of the land reform programme, there arose 'dissenting' musical voices, which disseminated information on the realities of the Zimbabwean society. These music activists who sang in 'discordant voices' were in two groups: the first group clearly sang the political ideologies of the ruling party and the second of the opposition party. The ruling ZANU–PF suddenly discovered a confronting and conflicting band of musicians who critiqued government policies through published songs. This resulted in the legislation discussed above, with the ruling party as the major player in state media control and the movement of information and people in Zimbabwe. Members of society have a right to listen to the information they want and musicians should have the liberty to create and express themselves as free citizens.

In the FTLRP era the state controlled the production and dissemination of music to satisfy its egoistic ambitions, mortifying political plurality. Music was manipulated in Zimbabwe as a disguise for cultural and structural violence by political parties, musicians, the music industry and society at large during the land reform programme from 2000 to 2010. This greatly impacted on the general human security of Zimbabwean people. Music and violence from the indigenous school/ethos are known to be discordant or non-compatible. As concluded by Meki Nzewi, to disagree or struggle over an issue is human as long as human life is not (mentally, physically, psychologically and spiritually) destroyed under any ideological or circumstantial arrogance.[7] Violence was unleashed against the musicians and their creativity, against consumers of music and the electorate in general, polarising Zimbabwean society.

---

7. Meki Nzewi, interview, Pretoria, 13 July 2013.

References

Chikowero, M. 2008. 'Struggles over Culture: Zimbabwean Music and Power, 1930s–2007'. PhD diss., Dalhousie University, Halifax.

———. 2011. 'The Third Chimurenga: Land and Song in Zimbabwe's Ultra-nationalist State Ideology 2000–2007'. In *Redemptive or Grotesque Nationalism? Rethinking Contemporary Politics in Zimbabwe*, edited by S. Ndlovu-Gatsheni and J. Muzondidya, 291–313. London: Peter Lang.

Chinouriri, B. 2014. 'Singing the Third Chimurenga: An Investigation of the Use of Music as an Ideological Force in the Political Mobilization of Zimbabwe's Land Reform Programme, 2000 to 2010'. PhD diss., University of Pretoria, Pretoria.

Chitando, E. 2005. 'In the Beginning Was the Land: The Appropriation of Religious Themes in Political Discourses in Zimbabwe'. *Africa* 75(2): 220–39.

Commission on Human Security. 2003. *Human Security Now*. https://reliefweb.int/report/world/human-security-now-protecting-and-empowering-people.

Eyre, B. 2000. '2000 Interview [with Oliver Mtukudzi]'. *Rock, Paper, Scissors*. http://archive.rockpaperscissors.biz/index.cfm/fuseaction/current.articles_detail/project_id/205/article_id/3594.cfm.

———. 2001. 'Playing with Fire: Fear and Self-censorship in Zimbabwean Music'. http://www.kubatana.net/html/archive/artcul/011001be.asp?sector=ARTCUL&year=2001&range_start=.

Kangira, J. 2005. 'Negative Advertising as a Strategy of Persuasion in the 2002 Presidential Election Campaign in Zimbabwe'. *Zambezia* 32(1–2): 41–63.

Kwabena Nketia, J. 1990. 'Contextual Strategies of Inquiry and Systematization'. *Journal of the Society for Ethnomusicology* 34(1): 75–95.

———. 2005. *Ethnomusicology and African Music: Collected Papers, Volume 1*. Accra: Afram Publications.

Lynch, J.A. 2012. 'Music and Communal Violence in Colonial South Asia'. *Ethnomusicology Review* 17: 1–6.

Mano, W. 2007. 'Popular Music as Journalism in Zimbabwe'. *Journalism Studies* 8(1): 61–78.

Mararike, C.G. 1998. 'The Human Factor, Media and Politics in Southern Rhodesia (Zimbabwe)'. In *The Human Factor Approach to Development in Africa*, edited by C.G. Mararike and V.G. Chivaura, 211–28. Harare: University of Zimbabwe Publications.

Moyo, S. 1995. *The Land Question in Zimbabwe*. Harare: Sapes Trust.

———. 2013. 'The Scramble for Land in Africa'. Paper presented at the Round Table Dialogue on Land Reform, Land Grabbing and Agricultural Development in Africa in the 21st Century, 17–18 June, Addis Ababa, Ethiopia.

Moyo, S. and P. Yeros. 2007. 'The Radicalised State: Zimbabwe's Interrupted Revolution'. *Review of African Political Economy* 34(111): 103–21.

Muzondidya, J. 2009. 'From Buoyancy to Crisis, 1980–1997'. In *Becoming Zimbabwe: A History from the Pre-colonial Period to 2008*, edited by B. Raftopoulos and A. Mlambo, 167–200. Harare: Weaver Press.

Ndlovu-Gatsheni, S.J. 2009. 'Mapping Cultural and Colonial Encounters, 1880s–1930s'. In *Becoming Zimbabwe: A History from the Pre-colonial Period to 2008*, edited by B. Raftopoulos and A. Mlambo, 39–74. Harare: Weaver Press.

Ndlovu-Gatsheni, S.J. and W. Willems. 2009. 'Making Sense of Cultural Nationalism and the Politics of Commemoration under the Third Chimurenga in Zimbabwe'. *Journal of Southern African Studies* 35(4): 945–65.

Vambe, M.T. and B. Vambe. 2006. 'Musical Rhetoric and the Limits of Official Censorship in Zimbabwe'. *Muziki* 3(1): 48–78.

Part III

The Rise of Dancehall in Zimbabwe
Regarding Transdisciplinary Studies

CHAPTER 11

Dancehall Music in Zimbabwe
Youth Activism or Subalternity? Some Notes on the Politics of Music Based on Select Songs at the 2014 Zimdancehall Awards

Rekopantswe Mate

The Zimdancehall scene is a recent development in nascent urban youth music cultures that emerged in the 2000s out of the fractious socio-economic crises in Zimbabwe. Music 'scenes' are defined by Andy Bennett (2004) as consisting of promoters, artists, producers, fans and the media and entail a shared preference for and consumption of specific types of music. Today, music scenes are multidimensional, with transnational links and local idiosyncrasies (Bennett 2004). However, Bennett does not discuss how hybridised context contestations within a scene are resolved. Do international dimensions of a scene meld seamlessly into local contexts? If locals resist and remodel certain aspects, what is removed or reworked and why? These questions are especially important when it comes to understanding music genres performed by youth in gerontocratic and neo-patrilineal societies such as Zimbabwe.

This chapter discusses songs of two artists, Seh Calaz (born Tawanda Mumanyi) and Tocky Vibes (born Obey Makamure) who dominated several categories of the second Zimdancehall Awards at the end of 2014. Both were contenders in several categories, including 'most outstanding artist of the year'; 'best song of the year', Seh Calaz's 'Hatimisike' (We Are Unstoppable) and Tocky Vibes' 'Mhai' (Mother); 'best social song', Seh Calaz's 'Ndinochema' (I Cry/I Am Crying) and 'Kwatinobva' (Where We Come From) and Tocky Vibes' 'Mhai' and 'best video of the year', Seh Calaz's 'Simudza Maoko' (Raise up Your Hands). This chapter analyses some of the nominated songs in the context of intertextual debates between Zimbabwean and Jamaican dancehall; the latter's lyrics and messages have stoked controversy (Cooper 1998; Noble 2008) and there is pressure on the former to avoid the same controversy. Additionally, the content of the songs has to be understood in broader contexts characterised by contradictory stances by the state and broadcasters towards youth music in Zimbabwe (see Mate 2012; Viriri, Viriri and Chapwanya 2011).

This chapter argues that the awards shape the Zimdancehall genre by rewarding some music and some artists, while ignoring and sidelining others who are deemed subversive and anti-establishment, thereby undermining and challenging the ethos of dancehall as a genre concerned with subjectivities of marginalised youth (Noble 2008; Cooper 1998). The lyrics and messages of nominated songs point to deep-seated local anxieties about foreign influences apparently undermining 'Zimbabwean culture' and corrupting youth (Scanell 2001; Viriri, Viriri and Chapwanya 2011). These anxieties have been accentuated by post-2000 socio-economic changes in Zimbabwe, as discussed below. Suffice to say, Zimbabwean youth are increasingly resorting to performing arts in response to chronic unemployment and to media policies that privilege 'local content' since 2001 (Mate 2012). The motivation to produce entertainment products has also led to official surveillance of content and messages, to ensure compliance with what officials and the public see as important cultural and political values (Viriri, Viriri and Chapwanya 2011; Mate 2012). The surveillance itself raises questions about whose interests these performances address. This chapter tries to show that pre-emptive action by elites calling for 'cleaner' lyrics and image in Zimdancehall, for instance (Viriri, Viriri and Chapwanya 2011), stifles the publicisation of performances that showcase the reality of survivalist livelihoods typical of low-income urban areas, commonly referred to as the 'ghettos' in both Jamaican and Zimbabwean dancehall. Often survival in the ghetto depends on young people living by their wits, passing time and having fun through illicit and sometimes criminal practices, such as petty crime (Biaya 2005). These emergent survival strategies deviate from ideals of respectability, characterised by wage work, marriage and having a family, guided by Judeo-Christian norms, preferred by older generations (Miller-Young 2008; Noble 2008).

This chapter uses Gramscian notions of subalternity to argue that contradictory responses to Zimdancehall (and youth performances in general) are embedded in relations of domination (Coronil 1994), by age and class. The dominated – poor youth in this case – find that their language, signs and symbols are outside mainstream discursive conventions, open to misinterpretation and ignored as non-speech (Maggio 2007). The dominant – adults in this case – insert themselves everywhere, thus shutting out alternative views (Smith 2010; Green and Ives 2009). This dominance leads to persistent criticism of young people as deviant or misguided by foreign influence and justifies interventions under the guise of giving guidance, supporting and mentoring. Thus, as this chapter shows, youth music that receives airplay and is nominated for awards affirms gerontocratic and class interests of those in positions of influence, such as radio stations, newspapers and sponsors. These acts of gagging and sidelining messages of youths are not value neutral. In keeping with the concern of subaltern studies to call attention to the drowned voices of the marginalised and point out the hypocrisy of those in power, the agency of youth music can only be seen when researchers excavate its politics by critiquing officially accepted messages and stances.

The subalternity of youth music in sub-Saharan Africa

Subalternity refers to relational conditions characterised by inequality, which perpetuate oppression, exclusion, invisibility and inaudibility of the oppressed, weak, dominated and excluded (Maggio 2007: 422). Fernando Coronil (1994: 649) explains it thus: 'Subalternity defines not the being of a subject, but the subjected state of being.' Domination silences, denigrates the actions of the dominated and leaves them open to being misconstrued and misinterpreted as deviant or ignored as insignificant (Coronil 1994; Maggio 2007; Green and Ives 2009: 22). Control of the dominated leaves them fragmented and passive while their exclusion means not being familiar with the workings of power. This is especially accentuated by the development of neo-liberalism, which has left many young people stuck indefinitely in liminality, neither recognised as adults because they lack resources, economic and political clout nor as children dependent on adults (see Honwana 2012 for a detailed discussion). Such indefinite social immobility, characterised by an inability to fulfil aspirational roles, can create disregard for social norms, seen in defiant pastimes such as the evolving street culture by seemingly leisured persons, as happens with youths who have no social role (Biaya 2005; Stanley Niaah 2008). While researchers argue that young people have agency to change and/or impact on their circumstances and society itself, this agency is sometimes directed at passing the time through the consumption of alcohol and other stimulants and playing games in street corners, cafés or bars, much to the disapproval of those in authority (Mains 2007; Carrier 2005). Not only are these pastimes incomprehensible to adults, adult indignation blames the youth for their circumstances, or accuse them of arrogance and/or a sense of entitlement to a better life (Mains 2007). Actions embedded in the performing arts are dismissed for not complying with the exacting demands of a real discipline. This prevents the development of organic intellectuals, but also allows criticisms of artists, as examples from sub-Saharan Africa show.

The growing availability of digital technologies democratised recording opportunities across sub-Saharan Africa, with many young people adapting rap, hip-hop and dancehall to create kwaito in South Africa (Steingo 2005; Stanley Niaah 2008), *bongo flava* in Tanzania and also in East Africa in general (Perullo 2005), *ndombolo* in the Democratic Republic of Congo (Biaya 2005) and urban grooves in Zimbabwe (Mate 2012; Kellerer 2014). Digital recording means that artists dispense with the need to learn or to play conventional music instruments. Vocalisations and chants over digital music extend music production to persons without formal training in music. The output is subversive music – hence, rap, dancehall and their variants across the world are seen by the establishment as 'noise', rather than music, because of the combination of inaccessible street language, the absence of traditional or Western musical instruments and apparently being off-beat (Cooper 1993; Gueye 2013; Perullo 2005). These types of music are dominated by the ethic of having fun and enjoyment, but can also be satirical.

The ethic of enjoyment or having fun can be misconstrued as hedonism when in fact, dominant groups prefer it when enjoyment occupies young people and makes it difficult for them to take action against or engage with structural causes of their marginalisation (Stanley Niaah 2008). Fun and enjoyment can be an escape from the dreariness of impoverishment (Gueye 2013). Substance abuse enhanced these escapes, much to the disapproval of adults. In some cases, enjoyment and political engagement are combined through satire, making the divide between enjoyment and political critique fuzzy. In this respect, Alex Perullo (2005) talks about Tanzanian youth critiquing the false promises made by politicians to which their followers are expected to agree by saying '*Ndio Mzee*', Swahili for 'Yes Sir', even when they know that the promises are empty. Not only does the culture of 'Yes Sir' undermine democracy, it perpetuates gerontocracy, patronage and corruption when most people yearn for change. In Dakar, (Senegal) young people protested against President Wade's third term through the Enough Is Enough movement, which was characterised by rap music played loudly during street marches, despite the erstwhile marginalisation of rap as a type of music (Gueye 2013; Fredericks 2014). The protest songs became a form of voter education, raising awareness about the concerns of the poor and marginalised. President Wade lost the 2012 elections and subsequently conceded defeat. In Côte d'Ivoire, student protests against poor service delivery and the deteriorating quality of education not only created protest music called *zouglou*, the music became a rallying call for democracy and multiparty transition (Konate 2002).

In the Democratic Republic of Congo's capital of Kinshasa, erotic dance moves of *ndombolo* give evidence of the fact that Congolese rumba music is an incisive critique of undemocratic transitions to power (Biaya 2005). Tshikala Biaya says *ndombolo* started on the street among unemployed youth born after independence, who are largely seen as work-averse. Some were homeless, others addicted to drugs, and many spent their time drinking, making money by hook or by crook and plotting clandestine entry into Belgium or France, where they imagined the realisation of their dreams for a better life. *Ndombolo* moves were a satirical representation of apparently unrefined body movements of mating apes. Out of the forest, the apes copulate obliviously, in full view of refined and disapproving residents of Kinshasa, with child soldiers incongruously commenting on events. This was in oblique reference to Laurent Kabila, a former exile whose ascent to power without elections and subsequent authoritarian rule and insurgency were much despised for their disruption of city life and leisure pursuits of young city residents. Kabila censored the dance as crude, but not before it became known internationally, where perhaps its deeper meanings are lost or it is seen as pointing to hypersexuality and hedonism in African youth. Clearly, enjoyment is not value neutral. In the Democratic Republic of Congo, Kabila and other politicians use musicians as praise singers and take advantage of the mobility of music to campaign for office and their causes (White 2014). Through being praise singers, artists earn patronage and income. In Kenya, the defiance and invincibility expressed through song by two unemployed young people, who went by the stage names Gidi and Maji, created an unexpected theme song for the 2002 general elections in Kenya (Nyairo and Ogude 2005: 226). The lyrics of the song struck a chord with public sentiment and catapulted the pair to stardom.

Even when youth performances do not become famous or notorious, they still remain political when dismissed as signalling pathology, literally or metaphorically, because they question, challenge or insult elders, social etiquette or the existing social order (Gueye 2013; Perullo 2005; Biaya 2005). This is used to justify attempts to control young artists, to ban their music as deviant, dismiss it as a nuisance (Mate 2012), or as 'noise' that disrupts peace and causes distress through noise pollution, thus requiring regulation by urban authorities. Loud music in public can be threatening, even more so when the lyrics challenge authority (Fredericks 2014) or when it is a new genre that goes against familiar local forms of music. In addition, youth music is intrusive by its rhizomatic circulation or its imposition, especially when played in confined spaces of informal public transport where passengers do not choose what to listen to (Mate 2014). These methods of circulation defy official controls.

In addition to subverting gerontocracy, youth artists also sing about gender relations, often telling off apparently wayward female peers (Perullo 2005; Prince 2006). This speaks to the dilemma that many young men find themselves in: they aspire to achieve ideal masculinities, but lack resources to do so. They tell off elders and female peers for their relentless demands and are criticised for being misogynistic. In sub-Saharan Africa the subalternity of these emergent activisms is seen in the fact that they do not lead to significant change, as young people are censured for being wayward or co-opted through patronage (White 2014; Kellerer 2013).

Methodological issues and debates
Understanding the politics of music is, of course, challenging because of what some refer to as the double entendre, the artistic licence to give multiple meanings that are deliberately left to consumers to decipher. Researchers, much like fans, have to read between the lines and come to their own conclusions. Whereas some studies prefer observing and decoding the performance of music, doing ethnographies of sites of performance, a lot of work also focuses on lyrics as potent messages, which even when presented as playful, cannot be taken as value neutral (Noble 2008; Cooper 1993; Perullo 2005; Gueye 2013; Fredericks 2014). A lot of these analyses are post-structuralist and see performativity in words and action as politically significant critiques, protests and speaking truth to power, thus (potentially) creating new realities. Marame Gueye (2013) observes that texts and words can be seen as activism, not merely reacting to something, but also initiating change by presenting new arguments and ways of thinking and critiquing existing arguments. Since texts, words and actions are open to interpretation, this creates contestable readings of young persons' performances of their nuanced meanings about their realities or experiences of marginalisation. At the same time, post-structural arguments are easily dismissed as much ado about nothing.

A note on Jamaican dancehall as the origin of the musical style
Dancehall evolved from and is often contrasted with reggae for its messages and expression of black ontologies. It is distinct by its use of *riddims*, instrumentations or digital music based on cut-and-paste-and-repeat formats, to which chants and vocalisations are added (Manuel and Marshall 2006). *Riddims* are easier to

produce and circulate because of digital technology (Cooper 1998: 161). *Riddims* are used repeatedly, can be modified to change tempo and chanters/vocalisers give *riddims* new dimensions. There are specialist *riddim* producers, chanters/vocalisers and sometimes also specialist poets who produce lyrics for chants. Voices that are discounted in conventional singing as not good enough (such as husky, gravelly voices) are welcome in dancehall. A lot of the chanting is out of tune, but deliberately so, hence it is often perceived as not well arranged to those formally schooled in music or as 'noise' (Cooper 1993; Manuel and Marshall 2006: 460). A good *riddim* attracts a following, just as a good chant/chanter has a following. Collaborations among chanters, *riddim* producers and poets are the bases of 'sound systems' (Pereira 1998) and rivalries among different collaborating teams are common. 'Sound systems' entail more than *riddim* and vocaliser/chanter collaborations; they suggest hardware such as turntables and public address systems, which entail more collaborators. These collaborations point to the origins of dancehall in poverty and in the marginalised sectors of Jamaica, where preoccupations with enjoyment were an important political activity to pass the time (Stanley Niaah 2008) during Jamaica's past political morass, when funding such activities was a challenge.

In Jamaica, dancehall is associated with rebellious young men, generally described as 'raggamuffins', 'rudies' or 'rude *bwais*' (Cooper 1998), who are described as disorderly, subversive and incorrigible in their deviation from social etiquette. Erin Mackie (2005: 30) says that these youths' code of ethics is transgression, celebrating survival and personal bravado. These traits are globally glamourised through the circulation of dancehall and the success of some of its artists.

Controversies of Jamaican dancehall
Dancehall has been criticised internationally for being homophobic, misogynistic and racist, but this is sometimes countered as criticising black art forms, ontologies and stereotyping blacks as conservative and intolerant (Noble 2008: 109). In addition, attempts at explaining the wordplay of lyrics leads to researchers being accused of making excuses for hate speech (Noble 2008). These controversies emanate from the fact that dancehall reflects a changing world and politics of (re) presentation as well as dissonance between the concerns and realities of today's young people, such as unemployment, social mobility and aspirations to participate in a global culture defined by consumer ethics, which privilege sex, sexuality, hedonism and free-spiritedness (Bauman 2004; Attwood 2006). Meanwhile, older

generations of blacks are preoccupied with respectability (Miller-Young 2008; Noble 2008), following decades of political struggle. However, grinding poverty challenges the performance of respectability for the young and music is a way out of the ghetto and grinding poverty, thus allowing them to be respectable. Consequently, dancehall's performance by youth can be seen as a protest against gerontocracy and Eurocentric notions of respectability (Noble 2008; Cooper 1993).

Jamaican dancehall is associated with 'slackness', seen in sexually explicit lyrics and erotic dancing by scantily dressed female dancers. Debates abound over whether or not such dances objectify women, are an illicit and/or crude display of black bodies, a celebration of previously marginalised black sexualities or portray black people as hypersexual and hedonist, thus playing into racist stereotypes (Noble 2008; Cooper 1993, 1998; Pereira 1998; Stanley Niaah 2005, 2008; Mackie 2005; Miller-Young 2008). There are complaints about subversive language and the fact that dancehall artists shun 'conventional' wage work (Cooper 1993:142). While these debates show that what gets highlighted is neither value neutral nor objective (Stanley Niaah 2005: 62–3; Noble 2008), they point to some threatening aspects of the genre for conservative neo-patrilineal culture brokers in Zimbabwe. In this respect, lyrics of songs in the second Zimdancehall Awards nominations are value-laden and necessitate questions about whose interests they represent.

The Zimdancehall scene: The socio-economic and political context of its genesis
Zimdancehall emerged in the recent deep economic and political crises, seen in the '75 per cent local content' media policy, details of which are beyond the scope of this chapter (Mate 2012). It is created, performed and consumed by 'ghetto yutes' (ghetto youths) to whom it appeals in newfound civic pride showcasing self and neighborhood (see Mate 2014).[1] The 'ghetto youths' that the lyrics refer to or call on in chants and taunts are male, unemployed residents of low-income/high-density residential areas in Zimbabwe's urban areas. Ordinarily, referring to high-density suburbs as 'ghettos' is politically incorrect. I use the term as Zimdancehall artists such as Winky D do (Manase 2011; Mate 2014) and newer artists such as Tocky Vibes and Seh Calaz have followed suit. Reference to 'ghettos' in Jamaican dancehall is itself political; an 'anti-euphemism', according to Sonjah

---

1. 'Ghetto yutes' was a term used in 'Lady Squanda and Lady Bee Settle Score', *H-Metro*, 6 November 2013 and 'Carlos Green Attempts Suicide', *H-Metro*, 24 October 2014.

Stanley Niaah (2008: 44), referring to the degeneracy of residential areas of poor black people, which politicians prefer to hide the appalling conditions by using euphemistic terms. Another anti-euphemism used in Zimdancehall is a colonial reference – 'location' or *rokesheni* in Shona (plural is *marokesheni*). It is rarely used in formal discussions (Mate 2014). In Zimbabwe euphemisms such as 'high-density areas' and occasionally 'low-income residential areas' are used to erase memories of racial inferiorisation in the colonial era, to give an impression of decent standards of living and mutual respect, but where socio-economic reality points to the contrary. Zimdancehall's anti-euphemisms remind listeners of existences based on cultures of survival, including the defiance of illicit pleasures such as gambling, dancing, drinking in unlicensed venues and other grey economic activities – hence *kukiya-kiya* documented by Jones (2010).[2] The majority of residents of 'ghettos' and *marokesheni* are implicated in *kukiya-kiya* because of limited opportunities. These activities defy respectability that elites prefer to highlight in the post-independence era.

In addition, ghettos and *marokesheni* have had to contend with poor service delivery, as seen in prevailing chronic water delivery, sanitation and electricity supply challenges. These conditions impinge on public health (Youde 2010) and transitions to male adulthood for chronically unemployed young men. Consequently, Zimdancehall is a pastime that offers marginalised young men a means to reimagine themselves by either providing a diversion through fun and enjoyment or, if successful, a means to claw their way out of the margins to recognition, status and some fame, albeit having to tenaciously struggle daily to provide for themselves because of low earnings. Contradictions inherent in the performance of dancehall, such as class, age and gender and postcolonial politics, come into relief in the Zimbabwean context because of the imperative of local music content, the generation gap and gender relations in a state of flux.

Subalternity in Zimbabwe's youth music
Zimdancehall owes its performance and politics to elusive quests for 'local music' (Scannell 2001). Debates about which media and music are Zimbabwean have a

---

2. The idea of *kukiya-kiya* captures emerging and pervasive survival strategies in urban areas, based on taking advantage of opportunities and other people through trickery, pilfering, scheming and scamming because of widespread unemployment and the shortage of basic commodities (Jones 2010: 286–7).

long history, accentuated in the past couple of decades by debates about English language public radio stations that are allowed to play 'international' (foreign or non-Zimbabwean) music (Scannell 2001; Zilberg 1994; Chikowero 2008). The debates have undercurrents of fear of foreign cultural influences and yet no culture is static or insular (Scannell 2001: 19). The debates intensified following the '75 per cent local content' media policy of 2001 (Mate 2012). Thus, as far as local music is about lived realities of Zimbabweans telling their own stories (Scanell 2001: 23), Zimdancehall should suffice. In Zimbabwe the domination of youth and their performances are seen in reaction to so-called 'inappropriate' lyrics (Mate 2012; Viriri, Viriri and Chapwanya 2011); DJs and radio stations apparently practise self-censorship even when there is no explicit ban on lyrics (Eyre 2005; Viriri, Viriri and Chapwanya 2011). Lyrics that are obliquely anti-government are likely not to receive airplay while those explicitly singing praises of the government or President Mugabe, such as songs by the Born Free Crew, receive a lot of airplay (Kellerer 2013: 55).

Complaints abound about violence in lyrics, following the initial success of pioneering dancehall artists such as Winky D, who sang about interpersonal violence and personal bravado in dealing with intransigent peers. These complaints seem to have swayed many artists to stay away from incendiary, chest-thumping lyrics (Manase 2011). The use of subversive language too has led to criticism and bans from airplay of certain songs (Viriri, Viriri and Chapwanya 2011). Concerns with 'clean' lyrics, messages and images by media institutions and the public are tantamount to erasure of the view from the ghetto and its lifestyles because of class sensibilities, but also age and gender discrimination. Furthermore, despite the evident need to showcase 'the ghetto' as a space of creativity, beauty, bravery and survival, as in what is globally popularly known as 'ghetto fabulous' (Stanley Niaah 2005; Noble 2008: 112–13), seen in ghetto women's pretty hairstyles, make-up and creatively painted nails, men's clothing, haircuts and manner of speech, 'ghetto fabulous' seems hard to perform in Zimbabwe's economic crises unlike in South Africa, Nigeria and elsewhere.[3] Discussions of the underbelly of the ghetto and ghetto survivalism are perceived as embarrassing exposure – elites find it tasteless.

---

3. In South Africa, 'loxion kulture' and 'lokshin bioscope' have helped to mobilise popular culture's gaze in ways that see and acknowledge low-income existences. Nigeria too has an active youth culture, supported by electronic media, movies and music.

Thus, despite dancehall being for and about 'ghetto yutes', the ghetto and its experiences cannot be showcased. 'Ghetto feminism', noted in Jamaican dancehall (Noble 2008: 166), seen in 'rude ghetto *gyals*' speaking back at 'rudies' and 'rude *bwais*', is silenced in Zimbabwe. If there are artists that follow the ghetto feminism ethic, they receive even less airplay and are thus snubbed as deviant. Evident in the 2014 nominations, the agency of rude *gyals* had been nipped in the bud, with some female artists already criticised for foul lyrics, apparently fit only for pub crowds.[4] Such conclusions are moral statements, judging the female artists' social standing and very stigmatising. As many ordinary Zimbabweans resort to fundamentalist Christianity, where ideal femininities are simplified to being subordinate to men, who are imagined as heads of household and also breadwinners (Mate 2002), there is very little support for the rude *gyal* and ghetto feminism.

Perhaps emulating Jamaican styles, Zimdancehall also has sound systems and stables defined by different artists' styles. Artists come from different 'ghettos', mobilise themselves around distinct styles they create in their neighborhoods and showcase them in 'clashes' and 'fests', much like in the Jamaican version (Pereira 1998). This fosters rivalries, which in turn sometimes leads to violence, which sometimes erupts as fans boo rival artists off the stage. Fans who support a particular star also volunteer to spread the word about him/her, including playing his/her music in public transport. Often this also creates interest and discussion about the artist, his/her style and lyrics. Thus stables have coded chants recognised by fans. For example, *'maninja'* (ninjas, as portrayed in Hollywood movies) are associated with Winky D to refer to the nimbleness and ability to navigate difficult socio-economic challenges on the part of the artist and his adoring followers. Those whose toasts start with 'Check, check, check, revise your manners' are with Seh Calaz, who refers to himself, his friends and fans as *'mabhanditi'* (convicts or outlaws). Metaphorically, an outlaw persona points to someone with no regard for social norms and structure, suggesting that peers who are comfortable in their success have to deal with his achievements. In this sense, he tries to show that he is better than other established artists.

The subalternity of Zimbabwean youth music can be seen clearly in the challenges of distribution, poor sound quality and packaging (Scannell 2001), which make it very difficult to distribute the music internationally. While searching

---

4. 'Lady Squanda and Lady Bee Settle Score', *H-Metro*, 6 November 2013.

for the songs and albums discussed in this chapter, I went to a music shop in Mount Pleasant, an upmarket residential area in Harare. I chose the shop for its proximity to the university and on the assumption that it is an established outlet, which likely follows ethical business procedures. However, the music was not available. The shop attendants assured me they could source it. It took more than four weeks of their calling suppliers, to no avail. What I eventually got were CDs not too different from pirated copies sold on the streets.

The CDs have no date of production/release and the compilations look improvised. Some songs are not properly listed, but merely referred to as 'and many others'. Consequently, one identifies songs by listening, as opposed to going by the list. It seems the CD designers could not reduce the font to list all the songs on the CD or they did not think it was important. On one of the CDs some songs are repeated, for unexplained reasons. In addition, even listed songs are misspelt – thus Seh Calaz's 'Hatimisike' is listed as 'Hatipisike', which in translation could be impolite and self-debasing.[5] The recordings are of poor quality and some songs are inaudible.

There are no credits given for different aspects of the production. Possibly, it is assumed that those closely involved in/with the scene will know, as long as the stable or studio is mentioned. This points to a lack of concern for posterity or the fact that artists have no resources to hire professionals to handle the business side of their creations. The packaging points to concerns with volumes sold, rather than the legal niceties of ownership and royalties. The poor quality of recordings, poor packaging and mislabelling speaks of marginality, a lack of resources and the chronic challenges of piracy.

Organisation of the Zimdancehall scene

Zimdancehall has had the mixed blessing of having media support in the form of a radio programme with a private radio station, Star FM, and its affiliated tabloid newspaper, *H-Metro*.[6] Star FM has an evening show called Dancehall Overdrive, which showcases local talent. It also has phone-in shows so as to involve fans.

---

5. The Shona verb *kupisika* means to wipe oneself after using the toilet. It is not used in polite company. Thus this spelling mistake means 'we not wipe after using the toilet' and is therefore self-debasing, instead of the desired chest-thumping.
6. The newspaper and the radio station are owned by ZimPapers, a media group in which the government has a 49 per cent stake.

Some of the debates carry over to *H-Metro*, which also has a regular column on the dancehall scene. Many young artists desire to be featured positively in these media and so have to comply with demands for music of quality good enough for airplay. They cover events such as shows and awards and commentary against explicit lyrics and calls for artists to be responsible are conspicuous. However, calls to 'clean up' Zimdancehall belie the reality of structural violence in the ghetto because of pervasive degeneracy, in part as a result of poor service delivery and the challenges that budding recording artists face.

Fans are kept up to date about developments in the Zimdancehall scene, including fests and clashes mentioned above, through the media (radio and tabloid newspaper as well as social media). Events are held at affordable venues in high-density areas, usually sports stadiums or parks, such as Gwanzura Stadium in Highfields, Chitungwiza Aquatic Centre or Harare Gardens. Artists are allowed to have stalls to sell their music, but these compete with parasitic stalls selling pirated copies on street corners. Apparently, by selling directly, artists remove middlemen and pocket the profits themselves. However, tax authorities are riled by these arrangements. There are also controversies about who profits from ticket sales and beverages sold at such events. Popular artists perform abroad, following the Zimbabwe diaspora – in the United Kingdom, Australia and neighbouring South Africa and Botswana. However, many artists live from hand to mouth and get by on cash payments from live shows.

Zimdancehall circulates through informal networks dominated by unemployed 'ghetto yutes', such as street-corner stalls selling pirated versions; it is played in commuter minibuses, as well as on radio as a result of the 75 per cent local content electronic media policy (Mate 2012). Similar to youth music elsewhere in sub-Saharan Africa, Zimdancehall is created in proliferating studios of uneven sophistication. Some artists own the studios and the availability of digital technology has made these studios easier to establish. Informal distribution means that availability of music through formal distribution channels is challenged.

Discussion of 2014 nominated songs
The dancehall characteristics of the nominated songs are the chanting/vocalisation and *riddim* aesthetic, as defined by Peter Manuel and Wayne Marshall (2006). The fact that the songs use Shona lyrics places them in Zimbabwe. Beyond these elements, the songs do not have any of the characteristics of dancehall, such as celebrating the ghetto's bravery, survivalism and fabulousness or its post-feminist

ethic on the part of female artists (Noble 2008). Instead, when looking at the social song category, what we see in Tocky Vibes' 'Mhai' is a well-worn, if not limp, celebration of neo-patrilineal filial piety, in which sons take care of their mothers and celebrate mothers' selflessness. We hear a mother's plea 'Tocky, *pazvinenge zvanaka usandikanganwe*' (Tocky, when things become better [economically or when your economic fortunes improve] do not forget me). The lyrics argue that mothers are self-sacrificing through, for instance, carrying pregnancies to term and tirelessly defending their children where others find fault. Furthermore, mothers pray for their children's success in the face of intractable socio-economic challenges typical of the ghetto. What is not stated is that prayer is the only thing available to poor mothers with aspirations of a better life for their children. They have no resources to fund their children's aspirations; economic conditions are bleak. Tocky Vibes presents filial piety as inevitable because the opposite is unthinkable. This simplistic view excludes challenges the economy presents for filial piety – that is, how do young men who feel obliged to help their mothers do so when they are unemployed? Tocky Vibes' alter ego insists, '*Vasiri'vo ndingadai ndisipo*' (If it was not for her [my mother], I would not be here). Thus metaphorically and literally, without his mother, the artist would not exist. Not only does the song put the artist in the neo-patrilineal fold, its nomination serves as a reminder to all young people that filial piety is essential. It gives mothers permission to claim their dues because, whatever their circumstances, they have played a role in their children's success. The song neither challenges the status quo nor realistically appraises poor mothers' difficulties in supporting their sons' transitions to adulthood in the ghetto.

Under neo-liberal globalisation, receding state capacity means that parents have to make decisions and fund their children's navigation of hurdles in transitions to adulthood in the ghetto, under circumscribed economic conditions, including credentialism and chronic unemployment. Praying is presented as appropriate parental support under these circumstances. The implication for less successful artists and young people might be that their mothers have not prayed enough. This allows young people and elders not to confront economic and political impediments characteristic of life in the ghetto and how young men overcome these challenges. Take, for instance, reactions to Winky D (a leading Zimdancehall artist) whose lyrics celebrate the invincibility of young people who survive by hook or by crook, cheating and fighting others or in altered psychological states because of substance abuse, as well as artists who celebrate hedonism, such as all-night drinking and partying. They are dismissed as overly violent, anti-social and lacking in appropriate messages (Viriri, Viriri and Chapwanya 2011; Mate 2012). The reality is that there are many young people, prayerful or not, who are unable to fulfil their filial obligations because of the depth of poverty – a result of chronic unemployment, low wages or unpredictable returns of informal sector work and many who illicitly try to resolve their problems through substance abuse and hedonism.

Seh Calaz's 'Hatimisike' (We Are Unstoppable), nominated for 'best song of the year', is a chest-thumping song that hides behind Christian faith as the driving force behind personal bravado and achievements. God is mentioned as a power that is especially potent against rivals, the supernatural wind beneath Calaz's artistic wings. The more his rivals fight him and his mates, the more they succeed. He says his rivals do not know where he gets his stamina to endure challenges, saying, '*Simba raMwari usaridherere*' (Do not take for granted/take lightly God's power). Later in the chorus, the line changes to '*Mabhanditi musandidherere*' (Fellow outlaws, do not take me for granted) because of God's intervention.

Maskiri, another artist, was criticised for singing about God using colloquial Shona, referring to God as '*Dhara rangu*' (Viriri, Viriri and Chapwanya 2011), which can be interpreted as 'My patron',[7] a benevolent older person, who listens and responds favourably, regardless of circumstances. He was criticised for using unrefined and subversive language to refer to God as a benevolent being and the song was barred (by public demand) from airplay. In fact, many Christians have adapted indigenous praise names for African deities, including some that are borrowed from ancestral worship and now customised for Christian worship. In the song 'Simudza Maoko' (Raise up Your Hands) Seh Calaz calls on fellow partygoers to raise their arms if God has been good to them. He asks them to jump up in joy and praise God, saying, '*Handirarame neraki*' (It is not by chance that I am where I am, meaning that God is responsible for his success).

The nominated songs show adult influences and keenness to uphold a version of 'clean lyrics'. The dominant view seems to be that colloquial language of the youth may not be used for Christian praise, as it dilutes, pollutes or undermines Christian subjectivities. As more and more Zimbabweans turn to Christianity, especially Pentecostal variants, in the face of pressing economic problems,

---

7. My understanding is that when young people say '*dhara rangu*' in everyday speech it refers to someone they have good rapport with, who is sympathetic and responds favourably to them.

musicians – including youth artists – attribute their success to God's miraculous ways. Testimonials stated in languages stereotyped as subversive are disavowed as antithetical to Christianity while those stated in conventional language, such as this 'Simudza Maoko' by Seh Calaz are embraced. This unevenness speaks to biases that divide the genre and point to power inequalities between artists and those who judge the music. Artists who seek success have no choice but to comply.

In Seh Calaz's 'Kwatinobva' (Where We Come From), we see toned-down chest-thumping, celebrating endurance and persistence on the part of artists seeking recognition. Seh Calaz repeatedly refers to opportunities to perform in the United Kingdom and his preparedness for this higher level of recognition. He boasts about fellow outlaws, '*mabhanditi*', in the form of fans and promoters, paying for his airfare to perform abroad. Air travel abroad signposts achievement as it is ordinarily out of reach for ghetto youths. There is a lot of boastfulness and one-upmanship – for example, Seh Calaz's 2015 album titled *Check, Check, Check*. The chest-thumping songs include thinly veiled slights against fellow artists who have criticised 'ghetto yutes' as scruffy and lacking street smarts. For example, a rap or hip-hop artist attempted suicide after he made public comments to the effect that ghetto youths were dirty and unsophisticated, saying, '*Maghetto yutes hamugeze*'.[8] The artist's comments riled his mates who subsequently criticised and it seems also isolated him. Seh Calaz hits back in a broadside against this trope with 'Sauro' or 'Saul' in English (a fictional name), whom he warns that he should be careful because there is no let-up on the challenge and struggle to be successful:

Ndamuona anotemba nemaninja
Vanogeza tisu mabhanditi.
I can see that he counts on his ninjas
We are smarter than you are.

Conclusion: Subalternity or youth activism?

If the Jamaican dancehall scene is a critique of colonial power structures, gerontocracy and Eurocentric definitions of respectability, which the Jamaican middle class has adopted (Noble 2008: 109), in Zimbabwe this is either lost in translation or too sensitive to deal with and middle-class sensibilities hijack

---

8. 'Carlos Green Attempts Suicide', *H-Metro*, 24 October 2014.

the genre. Not only have Zimbabwean elites imposed standards by calling for a 'clean image' and lyrics, they also sponsor and preside over awards to outstanding (read compliant) artists. Similarly, whereas Jamaican dancehall is about ghetto subjectivities (Noble 2008), these subjectivities are stifled in the Zimbabwean variant. It seems the anti-euphemisms of Jamaican dancehall are unsettling for Zimbabwean elites. Furthermore, the poverty of ghetto youths is such that they have neither access nor control over the means to publicity, such as radio, television and newspapers. Zimbabwean artists acquiesce to elite demands in order to get airplay and recognition, thereby colluding with the erasure of possibilities to publicise ghetto subjectivities. The complaints about violence, such as those raised against Winky D (Mate 2014; Viriri, Viriri and Chapwanya 2011) belie the fact that interpersonal violence is often used to settle scores, to avenge slights and to prove masculinity in low-income areas. Likewise, the ghetto feminism of Jamaican dancehall challenges ideal femininities, which in Zimbabwean contexts are increasingly shaped by Pentecostal Pauline doctrines (Mate 2002). Female artists cannot talk back to men and patriarchal culture without being criticised as deviant and fallen women.

In addition, what we see in Zimdancehall is a concerted effort to smuggle God into the dancehall, into spaces of enjoyment and defiance, thereby neutering the politics of the music based on defiance and invincibility, and its performance and origins in poverty. When God is introduced in places of enjoyment, He is celebrated for making the fun possible, without acknowledging the type of fun as an antidote to poverty. The impression we get is that for ghetto youths, prayer and faith can improve their lives. This impedes critical engagement with the prevailing socio-economic and political conditions, which perpetuate poverty. It is convenient for elites. Middle-class sensibilities, which are patriarchal, neo-patrilineal and homophobic, have infiltrated and dictated Zimbabwean dancehall music. For example, homophobic references go unchallenged in the media and elsewhere. Seh Calaz's alter ego says in one of his songs *'handitukane nengochane'* (I do not have arguments with/answer back to gays), suggesting arrogantly that he has no time for his gay peers. This is in the face of rumours that some of Zimdancehall artists secretly engage in same-sex relationships. These coded silences need to be unpacked.

Although Zimdancehall is political in as far as it has attracted the interest of elites, media debate and commentary, the politics of its current performance are to consolidate the marginalisation of poor youth's subjectivities because youths cannot use the music as a platform to talk about the underbelly of their existence in low-income neighbourhoods. Elites have erased bits of the genre that are not politically conducive to the realities they seek to perpetuate. This speaks to prevailing conditions in Zimbabwe, where ordinary people cannot speak truth to power. Thus one can conclude that Zimdancehall perpetuates subalternity, rather than youth activism.

Postscript: The Zimdancehall Awards continue, with a fourth ceremony held in 2017. The awards now have over 30 categories, with fans actively voting for their favourites through social media and entertainment news websites. The category 'social message' still exists, while other categories are concerned with other aspects of the music scene, such as fashion – 'best dressed' male or female artist, best MCs, new talent, videos, producers and so on.[9]

References

Attwood, F. 2006. 'Sexed up: Theorising the Sexualisation of Culture'. *Sexualities* 9(1): 77–94.
Bauman, Z. 2004. *Wasted Lives: Modernity and Its Outcasts*. Cambridge: Polity Press.
Bennett, A. 2004. 'Consolidating the Music Scenes Perspective'. *Poetics* 32: 223–34.
Biaya, T.K. 2005. 'Youth and Street Culture in Urban Africa: Addis Ababa, Dakar and Kinshasa'. In *Makers and Breakers: Children and Youth in Postcolonial Africa*, edited by A. Honwana and F. de Boeck, 215–28. London: James Currey.
Carrier, N. 2005. '"*Miraa* Is Cool": The Cultural Importance of *Miraa (Khat)* for Tigania and Igembe Youth in Kenya'. *Journal of African Cultural Studies* 17(2): 201–18.
Chikowero, M. 2008. '"Our People Father, They Haven't Learned Yet": Music and Postcolonial Identities in Zimbabwe'. *Journal of Southern African Studies* 34(1): 145–60.
Cooper, C. 1993. *Noises in the Blood: Orality, Gender and the 'Vulgar' Body of Jamaican Popular Culture*. New York: Macmillan.
———. 1998. 'Ragamuffin Sounds: Crossing over from Reggae to Rap and Back'. *Caribbean Quarterly* 44(1–2): 153–68.
Coronil, F. 1994. 'Listening to the Subaltern: The Poetics of Neocolonial States'. *Poetics Today* 15(4): 643–58.
Eyre, B. 2005. *Playing with Fire: Fear and Self-censorship in Zimbabwean Music*. Copenhagen: Freemuse.
Fredericks, R. 2014. '"The Old Man Is Dead": Hip-Hop and the Arts of Citizenship of Senegalese Youth'. *Antipode* 46(1): 130–48.
Green, M.E. and P. Ives. 2009. 'Subalternity and Language: Overcoming the Fragmentation of Common Sense'. *Historical Materialism* 17(1): 3–30.

---

9. See, for example, http://www.thezimtainment.co.zw/zimdancehall-awards-winners-list/.

Gueye, M. 2013. 'Urban Guerrilla Poetry: The Movement *Y'en Marre* and the Socio-political Influence of Hip Hop in Senegal'. *Journal of Pan African Studies* 6(3): 21–42.

Honwana, A. 2012. *The Time of Youth: Work, Social Change and Politics in Africa*. Sterling, VA: Kumarian Press.

Jones, J.L. 2010. '"Nothing Is Straight in Zimbabwe": The Rise of the *Kukiya-Kiya* Economy 2000–2008'. *Journal of Southern African Studies* 36(2): 285–99.

Kellerer, K. 2013. '"Chant down the System 'till Babylon Falls": The Political Dimensions of Underground Hip-Hop and Urban Grooves in Zimbabwe'. *Journal of Pan African Studies* 6(3): 43–64.

Konate, Y. 2002. 'Generation Zouglou (Zouglou Generation)'. *Cahiers d'Études Africaines* 42(168): 777–96.

Mackie, E. 2005. 'Welcome the Outlaw: Pirates, Maroons and the Caribbean Countercultures'. *Cultural Critique* 59: 24–62.

Maggio, J. 2007. '"Can the Subaltern Be Heard?" Political Theory, Translation, Representation and Gayatri Chakravorty Spivak'. *Alternatives: Global, Local and Political* 32(4): 419–43.

Mains, D. 2007. 'Neoliberal Times: Progress, Boredom and Shame among Young Men in Urban Ethiopia'. *American Ethnologist* 34(4): 659–73.

Manase, I. 2011. 'The Aesthetics of Winky D's Zimbabwe Urban Grooves Music and an Overview of His Social Commentary on the Post-2000 Experiences in Harare and Other Urban Centres'. *Muziki* 8(2): 81–95.

Manuel, P. and W. Marshall. 2006. 'The *Riddim* Method: Aesthetics, Practice, and Ownership in Jamaican Dancehall'. *Popular Music* 25(3): 447–70.

Mate, R. 2002. 'Wombs as God's Laboratories: Pentecostal Discourses of Femininity in Zimbabwe'. *Africa* 72(4): 549–68.

———. 2012. 'Youth Lyrics, Street Language and the Politics of Age: Contextualising the Youth Question in the Third Chimurenga in Zimbabwe'. *Journal of Southern African Studies* 38(1): 107–27.

———. 2014. 'Encountering *Rokesheni* Masculinities: Music and Lyrics in Informal Urban Public Transport Vehicles in Zimbabwe'. In *The Acoustic City*, edited by M. Gandy and B.J. Nilsen, 114–23. Berlin: Jovis.

Miller-Young, M. 2008. 'Hip-Hop Honeys and da Hustlaz: Black Sexualities in the New Hip-Hop Pornography'. *Meridians* 8(1): 261–92.

Noble, D. 2008. 'Postcolonial Criticism, Transnational Identifications and the Hegemonies of Dancehall's Academic and Popular Performativities'. *Feminist Review* 90: 106–27.

Nyairo, J. and J. Ogude. 2005. 'Popular Music, Popular Politics: *Unbwogable* and Idioms of Freedom in Kenyan Popular Music'. *African Affairs* 104(415): 225–49.

Pereira, J. 1998. 'Babylon to Vatican: Religion in the Dancehall'. *Journal of West Indian Literature* 8(1): 31–40.

Perullo, A. 2005. 'Hooligans and Heroes: Youth Identity and Hip-Hop in Dar es Salaam, Tanzania'. *Africa Today* 51(4): 75–101.

Prince, R. 2006. 'Popular Music and Luo Youth in Western Kenya: Ambiguities of Modernity, Morality and Gender Relations in the Era of AIDS'. In *Navigating Youth and Generating Adulthood*, edited by C. Christiansen, M. Utas and H.E. Vigh, 117–52. Uppsala: Nordiska.

Scannell, P. 2001. 'Music, Radio and the Record Business in Zimbabwe Today'. *Popular Music* 20(1): 13–27.

Smith, K. 2010. 'Gramsci at the Margins: Subjectivity and Subalternity in a Theory of Hegemony'. *International Gramsci Journal* 2: 39–50.

Stanley Niaah, S. 2005. '"Dis Slackness Ting": A Dichotomising Master Narrative in Jamaican Dancehall. *Caribbean Quarterly* 51(3–4): 55–76.

———. 2008. 'A Common Space: Dancehall, *Kwaito* and the Mapping of New World Music and Performance'. *The World of Music* 50(2): 35–50.

Steingo, G. 2005. 'South African Music after Apartheid: *Kwaito*, the "Party Politic" and the Appropriation of Gold as a Sign of Success'. *Popular Music and Society* 28(3): 333–57.

Viriri, A., A. Viriri and C. Chapwanya. 2011. 'The Influence of Popular Music, in Particular Urban Grooves Lyrics, on the Zimbabwean Youth: The Case of the Troika, Maskiri, Winky D and Extra Large'. *Muziki* 8(1): 82–95.

White, B. 2014. 'Singing Praises of Power'. In *The Acoustic City*, edited by M. Gandy and B.J. Nilsen, 131–5. Berlin: Jovis.

Youde, J. 2010. '"Don't Drink the Water": Politics and Cholera in Zimbabwe'. *International Journal* 65(3): 687–704.

Zilberg, J. 1994. 'Yes, It's True: Zimbabweans Love Dolly Parton'. *Journal of Popular Culture* 29(1): 111–25.

CHAPTER 12

Performing Manhood in Zimdancehall
Music as Patriarchised Space in Zimbabwe

Manase Kudzai Chiweshe and Sandra Bhatasara

The growth of Zimdancehall provides an important medium to understand the social significance of this art form in terms of youth identities in Zimbabwe. The genesis of the genre has opened up a space for the celebration and acting out of marginalised identities. Our concern with masculinities in this chapter seeks to go beyond the moralising critiques of Zimdancehall as a vulgar, violent and sexual art form. Our endeavour is not to act as a moral police, but rather to place the genre within a specific social context. Despite the acknowledgement of the significance of this growing popular cultural space, prominent attention to Zimdancehall is mostly limited to journalistic comments. Broadly speaking, scholarly inquiry into dancehall performance, practice and culture has been sparse in the disciplines of sociology and anthropology. In this chapter we focus on how Zimdancehall has emerged as a patriarchalised space, in which performing and proving one's manhood is an important part of the music. To this end, the chapter begins with a brief outline of the historical development of Zimdancehall as a distinct music genre in Zimbabwe.

Popular art forms often act as spaces in which specific identities are performed, contested and valorised. In this chapter we use music to highlight how lyrics, chants, behaviours and actions in the genre of Zimdancehall embody a particular practice of manhood steeped in patriarchal beliefs of male dominance. We focus on purposively sampled songs, videos, chants, behaviours and acts to highlight how artists are performing and valorising patriarchy, women's inferiority and male dominance. Over the past four years, Zimdancehall has emerged as the most popular music form in urban Zimbabwe, especially among the poor. This chapter outlines the evolution of this genre, which has roots in Jamaican reggae and raga music and shows how songs and catchphrases highlight how this music celebrates and valorises certain hegemonic masculinities. Our work views music as an important communicator and transmitter of social values. Young men and women from mainly poor urban households in Harare and other major cities have turned to music as a source of livelihood, as unemployment and underemployment remain high in Zimbabwe. Zimdancehall has emerged as a space to speak to everyday experiences of these young people. These experiences include ways of acting that can provide an understanding of the social context in which the music is created.

Evolution of Zimdancehall in Zimbabwe

The evolution of Zimdancehall in Zimbabwe is contested. The pioneers of the genre are numerous and often the stated origins depend on who is making the argument. It is therefore rather a problematic task to provide an accurate historical analysis of this music genre. We depend on various discussions online and elsewhere by singers, fans and a number of other stakeholders to highlight the diverse versions of the origins of Zimdancehall. What is not disputable, however, in all these debates and discussions is that Zimdancehall is based on Jamaican reggae and raga music. Bob Marley's performance at the celebration of Zimbabwe's independence in 1980 is seen as the birth of the country's love affair with reggae music. Over the years Zimbabwe has hosted many other Jamaican musicians, including Shabba Ranks whose songs and performances provide a significant touchstone for the macho nature of dancehall music. As with Jamaican dancehall music, Zimdancehall has emerged as a transmitter of the feelings, hopes and dreams of disenfranchised groups. Agostinho Pinnock (2007) argues that reggae music is an important tool for marginalised groups to celebrate and affirm their identities. For young people living under harsh economic conditions in Zimbabwe, where formal unemployment is over 80 per cent, Zimdancehall has provided a way of telling their stories while earning a livelihood.

Kumbie Shonhiwa (2015) argues that after Marley's performance and subsequent visits by other stars, including Sizzla and Cappleton, reggae grew in Zimbabwe, which also witnessed a growth in the 1990s of local artists, such as Major E, Booker T, Potato and Yappie Banton, with their own brand of mimicking Jamaican artists. In this era there were also recording artists, including Wappy. Other sources, however, trace the genre's origins to the 1980s when there was an emergence of local sound systems, such as A1 Sound and Startime, which exposed mic chanters such as Culture T, Allan Ranks and Dudz.[1] There was marginal

---

1. https://en.wikipedia.org/wiki/Zimdancehall.

success for most of these artists, as they remained outside the mainstream, with the exception of a few, especially Major E and Malvern S, and collaborations with Innocent Utsiwegota providing the hit song 'In My Dreams'. The vast majority of the artists did not gain any commercial success because recording companies did not see the commercial appeal of artists branded as Jamaican copycats. There were various attempts to record and sell music by many of the artists, with little success, except for Transit Crew whose success was mainly international. However, there were many bands at home that played reggae music regularly, such as Trevor Hall's Crucial Mix and Black Roots. It is also important to note the contribution of sound systems such as Stereo One, Judgement Yard; clubs such as Rumors, lately Red Fox, and individuals such as Templeman, Jackie Bango and Gary B. The genre developed a small but loyal fan base that kept it going through hard times, ensuring that it never died. What is critical to note even at these formative stages is the male-dominated nature of the genre.

Zimdancehall has recently overshadowed urban grooves as the most popular music among youths. Yet, in essence, it was the emergence of urban grooves that carved a niche and paved the way for Zimdancehall. The growth of independent studios and recording companies after 2000 opened the way for a new crop of urban chanters, most notably Donald Chirisa (Sniper Storm) on the Chigutiro compilation. Depending on whom you ask, it was Sniper Storm's 2004 album that changed the way dancehall music was received in Zimbabwe. The album, *Ndakabata Mic*, showed that the key to mass appeal for dancehall and reggae music was to sing in a vernacular language and to mimic Jamaican accents and language. While there were many other artists working hard in the background, it was at this juncture that people began to take note of dancehall and this popularity was cemented as artists such as Winky D, King Labash, Freeman and Shinsoman began to emerge and record popular songs, which gained constant rotation on local radio stations.

The name 'Zimdancehall' can be traced to 2006 when Slaggy Yout, a Zimbabwean artist based in the United Kingdom, created a website called Zimdancehall to promote upcoming artists who were not receiving any airplay or being booked for shows.[2] Anecdotal evidence provides counter-narratives for the naming of the genre, with various people claiming the accolade. What is important,

---

2. https://en.wikipedia.org/wiki/Zimdancehall.

however, is that, in Harare the emergence of backyard studios has seen a growing number of artists' studios, such as Chillspot in Matapi Flats, Mbare, which have provided hit songs and *riddims* (a beat or tune where a number of artists sing different songs). This has also seen the rise of new stars, including Soul Jah Love, Seh Calaz, Lady Squanda, Kinnah and Killer T. The artists have become household names and are now performing regularly across the country. There are now also annual awards focusing on Zimdancehall. Commercial success has been steadily increasing, with most artists touring South Africa, England and Australia. This brief history, while not detailed, provides important insight into how the genre of Zimdancehall has evolved into an important part of Zimbabwe's music landscape, reaching almost half of airplay on radio.

Music as a patriarchal form in Zimbabwe
Historically music has been a medium for human social expression, which can take many forms, from triumph and hope to utter frustration and despair (Adams and Fuller 2007). Music is not merely for leisure or entertainment, but a site in which fundamental aspects of social formation are confronted and negotiated. If there is one thing we can say with conviction it is that one of the fundamental aspects of social formation is patriarchy. Music plays an important role in patriarchal signification and representation. The significance of patriarchy can be seen in the construction of the popular music history: the perceived masculine or feminine nature of particular genres/styles, audiences, fandom, record collecting, the occupation of various roles within the music industry, youth subcultures and gender stereotyping in song lyrics and music videos (Shuker 2005).

In a global context, Thomas Maxwell Shore (2009) is of the view that the Rolling Stones songs 'Under My Thumb' (1966) and 'Yesterdays Papers' (1967) exhibit an identity of women as subservient preachers of domesticated suburbia. In misogynistic rap music, African American women are generally presented as money-hungry, scandalous, manipulating and demanding. In such circumstances, rap music serves as an ideological support mechanism that legitimises the mistreatment and degradation of women (Adams and Fuller 2007). Hence, gender hierarchies inherent in Western patriarchal societies manifest in music. However, some scholars depart from the male-domination perspective that has been used to read popular music, referencing other versions of femininities present. For instance, female artists such as Madonna or Britney Spears are portrayed as independent, sexualised, bold and ambitious women.

However, the patriarchal view is clearly dominant in both the West and elsewhere. In China and Taiwan, men are projected as energetic, hard-hearted, considerate, tolerant and free like the wind, while women are portrayed as emotional, meek, illogical, frail and dependent on men, childish, agreeable, yielding, passive victims to men's caprice and pretty (Moskowitz 2009). In the Dominican Republic, Pedro Antonio Valdez (1999) drew a connection in Bachata music between the emotionalism of the male characters and the physical and psychological violence carried out against the females. Similarly, in Jamaica, the construction of sexuality in some dancehall lyrics effaces women as social, political and sexual beings, producing a masculinised narrative of unified national identity (Saunders 2003). This is echoed by Jarret Brown (1999), who notes that the way some male artists in the dancehall community in Jamaica describe the female body, sex and other categories of men and the way some female artists respond to this description or even describe themselves, can be seen as a direct result of the patriarchal views that pervade the society. To illustrate this, he observes that Buju Banton's song 'Gal fi Beg' 'seems to be the anthem for manhood, portrays unmistakable violence and relegates the female identity to the category of sub-human' (Brown 1999: 7–8).

Various studies in Africa also regard music as implicated in the production and reproduction of patriarchal practices and hierarchies. Consistent with international trends, popular music has been severely criticised. For instance, in Cameroon, similar to some countries in West Africa, Divine Fuh (2011) detected that popular songs promote the phallus, defile femininity, disparage women as objects of contemplation, portray patriarchy and yet also reveal men in crisis. In South Africa during the migrant labour system in the 1940s and 1950s, there was a masculinisation of popular music performance buttressed by the state apparatus, which put men into positions of complete dominance (Ballantine 2000). Similarly, Malawian popular music is conceived as male dominated, with class and gender dynamics serving to reproduce dominant gendered power relations between male and female performers and fans (Gilman and Fenn 2006). Likewise, Evan Mwangi (2004) confirmed that East African hip-hop is haunted by notions of hegemonic masculinity.

Thematically, music in Zimbabwe focuses on a range of issues, such as the economy, politics, society and religion. Singers articulate social norms relating to marriage, relationships, love and death. Music in Zimbabwe is diverse, ranging from traditional and gospel to *chimurenga* and popular music. Although traditional music involves practices and cults that are patriarchal (Bourdillon 1987), some argue that women occupy central positions (Chitando 2002). In our view, one aspect that is often embedded in Zimbabwean popular music is misogyny. Misogyny is the promotion, glamorisation, support, humorisation, justification or normalisation of oppressive ideas about women (Adams and Fuller 2007). Misogyny has its roots in patriarchy. The notion of patriarchy is not purely in the sense of family lineage being traced through the father, but in the sense of domination and rule by men. This domination involves the domination of women, but also of men by other men. In this regard, patriarchy is entrenched in most Zimbabwean cultures. Although women can still play important roles within these patriarchal cultures, overall men are idolised whereas women are minimised (Chitando and Mateveke 2012). Patriarchy looms large because it acts as a metanarrative that interacts iteratively with micronarratives, social milieus and lived experience (Brown 1999).

Misogyny, as reflected in most genres of Zimbabwean music, often casts women as inferior, helpless, vain and unfaithful: 'The key stereotypical images produced and dispersed through songs by male singers are those that present women as hopeless victims of social circumstances, dangerous and loose' (Vambe 2000: 82). It is evident that most songs by male artists in Zimbabwe reveal a deep concern for society's need to control female sexuality. In one popular music genre called *sungura*, women are posed and marketed as uncultured prostitutes and sex objects while their male counterparts are depicted with decency (Machingura and Machingura 2011).[3] Pertaining to another genre that has been popularised by male urban youth, urban grooves, the frequent articulation of gender stereotypes is horrifying. The reproduction of the dominant patriarchal power relations has also been inexorable (Keche and Manatsa 2015). Tendai Chari (2009) is of the view that sex, simulated sex, sexual dancing, coarse humour and obscenities are the main features of urban grooves music. Soft violence, which is verbal, is what ordinarily characterises the music of singers such as Stunner and Nasty Trix, where they reveal beauty in pejorative imagery (Chari 2009). At the same time, music not only celebrates, but also institutionalises and solidifies hegemonic masculinities in Zimbabwe. Urban grooves artists deploy a normative standard against which other men position themselves. This is based on the belief of male superiority,

---

3. *Sungura* is a common name for a Zimbabwean style of popular music that draws heavily on Congolese rumba. The music uses instruments that include drums, guitars and keyboard (Machingura and Machingura 2011).

heterosexuality and multiple sexual partners, among other things (Chiweshe and Bhatasara 2013). Other forms of sexualities are subordinated to this superior manliness.

The music industry in Zimbabwe has also been masculinised. The masculine-dominated nature of the music industry is also notorious in that it has created masculine genres. Francis Machingura and Jesca Mushoperi Machingura (2011) observe that men have crowned themselves kings of *sungura* and queens seem unwelcome. They argue that the media has generated a gendered space that women have yet to break into. Women who venture into the performing arts in Zimbabwe face serious censure from patriarchy and those it has conscripted into its version of reality, including fellow women (Chitando and Mateveke 2012). Various factors converge to explain why women are excluded. For instance, the construction of respectable womanhood and the cultural stereotypes associated with popular music also restrict women. Shona people generally perceive sexually appealing dances, as in most *sungura* performances, as taboo or appalling (Mashiri, Mawomo and Tom 2002) and are of the opinion that respectable women ought to shun those dances. Gender stereotypes regarding the roles of women also confine women to the private sphere and limit their choices with regard to respectable and non-respectable work. Because of the prevailing patriarchy, public space, especially in urban contexts, is constructed in masculine terms (Chitando and Mateveke 2012). This is alienating for women, in that it confines them to the domestic sphere, thereby imposing their subservience to men (Keche and Manatsa 2015).

However, women's agency is evident in how they navigate and reconfigure patriarchal spaces: 'Patriarchy is a dynamic system constantly reproduced and re-constituted through gender relations under changing conditions, including resistance by subordinate groups' (Carrigan, Connell and Lee 1985: 598). Kerstin Bolzt (2007) confirms this view in her study of the status of women's creativity in various media in precolonial, colonial and postcolonial Zimbabwe. In terms of music specifically, over the years, there has been an increase in women singers performing in the sacred or respectable spaces of gospel music. Undoubtedly, gospel music has opened spaces for women to be accepted as singers, to enjoy a good image and to talk about some of the broader challenges affecting women. Nonetheless, whereas this is uncritically conceived as progressive, only a few scholars have realised that gospel music has its own problematic ideological element of conservative Christianity. Articulating the connections between Christianity and patriarchy, Ezra Chitando and Pauline Mateveke (2012) argue that since patriarchy remains dominant in the religious sphere, women have had to contend with its deleterious effects. Chitando (2002) draws attention to how gospel singers still have their morals questioned by patriarchal puritans.

Apart from gospel music, women also confront patriarchy in *mbira* music. Singers such as Stella Chiweshe (and her daughter Virginia Mkwesha), Busi Ncube, Hope Masike and Chiwoneso Maraire, although not feminists, have mounted major challenges to patriarchal practices and attitudes. Female singers have also challenged these practices by venturing into *sungura* and urban grooves music. Importantly, David Kerr (2009) draws attention to the numerous Zimbabwean male artists who have supported female struggles with patriarchy, such as Cde Chinx and Oliver Mtukudzi. Early pioneers of urban grooves music such as David Chifunyise also supported women's concerns in the context of HIV and AIDS. Mtukudzi directly attacked patriarchy (or rather, drunken patriarchies) in his song 'Tozeza Baba' (We Are Scared of Father) in which he sings about male violence against women.

It is within this broader patriarchal context that contemporary Zimdancehall music has proliferated. Despite this genre gaining momentum, it has not yet attracted sociological and anthropological inquiry and from the very few sources – at least the ones we managed to locate – concrete conclusions cannot be drawn. The role of male artists and the construction (and redefinition) of masculinities (in ways that incorporate myriad themes that engender multiple dialectics of meanings) in the patriarchal space of Zimdancehall have not received significant critical attention. At a very general level, it seems Zimdancehall has not broken from the misogynistic inclinations created and perpetuated by other genres. It has also been linked to the reproduction of male hegemony and celebration of tough masculinities. Irikidzai Manase (2011), in his study of Zimdancehall singer Winky D, points out that the song 'Vanhu Vakuru' (Big People) expresses Winky D's survivalist identity by bragging that he is the most wicked man in town, a big fighter and a man of high class who is loved by all beautiful girls. Winky D venerates violence, tough masculinity and associated 'heroic' qualities. This resonates with remarks in *Panorama* magazine:

> These young dancehall artistes are unapologetic about their drunkenness, sex tapes and pornography. Their negative role modelling has seen many disrespect women as was the case at one time with hip-hop where the lyrics were powered by an abundance of expletives and has potential to destroy

the positive energy that is often associated with the foundation of dancehall music, notably Rasta, Reggae and Resistance.[4]

A possible method to analyse masculinity in Zimdancehall

Our analysis in this chapter is qualitative in nature, focusing on the the dances, dress, lyrics and spaces of Zimdancehall music artists to understand how these are implicated in the construction, reconstruction and negotiation of masculine identities in a context where they are denied real access to resources and power in the formal structures of society. Most of the studies on Zimbabwean music pay most attention to song lyrics. Therefore, what we seek to do in this chapter is to expose some of the missing nuances that stay buried when we focus our attention merely on lyrics and not the everyday or the every-night practices of its participants. According to Sonjah Stanley Niaah (2004), the dance arena (and the associated spaces and adornments of dancehall artists) has been grossly underexplored, yet it can yield important insights into how disenfranchised citizens create spaces of celebration, renewal and transgression. We have focused on purposively sampled popular songs and videos of the Zimdancehall genre released in the last five years. This includes songs played on radio and also those deemed to be inappropriate for radio, but very popular on the streets. The purposive sampling technique is the deliberate choice of respondents or cases because of the qualities they possess. Hence, we selected songs and videos based on the idea that they could best allow us to advance our argument.

The focus of this chapter is on understanding the songs and videos, their meanings and the context in which they are produced, so we used a critical qualitative analysis technique. We conducted qualitative content analysis and critical discourse analysis. Researchers regard content analysis as a flexible method for analysing text data (Cavanagh 1997). The specific content analysis approach chosen by a researcher varies with the theoretical and substantive interests of the researcher and the problem being studied (Weber 1990). Content analysis allows researchers to scrutinise large volumes of data in a systematic fashion and with relative ease. We applied conventional content analysis by sifting through the content of various songs, identifying the lyrics, the melodic phrases and language

---

4. http://www.panorama.co.zw/index.php/archives/119-perspective/792-revisiting-zimdancehall.

used. We also examined videos to identify the dances, dress and adornments of the artists and the audiences and the venues as spaces in which dancehall music is performed. We then applied critical discourse analysis to establish the meanings, representations and gender nuances in the entire context analysed.

As described by Norman Fairclough (2002), critical discourse analysis focuses on body language, utterances, symbols, visual images and other forms of semiosis (signs and symbols) as means of discourse. Given the power of the written and spoken word, Allan Luke (1997) contends, critical discourse analysis is necessary for describing, interpreting, analysing and critiquing social life reflected in texts. Likewise, Nancy Naples (2003: 106) espouses a feminist approach to critical discourse analysis and alludes to the idea that 'the approach involves looking at structural patterns of domination to render visible those issues about women that are underrepresented'. Critical discourse analysis is concerned with studying and analysing written texts and spoken words to reveal the discursive sources of power, dominance, inequality and bias and how these sources are produced, maintained, reproduced and transformed within specific social, economic, political and historical contexts (Van Dijk 1993). In other words, the text becomes more than just words on a page; it divulges how those words are used in a particular social context (Huckin 1997). Jan Blommaert and Chris Bulcaen (2000) state that discourse is socially constitutive, as well as socially conditioned. 'The purpose of critical discourse analysis is to analyse opaque as well as transparent structural relationships of dominance, discrimination, power and control as manifested in language' (Wodak 1995: 204).

Findings and discussion
Zimdancehall as a male-dominated space
Zimdancehall is a space dominated by men it terms of the artists, fans who attend shows and promoters. While the Jamaican dancehall scene has some female artists, it is also male dominated and Zimbabwe's interaction with reggae has largely been through male vocalists. This is reflected in Zimdancehall, as women have largely remained on the periphery, with a few exceptions. Manase Kudzai Chiweshe and Sandra Bhatasara (2013) cite King Shady's chant 'Ndezve Varume Izvi' (This Is for Men) to highlight the masculine nature of urban music in Zimbabwe. Consistently, Zimdancehall reflects the patriarchal nature of Zimbabwean society, in which men dominate the public life. The majority of people attending Zimdancehall concerts are male youths, mainly because of the violence associated with the shows. Women

often face harassment from rowdy and drunken men, which limits the number of people the music genre can appeal to in terms of live shows. The marking of this space as masculine is also portrayed in the lyrics, performances and actions of the singers, both male and female. Zimdancehall is portrayed as a warzone with generals, ninjas, presidents and soldiers. Linked to this is that the predominantly male actors in this music genre bear unmistakable traces of the economic, social and political transformations in Zimbabwe as a whole. It is within this framework that we understand how manhood is valorised and celebrated and, sometimes, negotiated.

Performing manhood: Lyrics, names, chants and performance

In this section we note five ways in which manhood is performed and valorised in Zimdancehall. As argued by Mwangi (2004), patriarchal masculinity is arbitrary and assumptive, such that it has to be constantly performed to retain its hegemonic hold on both men and women. Therefore, we explicate how this occurs in Zimdancehall by discussing hyper-heterosexuality and homophobia, misogyny and hegemonic masculinities. Firstly we discuss how hegemonic masculinities are contained in the struggle for dominance and self-naming among male artists. In this regard, hegemonic masculinity ceases to be merely about patriarchal domination by men over women, as originally conceived by R.W. Connell (1995). Some male artists use masculine nicknames to highlight their dominance over other males and to highlight attributes of a desired form of masculinity, including dominance, power and authority. Most names are borrowed from everyday usage where they also carry patriarchal overtones of authority and domination. Soul Jah Love calls himself 'Chibaba' (The Father). *Baba* in Shona culture is the head of the family, traditionally the breadwinner and decision-maker. Such names highlight how the need to perform tasks accompanying manhood is an important part of Zimdancehall. Killer T calls himself 'The Chairman'; Winky D is 'Big Man', while Sniper calls himself 'Soldier'. These names highlight how manhood has to be reflected in the names artists give themselves. What is striking is that Killer T, Winky D and Sniper are already their performance names and both these names and the second names given above are expressive of a macho masculinity, so the double naming is a performance of hyper-masculinity. Hegemonic masculinities are also played out in the hyper-sexual nature of the songs and lyrics. This confirms dancehall's fundamental preoccupation with sex and sexuality detected by Pinnock (2007) and Stanley Niaah (2005).

As a genre, Zimdancehall encompasses multiple messages that speak mainly to the everyday experiences of young people, including poverty, HIV, unemployment, wishes for a good life, dance songs, love, hate, conflict and religion. There is, however, another theme of the music that celebrates and venerates sexual prowess. These songs explicitly promote masculinity as being irretrievably linked to sexuality. Sexual prowess laced into the lyrics is part of playing man and provides evidence of masculine credentials. Being sexually active with multiple partners is part of this culture that mainly portrays and views women as objects of male sexual power and satisfaction. This way, artists ritualise, through music, sexuality as a discourse of power in society. The explicit content of Zimdancehall songs may be interpreted as 'slackness' (regarding sex and women as important ingredients in masculine performance), a master narrative in Jamaican dancehall (Stanley Niaah 2005; Brown 1999; Cooper 1994). Guspy Warrior's song 'Seunononga' (Like You Are Bending) became a national hit, despite its sexually loaded message. Platinum Prince's 'Bhendakunge Banana' (Bend Like a Banana) and Ricky Fire's 'Ndiratidze Zvaunoita' (Show Me What You Can Do) are sexually loaded songs with provocative videos featuring popular adult dancers/strippers Zoe and Bev respectively. Soul Jah Love's personal life, as reported in the tabloids, is tainted with controversial sexual escapades. In his song 'Gumkum' (colloquial name for an iguana), his lyrics subtly promote sexual violence through the use of force to get sex: '*Usade kundimisa iwe endewabvira kudhara uchida kundityisa asi nhasi ndokurwisa iwe babe*' (Do not try to stop me [having sex with you], you have been trying to scare me, but today I am going to fight you, babe [use force to have sex with you]). The innuendo of the message is clear and worrying, given that over 27 per cent of women report to have been forced to have sex against their will (U.S. Department of State 2013).

Related to the above is another important theme that shows the playing out of manhood in Zimdancehall, which is the celebration of heteronormativity and homophobia. Zimdancehall depicts a rampant and very publicly advertised male heterosexuality, as well as a vocal denunciator of male homosexuality (Pinnock 2007). Homosexuality is shunned in songs, chants and interviews by the various singers in this genre – for example, Tocky Vibes' song 'Vakafa Havana Chavakaona' (Those Who Are Dead Are Missing Out):

Hobho varume ave masistrani
Tirikutambisa nguva tichimuti jah man

Mukadzi wekamwe kamuIndian
Kuita hungochani opihwa ten mari
Nhai vanhu vaMwari nei musinganyare?
Diva kutora chinzvimbocha Memory
Ingava million, in handizvigone
Kushora Mwari kuda kunzi mukadzi
Enda munombotarisa pamirror
Unganzi maimwana here zvigoita?
Ngochani tinopisa?
Many men are now women
We are wasting time calling them men
He is a wife to some Indian
Being gay to get ten dollars
Why are God's people not ashamed?
David [male] taking the place of Memory [female])
Even if it is a million dollars, I can never do it
Shaming God by trying to be a woman
Look in the mirror
Is it possible to be called someone's wife?
Why don't we burn gays?

This song is a clear example of how homophobia is a signature of this musical genre, where anything deemed to divert from the norm is shunned. This is not surprising, given dancehall's long associations with a militant anti-homosexual culture (Pinnock 2007). However, what is interesting is that homosexual men are regarded not as alternative masculinities in the song above, but as women, females and wives. Similarly, during Guspy Warrior's album launch in May 2014 at Harare Gardens, Dhadza D and Soul Jah Love took turns to chant homophobic messages with the crowd responding positively to the message. Seh Calaz has a song titled 'Ndopisa Ngochani' (I Burn Gays). There is thus an established culture of homophobia, which can be attributed to two things. Firstly, this can be traced back to the Jamaican roots of the genre in which artists are openly homophobic and there are many songs denouncing gays. For example, Patricia Saunders (2003) makes reference to the homophobic lyrics in the song 'Boom Bye-Bye' by Jamaican singer Buju Banton. Secondly, in the Zimbabwean context homosexuality is largely denounced as sinful and uncultured. Singers tend to mirror the social context within which they exist and Zimbabwe is largely homophobic, starting with the president, as well as traditional and religious leaders. Ricky Fire cements this heteronormativity in his song 'Hakuna asingade' (Everyone Wants Sex), in which he claims, '*Kana usingade zvimoko urichirema nhai*' (loosely translated, if you are gay, then you must be disabled). Therefore, perhaps what we are seeing in these songs is that dancehall music represents the 'unofficial' cultural code of conduct, both lyrically and literally (Noel 1993). Furthermore, it is how heteronormative masculinity, as practised in dancehall popular culture, demands as a significant part of its construction and consequently its performance of heterosexuality, the creation of homosexual beings. More so, if the above song is anything to go by, it also reveals the anxiety felt by those who uphold heterosexual assumptions because of the realisation that homosexuality threatens patriarchy and its ability to reproduce itself and discourses of masculinities. However, although the homophobic tendencies are clear, we concur with the assertion by Pinnock (2007) that condemnations of male homosexuality do not, by themselves point to the absence of homosexual practices among men and women, whether in dancehall or elsewhere in the Zimbabwean society. In fact, the fundamental paradox is that by singing about homosexuals and homosexuality, the singers are ironically admitting to their existence.

Lastly, expressions of manhood in Zimdancehall are expressed through misogynistic messages and behaviours. Women are often described in disparaging terms and in most cases as sexual objects. Therefore, we agree with the observation by Carolyn Cooper (1993) that it is the sexuality of women, much more so than that of men, which is both celebrated and devalued in the culture of the dancehall. Donna Hope's (2004) 'femiphobia' thesis posits that the construction of the female body is a key part of how dancehall defines its concepts of masculinity. Sexual depiction of the female body is linked to how women are viewed as sexual toys (Chiweshe and Bhatasara 2013). Women are also portrayed as materialistic and immoral – for example in Maggikal's song 'Unodazvinhu':

Babe, *unodazvinhu*
Ndiwe wakanzi nemaroja urimuti wemusango
Haunahunhu
Uri nzirayekutoyazi
Wese anenge achiti ndambobvako
Usadakuzviita sister, wakachipa
Mai vemwana muriveBacossi.

> Babe, you are materialistic and loose
> You are like a tree in the forest without an owner
> You do not have any morals
> You are like a path to the toilet
> Everyone says they have been with you
> Do not act like a Christian because you are cheap
> You are like Bacossi products.[5]

These lyrics highlight the general sentiment about women in most Zimdancehall songs. Women are portrayed as whores, witches, wayward and various other disparaging misogynist stereotypes. In his song 'Babe Wakachipa' (You Are Loose) G Brendon conveys the same message when a girl is considered as cheap as second-hand clothes. Junior PC in a song titled 'Pfuma Ndakabvisa' (I Paid Lobola) portrays a wife that has changed after marriage to become troublesome, yet he paid brideprice for her. Therefore, women are central in dancehall lyrics, as objects of desire and the subjects for the performance of masculinity (Saunders 2003).

Aspects of manhood portrayed in Zimdancehall are not always negative, but also build on certain aspects of being a man, such as providing for the family, hard work and making it in life. The male artists whose songs convey these meanings may be called responsible masculinities. There are many songs and performances that promote these more positive aspects of manliness, such as Freeman and Shinso's collaboration on 'Ndinomira Semukono' (I Will Stand Like a Man), Tocky Vibes' 'Mhai' (Mother), 'Usakanda Mapfumo Pasi' (Do Not Give Up) and 'Tocky Aenda Nenyika' (Tocky Has Made It to the Top). In the song 'Kubasa' (My Workplace), Freeman highlights how singing is the source of his livelihood, providing his food and clothing. In the song 'Ndini Uyauya' (I Am the One), Soul Jah Love narrates an ordeal of moving from poverty to relative success, praising God and those who helped him through hard times. Ras Pompy, whose father died when he was thirteen, has been providing for his mother and family through shows and performances. There is, however, a paternalistic aspect of this performance of manhood, in that while it promotes responsibility in males, it infantilises women

---

5. Bacossi (Basic Commodities Supply Side Intervention) is a programme initiated by the government of Zimbabwe to provide cheap basic products. The name has now been appropriated to mean all cheap things.

and portrays them as in need of protection and care from men. In a song called 'Soja Riripo' (A Soldier Is Here), Buffalo Soulja sings: '*Uri bhodho rinopwanyika ukabatwa* rough' (You are pot that will break if not handled with care). The implication here is that women need men for protection and for all their needs to be met. Women are equated to fragile property, which needs careful handling.

Testing testosterone: Rivalry as part of being man

Another important part of performing manhood in Zimdancehall is the aspect of rivalries that often lead to violence and conflict. Rivalries are used as spaces to test manhood and often promoters have buttressed these conflicts to sell shows. The genre seems to thrive on antagonistic conflicts and many songs have been written about fights and hatred among artists. We focus on the rivalry between Seh Calaz and Soul Jah Love to highlight how rivalries are played out as part of manliness in Zimdancehall. The rivalry between the two came to a head during a Sting festival at Harare City Sports Centre, which left a number of people injured after violent clashes between fans of the two singers. The concept of 'Sting' is borrowed from Jamaica, where artists clash on stage. Below is an excerpt from *The Herald* newspaper report on the incident:

> Some music fans were at the weekend seriously injured in a stampede that occurred at the much-hyped Sting 2014 held at City Sports Centre in Harare. Several show-goers escaped with bruises while others dislocated their hips and ankles in a melee caused by the police who fired teargas into the packed auditorium during the tune-for-tune Zimdancehall battle . . . Soul Jah Love confronted Sir Calaz, who was already making his way to the backstage. A scuffle then ensued and the bouncers had to restrain Soul Jah Love from fighting Sir Calaz. In the midst of all that there were sporadic fights among the fans. As the situation got worse, the police fired teargas and all hell broke loose (Mbiriyamveka 2014).

The singers have multiple songs disparaging one another. The songs are meant to demean other men and to show dominance, although some artists (such as Winky D) have said they will not waste valuable studio time 'dissing' other people. Such songs of rivalry are called 'diss songs' and have a long history in the Jamaican music scene. Soul Jah Love has a song called 'Calaz Ndakamukwapaidza' (I Beat up Calaz):

Ndakamurakidza kuti ndirichibaba
Ndiri munhu mukuru, ndakadya nduru
Ndiri bhuru rine uturu
Mucity sports centre, ndakamusiya asurrender
Ndakangotanga nekumukwapaidza Calaz
Handina kumupa nguva yekubatanidza.
I showed him that I am a father/man
I am a big person, I ate bile duct
I am an angry bull
I made him surrender at the city sports centre
I started by clapping him, Calaz
I did not give him a chance.

Seh Calaz has his own diss songs, but here we sample part of one of his songs titled 'Sauro Une Pamutauro' (Soul Jah Love, You Are Troublesome):

Ndamuona arikutemba nema ninja
Manje handikwate ndinovadhedha
Madiss anoita kundivava
Wakazvitangirei uchatosvava
Ndini mambo wehondo warivara
Sauro, sauro, sauro une pamutauro
Mugunduru wabata gauro
Chimhanya unogeza tora tauro
I see that he depends on ninjas [Wink D's nickname]
But I am not afraid of them, I will cut them up
I am a master of dissing
You will regret starting this
I am the king of war
Soul Jah Love you talk too much
A homeless person now has a place to sleep
Take a towel and go bath.

As can be seen in these examples, many Zimdancehall songs are punctuated by violent threats, claims of physical prowess and often disparaging remarks about other artists. This 'thugged out' masculinity is not unique to Zimbabwe. Defending the 'rudey' (rudeboy) identity in dancehall is very important in defining territory, as well as advertising masculine prowess and authority in Jamaica (Tafari-Ama 2006). Indeed, Cooper (2004) is also right to claim that masculinity is constructed in a discourse of violence. The two artists were once friendly and have collaborated musically in the past, yet this rivalry shows how egos and masculinities are built around the need to dominate and be seen as the best. Rivalries have often turned physical, with singers attacking each other. Another example is the rivalry between Lady Squanda and Ninja Lipsy, in which the former attacked the latter. Lady Squanda released a song promising more violence towards Lipsy called 'Morefire'. Seh Calaz was also involved in a fist fight with Qonfused.

Coupled with violence is the controversy over the use of illicit drugs, especially marijuana. Within the ideological space of inner cities and dancehall, the underlying discourse of illegality and violence is of particular importance in solidifying the status and power of this incarnation of masculinity (Hope 2004). The smoking of marijuana by Zimdancehall artists is seen as part of reggae culture, as is the case with the Jamaican singers, including Bob Marley. Many singers have songs openly celebrating smoking marijuana, the most popular being Seh Calaz's 'Mumota Menyu Muri Kubvira' (There Is Something Burning in Your Car) that glorifies the use of marijuana. Ricky Fire has a song called 'Ndinokuda Sechamba' (I Love You Like Marijuana) in which he compares his love for his girlfriend with his love for marijuana. Anecdotal reports during the course of this research highlighted how at one time Winky D became unpopular among other artists and fans because of his song 'Mafira Kureva' (Kill the Messenger), which speaks out against the use of illicit drugs and claims that most artists are users.

Yet, at one time, Winky D had songs glorifying marijuana, such as 'Mzii' (Marijuana) and 'Ndiri Rasta' (I Am a Rasta). Empress Fina and Mega B have a song dedicated to the love of marijuana called 'Chamba' (Marijuana). In the video they are smoking and passing around what one can assume to be marijuana, although it is illegal to use the drug in Zimbabwe. Viviuun also has a song celebrating smoking marijuana called 'Ndinoputa' (I Smoke) and Guspy Warrior sings 'Timonemone' (Let us Roll the Marijuana). This is the reality of most disenchanted and disenfranchised masculinities in the ghetto: men who resort to using illicit drugs to escape the everyday realities of poverty and unemployment. It can be argued that with a dire shortage of appropriate yardsticks for manhood, namely, the ability to work and provide for one's family and self, drug abuse appears the easy way out. Another interpretation is that while male artists often exhibit tough masculinities, calling themselves soldiers and ninjas, vulnerable, fragile and ambivalent masculinities are also evident. Therefore, we argue that men are also oppressed by the patriarchal models to which they are expected to conform.

Situating female dancehall artists in the debate

Female Zimdancehall artists occupy a complex and curious space within this debate. In a male-dominated industry sexism tends to be rampant, as women are largely seen as 'invading' men's space, yet Zimdancehall has seen the rise of numerous female artists. They face serious challenges, despite many of them proving that they have the talent and ability to make an impression in the industry. Zimdancehall, like *sungura*, has largely been given an occupational gender stereotype. Women are seen as weak and unable to compete in a ruthless industry. Given the violence and 'bad boy' image associated with Zimdancehall, this may be seen as an unsafe space for women to be. In an interview in the *Chronicle* newspaper, arguably the most successful female Zimdancehall artist, Lady Squanda noted: 'Zim dancehall is not for the faint hearted. It's for men which is why I call myself a man. There is nothing that can be done by a male Zim dancehall artiste that I cannot. Where they swim, I swim and where they hunt I hunt' (Ndlovu 2014).

This masculinised nature in Zimdancehall is present across music genres in Zimbabwe. As already mentioned, music remains a male-dominated space and there is stigma associated with women who involve themselves in the industry. Nightclubs and bars are not spaces where 'decent girls' should be found. This means that to be involved in this industry, women have to assume the masculine traits and ignore social stigma. In an interview, Bounty Lisa highlighted how female artists are often forced to sleep with promoters to get booked for shows, which points to high incidences of sexual abuse in the industry (Ndlovu 2014).

Female artists, such as Lady Squanda, have thus assumed the vulgar, misogynistic and sexual content of their male counterparts with chants and songs such as 'Dhodhi Reguava' (describing the difficulty of going to the toilet after eating guavas) and 'Fuck You'. Another highly controversial female artist who thrives on vulgar and sexual innuendo is Lady Bee, with songs like 'Mupunduru' (colloquial word for buttocks or backside), which has a very sexual video. The song and the video are about body parts and sex and promote the objectification of women as sexual objects. This is an important part of the debate about how we construct women who are involved in spaces deemed to be misogynistic. Another video that taps into women's sexual appeal is Ninja Lipsy's 'Ma Babe Anoita' (Fine

Women), which shows scantily dressed women dancing while washing cars and wearing wet clothes.

Does one then paint female dancehall artists as victims of a patriarchal system that forces them to promote messages that are detrimental to their sex to survive? As active agents creating space in a male-dominated industry using multiple resources at their disposal? Or as defying patriarchy? We argue that there are a myriad of responses to the above questions. First, their mere presence in Zimdancehall and their adoption of vulgar lyrics may be regarded as potentially the politics of subversion; a metaphorical revolt against law and order and an undermining of consensual standards of decency (Cooper 1993). Second, these women can be interpreted as representing an emerging radical confrontation with the patriarchal gender ideology and the pious morality of fundamentalist Zimbabwean society. After all, as Bibi Bakare-Yusuf (2006) argues, dancehall shows no conformity with even the basic existential and social hierarchies.

Third, making reference to the videos cited earlier, notions of sexual vulnerability are discarded in favour of a 'bad girl' image. This confirms that women in dancehall culture exhibit a strident confidence that seeks to oppose and disrupt the chaste and respectable (Bakare-Yususf 2006) image of the monolithically defined Zimbabwean woman. These videos attract predominantly the male gaze, which may lead to interpretations of sexual objectification or sexual availability. However, this can also be regarded as ways in which female artists are showing their agency, limited as it may be. They are disrupting the pervasive constructions of respectable (non-sexual, passive and maternal) and non-respectable (sexualised) femininities. Hence, drawing on motifs of deviant sexuality and symbols of excessive femininity allows dancehall women to express sexual power, though also affirming their sexual objectification at the same time.

Fourth, these artists are actively invading male spaces, challenging pervasive notions of respectable and non-respectable work that seek to exclude women from Zimdancehall as a male space. Whether these women use their voices or their sexuality (as commodified, gendered capital) is a moot point in this regard. What is important is that this translates into economic power (Hope 2006). Fifth, these artists can be said to be questioning existing patriarchal practices, such as violence and abuse, in the same manner that female *mbira* or *sungura* artists are doing. Lastly, it is clear that whatever else can be said, these women are reinforcing misogynistic tendencies and the sexual objectification of women. It may be argued, then, that women also take part in the valorisation of the highly sexualised and commodified identities of the female body in dancehall through their own support for and participation in such spaces (Pinnock 2007).

Conclusion

Music as an art form is a space in which identities are played out in various performative ways. In this chapter we have highlighted how manhood is performed in Zimdancehall in various aspects of the genre. Our analysis focused on songs, chants, interviews, performances and literature reviews to highlight how definitions of manhood are created in performance arts. The focus of our chapter was not to provide a moralistic critique of the music genre, as many music critics have done, but rather to focus on music as a space where gender is performed and contested. Hence, an examination of Zimdancehall reveals multiple discourses at work, including the construction of Zimdancehall as a masculine space; heavy emphasis on sexuality and sex-play; and deep linkages between masculinities, violence, misogyny and illegal drug use; and the contradictions generated by the presence of female artists.

We argue that Zimdancehall is a cultural site for the creation and dissemination of symbols and ideologies that reflect and legitimise the lived realities of its adherents. Our reading of this music genre also points to deep-rooted challenges in the fight against gender inequality. The valorisation and celebration of certain aspects of masculinities provides a toxic context in which the objectification and abuse of women becomes accepted as a norm. It is time to move beyond the beat and seriously consider the effect that the negative imagery produced in Zimdancehall music has on men, women and society at large.

References

Adams, T.M. and D.B. Fuller. 2007. 'The Words Have Changed but the Ideology Remains the Same: Misogynistic Lyrics in Rap Music'. *Journal of Black Studies* 36(6): 938–57.

Bakare-Yusuf, B. 2006. 'Fabricating Identities: Survival and the Imagination in Jamaican Dancehall Culture'. *Fashion Theory* 10(4): 461–84.

Ballantine, C. 2000. 'Gender, Migrancy and South African Popular Music in the Late 1940s and the 1950s'. *Ethnomusicology* 44(3): 376–407.

Blommaert, J. and C. Bulcaen. 2000. 'Critical Discourse Analysis'. *Annual Review of Anthropology* 29: 447–66.

Bolzt, K. 2007. *Women as Artists in Contemporary Zimbabwe*. Bayreuth African Studies No. 84.

Bourdillon, M.F.C. 1987. *The Shona Peoples: An Ethnography of the Contemporary Shona People with Special Reference to their Religion*. Gweru: Mambo Press.

Brown, J. 1999. 'Masculinity and Dancehall'. *Caribbean Quarterly* 45(1): 1–16.

Carrigan, T., R. Connell and J. Lee. 1985. 'Toward a New Sociology of Masculinity'. *Theory and Society* 14: 551–604.

Cavanagh, S. 1997. 'Content Analysis: Concepts, Methods and Applications'. *Nurse Researcher* 4(3): 5–16.

Chari, T. 2009. 'Continuity and Change: Impact of Global Popular Culture on Urban Grooves Music in Zimbabwe'. *Muziki* 6(2): 170–91.

Chitando, E. 2002. *Singing Culture: A Study of Gospel Music in Zimbabwe*. Research Report No. 121. Uppsala: Nordiska Afrikainstitutet.

Chitando, E. and P. Mateveke. 2012. 'Challenging Patriarchy and Exercising Women's Agency in Zimbabwean Music: Analysing the Careers of Chiwoniso Maraire and Olivia Charamba'. *Muziki* 9(2): 41–52.

Chiweshe, M.K. and S. Bhatasara. 2013. '*Ndezve Varume Izvi*: Hegemonic Masculinities and Misogyny in Popular Music in Zimbabwe'. *CODESRIA Africa Media Review* 21 (1–2): 151–70.

Connell, R.W. 1995. *Masculinities*. Cambridge: Polity Press.

Cooper, C. 1993. 'Slackness Hiding from Culture: Erotic Play in the Dancehall'. In *Noises in the Blood: Orality, Gender and the 'Vulgar' Body of Jamaican Popular Culture*, edited by C. Cooper, 136–73. London: Macmillan.

———. 1994. '"Lyrical Gun": Metaphor and Role Play in Jamaican Dancehall Culture'. *Massachusetts Review* 35(3–4): 429–47.

———. 2004. 'Enslaved in Stereotype: Race and Representation in Post-independence Jamaica'. *Small Axe: A Caribbean Journal of Criticism* 16: 154–69.

Fairclough, N. 2002. 'The Dialectics of Discourse'. *Textus* 14(2): 3–10.

Fuh, D. 2011. *'Quand la Femme se Fache': Popular Music and Constructions of Male Identity in Cameroon*. Basel: Institute of Social Anthropology/Centre for African Studies, University of Basel.

Gilman, L. and J. Fenn. 2006. 'Dance, Gender, and Popular Music in Malawi: The Case of Rap and Ragga'. *Popular Music* 25(3): 369–81.

Hope, D. 2004. 'The British Link-up Crew: Consumption Masquerading as Masculinity in Dancehall'. *Interventions* 6(1): 101–17.

———. 2006. *Inna di Dancehall: Popular Culture and the Politics of Identity in Jamaica*. Mona: University of the West Indies Press.

Huckin, T.N. 1997. 'Critical Discourse Analysis'. In *Functional Approaches to Written Text: Classroom Applications*, edited by T. Miller, 78–92. Washington, DC: United States Information Agency.

Keche, K. and P. Manatsa. 2015. 'A Critical Analysis of the Manifestation of Patriarchal Power Relations in Zimbabwe's Urban Grooves Music'. *Journal of Humanities and Social Science* 20(4): 72–6.

Kerr, D. 2009. 'Book Reviews: *Women as Artists in Contemporary Zimbabwe*, by Kerstin Boltz, ed. Susan Arndt, Eckhard Breitinger, and Marek Spitczok von Brisinski *Theatre, Performance and New Media in Africa, 2007*'. *Research in African Literatures* 40(1): 166–70.

Luke, A. 1997. 'Theory and Practice in Critical Science Discourse'. In *International Encyclopedia of the Sociology of Education*, edited by L. Saha, 50–6. New York: Pergamon.

Machingura, F. and J.M. Machingura. 2011. 'Women and Sungura Music in Zimbabwe: Sungura Music as a Culturally-Gendered Genre'. *Journal of Research and Discussion* 4(1): 21–43.

Manase, I. 2011. 'The Aesthetics of Winky D's Zimbabwe Urban Grooves Music and an Overview of His Social Commentary on the Post-2000 Experiences in Harare and Other Urban Centres'. *Muziki* 8(2): 81–95.

Mashiri, P., K. Mawomo and P. Tom. 2002. 'Naming the Pandemic: Semantic and Ethical Foundations of HIV/AIDS Shona Vocabulary'. *Zambezia* 29(2): 221–34.

Mbiriyamveka, J. 2014. 'Chaos at Sting 2014 Clash'. *The Herald*, 10 November. https://www.herald.co.zw/chaos-at-sting-2014-clash/.

Moskowitz, M.L. 2009. *Cries of Joy, Songs of Sorrow: Chinese Pop Music and its Cultural Connotations*. Honolulu: University of Hawaii Press.

Mwangi, E. 2004. 'Masculinity and Nationalism in East African Hip-Hop Music'. *Tydskrif vir Letterkunde* 41(2): 5–20.

Naples, N. 2003. *Feminism and Method: Ethnography, Discourse Analysis and Activist Research*. London: Routledge.

Ndlovu, B. 2014. 'Zim Music: A Man's Game?' *Chronicle*, 11 October.

Noel, P. 1993. 'Batty Boys in Babylon: Can Gay West Indians Survive the "Boom Bye Bye" Posses?' *Village Voice*, 12 January.

Pinnock, A. 2007 '"A Ghetto Education Is Basic": (Jamaican) Dancehall Masculinities as Counter-Culture'. *Journal of Pan African Studies* 1(9): 42–75.

Saunders, P. 2003. '"Is Not Everything Good to Eat, Good to Talk": Sexual Economy and Dancehall Music in the Global Marketplace'. *Small Axe* 7(1): 95–115.

Shoniwa, K. 2015. 'The Rise of Zimdancehall'. *Music in Africa*, 20 January. https://www.musicinafrica.net/magazine/rise-zim-dancehall.

Shore, T.M. 2009. 'Androgynous Geographies of the Body: Popular Music and 1960s Counter-Culture'. http://thomasmaxwellshore.wordpress.com/androgynous-geographies-of-the-body-popular-music-and-1960s-counter-culture/.

Shuker, R. 2005. *Popular Music Culture: The Key Concepts*. London: Routledge.

Stanley Niaah, S. 2004. 'Making Space: Kingston's Dancehall Culture and Its Philosophy of "Boundarylessness"'. *African Identities* 2(2): 117–32.

———. 2005. '"Dis Slackness Ting": A Dichotomizing Master Narrative in Jamaican Dancehall'. *Caribbean Quarterly* 51(3–4): 55–76.

Tafari-Ama, I.M. 2006. *Blood, Bullets and Bodies: Sexual Politics below Jamaica's Poverty Line*. Kingston: Multi Media Communications.

U.S. Department of State. 2013. 'Country Reports on Human Rights Practices for 2013: Zimbabwe'. https://www.state.gov/j/drl/rls/hrrpt/2013humanrightsreport/index.htm?year=2013&dlid=220176#wrapper.

Valdez, P.A. 1999. *Bachata del ángel caído*. San Juan: Isla Negra Editores.

Vambe, M.T. 2000. 'Popular Songs and Social Realities in Post-independence Zimbabwe'. *African Studies Review* 43(2): 73–86.

Van Dijk, T. 1993. 'Principles of Critical Discourse Analysis'. *Discourse & Society* 4(2): 249–83.

Weber, R.P. 1990. *Basic Content Analysis*. Beverly Hills: Sage.

Wodak, R. 1995. 'Critical Linguistics and Critical Discourse Analysis'. In *Handbook of Pragmatics*, edited by J. Verschueren, J.O. Östman and J. Blommaert, 204–10. Amsterdam: Benjamin.

CHAPTER 13

The Depiction of the Unsung African S/hero or Heroine in Post-2000 Zimdancehall Music Lyrics
A Critical Analysis

Ruby Magosvongwe

This chapter redefines images of the African s/hero as understood, lived and appreciated in popular Zimdancehall music in the Zimbabwean language of Shona. Zimdancehall, as social commentary, in many ways symbolises vulnerable youths' conceptions and perceptions about dominant cultural attitudes, as well as the youths' own vision and aspirations, especially their views regarding the black African s/hero/heroine. Because of the experiential thrust embedded in the selected lyrics, this chapter uses content and discourse analysis from an Afrocentric standpoint in its examination of depictions of the s/hero by the selected male dancehall artists. The selected lyrics are understood within the broader Zimbabwean context and the instabilities characterising the age group within which Zimdancehall enjoys and solicits an increasing audience. This chapter deliberately focuses on the philosophical underpinnings and cultural moorings that have buoyed the average Zimbabwean's spirits in the face of the bludgeoning economic environment of the post-2000 hyperinflationary crisis years, including the accompanying scourge of vulnerable livelihoods, adversities, catastrophes, diseases and maladies. This chapter uses the lyrics of selected Shona songs taken from albums by Tocky Vibes, Shinsoman and Killer T in its examination of the depictions and popular images of women, especially in the new millennium, at a time that Zimbabwe is hotly pursuing indigenisation and empowerment programmes.

The s/hero or heroine in the lyrics of Shinsoman
Shinsoman prides himself on being the father of Zimdancehall. This section focuses on the lyrics of two songs by Shinsoman that pay tribute to important female figures in his life. The songs are 'Baby Help' and 'Mama', produced in 2013 on the album

Shinsoman: Singles Collection. Other songs on the album showing the artist's and his persona's dedication and commitment to recuperating women from lurid sexual depictions rendered elsewhere include 'Kamwe Kabhebhi' (Another Girl), 'Kukunakidza' (It's Exciting), 'Ndodiwa Mhani' (I Am Loved) and 'Ndoshandira Iwe' (I Work for You). Songs such as 'Kamwe Kabhebhi' show deep admiration for a woman, not necessarily as a sex object or a prized conquerable possession, but as desired companionship. 'Kukunakidza' and 'Ndoshandira Iwe' depict an awareness and consciousness to serve, contrary to the manipulation, exploitation, extortion and other disparaging elements so often depicted in urban grooves music. The conscious commitment to serving female figures in Shinsoman's lyrics makes the black woman the motivation and centre of his world, thereby making her the unsung s/hero of his lyrics, as can be seen in 'Baby Help':

Huya undinyurure, Baby
Rudo rwako, Baby, runondiita bhoo
Handichadi kufeedwa nemanext door
Iwe uripo, Baby
Huya undiburitse, undinyurure ×4
Huya undisimudze, Baby ×4
Baby, usandikanganwa
Tive bhurukwa nebhande.
Please come rescue me, Baby
Your love, Baby, makes me whole
I refuse to continue depending on neighbours' handouts
Knowing you can do better for me, Baby
Come and rescue me, save me ×4
Lift me up, Baby ×4
Baby, forget me not
You and I should be one.

Shinsoman shows that hope for his life lies with his lover, who is his inspiration and source of strength. He is alluding to the stability that comes with marriage from a Shona cultural perspective. The depiction of his lover as 'Baby' departs from and subverts the negative characterisation of women as gold-diggers so often found in urban grooves lyrics. Rather than focusing on the negativity embedded in the infantile image of 'Baby', Shinsoman subverts the stereotype, appropriating life-giving attributes that the female lover is endowed with. By accentuating positivity, focusing on the constructive contributions women make in his life, Shinsoman shifts the gaze to the life-giving properties that have received no recognition in a society sinking in moral nihilism. The Shona collocates *'kuburitsa'*, *'kunyurura'* and *'kusimudza'* (*'undiburitse'*, *'undinyurure'* and *'undisimudze'* in the lyrics) paint a desperate situation that can only be redeemed with the woman's efforts and help. The persona cannot continue to survive on neighbours' handouts. Introspection could point towards the need to acknowledge the failure of male dominance in a society with a fragile economy and to seriously consider female participation and muster courage to give women space to contribute positively in family, community and nation building. Home, family, community and nation building are not man's preserve alone. Furthermore, without family as an anchor, a man is destined to sink (*kunyura*). Traditionally, among the Shona, it is the women in marriage who give stability and dignity to men's lives and existence. The centrality of traditional institutions cannot be trivialised if Zimbabwe as a society is to survive current threats and difficulties.

Indirectly, Shinsoman challenges women to consider taking up their traditional roles and responsibilities as carers, nurturers, love-givers, homemakers, moral anchors, providers of sustenance and repositories of values. Women, especially mothers, have withstood pressures, making themselves pillars of strength in the faltering and crumbling world of post-2000 Zimbabwe, in which men and society in general are groping for hope, sustainable livelihoods and meaningful sustenance. Not to mention that without the woman coming to raise him up (*kusimudza*), to rescue him (*kunyurura*) and taking him out (*kuburitsa*), it appears the male persona's fate has been sealed. These terms are collocates denoting dependence and a need for rescue. It is ironic that the universally represented weaker sex, the woman, in Shinsoman's lyrics, is the only person endowed with the strength and ability to deliver him from peril. This depiction, definition and conception of the black woman is critical. It entails a revision of perceptions and conceptions of the black woman as the socially 'dispensable other', predicated as an appendage, inferior other, denigrated as grovelling for social relevance. Elsewhere I have argued: 'Women . . . have an indispensable responsibility in nation-building, contrary to views that negate women's direct involvement in the affairs of their families [, communities] and the nation' (2008: 83).

The manner in which Shinsoman defines his own unsung black s/hero or heroine can influence attitudes towards women in society. Such lyrics rejuvenate views of women in a world plagued by contradictions in values and world views.

Proper naming precedes attitude change. Toni Morrison (1988: 190) surmises: 'Definitions belonged to the definers – not the defined.' Definitions empower and emancipate or disempower and deflate a sense of being and human worth. Quite clearly, Shinsoman directly subverts popular images of disempowered women surviving at the mercy of men, removing distortions peddled to downplay/trivialise women's roles and responsibilities in building the family and society.

Shinsoman acknowledges that left to his own devices and survival approaches, man could self-destruct by overdependence on external help, an indication of psychological insecurities. Philosophically, what is brought to the surface is the African view that man alone is incomplete, as he desperately needs a woman to stabilise him in life. Bachelorhood in Shona culture shows deficient manhood. Shinsoman's depiction echoes the proverbial adage: 'Behind every successful man there is a woman.' Could the underachievement in the private and public sectors of politics and the economy be indicative of the results of little or no participation by women in programmes that impact on sustainable development? Shinsoman's lyrics unwittingly solicit candid debate, dialogue and discussion on how far, and in what constructive ways, women can influence family, community and broader social development. Re-enforcing the traditional roles of women as unsung heroines? Maybe/indeed! It is not uncommon that people, academics in particular, 'infuse a popular singer's lyrics with their own meaning simply to reach their own political goals' (Chirere 2008: 122). Acknowledging Shinsoman's depictions of women shows that it is self-deluding for any audience to register only the literal meanings of music and its lyrical content. While listeners have the freedom to process their preferred meanings, it is prudent never to discard the empowering, evasive and symbolic cultural meanings that Zimdancehall embraces, especially in the case of the youth, who often see the imaginary state and political and cultural control of adults as ideologically constricting in a global world. However, critics should not be 'prescriptive' (Rutherford 1992: viii) about how audiences should read or respond to cultural phenomena/environments.

Shinsoman's song 'Mama' is a tribute to his mother:

God bless you Mama, I love you Mama
Haiwaiwa Mama
Nhasi ndawana mukana
Wekutenda imi makandipa mukana
I love you Mama

Nhasi ndave baba
Kugona kwevakandipa mukaka
I remember *ndanga ndiri dofo*
Muchinditi mwana wangu zvichaita bho-o
Muchindiudza zvese zvichaita bho-o
Maindigeza nyangwe pasina sipo
Nyangwe zvakaoma maishingirira
Yowe amai-we-e
Makandichengeta kusvika nhasi
Haiwaiwa Mama, yuwi Amaiwe-e
God bless you Mama, I love you Mama
I love you Mama
Today I have an opportunity
To thank you for giving me opportunity
I love you Mama
Today I am a father and head of the family
Evidence of your achievements as my nurse and nurturer
I remember I was dull in school
You assured me: 'My son, don't lose heart, you will make it'
Repeatedly assuring me, 'All will be well'
You bathed me even without basics like soap
Even in the toughest of times, you persevered
Oh my Mama
You have looked after me till today
I love you Mama, God bless you Mama

Evident from these lyrics is the absence of a father figure. With Shinsoman consciously editing his father out of his childhood, it is not surprising that critics could view the artist as a father slayer. Nevertheless, if the father was perpetually absent, the question is: 'Who slays who?' The extent to which Shinsoman's lyrics silence fathers makes political and social commentaries on the socio-cultural developments that Zimbabweans are grappling with. Even when some fathers are physically present, after their economic emasculation because of the maladies characterising the hyperinflationary period and its aftermath, most fathers have found themselves becoming mere procreation bulls. They cannot financially provide for and sustain their families. Furthermore, because of the economic scourge, most families found themselves headed by a single parent, with spouses splitting for job-hunting in the diaspora. It is the mothers who mostly stayed behind with the family and children. In the ghettos and rural areas, mothers also became expert vendors and traders in a multiplicity of wares in order to support their families. What was characteristic of rural households from early colonial days was that homesteads remained in the charge of the eldest female figure while males went looking for wage-earning labour. This has also become the norm in the ghettos, where most families have absentee and visiting fathers. The frustrating and paralysing harsh economic environment, coupled with male pleasure-seeking tendencies, explored by Valerie Tagwira's novel *The Uncertainty of Hope* (2008), reduces men to infantile capacity, forcing them to be financially dependent on women to sustain the family. With gender roles having shifted in this way, it comes as no surprise that the s/hero in Shinsoman's 'Mama' is the persevering mother. In addition to the economic catastrophes, one of the reasons why Zimbabwe established the Matrimonial Causes and Maintenance Act (1985) is to compel fathers to contribute towards the upkeep of their children, whom they have a tendency to forget about or ignore in their pursuit of personal fleeting pleasures. The case is different for a mother – the bringer, bearer and nurturer of human life from infancy till adulthood, conditions notwithstanding. To this end, the s/hero in Shinsoman's life is his mother. Victor Muzvidziwa (2005) explores the invaluable contributions that enterprising Zimbabwean 'women without borders' made to sustain families at the domestic level at the peak of Zimbabwe's economic woes between 2006 and 2008. They also enhanced transnational trading in the SADC (Southern African Development Community) during the same period. No wonder Shinsoman's lyrics project deeply felt personal reasons why mothers are celebrated, while the silence about fathers edits them out of family structures as defenders of the home. The lyrical content is self-explanatory. Muzvidziwa (2005: 3) observes that his study 'revealed a multiplicity of strategies that women traders used in their attempt to extract themselves from poverty. Not only did the women . . . devise coping mechanisms and investment strategies, but [they] also . . . sought to escape or prevent themselves from being trapped in the cycle of poverty'. While it is generally recognised that cross-border trade is the most successful coping strategy to be pursued by urban women, the effects have not been uniform.

Further, because mothers are perceived and believed to be naturally gentle nurturers, they become beacons of hope in times of crisis, an aspect that Shinsoman highlights in the lines from 'Mama' below:

> I remember *ndanga ndiri dofo*
> *Muchinditi mwana wangu zvichaita bho-o*
> *Muchindiudza zvese zvichaita bho-o*
> I remember I was dull in school
> You assured me: 'My son, don't lose heart, you will make it'
> Repeatedly assuring me, 'All will be well'

Shinsoman's 'Mama' exudes an unshakeable faith and confidence in the youth who are the country's future: '*Zvese zvichaita bho-o*' (All will be well). With this transcendental attitude, every problem becomes surmountable, instilling self-confidence and a positive self-esteem. Such attributes boost one's positive sense of self and human worth. With self-respect, self-confidence and maternal support, children can overcome what might be viewed as insurmountable obstacles. This becomes part of a self-naming and self-defining process, breaking any bonds and prejudices that could be psychological encumbrances. Shinsoman's mother is the architect behind his successes and celebrity identity. Self-naming and self-definition 'speaks to [the] conviction that unless African people are critically aware of who they are, which, to a large extent is a product of what happened to them and what they accomplished or could not accomplish, they will remain oblivious [to] what they are capable of achieving' (Gwekwerere, Magosvongwe and Mazuru 2012: 97–8).

In 'Mama' Shinsoman eulogises the female figure as s/hero, a trope that Tocky Vibes takes up, giving all credit to *Mhai*/Mother for nurturing him into becoming the celebrity whose talent Zimbabweans enjoy today. Tocky Vibes is generally viewed as a social delinquent, a misfit groping for relevance in the ghetto, but this chapter focuses on another view of him, as revealed in some of his lyrics in songs such as 'Mhai' and 'Ndazokundikana'. In the latter song, Tocky Vibes uses lewd language and images, showing an unrestrained libido to the point of bedding his own brother's wife. The song shows the collapse of family ties and the general degeneration of traditional cultural values within the ghetto/urban spaces. In Shona there are two sayings: '*Charehwa mutupo chaera*' and '*Mukadzi weumwe ndaambuya*', which both loosely mean that another man's wife is sacred ground that should not be transgressed. In 'Ndazokundikana' Tocky Vibes strikes an image of a struggling and traumatised soul, not the delinquent youth strutting the ghetto streets as a mock-hero:

Nda-nda-zokundikana
Mukoma musandidzosera kumusha.
I-I-I have capitulated
Brother, don't send me back to the rural home.

The failure of the individual to uphold communal morality is analogous to the failure of national projects. The song suggests that authorities and the adult world should take stock of failed national projects that seemingly exclude the youths. The artist urges a re-examination of strategies that are more inclusive, more radical and more empowering. J.D.Y. Peel (1995: 587) rightly argues that self-narrative empowers because it enables its possessor to integrate memories, experiences and aspirations in representation and hopefully reclaim control of their own life. Looking back, into and beyond the present cultivates a transcendental attitude that Zimbabwean society needs in order to come out of the quagmire that has seen many families disintegrating. Tocky Vibes' rationality becomes even more poignant in this extract from the lyrics of 'Simudza Maoko' (Raise up Your Hands):

Kuti usvike
Wotozvipinza jeri
Simudza usakande mapfumo pasi
Kungava kure asi tinosvika badzi
Usafunge kugara pasi
Pfeka mweya wehurume kubva nhasi.
If you want to succeed
Consciously commit yourself to diligent honest work and sacrifice
Persevere and soldier on
It may be arduous, but we will make it in the end
Never dream of giving up
Put on manly courage and soldier on from today

The song exhorts listeners not to give up on their dreams, but the hope, bravery and boldness is depicted using masculine imagery. Characterising the lyrics is a tone of resilience and defiance against all daunting odds. The lyrics speak to a target audience, which may not have been given the requisite skills and tools to help them navigate the world confidently, especially in the unprecedented hostile economic environment. The fact that Tocky Vibes borrows from and appropriates the rich indigenous idiom '*Usakande mapfumo pasi*' (Never give up on your efforts/Continue exerting yourself) as a navigating tool shows the deeply etched values that he subtly exalts. The s/hero once more becomes amorphous. The victor is rewarded for commitment to hard honest work, thrift, respect for communal values and discipline, including submission to tested societal values. This earns Tocky Vibes commendations from both the youth and adult worlds. Similarly, his song 'Mhai' places every mother on a pedestal:

> *Nzombe huru yakabva mukurerwa wani*
> *Ichi chitsidzo chandakaita inini amai*
> *A-a, Iwe Tocky Tocky*
> *Pazvinenge zvanaka*
> *A-a Mhai ndopika handikukanganwe*
> *Mhai mirai nditende mhaiyo-o*
> *Mai kudai musirimi dai ndisiri mudariro.*
> Every big/influential man was suckled and nurtured by his mother
> This is the vow I made to you, my mother
> A-a, Iwe Tocky Tocky
> Never forget us when all has gone well for you
> I swear, I will not forsake you Mother
> My mother, let me thank you, Mother
> Were it not for you, your sacrifices, I wouldn't be who I am today.

In these lyrics Tocky Vibes acknowledges the fact that the supportive and compassionate nurturing from his mother accounts for his achievements. With his vow to reciprocate the good that his mother invested in him, the speaker gives assurance for a secure adulthood and future in the hands of the conscientious youths. That the lyrics resonate with cultural and national expectations, couched in morally acceptable language, gives assurance to the older generation that the youths will struggle with determination against domination, underdevelopment, poverty and misery. This struggle could raise Zimbabwe and Africa to better, secure and more sustainable livelihoods. The song implies that the present-day youth are taking social accountability and moral responsibility to work hard for their parents, and indeed their country. In this regard, Tocky Vibes represents the embodiment of change, attitude renewal and behavioural transformation that many parents hanker to see in the youths. Together, the artist and the mother are to become the s/hero that post-2000 Zimbabwe desperately needs. If the youth choose not to forget their humble beginnings, their roots, and promise to give back in recognition of the investments that have been made into their lives, taking mutual responsibility for their respective families' and homes' sustenance together with their parents, there is every reason to keep hoping for a brighter Zimbabwe.

In the line '*Nzombe huru yakabva mukurerwa wani*', Tocky Vibes' lyrics become double-edged, reminding his audience about the principle of sowing and harvesting, fundamental to Shona philosophy. Parents cannot expect positive returns from children they neglect. The converse also holds true. Children should care for parents who made sacrifices to guarantee sound foundations for their eventual successes and life achievements. Tocky Vibes' song sounds a pertinent and timely reminder to society in general – opening their eyes (*kuvhura maziso*) – leading to another one of his didactic albums, *Ndivhurei Maziso* (Enlighten/Guide Me). These didactic lyrics instil hope in the ghetto and rural youths in their struggles for survival. Ironically, like most youths taking to Zimdancehall music, Tocky Vibes is himself in pursuit of survival, but within morally and culturally acceptable limits, for society's greater good.

Killer T claims on the label that his album *Ngoma Ndaimba* (I Have Poured My Heart out into/Given My Best in This Album) is 'The Zim Best'. The intricately woven stunning and stinging lyrics selectively drawn from Shona rhyming maxims echo the inexorable wisdom of the elders. The lyrics echo the voice of the s/hero pouring out gleaned, experiential, tested wisdom. His song 'Unozoona Kukosha Kwechikorobho Warasa Mvura' (You Will Discover the Invaluable Worth of My Advice When It Is Too Late) with lyrics below, depicts the importance of taking and heeding advice, especially when it is given by elders:

Mwanangu ita unditeerere
Usaite sekunge dzakambotamba nepwere
Hauna kungwara, usazvinyepere
Kana zvaoma usazondichemere
Uchazoona kukosha kwechikorobho warasa mvura
Hauteerere kana ndichikutsiura
Mukana inguva uyu unopfuura
Uchazoona kukosha kwezvandaireva
Mwanangu pangu ndakashanda kare

Inzwa, unopindura kana wabvunzwa
Wotomubatisisa anotumbura munzwa
Achazooneka nembonje pahuma ndambakunzwa
Muromo wevakuru hauwiri pasi
Hakuna munhu asina basa kubvira nhasi
Usava nemunhu waunozotarisira pasi
Nekuti mangwana haasi nhasi
Idzo nungo dzinouraya watenzi nenzara
Unofanira kudyawo zvaunenge wadyara
Kwete kuda kuguta asi wakagara
Upenyu hwakanaka hahuuye wakagara
Pauchazotsvaka bako unenge wanaiwa ha-ha
Ipapo uchanditsvaga asi uchandishaiwa ha-ha.
My child, pay attention to me
Do not behave like an imbecile
You are not clever, don't fool yourself
Do not bother me when life goes sour
You will discover the invaluable worth of my advice when it is too late
You never listen when I correct you
Opportunity comes only once in life
You will discover my invaluable advice late
My child, I have since played my part
Listen, it is rude interjecting when I am talking
Treasure the counsellor who warns you
A delinquent always reaps trouble
The elders' wizened advice never fails
Everyone deserves respect
Never look down upon anyone
Because tomorrow you may need their help
Those who don't work should take leave of eating
Always survive on the proceeds of your labour
Never desire to survive on exploiting and abusing others
Good life does not drop from the sky
You will seek this advice a little too late, ha-ha
Then you will seek me in vain, ha-ha.

Cumulatively, indolence never pays: '*Idzo nungo dzinouraya watenzi nenzara / Upenyu hwakanaka hahuuye wakagara*' is a bedrock of Shona philosophy – 'Life is a struggle that should be tamed', exhorting listeners to commit themselves to diligent work. Speaking to each of the respective lines, living on handouts is self-destructive. The exhortation in Killer T's lyrics is also reminiscent of the proverbs of the wisest king in the Bible, King Solomon:

> That men [sic] may know wisdom and instruction, understand words of insight, receive instruction in wise dealing, righteousness, justice, and equity; that prudence may be given to the simple, knowledge and direction to the youth – the wise man [sic] also may hear and increase in learning, and the man [sic] of understanding acquire skill, to understand a proverb and a figure, the words of the wise and their riddles (Proverbs 1:2–6).

While commending Killer T, one also has to acknowledge the master philosopher behind his profound message and advice. The succinct message is for individuals not to wholly rely on their own judgement, not to disregard the exhortations of parents and elders or take them for granted. Their commonplace maxims provide guidance. The cited lyrics exhort youths to treasure their mothers' sacrifices in raising them. Their mothers' 'wizened advice', gleaned from experience, should therefore be heeded. The mothers are providing guidance, seeking to stabilise their children's lives. The lyrics address every listener, not only biological children. Every listener becomes the child who should be prudent to avert avoidable encumbrances. Sadly, the lyrics' translations give approximate meanings, so much of the Shona originals' rich meaning and rhythmic effect are lost.

Conclusion

The lyrics in these songs by Shona Zimdancehall artists reflect a deep belief in African values symbolically and spiritually, especially in their depiction of the African s/hero during the post-2000 socio-economic difficulties in the country. Discourses from selected songs by Shinsoman, Tocky Vibes and Killer T buttress the view that these lyrics subvert stereotypical negative representations of black women. Selected lyrics in this chapter aim to highlight the downplayed narrative of the unsung s/hero or heroine, who is the anchor of individual family members, the home, the community and the nation. Every listener is exhorted to plough and give back to family and community. Greed, self-centredness and self-aggrandisement are subtly attacked in the songs discussed above. In this way, the corrupt community and national leaders are dealt a subtle blow.

The songs analysed in this chapter reaffirm the African maxim that Okot p'Bitek (1986: 19) aptly captures: 'Man [sic] is not born free. He [sic] cannot be free . . . He [sic] has a bundle of duties which are expected of him [sic] by society and his [sic] family.' This philosophical principle has sustained and kept families and communities closely knit, avoiding the most violent of threats. The embedded perspectives that valorise women as s/heroes or heroines require further investigation, so that their potential can be fully maximised for building communities and the nation. The youth themselves – in their introspective and reflective lyrics – could be equally the s/hero that present-day Zimbabwean families need. Gagging and censoring Zimdancehall artists could rob Zimbabwean society of the messages and litmus test that society needs for regeneration and rejuvenation.

Generally speaking, in African traditional culture, there is a place for all at the rendezvous of knowledge (Césaire 1995). The selected lyrics in this chapter have been deliberately chosen to project how the selected artists almost deify the mother figure, challenging stereotypes that objectify and commoditise African mothers. The artists' depictions, based on personal experiences and lived reality in the ghetto and rural areas, accord with Rudo Gaidzanwa's (2006) acknowledgement of opened spaces that have allowed formerly excluded Zimbabwean women to legally participate and contribute towards building the community and nation.

The images that the respective artists project sharply challenge images of indolent African mistresses, wives and mothers, who survive at the mercy of their economically emasculated African men. Artists' mining from commonly held philosophies about mothering in the traditional Shona world view could also partly explain how ordinary Zimbabweans have had their spirits buoyed despite the ongoing socio-economic woes. In examining Tocky Vibes, Shinsoman and Killer T's treatment of women in their lyrics, this chapter ascertains the extent to which popular youth culture subtly influences views and attitudes about certain sections of society. Merely by focusing on women's creativity, potential, resilience and positive attitudes in building families at a domestic level, the lyrics inject seamless and timeless energy into the minds and bodies of Zimbabwean s/heroes or heroines. The latter accomplished, society, especially the generally unacknowledged and sidelined s/hero, would be intellectually, mentally, psychologically and spiritually rejuvenated.

References

Césaire, A. 1995. *Notebook of a Return to My Native Land*. Newcastle upon Tyne: Bloodaxe Books.

Chirere, M. 2008. 'To Whom Does Oliver Mtukudzi Belong?' *Muziki* 5(1): 111–23.

Gaidzanwa, R. 2006. 'Continuity and Change in Women's Shona and Ndebele Writing in Zimbabwe: A Gender Analysis'. In *African Womanhood in Zimbabwean Literature: New Critical Perspectives on Women's Literature in African Languages*, edited by Z. Mguni, M. Furusa and R. Magosvongwe, 195–211. Harare: College Press.

Gwekwerere, T., R. Magosvongwe and M. Mazuru. 2012. 'An Analysis of the Africana Womanist Emphasis on Self-naming and Self-definition'. In *Rediscoursing African Womanhood in the Search for Sustainable Renaissance: Africana Womanism in Multidisciplinary Approaches*, edited by I. Muwati, Z. Mguni, T. Gwekwerere and R. Magosvongwe, 93–102. Harare: College Press.

Magosvongwe, R. 2008. 'Contrasting Discourses of Emancipation and Empowerment in Selected Albums by Hosiah Chipanga and Fungisai Zvakavapano'. *Muziki* 5(1): 75–91.

Morrison, T. 1988. *Beloved*. New York: Plume Books.

Muzvidziwa, V.N. 2005. *Women without Borders: Informal Cross-Border Trade among Women in the Southern African Development Community Region (SADC)*. Addis Ababa: OSSREA.

p'Bitek, O. 1986. *Artist the Ruler: Essays on Art, Culture, and Values, Including Extracts from Song of Soldier and White Teeth Make People Laugh on Earth*. Nairobi: Heinemann.

Peel, J.D.Y. 1995. 'For Who Hath Despised the Day of Small Things? Missionary Narratives and Historical Anthropology'. *Comparative Studies in Society and History* 37(3): 581–607.

Rutherford, A. (ed.). 1992. *From Commonwealth to Post-Colonial*. Sydney: Dangaroo Press.

Tagwira, V. 2008. *The Uncertainty of Hope*. Harare: Weaver Press.

CHAPTER 14

The Political Underpinnings of Zimdancehall Music
Analysing Selected Songs of Winky D and Tocky Vibes

Itai Muwati, Tinotenda Mwamuka and Charles Tembo

This chapter is a critical analysis of the political inclinations of Zimdancehall music. Anchoring the exegesis in selected songs by Winky D and Tocky Vibes, the chapter argues that Zimdancehall is far from being politically and philosophically sterile. Rather, it is a genre that is coterminous with the hopes, frustrations and anger of the majority of people in Zimbabwe. The music of Zimdancehall eschews the objectification and silencing of the subaltern at the hands of the oppressive state. It is strategically positioned in the trenches of intellectual warfare, relentlessly unleashing satiric missiles and fighting running discursive battles with those in positions of unearned privilege. The artists under discussion seem to have jettisoned fear and trepidation, instead, fully exploiting the advantages arising from the fact that the majority of them produce music outside those zones that are easy to censor. While the genre has been dismissed as music for music's sake, this chapter argues that it is very much grounded in people's attempts to understand the oppressor and also to liberate themselves.

Zimdancehall is a nascent genre that sprouted and flourished in the post-2000 dispensation in Zimbabwe. The political and economic downturn that epitomises the post-2000 period has inspired an upsurge in artistic creativity, as artists have tried to come to terms with the marauding crises incessantly buffeting the nation. During this period, culture and modes of cultural expression have been in a continuous state of flux, expunging fixity. This is a clear reflection of the volatile socio-economic and political conditions in the country. The period is known in scholarly circles as the decade of crisis or the lost decade. In fact, in music, this decade has seen the most creative voices coming to the fore.

The tempestuous economic and political environment ruptures and destabilises conventions, while perforating settled ways of seeing, hearing and thinking. For instance, at the zenith of the crisis, inflation reached 89.7 sextillion per cent on 14 November 2008 (Nyota and Sibanda 2012: 131). Zimdancehall was born out of this volatile environment when illogicality seems to have become the new form of logic in economics, politics and social conduct. The other stimulating factor for the rise of this genre is the mushrooming of numerous recording studios that offer opportunities to the youth sector. Some of the studios are in backyards, which means that they are not officially recognised by the media authorities of Zimbabwe. Even if some of the most sensitive songs are not played on radio, they get popularised through social media, a new platform that is beyond the regulation of censorious officials. For that reason, it is not easy to impose an embargo on Zimdancehall music. While Zimdancehall has been viewed unenthusiastically and disapprovingly (as an expression of violence, promiscuity, drugs, sex and vulgar language) and has received negative media coverage, it is incandescent with powerful messages that increase people's awareness of their environment. Increasing people's consciousness is key to waging a struggle against forces of human degradation. It is also vital in enhancing citizen participation.

Using selected songs from Winky D and Tocky Vibes, this chapter observes that Zimdancehall spawns an artistic terrain where music and politics intersect. It represents, in a sense, 'the difficult process of the evolution of national consciousness and nation building. A seriousness in turn leavened by a controlled playfulness of spirit, an unerring eye for the absurd, and a gentle appreciation of the sharp ironies of post-colonial life' (Thelwell 1988: 4). Seen in this light, this chapter rescues Zimdancehall from a carnage of distortions and disorienting analyses. Remarkably, the selected lyrics are part of the conveyor belt of discourses that unleash satiric missiles against the state, indicting its scorched-earth policies, which engender mass pauperisation and mass victimhood.

The rise of Zimdancehall

Just like urban grooves, Zimdancehall has proved to be extremely popular with the youth, while receiving scathing remarks from the older generations. As previously mentioned, the old generations characterise it as 'filthy', 'uncouth' or just 'bubblegum' music. It is inspired by Jamaican dancehall – for instance, Philip Tagg (1982: 40) is of the view that 'dancehall music . . . originated from Jamaica in the late 1970s and became Jamaica's popular music'. Zimdancehall is a complex music genre and is difficult to define. What is straightforward, though, is that it is part of the evolution of the urban grooves genre in Zimbabwe, which hogged the limelight at the turn of the twentieth century. It triumphantly emerged at a time when mainstream urban grooves music was waning in popularity. In an interview, a producer at Wadzanai studio in Mbare, who chose to remain anonymous, said that Zimdancehall emerged around 2012 and 2013 as a contemporary music genre.[1] It also emerged from the same interview that Zimdancehall is believed to have become visible from the MC contest in the Communal Halls in the urban area, particularly in the 'ghetto'. Some Zimdancehall audiences and producers believe that Zimdancehall is a shift from urban grooves music. For instance, Godwin Muzari (2015), an entertainment editor for *The Herald*, opines that 'the decline of urban grooves did not mean an end to the benefits of the 75% local talent regulation that is when another genre that has been named Zimdancehall stormed the industry'.

Zimdancehall audiences and artists acknowledge artists such as Booker T, Major E and Culture T as the forerunners who brought dancehall music from Jamaica when they first sang dancehall music at Zimbabwe Hall back in the 1980s. Internationally, the term 'dancehall' is common, but the term 'Zimdancehall' captures the creativity and uniqueness of the genre and localises it. Artists such as Winky D, Tempo Man and Gerrie B are thought to have popularised Zimdancehall music in Zimbabwe in 2013. According to Tempo Man, as a 'response to the 75 per cent local content promulgated under the Broadcasting Services Act of 2001, we commercialised the MC contest, promoting youth through music and paving the way for talented youth to showcase their area of gifting'.[2] Similar views come from Max Mandeya (a music analyst), who says: 'Dancehall artists have domesticated the critical potentials of popular culture by using popular culture and the marketplace as the opportunity to arouse a comprehensive dialogue and evaluation about critical subjects that affect their communities'.[3] Munavo Gwashavanhu, a music analyst echoes these sentiments: 'The Zimdancehall genre has provided a significant spot for the inspection as well as analysis of the distribution of authority and power in the municipal setting'.[4] Music analyst Tapiwa Matangira summarises the numerous ways in which popular music challenges the status quo of racialised power dynamics: 'Zimdancehall has returned politics to youth culture

---

1. Anonymous, interview, Mbare, 4 December 2014.
2. Tempo Man, interview, Harare, 5 December 2014.
3. Max Mandeya, interview, Harare, 9 January 2015.
4. Munavo Gwashavanhu, interview, Harare, 3 February 2015.

as well, making political discourse "cool" with young people. Zimdancehall carries political discourses from the MCs who work as "organic intellectuals" of sorts to the masses, who then circulate the discourses in their communities and back again to the MCs'.[5] As Murray Forman (2002: 11) argues:

> It is not an empty claim to suggest that dancehall music and the spectacularity of the extended dancehall culture have been central factors in the notion of cultural counter discourses among youth and teens and in the contemporary transformations of African cultural identities and politics that are formed within the public sphere.

This is not to suggest a sort of determinism in which the politics on offer via MCs determine the political beliefs of listeners, but rather it is a dialogue in which members of the community participate and in which dancehall music is both a forum and a catalyst. Zimdancehall music has sometimes been described as aggressive, gangster-orientated, violent and vulgar. It has become common to associate it with moral bankruptcy and intellectual limitation. It has also been identified as an agent of cultural imperialism, shamelessly mimicking Jamaican artistic traditions. However, this chapter points out that although there are some unpleasant elements in this genre, the positives should not be ignored. The music engages with very sensitive issues that affect ordinary people and their everyday struggles. In other words, Zimdancehall is part of popular music that identifies with the marginalised, pointing out the relationship between those in power and the masses as a whole.

Subverting the logic of the state through critical engagement

The functionality of art in society shows that artists have an important role to play. They have critical obligations to the societies in which they function. Ideally, artists do not have the luxury to avoid the multiple challenges confronting their societies. Chinweizu, Jemie and Madubuike (1985: 225) reinforce this view and argue: 'The function of the artist in Africa, in keeping with our traditions and needs, demands that the writer, as a public voice, assume the responsibility to reflect public concerns in his writings, and not preoccupy himself with his puny

---

5. Tapiwa Matangira, interview, Harare, 15 February 2015.

ego.' Chinua Achebe (1989: 64) suggests that the function of art is tantamount to 'earthing' an electrical socket 'to ensure communal safety'.

Winky D

According to Tatenda Mangosho, Peace Mukwara and Doricah Mhako (forthcoming):

> Wallace Chirumiko a.k.a Winky D is a young dancehall-reggae artist. He was born on 1 February 1983 and grew up in the high-density suburb of Kambuzuma, which is in the capital city of Harare. He is also popularly known as 'Big Man' or 'The Ninja President'. Apart from radio, Winky D has featured on various platforms and has been a brand ambassador for various community initiatives, such as the male circumcision programme (*kuchecheudzwa*). At one point, he was a television presenter for *Rocker's Vibes*, a programme that aired reggae and dancehall music on Zimbabwe National Television.

Winky D identifies himself with the 'ghetto' struggle. He notes that ghettos are looked down upon and he claims, 'the harder the battle, the sweeter the victory'.[6] Winky D is fond of identifying himself through the phrase '*Ego figo*', which according to the artist, means 'unexpected man'. He stresses that people should not be predictable; instead, they must act like lightning, which strikes from any angle. Winky D and his music group are known as the Vigilance Band. The significance of the group's name finds revelation in the manner in which the artist raises very sensitive issues.

Through his songs, Winky D identifies the state as the chief architect of the Zimbabwean people's penury and misery. This becomes a function of the 'vigilance' in the group's name. The songs creatively exhibit engagement, rather than avoidance behaviour. Engagement behaviour is about a volition to bring about transformation, rather than to consecrate the status quo. It marks a conscious refusal to swallow holus-bolus (all at once) the logic and thinking of the state. Through such engagement behaviour, Winky D's songs create sufficient critical distance between the state and the suffering majority. This is a necessary condition

---

6. Winky D, interview, Harare, 11 October 2014.

in the struggle for justice and freedom, without which, the risk for misdirecting energy increases. Without such critical distance, a misleading and potentially stultifying set-up of the oppressor as the oppressed people's saviour arises. Achebe (1988: 6) is right in advising:

> To answer oppression with appropriate resistance requires knowledge of two kinds. Self-knowledge by the victim means in the first place an awareness that oppression exists, that the victim has fallen from a great height of glory or promise into the present depths. Secondly, the victim must know who the enemy is. He must know his oppressor's *real* name, not an alias, not a pseudonym, not a nom de plume.

This is the calibre of artistic commitment that Zimbabwe needs in order to overcome years of one-party oligarchy.

In the song 'Vashakabvu' (The Departed), Winky D uses the epistolary technique. The lyrics are in the form of a letter addressed to the departed, especially those who died in the 1970s, 1980s and 1990s. The epistolary technique is appropriate for the purposes of holding dialogue with the departed because of its transcendental qualities. It makes the ground between the two worlds quite navigable and it can be seen as a kind of libation for the ancestors. The letter is oxymoronically contoured in the sense that it creates a very superficial impression of simply informing the departed of the many changes that have taken place, yet it radiates a scathing satiric message. The lyrics are, in part, as follows:

> *Zvinhu zvachinja* rough
> *Foni kuzara muhomwe dzichiyuza mabatries*
> *MaChina ave muno ovhura mafekitari*
> ...
> *Mari yashandiswa muno ndeyeAmerica*
> *Zimdhora hapana kana achamboriyeuka*
> *Hakuchina macall box kwave nemacellullar*
> *Kombiyuta dzimba dzese tave kungogugula*
> *MaBoy-sky amakavaka aye takaputsa*
> *Zvakanzi haasi pamutemo asi imi hamunakutiudza*
> *Pave neUnity Government ndofungamakaudzwa*
> *Mapato enyika obatana nyika tosimudza*

Vanambuya Nehanda mobvamavaudza
Pangu ndasakura ndazunza.
Things have changed in a big way
Pockets are now full of phones that make use of batteries
The Chinese are now in the country and are opening factories
...
Zimbabwe now uses the American dollar as its currency
No one remembers the Zimbabwean dollar anymore
There are no more public phones, we now use cellphones
Every household now has a computer for surfing the Internet
We have demolished all the cottages that you built
They were outlawed but you did not inform us
There is a Government of National Unity, I am sure you were told
Political parties have joined hands and we are focused on national
 development
Tell Mbuya Nehanda
I have played my part.

Reference to the departed is an ontological necessity among the Shona people. The departed, who become ancestors, are a vital life force and a crucial palisade. The artist deliberately chooses to address the departed in order to inform them of some of the injustices that have taken place at the hands of the ruling ZANU–PF (Zimbabwe African National Union – Patriotic Front). It is also a Machiavellian way of rebuking the state and conscientising citizens about the excesses of the state. Such a strategy is triggered by an awareness that censorship exists. Remarkably, the song identifies and chronicles a litany of post-2000 events that highlight the pain, trauma and despondency of the majority. The selected events also mark the apogee of the crisis that engulfed the nation between 2000 and 2010. For instance, the song mentions the government's Look East Policy, the loss of the national currency, as well as Operation Murambatsvina.[7] The striking reality about these

---

7. Operation Murambatsvina, also officially known as Operation Restore Order, was a Zimbabwean government campaign to clear illegal structures in urban areas. It started in 2005 and, according to United Nations' estimates, has affected at least 700 000 people directly through loss of their homes or livelihoods and thus could have indirectly affected around 2.4 million people. The campaign met with harsh condemnation from opposition

events is that they symbolise the great human and economic disaster that ravaged people's lives. Embedded in the lyrics is political satire against the unfortunate developments that include the influx of Chinese citizens in Zimbabwe, who take over trading spaces and fill the markets with cheap products. Some Zimbabweans have not fully embraced the government's Look East Policy, which has opened up the economy to the Chinese. This policy was inaugurated at a time when relations between Zimbabwe and the West became strained as a result of alleged bad governance and human rights abuses. To those opposed to the government's thinking, the Chinese are seen as the new coloniser. For that reason, it can be argued that the song is an indirect protest against the invasion of businesses and social spaces by outsiders.

In a context in which foreigners seem to enjoy abundant business space and opportunities, Winky D is concerned about how this impacts on Zimbabweans. As mentioned above, the Chinese are often accused of shortchanging Zimbabweans by bringing into the country substandard products. More importantly, the song is dedicated to criticising those in charge of the affairs of the state for presiding over what Chinweizu (1987) calls 'imperialised development'. In the context of Chinese domination in commerce and other sectors of the economy in Zimbabwe, Winky D echoes Chinweizu's argument:

> What needs to be created is an integrated [Zimbabwean] economy oriented not to the needs of the economies of the West [or East], but to the needs of [Zimbabwe] as defined politically by the people. Anything short of that will prove incompatible with our aspirations for political and cultural autonomy (Chinweizu 1987: 286).

The artist satirises the government leadership for allowing the Chinese to invade the Zimbabwe economy and social spaces despite their spirited claims to sovereignty. In the same song, the artist advises the departed of the new monetary developments in the nation. He notifies them that Zimbabwe abandoned its currency for the United States dollar and a basket of other currencies. The Zimbabwean dollar was a symbol of national pride and identity. Seen in the context of the decade of

---

parties, church groups, non-governmental organisations and the international community (http://en.wikipedia.org/wiki/Operation_Murambatsvina).

crisis when the economy reached a nadir, the lyrics constitute an indictment of the ZANU–PF government for presiding over the collapse of the nation. The loss of the national currency constitutes a metaphor for bad governance, characterised by greedy and predatory economics. Hyperinflation, which officially reached a peak of 230 million per cent, eroded people's incomes and plunged the nation into unprecedented economic turmoil. Brian Raftopoulos (2009: 220) explains that life was made more difficult by 'hyperinflation [which] reached an official level of 230 million per cent by the end of 2008, devaluing both earnings and savings' and leading to the impoverishment of ordinary citizens.

The lyrical content, therefore, addresses grave economic and political issues. In this regard, it is trite to merely dismiss Zimdancehall as 'bubblegum' music. Evidence marshalled here demonstrates that the genre is steeped in the trenches of the painstaking struggle for justice. Reference to the departed becomes an appropriate technique the author adopts in order to escape censorship. The song thus slaloms tantalisingly past the watchful gaze of the state. The departed become a site for registering the failures of the state. While Winky D purports to be informing those who died in the 1970s, 1980s and 1990s about the changes in Zimbabwe, it is critical to note that he lays the blame on those in charge of the affairs of the state.

Operation Murambatsvina was launched in May 2005 at a time when the ZANU–PF government was already unpopular with urbanites. During this time, all indicators pointed towards a massive economic, social and political conflagration. The demand for housing, which had been escalating since 1980, exploded in the post-2000 dispensation when government simply ignored the mushrooming informal structures in the cities. The result was a chaotic form of urban planning. Alois Mlambo (2008: 19) provides a historical background to Operation Murambatsvina, emphasising that

> the failure of the government to live up to its earlier promises of providing health, education and housing for all by 2000 due to a number of factors, among which the poor performance of the national economy must rank very highly especially in the aftermath of ESAP [Economic Structural Adjustment Programme], which left the Zimbabwean economy worse off than before.

Be that as it may, Operation Murambatsvina was a strategy to split the urban vote by driving out of the urban zone all disgruntled voters. The unsettling of the urban demographic structure was inspired by political scheming, rather than the logical dictates of urban planning. According to Mlambo (2008: 10):

> Operation Murambatsvina destroyed whatever accommodation the urban poor had been able to establish for themselves in the context of the failure of municipalities to provide adequate housing. Murambatsvina also ruined many sources of livelihood by razing flea-market stalls and informal workshops to the ground. By most accounts, it was carried out with a high degree of insensitivity to the rights and needs of those affected and with such ferocious speed that local people began to speak of 'Zimbabwe's tsunami'.

This is what Winky D brings to the attention of the deceased in the lines: '*MaBoy-sky amakavaka aye takaputsa / Zvakanzi haasi pamutemo asi imi hamunakutiudza*'. It is clear that the artist views this move as inhuman. One possible interpretation is that he informs the deceased so that they can fight from the other side of the world.

The invocation of the spirit of the dead in the song is coterminous with the deathless and historically acclaimed pronouncement of Mbuya Nehanda (a very important spirit medium of the Shona people who inspired resistance against the British settlers in the 1890s): '*Mapfupa angu achamuka*' (My bones shall rise). Molefi Kete Asante and Ama Mazama (2009: 422) tell us that

> no medium has ever reached the significance or importance of Nehanda, who was the daughter of the founding King of the Mutapa empire. Her ritual marriage to Matope gave supernatural powers to the Mutapa Empire. After her death, she became a *mhondoro* spirit who could be appealed to by the mediums, *masvikiro*.

In Shona ontology, the dead are known to fight for justice from their graves. In most cases, they have to be called upon to intervene and this is exactly what the song 'Vashakabvu' is attempting to do. The legacy left by the deceased has been destroyed by a callous government, the lyrics subtly allege. Through demolishing the houses, the government potentially invited the wrath of *ngozi* (avenging spirit) to its doorstep. The song becomes part of the social and spiritual realm that the oppressed or suffering African appeals to in the search for justice. In short, the message here is: Rise and fight this regime, which has destroyed what you worked so hard for! In the final stanza of the song, Nehanda is invoked in the search for a breakthrough among a people who suffer under an oppressive, authoritarian and violent regime. The artist attacks the ruling elite for reversing the agenda for freedom that Nehanda and other legendary figures stood for. Bad governance and mismanagement of the economy by the political leadership is blamed for the plummeting standard of life that characterises Zimbabwean society. Nehanda thus becomes symbol for struggle, justice and victory.

Through song, Winky D also alludes to the 'Government of National Unity', which was 'primarily prompted by the political stalemate among Zimbabwe's political parties following the disputed results of the March 2008 harmonised elections and the violent presidential runoff of June 2008' (Muzondidya 2013: 40). Furthermore, the elections followed

> five months of incertitude . . . preceded by years of intense political combat between ZANU–PF and the MDC [Movement for Democratic Change] parties, violence and repression, decay of the national infrastructure and institutions of governance, serious economic and social decay characterised by hyperinflation, an unaffordable cost of living, the erosion of educational and health services and the high prevalence of epidemics such as cholera, typhoid, tuberculosis and other HIV/AIDS-related infections (Muzondidya 2013: 41).

Winky D uses his voice as an artist to articulate the history of a nation gripped by multifarious problems (economic, political and social). It is a voice that is aglow with critical consciousness. As Okot p'Bitek (1986: 40) tells us: 'It is the creative work of the artist that constitutes the mental pictures which guide men's lives, which make them human'. In this way, Winky D yields to the task of helping society to reflect on itself.

Another of Winky D's songs, 'Public Image', challenges people to be vigilant when dealing with prominent individuals in positions of authority (pastors, artists and even Members of Parliament). The call comes against the background of chronic power abuse by the powerful. Such power abuse is inalienably linked with the social and economic rot in the nation, as well as the tumbling living standards. The song provides a stern warning to people to guard against being misled by outside appearances. Though veiled, the voice castigates politicians for domineering and deceitful behaviour. It appeals for critical consciousness, urging people to ask questions and have doubt each time they transact with politicians. It thus encourages and cultivates a culture of speaking out, while expunging a culture of silence, which opposes critical thinking and critical engagement.

The song conscientises people regarding the need to guard against uncritical acceptance of politicians' purported capabilities in public. A sharp sense of betrayal resulting from irresponsible Members of Parliament who renege on the fundamental duty of serving the people who voted for them, to pursue self-aggrandising agendas, is expressed in the song in a manner that challenges the people to be observant:

Haikona kubhaizwa nepublic image
Kunze kwakanaka, mukati makatakura negative energy
Ndosaka kubva nhasi uya waunoti munhu kwaye pamwe haasi
Nyatsodzidza munhu umupindire mugirazi
Munhu haasi wekutarisira mugirazi
Kune mamwe maMP
Manyepo enyu handikwanisi kumamwisa tea
Ndikakupa vote *yangu ndiri pachokwadi*
Ndinokubvunza kuti, 'Ko chako chokwadi chiripi?'
Uko kumachechi, maPastor
Pakukanika message, imi baba kana mapfeka gemenzi musazofarisa
 kwakuzviidza Tenzi
Usazojaja munhu zvaari pavanhu anokubhaiza, kukupfekera kamwe
 kahunhu kunyanya vanhu vePublic munonetsa pahunhu
Ini handibhaizwi nesimairi, munhu chimwe chinhu saka ndisati
 ndapicker munhu ndomboridha hunhu
Papublic zvakawanda anoviga munhu
Ukaita patience mbijana ombodhiga munhu
Do not be deceived by the public image
The outside appearance is good. Yet the inside redounds with negative
 energy
That is the reason why from today you should know that the one whom
 you think is good is in fact not good at all
You should have knowledge of the individual

> Do not take people at face value
> There are some MPs
> Who are fond of telling lies
> If I give you my vote out of trust
> I will ask you this question: 'Where is your truth?'
> In the church
> When preaching the word and you have put on church regalia do not mock the Lord
> Do not judge someone in public, you will be misled by appearances
> He or she will put on superficial appearances, especially public figures
> I am not one to be deceived by a smile; a human being is something else so before I trust someone
> I must have knowledge of that person
> When in public, a person hides his/her true colours
> You must have patience so that you develop a better understanding of the person

The lyrics demonstrate Winky D's combative attitude and willingness to speak out on political issues. The stage is set for a community that is divided into leaders and followers. As expressed in the song, the leaders are bereft of moral rectitude. They show negative human qualities, such as infidelity and zero transparency and accountability. What is most instructive is that the song traces Zimbabwe's endless conundrums to unethical leadership nourished by jaundiced human values. Leadership without positive values, just like politics without morals, is threatening to human development. It is noteworthy that the song focuses more on inner behaviour as it searches for the solution to the nation's problems and challenges from within. The tendency is inherent in the ZANU–PF party to lay the blame on outsiders, in particular Britain and America, which are incessantly accused of undermining the government through the imposition of 'sanctions'. The condemnatory inclination in the song empowers the public masses. It intellectualises the politics of interaction between the leaders and the masses by pontificating on the urgent need for a change in the attitudes of the masses. Such a shift radically transforms people's perception of their leaders from being indispensable messiahs to crooks. It is hoped that that once the public is able to unmask the deceit and chicanery of the leadership, desired change in the nation can be brought about. The song joins the not-so-long list of songs that identify a leadership vacuum in the nation as Zimbabwe's Trojan Horse. For instance, the Member of Parliament in the song epitomises 'the absence of effective, in the sense of quality, leadership both politically and intellectually' (Johnson 1997: 250). The artist exposes and scorns Members of Parliament who betray the trust bestowed on them by the people. Rather than serve the people, such politicians desert their obvious duties and in the process compromise service delivery and national development. Thus, Winky D's song 'Public Image' reveals sound political consciousness, given that it articulates and grapples with a cancer that is destroying African societies, such as irresponsible leadership. Peta Ikambana (2007: 257) pointedly argues:

> Hundreds of millions of Africans throughout the continent are trapped in poverty and paying the price for their countries' government mismanagement. These people are not the primary beneficiaries of many promises made by their governors when they seize power. On the contrary, these governors quickly become their worst nightmare, unable to fulfil their legitimate dream for better lives, in a rich continent . . . Africans are obliged by their own governors to live in constant and profound economic and social misery, while those in power are increasingly concentrating on their wealth.

The lyrics of 'Public Image' bemoan a lack of reciprocity between voters and those who are voted into power. The irresponsible Member of Parliament does not go unchallenged because the song seizes the initiative to question the Member of Parliament on delivery of election promises. The Member of Parliament is unequivocally reminded that prevarication undercuts efforts aimed at development. Winky D's agenda is to change society, so he does not simply report on the crisis of leadership, but uses his voice to restore sanity in an environment characterised by grotesque absurdity and non-commitment, especially among those who are elected into public office. Through challenging the Member of Parliament to articulate the truth, the lyrics agitate for agency and confrontation. It can be argued that good art must be agitative because without such agitation change remains a mirage. 'Public Image' scorns politicians who are 'preoccupied with filling pockets as rapidly as possible [and in the process] the country sinks all the more deeply into stagnation' (Fanon 1968: 165). The artist's voice is the voice of reason in an environment characterised by a crisis of leadership. Echoing Chinweizu (1987: 388), the song is satirising political leadership for failing the people:

> When our elite deserts its obvious duties ... when it does not do what it must do to win the hearts of our people, namely, feed their hunger, raise their political consciousness, make them more aware of the ultimate causes and hidden modes of perpetuating their impoverishment, and raise their power and self-esteem in practical ways; when the nation's interests are, with nervous greed, sacrificed for the false grandeur of a few, it is time for profound concern. Such quisling tendencies in her elite are a manifest danger to the welfare of Africa.

In Winky D's 'Public Image', reluctant and irresponsible leadership is called upon to execute the duties expected of them by society. Dishonest leadership is castigated because of its negation of the struggle for collective socio-economic transformation.

Images of power abuse in Tocky Vibes' 'VaMayaya' and Winky D and Shinsoman's 'Survivor'

Like Winky D, Tocky Vibes unleashes a total blitzkrieg against the state and its institutions, particularly the police, for making life very difficult for the already struggling citizens. Of particular interest is the song 'VaMayaya', which derives its title from the popular drama in Zimbabwe known as 'Sabhuku Vharazipi 2' (Village Head, Close Your Zip 2), in which there is a shamelessly corrupt police officer, VaMayaya. The song gyrates around the much-talked-about subject in Zimbabwe of a violent and unscrupulous police force that makes the business environment extremely difficult to operate in. In the song, Tocky Vibes assumes the voice of an individual who is unhappy with the disturbing police operations on the road and at pick-up points. It is a voice of resistance against an oppressive and violent regime, symbolised by the police. The song exposes and attacks the police for their violent and confrontational policing methods. In fact, the police officer in the song is presented as a potential instigator of anarchy in the nation, who flagrantly attacks citizens who are trying to eke out a living in difficult economic circumstances. By extension, the police officer also symbolises the readiness of the state to use violence against a restive population. VaMayaya (the notorious police officer) embodies and simultaneously personifies both the history and philosophy of violence that has haunted the neo-colony since the days of independence. The song thus cautions the state against using violence when dealing with the people, whose side of the story is represented by commuter minibus operators. The environment is epitomised by lawlessness and nonchalant disregard of civilised conduct, as revealed in the following lyrics:

VaMayaya, aaahaaaah VaMayayaka! Aaahaaah
Heeee, Tocky Vibes
Officer musakoke mboma
Mapwanya screen Taakutoshanda imimi
Tinotaurirana musarova madzinhi
Officer, hamunete nekutimhanyisa
Ipeturu ipi isingambosinker?
Nguva yareba muchingotityisa
Tese tiri kuda kushanda
. . .
Aaa haiwa Officer musandibata
. . .
Muromo handivhare hauna zipi
Ndikavhara mobva manditi teki teki
Muchakuvara ndapinda nemumadhangi
Ndofa nenzara rikanyura ndisina cent
Inzwai, mapassenger atoisa complaint
Makandidzvanya kupinda nemulocation
Totsika vana maOfficer mirai mheni
Tatouraya suspension
   Ooyi hwani mari mombononwawo can
   Tese tiri kuda kushanda.
VaMayaya, aaahaaaah VaMayayaka! Aaahaaah
Heeee, Tocky Vibes
Officer, do not position your baton stick for a strike
Now you have smashed my car windscreen
We are now working for you
Let's talk – do not hit my car
   Officer, you never get tired of chasing after us
   Where do you get the petrol from?
You have been initimidating us for a long time now
We all want to work
. . .

> No, Officer! Do not touch me
> ...
> I will not keep quiet because the mouth has no zip
> If I keep quiet, you then come after me
> You will get injured one day
> I will starve if the day ends without me working
> Even passengers are complaining
> > You pursue me even into the suburbs
> > We risk running over children
> We are damaging the car's suspension
> Here is one dollar so you can have a drink
> We all want to work.

The song presents a young man in the city of Harare who is tirelessly fending for his family. He is working as a commuter minibus conductor, as well as vending in the streets of Harare, specifically Charter. His efforts are rendered futile as a result of a brutal police force and a punitive city council. The cruelty of both the police and the city council lies in the arrest of the breadwinner. Such a situation renders the family vulnerable to hunger. Despite threats and frustrations that confront the man in the city, he refuses to submit. He thus represents the multitudes who have resisted the inducement to succumb to oppression and violence in the city. He exudes optimism and is prepared to defend his family 'by any means necessary'. The voice of the artist represents a cornered and tormented citizen. The voice pleads with the police to spare his commuter minibus, so that he can survive because it is his only source of livelihood. It is apparent that the environment is very hostile as a result of a police force that has turned predatory. The ubiquitous violence, symbolised by the smashing of windscreens, intimidation (*nguva yareba muchingotityisa*) and corruption (giving a dollar to the police officer for a drink), exacerbates the people's condition. While this is the case, the voice fearlessly canvasses for the need to negate inaction and seize the initiative to resist the machinations of a police force that makes life extremely difficult. The sad situation is portrayed by Frantz Fanon (1968: 172) as follows:

> In these poor, underdeveloped countries, where the rule is that the greatest wealth is surrounded by the greatest poverty, the army and the police constitute the pillars of the regime; an army and police force which are

advised by foreign experts. The strength of the police force and the power of the army are proportionate to the stagnation in which the rest of the nation is sunk . . . there is not a soul down to the simple policeman or the customs officer who does not join in the great procession of corruption.

In 'VaMayaya' Tocky Vibes reflects on the stark realities in Zimbabwe in which the police are often involved in 'heated battles' with commuter minibus operators. The collapse of industries in Zimbabwe in the post-2000 period has forced desperate citizens to create an informal sector.

The difficulties facing the people of Zimbabwe and the unprofessional conduct of the police force has also prompted reactions from other Zimdancehall artists. For instance, in the song 'Survivor' by Winky D and Shinsoman, the two artists expose the frightening level of unemployment, which has rendered most young people idle:

Vakationa takaleza pakona
Vanoti hatina zvatinogona
Kumaghetto youth *mikana mishoma*
Hakuna ghetto youth *risina zvarinogona*
Saka Shinso ndopa mhiko
Kusapota ghetto *asi hakuna iriko*
Takumiririra vanhu kunge Steve Biko
Ukaona Bigman
Ukaona Shinso
Pane hobho vanenge isusu vane zvipo
Maghetto youth *gozha*
Vanomhanya nemaiki, anotamba bhora
But *hapana zviripo*
Ndati ndizame chiconductor porisi iri kurova nemboma apa
Ndironge musika panaCharter dhimoni rekanzuru rabva rabata
Shinsoman the dancehall father *ndabatwa*
Biggy mucentral police *ndavata*
Zvakaoma kudaro, tiri masurvivor isu tiri masurvivor
Ende futi tine nharo tinenge Magaivha isu tinenge Magaivha
Saka Shinsoman *neni Biggyman*
Mukadzi nemwana vakamirira kumba

Baba vachadzoka kubasa
Ini ndakandwa mukabiyasi
Tariro handife ndakarasa
Ndichangoramba ndichishingirira
One day *tichabudirira*.
When they see us seated at the street corner
They think we are incapable of doing anything
There are very limited opportunities for the youth in the city
There is no youth who is not capable of doing something
So Shinso, I swear
I support the ghetto but there is nothing
We now represent the people like Steve Biko
If you see Big Man
If you see Shinso
There are many just like us, who are gifted
Ghetto youths are talented
They are gifted musicians, they play soccer
But there is nothing
If I try to be a bus conductor, the police smash windscreens with their baton sticks
If I set up a stall along Charter Street, municipal police unleash violence
Shinsoman the dancehall father has been arrested
I spent the night at Harare Central police station
Though things are tough, we are surviving, because we are survivors
We have a tenacious spirit like MacGyver, we are like MacGyver
So you Shinsoman and me Biggyman
My wife and the kids are waiting at home
Waiting for father to come back from work
Yet I have been arrested
But I will never lose hope, I will remain steadfast
One day we shall conquer.

The song's title, 'Survivor', suggests that the individual in the song is facing a lot of challenges resulting from an environment that has turned life-threatening. It is an environment that requires much energy in order to transcend the problems affecting the society. It fundamentally brings out the resilience, determination and toughness of the character of the youth. It is a galactic expression of struggle and victory. The song begins by capturing the plight of unemployed urban youths who spend substantial time on the streets. Remarkably, the song avoids the chronic victim-blame syndrome. Rather, the young man in the song attributes the situation to limited opportunities that render them vulnerable to poverty and manipulation. Winky D and Shinsoman reiterate the critical need to remain hopeful and confront the problems because helpless victimhood works to the advantage of the architects of poverty and misery. They are not doubtful that 'elites come and go. There is nothing permanent or sacrosanct about any elite. And an elite is expelled most disastrously when they have left undone those things which it ought to have done, and has done those things which it ought not to have done' (Chinweizu 1987: 351).

In these songs Tocky Vibes and Winky D and Shinsoman are interrogating the authoritarian regime that presides over the police force, an arena in which the public have no say about unlawful punishments. It is a scathing attack on a police force that holds absolute power and does not accept any form of advice given outside their sphere. The singers satirically castigate authoritarianism as the chief cause of misery in the polity.

Conclusion
This chapter finds its fountainhead in an intense interest in political issues manifesting in selected Zimdancehall music. It has established that the artists use their voices to lampoon the leadership for grand mismanagement, corruption and ultimately turning the nation-state into a mere jungle in which life is very difficult. The chapter marshalls a reverse argument about the place and significance of Zimdancehall music – the commonplace view about Zimdancehall is that it is vapid, ideologically bankrupt and morally reprehensible. Yet this chapter evinces that the genre is gravid with political innuendos. It abets the struggle for justice by increasing a people's awareness about the existence of oppression. The selected songs reflect a never-say-die spirit. The artists have no vacillation whatsoever when it comes to rebuking authority. They even go to the extent of urging confrontation. Given that this is a genre that is popular with the youth, it has the potential to galvanise political participation of the youth in Zimbabwe's turbulent politics. Through song, the artists become an inevitable part 'of that popular energy which is entirely called forth for the freeing, the progress, and the contentment of Africa' (Fanon 1968: 206).

References

Achebe, C. 1988. 'Spelling Our Proper Name'. In *Black Writers Redefine the Struggle: A Tribute to James Baldwin*, edited by J. Chametzky, 5–12. Amherst: Massachusetts Institute for Advanced Study in the Humanities.

———. 1989. *Hopes and Impediments: Selected Essays*. New York: Anchor Books.

Asante, M.K. and A. Mazama, eds. 2009. *Encyclopedia of African Religion*. Thousand Oaks: Sage.

Chinweizu, I. 1987. *The West and the Rest of Us: White Predators, Black Slavers and the African Elite*. Lagos: Pero Press.

Chinweizu, I., O. Jemie and I. Madubuike. 1985. *Toward the Decolonisation of African Literature: African Fiction and Poetry and Their Critics*. London: KPI.

Fanon, F. 1968. *The Wretched of the Earth*. New York: Grove Press.

Forman, M. 2002. *The 'Hood Comes First: Race, Space, and Place in Rap and Hip-Hop*. Middletown, CT: Wesleyan University Press.

Ikambana, P. 2007. 'On Governance, Personal and Military Power in Post-independent Africa'. In *Africa in the 21st Century: Toward a New Future*, edited by A. Mazama, 257–62. New York: Routledge.

Johnson, C.S. 1997. 'Cornel West as Pragmatist and Existentialist'. In *Existence in Black: An Anthology of Black Existential Philosophy*, edited by L.R. Gordon, 243–62. New York: Routledge.

Mangosho, T., P. Mukwara and D. Mhako. Forthcoming. 'Protest and Subversion in Zimbabwe's Dancehall Music: The Case of Winky D'. In *Singing Nation and Crisis: Music and the 'Decade of Crisis' in Zimbabwe, 2000–2010*, edited by I. Muwati, T. Charamba and C. Tembo, 75–87. Gweru: Midlands State University Press.

Mlambo, A. 2008. 'Historical Antecedents to Operation Murambatsvina'. In *The Hidden Dimensions of Operation Murambatsvina in Zimbabwe*, edited by M. Vambe, 9–24. Harare: Weaver Press.

Muzari, G. 2015. 'From Urban Grooves to Zimdancehall'. *The Herald*, 16 April.

Muzondidya, J. 2013. 'The Opposition Dilemma in Zimbabwe: A Critical Review of the Politics of the Movement for Democratic Change (MDC) Parties under the GPA Transitional Framework 2009–2012'. In *The Hard Road to Reform: The Politics of Zimbabwe's Global Political Agreement*, edited by B. Raftopoulos, 39–70. Harare: Weaver Press.

Nyota, S. and F. Sibanda. 2012. 'Digging for Diamonds, Wielding New Words: A Linguistic Perspective on Zimbabwe's "Blood Diamonds"'. *Journal of Southern African Studies* 38(1): 129–44.

p'Bitek, O. 1986. *Artist the Ruler: Essays on Art, Culture, and Values, Including Extracts from Song of Soldier and White Teeth Make People Laugh on Earth*. Nairobi: Heinemann.

Raftopoulos, B. 2009. 'The Crisis in Zimbabwe, 1998–2008'. In *Becoming Zimbabwe: A History from the Pre-colonial Period to 2008*, edited by B. Raftopoulos and A. Mlambo, 201–32. Harare: Weaver Press.

Tagg, P. 1982. 'Analysing Popular Music: Theory, Method and Practice'. *Popular Music* 2: 37–67.

Thelwell, M. 1988. 'Introduction'. In *Black Writers Redefine the Struggle: A Tribute to James Baldwin*, edited by J. Chametzky, 2–4. Amherst: Massachusetts Institute for Advanced Study in the Humanities.

CHAPTER 15

Patterns of Ndebele Zimdancehall Music

Zifikile Makwavarara and Albert Nyathi

It is interesting to note that since the majority of dancehall artists hail from Harare, they use the dominant language Shona, which is spoken by more than ten million of Zimbabwe's population. Very few musicians have tackled this genre in Ndebele, which, according to the 2012 population census, is spoken by close to four million people – hence the view that Bulawayo (predominantly Ndebele) is isolated from the Zimdancehall arena. Artists resident in Zimbabwe's second largest city, Bulawayo, have largely preferred to incorporate the Shona language into their performances, as this puts them in an advantageous position in terms of receiving airplay and therefore reaching a wider audience.

The music industry in Bulawayo has largely been influenced by neighbouring South Africa, hence the dominance of kwaito and *kasi* (township) and house music. Of note also is that Bulawayo musicians have historically imported music from South Africa. This comes as no surprise, for the Ndebele people of Zimbabwe have strong cultural, historical and economic ties with the people of South Africa, from where their ancestors migrated in the nineteenth century. The Ndebele inhabit mainly Bulawayo, the Midlands and the two Matabeleland provinces. As a nation, they came into existence through a process of conquest and incorporation of various ethnic groups, such as the Sotho, Tswana, Kalanga, Tonga, Nambya and Venda, as well as the Shona-speaking groups. Ndebele history is associated with heroic militarism, as it recounts their precolonial raids into Shona and other territories, mainly in search of grain and livestock. However, some historians (see Beach 1986) have challenged these historical accounts, as other Nguni kings, such as Soshangane and Zwangendaba, had passed through this same territory on their way to Mozambique and Malawi, respectively. This scenario was common practice in southern Africa during the Mfecane. What is of no doubt, though, is that in post-independence Zimbabwe, the Ndebele's relationship with the predominantly Shona ruling elite has been punctuated by tensions amid deliberate peripherisation of Ndebele contributions to the struggle for national independence and their role in national development. This may also be why there is limited airplay on music from Matabeleland on national radio stations.

It is arguable that dancehall was imported from Harare to Bulawayo. As a result, dancehall performers whose lyrics are in Shona have tended to enjoy more airplay than their Ndebele counterparts, leading to an outcry that Harare musicians are taking centre stage. It is also interesting to note that this genre has been mainly a preserve of young male performers, with only a handful of female performers, such as Lady Squanda and Lady Bee, taking to the stage in recent years.

Zimdancehall, as is the case with its Jamaican predecessor, has often thrived in poor communities as a form of protest art – hence the use of rough language associated with ghetto life. In Harare, most dancehall musicians reside in the townships or high-density suburbs, while youngsters hailing from upmarket, northern suburbs are attracted to urban grooves, a genre that was basically inspired by, and is almost an imitation of, American music, such as R & B, hip-hop and house music. Once in a while, urban grooves musicians perform in middle-class venues such as Pablo's Bar in Borrowdale, the Zimbabwe German Society in Milton Park or Alliance Française in the city. However, the genre has failed to sustain a large following, especially among the township youths, probably because of its preoccupation with material gains – such as the flashy limousines evident in some of the videos. Urban grooves musicians exhibit a consciousness that is far removed from the major concerns of most Zimbabweans. Zimdancehall music, on the other hand, has responded to the realities of the times – for instance, through the musicians' awareness of Zimbabwe's perennial challenges, such as endemic poverty, corruption, social immorality and other related issues that have plagued post-independence Zimbabwe.

It can be argued that dancehall music has provided the youth with opportunities to air their views and to register a strong protest about their conditions. This is more so since such music is mostly produced and recorded in backyard studios that are not registered, thus making it difficult for authorities to keep track or censor the lyrics and the performances that are quickly and widely disseminated for public consumption largely through social media. The genre has also afforded unemployed youths some form of employment in a country where young people are the hardest hit in terms of unemployment. The *Zimbabwe Country Report for the 2014 Ministerial Conference on Youth Employment* makes the following crucial observations: according to the 2012 population census, Zimbabwe has a young population. Of the total population of 13 061 239, 77 per cent are children and youth below 35 years of age. Youth aged 15–34 make up 4 702 046 individuals, which constitutes 36 per cent of the national population and those aged 15–24 years are 20 per cent. The youth aged 15–34 years constitute 56 per cent of the economically active population.[1]

Unemployment is one of the major challenges confronting young people in Zimbabwe. Available data indicates that despite being in the majority, young people are mostly unemployed. The 2012 population census data shows that the youth aged 15–34 constitutes 84 per cent of the unemployed population and those aged 15–24 constitute 55 per cent. The statistics also indicate that the highest concentration (31 per cent) of the unemployed is between the ages of 20 and 24.

It is worth noting that despite the increasing popularity of dancehall music among the youth in Zimbabwe, this music genre has received very little critical attention, as most researchers have tended to focus on established musicians in their respective genres. One possible explanation is that dancehall is not only a relatively new music genre in Zimbabwe, but is also steeped in controversy. Researchers have tended to dismiss it without paying due attention to its dynamism or its potential as a tool for conscientising society, particularly the youth. For instance, some critics, including one leading Zimbabwean music critic, Fred Zindi (2014), are of the view that dancehall lyrics lack maturity and rather than being helpful, as expected of art in an African context (see Kwabena Nketia 1990), the lyrics are nonsensical, vulgar, uncouth and, in some instances, mere noise. Others have accused Zimdancehall musicians of being copycats that blindly and shamelessly imitate Jamaican art, despite the fact that in Jamaica this genre is associated with marijuana, violence and sexual abuse. One of the leading dancehall musicians, Winky D, 'has been loosely rated by critics as a ghetto chanter who sings about violence, women and drugs, thriving on imitating international Dancehall icons' (Mangosho, Mukwara and Mhako 2014: 78) – in spite of the fact that he has taken to the stage to raise society's consciousness about critical issues such as the need to curb the spread of HIV and AIDS, which have wreaked havoc in Zimbabwe and the rest of southern Africa.

Scholarship on Zimdancehall is therefore of the view that dancehall musicians are merely engaged in the glorification and promotion of moral decadence, which

---

1. See http://www.adeanet.org/min_conf_youth_skills_employment/sites/default/files/u24/Zimbabwe%20Country%20Report_0.pdf.

does not augur well for the moral fibre of Zimbabwean society, particularly the youth. What is undeniable is the fact that some lyrics are not only uncouth and bordering on vulgarity, but are also accompanied by outrageous and indecent dancing styles, as well as semi-nude youngsters, including girls simulating sex, as is the case with Lady Bee's videos, 'Murume' (A Husband) and 'Mamisa' (To Cause Someone to Mess Themselves up). Although the exploitation of sexuality could be for the purpose of 'attracting wider audiences and receiving more attention' (Thielen 2010), it is seen as immoral in the face of indigenous cultural tradition that considers the human body, particularly the female body, as sacred. Such music fits Bridget Chinouriri's (2013: 113) observation that 'in the contemporary milieu, music creativity and music development have been directed to entertainment and self-gratification by both creators and consumers of musical arts. The established utilitarian role of musical arts in society has been reduced to a greater extent to a mere art for art's sake.'

Although the critic's views are rather extreme, there is no denying that such music represents a marked departure from the traditional role of art in African communities, where 'the performer has always been the voice of society from time immemorial' (Chinouriri 2013: 115) and has been expected to 'be resolute and militant regarding his divine assignment of representing the silent voices of the people, even in a difficult environment' (116). To foreground the critical role that music plays in society, particularly in the African context, Niyi Osundare (2002: 6) observes:

> You cannot keep quiet in the kind of countries we find ourselves in. In Africa you wake up and there is no running water when you have power outages for days and nights, no food on the table . . . no peace of mind . . . There is no other way than to sing about this in an attempt to change the situation for the better.

Zimbabwe's socio-political environment is the reality that the artist grapples with. Like other forms of art, Zimdancehall, therefore, cannot be fully appreciated outside the context that has given rise to it and continues to shape it.

Zimdancehall in Ndebele

This chapter is a critical analysis of Zimdancehall in Ndebele, using selected songs from one Bulawayo-based musician, Senko, as a case study. Senko has been selected for a number of reasons. Firstly, he is one of the few of Bulawayo's rising Ndebele Zimdancehall artists who, by virtue of their pioneer status, are likely to influence the direction of Zimdancehall in the Ndebele language. Secondly, he has produced a sizeable number of tracks in Ndebele, compared to other artists in this genre, most of whom have not gone beyond one or two songs. Thirdly, his initial dancehall performances were a mixture of three of Zimbabwe's major languages: English, Shona and Ndebele, but he has since made a conscious decision to focus on producing dancehall in Ndebele. For these reasons, it is important to subject his music to scholarly analysis. As already noted, the bulk of dancehall music in Zimbabwe is in Shona, hence the observation by Bruce Ndlovu (2015) that Senko comes from 'a different breed of Zimdancehall artistes' and is bringing 'a different flavor' by virtue of the fact that 'he tackles the popular genre with lyrics mainly chanted in the Ndebele language'. Ndlovu goes on to say that Senko consciously chose to 'tackle the popular genre in a language that people are not used to' as a way of distinguishing himself from the rest.

As is the case with most forms of music, dancehall is in essence poetry and poetic techniques, such as alliteration and assonance, which accentuate the rhythmic aspect of this semi-chanted music genre. However, music is not just about rhythm, but also about words, that is, the message. In line with the prime role of the artist in Africa, the focus of this chapter is on the lyrical content of the music, as opposed to the rhythm and other elements. As is the case with artists whose chants are in Shona, Ndebele musicians draw heavily from – and in some cases imitate – Jamaican dancehall wholesale in terms of rhythm and the thematic aspects of their performances, the only major difference being their chosen language of communication. Zimdancehall rhythm and themes therefore cut across language boundaries. This means that Zimdancehall in Ndebele has not deviated markedly from the Jamaican version in terms of rhythm and themes, and Senko is no exception. For instance, his 'Hit Track', whose lyrics are rendered predominantly in pidgin English, is a celebration of mindless entertainment which, according to critics of this genre, actively promotes anti-social behaviour. The song goes as follows:

> It's S.E.N.K.O. make a table an' bring mi da liquar deh
> Today it's a holiday we gonna party like we don't care
> Every gal give me a slow wine there
> *Ngendlela oshaker ngayo* (The way you shake your body)

> *Uphambanisa abantu ku-*dance floor (You disturb people on the dance floor)
> *Ngendlela oyenza ngayo* gal (The way you do it girl)
> *Ungiphambanisa ingqondo* (You disturb my brain)
> Babe, jus wine *yenza ngani wena awunamathambo* (Babe, just wine and pretend you have no bones)
> Babe, move your body come to me, jus wine babe ×15
> Shake it babe just move
> Shake it babe don't move now
> Babe come back it pan mi don stop
> Do it like you never did before.

In typical Jamaican style, the lyrics, which express the vocalist's sexual prowess, are a celebration of love, parties and the attendants' drunkenness. Notwithstanding that this is music for the youth, the elaborate description of erotic movements would be considered immoral from an African perspective. Perhaps this explains why the lyrics are predominantly in English, as any attempt to translate them into any of Zimbabwe's local languages would border on vulgarity. The lyrics call to mind Lady Bee's 'Ane Zihombe' (He Has a Huge One), which is in the Shona language. The suggestive title, which is also the refrain of the song, unmistakably alludes to the size of the male reproductive organ. This is unacceptable in African culture, even more so since it comes from a female musician. Women in Zimbabwean culture are revered for their child-rearing and child-nurturing capacities. They are shapers of the society's morals and consciousness, mirrored in the proverb 'If you educate a man you educate an individual, but if you educate a woman you educate a family (nation)' (Suen 2013: 60). Also, as Chinouriri (2013: 17) observes, young people, perhaps as a result of their impressionable minds, tend to idolise their favourite music performers and blindly 'want to imitate everything they do – even if it is contrary to societal norms'. Perhaps it is for this reason that a Bulawayo-based Zimdancehall artist, Bovas, has urged all fellow artists to 'not use dirty lyrics'.[2]

However, it would not be correct to dismiss Zimdancehall as a genre that only promotes anti-social behaviour, thus 'propagating a ruinous mindset among

---

2. http://www.zbc.co.zw/news- categories/entertainment/56797-play-our-music-zim-dancehall-artists.

the youth' (Chinouriri 2013: 120), as some of the lyrics are indicative of the seriousness with which the artists view their role in society. To dismiss dancehall as an unnecessary evil produced by directionless young people would be unfortunate, for it would imply that contrary to real life, young musicians in Zimbabwe lack identity and cultural consciousness. Joseph Kwabena Nketia (1974: 20) holds that music should be appreciated in its socio-cultural context. This is important as it affords critics a deeper appreciation of both music makers and music users. An examination of Zimdancehall lyrics indicates that the artists are aware of their roles as the sensitive needle of society, evident in the fact that their compositions have serious messages not only for the youth, but for society in general. For instance, Winky D, arguably the most prominent dancehall musician in Zimbabwe, has taken it upon himself to contribute to voices that continue to raise awareness about the HIV scourge that has ravaged Zimbabwe and other countries in the region. In recognition for his positive influence on the youth, Winky D was appointed brand ambassador for male circumcision by Population Services International from 2011 to 2016. Many other dancehall artists draw attention to Zimbabwe's perennial problems that have adversely affected urban households, for instance, water scarcity, load shedding and sewage problems, which are bound to be worse for poor households. This is in line with Norman Stolzoff's (2000) findings based on dancehall culture in Jamaica that this genre has afforded young, black Jamaicans from lower classes the opportunity to articulate and also project a distinct identity in local, national and global contexts.

The seriousness with which Zimdancehall should be considered is amply demonstrated in the lyrical content of the majority of Senko's songs. For instance, his protest song sarcastically titled 'Amasela Emzilikazi' (Thieves of Mzilikazi) is a fierce defence of marginalised poor communities, from the negative attitude and the disparaging remarks that are often aimed at them by the rich:

Bakhuluma kabi ngeghetto lami
Bathi kuphuma amasela eMzilikazi
Bakhuluma kabi ngeghetto lami
Bathi kuphuma amawule eMakhokhoba . . .
Ngifuna ukubakwazi watshontshelwa ngabangaki
Owababona bethatha okungayisikho kwabo bangaki?
Owababona besenza izinto ezimbi?
Ngiyababona lababantu basithathela phansi

Babona angani akulalutho oluphuma ekasi
Bafuna ukusenza amasela bafuna ukusenza mawule
Manje mina ngiya ngithi fire burn dem no
USenko uphumaphi? UPeter Ndlovu uphumaphi? UMadinda uzelwe kuphi?
The late *Beater Mangethe uzelwe kuphi?*
Hayikhona ukuthi likhulume izinto elingazazi . . .
Abazi labafundisi silabo.
They speak ill of my ghetto
They say Mzilikazi breeds thieves
They speak ill of my ghetto
They say Makhokhoba breeds prostitutes
They speak ill of my ghetto
They say Mzilikazi breeds thieves
They speak ill of my ghetto
They say Makhokhoba breeds prostitutes . . .
I would like to know, how many have stolen from you?
How many have you seen taking that which does not belong to them? Or doing bad things?
I can see that these people have a low opinion of us
They think nothing good comes out of the townships
They want to turn us into thieves and prostitutes
As for me I resist this, saying *fire burn dem no*
Where does Senko come from?
Where does Peter Ndlovu come from?
Where was Madinda born?
What about the late Beater Mangethe?
Do not talk about things that you are not fully conversant with . . .
They do not know that we also have pastors/ministers of religion.

The song draws attention to the fact that the majority of black Zimbabwean urbanites have suffered almost a century and a half of endemic poverty, as evident from their continued marginalisation in terms of development priorities in the post-independence era. The musician mocks the assumption by the privileged that nothing good can come out of the poor, an indication of the ever-widening gap between the haves and the have-nots, as well as the resultant tensions. The gap is amply reflected in the sharp contrasts in terms of residential areas where the respective classes hail. Mzilikazi and Makokoba, which are mentioned in the song, are some of Bulawayo's oldest and most poverty-stricken former townships, referred to as high-density suburbs after independence. These are the ghetto areas that the musician is referring to. The geographical spread of the ghetto is extensive, covering all high-density suburbs, as is evident in another of Senko's song titled 'Bas Ah Blunk'. The title is a slogan that the ghetto youth use to identify one another. The political elite has inadvertently created a formidable force that has taken it upon itself to challenge the rulers who have been presiding over an economic system that has failed to transform the lives of the majority for the better. The ghetto stands in contrast to the low-density or leafy suburbs where the privileged reside. The artist challenges the assumption that the high-density areas are dominated by thieves and other people of low morals. He protests that the political and economic elite paint the majority poor with the same brush, that is, they are outsiders, gangsters and generally people of questionable morals, an indication that the rich neither sympathise nor empathise with the poor. He directly confronts the elite and sarcastically questions whether their negative pronouncements are informed by the reality on the ground, or are arising out of wilful ignorance – hence the series of direct questions, '*Ngifuna ukuba kwazi wantshontshelwa ngabangaki?*' (I wish to know how many have stolen from you). This disconnect between the privileged and the underprivileged is also pertinently reflected by the Amakhosi Cultural Centre director, who is reported in a state-owned newspaper to have criticised Andrew Langa, then minister of Sports, Arts and Culture for being 'too busy to stay and listen to artistes' concerns' (Ndlovu 2014). This confrontational approach is also evident in the tone of the song under discussion, which is a marked departure from the victim mentality commonplace in most protest art in Ndebele. The artist has used this genre that is often looked down on to wage a struggle against the elite in defence of the poor majority's dignity and self-worth.

While it is common knowledge that poverty can drive individuals into prostitution, the fact that there is no marked difference between the Makokoba of today and that of yesteryear in terms of economic and social well-being is an indication of the failures of the post-independence dispensation. Preben Kaarsholm (1999: 246) makes the following observation about the city of Bulawayo, almost twenty years after Zimbabwe's independence:

> Bulawayo today is a fascinating mixture of change and continuity. The townships (now high density suburbs) continue to display the old characteristics of poverty and deprivation, crime persists as an everyday problem, and the limited institutional cultural facilities continue to centre around beer gardens, shebeens, churches and community halls. The overwhelming impression a visitor now gets is of persistent segregation between the living conditions of rich and poor, proper citizens and tolerated ones.

This bears testimony to the fact that not much has been done to upgrade the lives of the poor majority in Zimbabwe. In the song in question, ironically for a moment the tables have been turned and the voice of the often misunderstood and downtrodden majority stands unchallenged in its determination to speak out on the conditions of the underprivileged. The voice represents some triumph by the downtrodden over the privileged elite who, because of their ignorance or callous attitude, often misunderstand and misrepresent the lives of the majority and paint a picture that runs contrary to the reality that has always been known by those who are looked down upon. The artist speaks fondly of the high-density suburbs, choosing to refer to them as *'ighetto lami'* (my ghetto). The song cites well-known names born and bred in the ghetto, among whom are celebrated musicians such as Senko and the late Beater Mangethe, national soccer stars such as Madinda Ndlovu and Peter Ndlovu. The song alleges that the rich want to turn the poor into thieves and prostitutes and is a reflection of a society deeply divided along class lines. One can sense anger and bitterness against the rich, while there is a fierce defence of the downtrodden or the 'masses', as they came to be collectively referred to after independence. This labelling makes it difficult, if not impossible, for its originators, including those who use or promote it, to treat people as individual human beings who deserve respect. Instead, they are simply lumped together as an indistinguishable mass, thereby impinging on their individual identity and seriously eroding their self-worth and self-confidence, as well as their humanity. This negative attitude of the wealthy towards those less fortunate than they are militates against national unity, national development and the well-being of society. It flies in the face of the lofty promises of the post-independence government to uplift the lives of the poor.

However, this negative attitude is not without foundation, for it is a well-known fact that social and economic inequality and poverty breed discontent and crime. The unprecedented socio-economic challenges that gripped the country during what has come to be known as the 'decade of crisis' (2000–10) led to a sharp decline in household incomes, as well as rising unemployment and increased poverty, in particular for urban dwellers (Hanke and Kwok 2009), with many families being forced to live on less than one US dollar per day. In an already divided country, this may lead to national instability.

In 'Khonapho Khonapho' (There and Then), Senko alludes to the economic hardships bedevilling the nation. The title could be an allusion to the get-rich-quick culture that appears to have replaced honest hard work in the new dispensation. While the artist appears to be boasting about the quality of his music and his popularity as a musician, it is also apparent that people have adopted this 'motto', as the musician calls it, as a survival strategy:

> Assassins *uzasithola* everywhere
> *Njenge traffic cop bazadiza* every *dei*
> *Ufuna ungafuni ngokwakho lokho*
> *Buya eghetto dats* our motto
> *Hamba ekhoneni uzabathola bebanga umsindo*
> *Sidinga imali akula ongasi* stopper.
> *Lapha esihamba khona siding' imali*
> *Asila ndaba sibhekwe ngubani*
> Assassins' *siyabe siding imali*
> One rand, two rands *siyabe siding' imali.*
> Assassins you will find us everywhere
> Just like the traffic police who line their pockets on a daily basis
> Whether you like it or not this is how things are
> Come to the ghetto that's our motto
> Go to every corner you will find them making noise
> We are looking for money, no one will stop us.
> We are looking for money wherever we go.
> We do not care who sees us
> Assassins we will be looking for money
> One rand, two rand we will be looking for money.

The praise name 'silent assassins', which the artist uses to refer to himself and his group, unfortunately has connotations of violence and death. It gives an image of invincible, larger-than-life figures, who will do whatever it takes to get money. The song is, however, an apt expression of the living conditions of people in the ghetto. While they strive to make an honest living out of selling a variety of wares on every street corner, the municipal police are quick to round them up and, in some cases, even confiscate their wares, thus leading to a further plummeting of their living standards. Zimbabwe's appalling socio-economic conditions have turned the country into a nation of vendors. Many people have hardened and developed an 'I do not care' attitude. This attitude that pervades the song gives credence to critics' perceptions that anarchy, which breeds corruption, reigns in Zimbabwe, and the people will do whatever it takes to earn income to sustain their families. In the song in question, it appears that the pursuit of money has overtaken all other aspects of their lives. The same attitude may be a pointer to a system that has dehumanised both the exploiter and the exploited, a situation that has serious repercussions for the nation's moral fabric. To compound the situation, the musician alludes to a variety of social ills that have pervaded post-independence Zimbabwe. For instance, reference to the traffic police is a pointer to the allegations of corruption that have been levelled against policemen who run roadblocks in Zimbabwe, who often demand bribes from unsuspecting motorists, in particular emergency taxi drivers. The comparison between the people's desire to get money with the traffic police is most unfortunate as it insinuates that the ordinary people (including musicians who do part-time vending), like the traffic cops, resort to unethical means to get an income. At the same time, it is a serious indictment on the police in general and the post-independence government in particular.

In another track titled 'Abafundisi' (Pastors), the musician protests against what he considers to be a raw deal that pastors receive from congregants in particular and from society in general. The rise of Pentecostalism and its various denominations has given birth to serious questions regarding the role of the church in Zimbabwean society. In particular, the emergence of prosperity pastors has led to serious allegations that some men of the cloth have deviated from their core agenda of preaching the gospel of salvation, to pursuing wealth, thereby preying on desperate churchgoers by converting congregants' hard-earned cash to their own use and, in the process, promising a non-existent heaven on earth. Surprisingly, the musician, perhaps a staunch believer, is on the side of the men of the cloth:

Bakhuluma kabi ngabo pastor *bethu. Bakhuluma kabi ngabafundisi* ×2
Manje mina namhla ngizalikhuluma iqiniso noma kanjani . . . ×2

Upastor angathenga imota yimali yechurch
Edrayive iskorokoro yimali yechurch. Kodwa ngicela ukubuza
I-one rand yenu ingathenga imoto enhle kanje. Athenge isudu yimali yechurch
Kodwa ubon' angani i-one rand yakho. Ingathenga isudu enhle kanje?
Ngizobakhuluma mina ng'zobakhuluma. Ngoba lababantu bakhuluma kabi
Kanti gobani lisebenze enkonzweni yechurch
Yini odiyabhorosi osatane lidingani enkonzweni . . .
Kodwa kusasa yini abokuqala ukuhlupha umfundisi ebusuku
'Pastor this, pastor dat', lifuna ukukhulekelwa.
Kodwa belikhuluma kabi
They speak ill of our pastors. They speak ill of our ministers ×2
As for me I shall say the truth today whatever happens . . . ×2
Why do you assume that if a pastor buys cars, he is using church money?
If he drives a dilapidated car, he is using church money?
But I wish to ask a question
Can your one rand buy such a good car?
If he buys a suit, he is using church money.
But in all honesty can your one rand buy such a nice suit?
I will say the truth about these people,
Because they speak ill [of our pastors]
You work for the church
Yet you are Satan the devil, so what do you want in church?
Yet you are the first to bother the minister, even at night
'Pastor this, pastor that', you are quick to request the pastor to pray for you
Yet you say bad things about him.

The last two lines are evidence of the fact that, faced with adverse economic and social circumstances, Zimbabweans have tended to turn to religion to find answers to life's challenges. Pastors of African independent/indigenous churches, as well as Pentecostal churches, have become controversial figures in Zimbabwe because of the powers they claim to have and the massive wealth that some have flaunted publicly. Although the song above is in defence of pastors and ministers of religion, it also unwittingly and ironically alludes to a culture of exploitation that has engulfed post-independence Zimbabwe. The church has become a site of struggle, with pastors competing to attract huge congregations allegedly for earthly fame and the accumulation of material riches. As a result, men of the cloth in Zimbabwe, as well as elsewhere on the continent and beyond, rank among the richest in their respective societies. In Zimbabwe, the desperation of the exploited churchgoers partly arises from abject poverty that has wreaked havoc in the country. The prevalence of individuals who can only afford one rand as church offering bears testimony to the adverse socio-economic conditions bedevilling the nation. The resort to a multi-currency system is a reminder of the demise of the local currency as a result of the unprecedented economic meltdown that gripped Zimbabwe at the height of the decade of crisis.

Furthermore, diseases such as HIV and AIDS are rampant in a country that has been plagued with a flight of human and material resources, in addition to the myriad of other challenges. Citing the 2010 United Nations Children's Fund (UNICEF) report, Belamino Chikwaiwa, Kefasi Nyikahadzoi and Abel Matsika (2013: 77) state that 'the HIV and AIDS pandemic has orphaned about 1.6 million children in Zimbabwe'. While modern medicine has found no cure for HIV and AIDS, traditional healers claim that a cure exists, while some men of the cloth claim that faith in God alone can cure any diseases, including HIV and AIDS. In her study of male reproductive health-seeking behaviour in Zimbabwe, Stanzia Moyo (2013: 16–20) avers that for various reasons, Zimbabwean men tend to have a negative attitude towards the use of modern healthcare facilities, with some resorting, instead, to religion. This represents a significant proportion of Zimbabwean society. Individuals in desperate need of a cure for incurable medical conditions have thronged to church healing schools and sessions. Such individuals have been told to 'look up to God for protection, prevention and curing of diseases' (8). It is no wonder therefore that the prosperity gospel that foregrounds earthly comforts and wealth has attracted millions of Zimbabweans who are in desperate need of cure, solace and comfort in these difficult times. Therefore, where modern medicine has failed, there is always religion to resort to, hence the musician's assertion that the very same people who criticise the pastor for using church funds for personal gain, are the ones who will bother the pastor by requesting prayers when faced with difficult circumstances. The people appear to be in a catch-22 situation. They believe that they are being exploited, yet because of their hardships, they cannot extricate themselves from the exploiter. The danger, though, is that the belief that there is a cure for AIDS may lead to the practice of high-risk behaviour associated with the spread of HIV and AIDS.

Conclusion

In Zimbabwe, dancehall music has generally been regarded as the music of Harare's ghetto youth. However, of late, it has been fast gaining popularity with Bulawayo's township youths, who can now identify with it, as its lyrics are being rendered in a language that they are familiar with. Although some critics have a tendency to dismiss this music genre as a corrupt and corrupting force in society, it has come to prominence as a form of protest against certain sections of society, as well as the establishment. As a socio-political force, it constitutes a critical interrogation of topical socio-political issues confronting lower-class urbanites in particular and Zimbabweans across the political, race, ethnic and class divide, in general. Furthermore, as an interrogative tool, it can be used to fight societal imbalances. Zimdancehall musicians appear to be carefully negotiating their identity as artists. While they would want to remain faithful to the originators of the genre in terms of lewd performance and lyrical content, they are also mindful of their role as artists in an African set-up. They are therefore mindful of the fact that they play a critical role in being the voice of the voiceless, as expected of the artist in African communities. Zimdancehall therefore strives to be relevant to its youthful consumers by speaking out on their concerns and interests. Of note is that the Ndebele people have felt that they have been treated as outsiders, not only in terms of limited airplay accorded to Ndebele music in various radio stations and on television, but also in all spheres of life. It therefore comes as no surprise that the Bulawayo youths are beginning to resonate with Zimdancehall being produced in Ndebele, as they identify with the language that defines them and also sets them apart as a distinct micro-nation within the larger Zimbabwean nation.

References

Beach, D.N. 1986. *War and Politics in Zimbabwe 1840–1900*. Gweru: Mambo Press.

Chikwaiwa, B.K., K. Nyikahadzoi and A.B. Matsika. 2013. 'The Determinants of Social Capital and their Role on Psychosocial Well-being of Orphans and Other Vulnerable Adolescents in Zimbabwe'. *Zambezia* 40(1–2): 77–88.

Chinouriri, B. 2013. 'Drawing from Indigenous Knowledge Systems: A Guide for Shona Creativity and Performance'. In *Africa and Beyond: Arts and Sustainable Development*, edited by P. Ebewo, I. Stevens and M. Sirayi, 109–21. Newcastle: Scholars Publishing.

Hanke, S.H. and A.K.F. Kwok. 2009. 'On the Measurement of Zimbabwe's Hyperinflation'. *Cato Journal* 29(2): 353–64.

Kaarsholm, P. 1999. '*Si Ye Phambili* – Which Way Forward? Urban Development, Culture and Politics in Bulawayo'. In *Sites of Struggle: Essays in Zimbabwe's Urban History*, edited by B. Raftopoulos and T. Yoshikuni, 227–56. Harare: Weaver Press.

Kwabena Nketia, J.H. 1990. 'Contextual Strategies of Inquiry and Systematization'. *Journal of the Society of Ethnomusicology* 34(1): 75–97.

———. 1974. *The Music of Africa*. New York: W.W. Norton.

Mangosho, T., P. Mukwara and D. Mhako. 2014. 'Protest and Subversion in Zimbabwe's Dancehall Music: The Case of Winky D'. In *Singing Nation and Politics: Music and the 'Decade of Crisis' in Zimbabwe, 2000–2010*, edited by I. Muwati, T. Charamba and C. Tembo, 75–87. Gweru: Midlands State University.

Moyo, S. 2013. 'Male Reproductive Health-seeking Behavior in a Rural Set-up: A Case Study of Mhondoro-Ngezi, Kadoma District, Zimbabwe'. *Zambezia* 40 (1–2): 1–24.

Ndlovu, B. 2014. 'Minister Gets Tongue Lashing from Cont Mhlanga'. Nehanda Radio. http://nehandaradio.com/2014/10/10/minister-gets-tongue-lashing-cont-mhlanga.

———. 2015. 'Senko Tackles Dancehall in isiNdebele'. *B-Metro*, 30 March. http://www.b-metro.co.zw/senko-tackles-dancehall-in-isindebele/.

Osundare, N. 2002. *Thread in the Loom: Essays on African Literature and Culture*. Trenton: Africa World Press.

Stolzoff, N.C. 2000. *Wake the Town and Tell the People: Dancehall Culture in Jamaica*. Durham: Duke University Press.

Suen, S. 2013. 'The Education of Women as a Tool in Development: Challenging the African Maxim'. *Hydra* 1(2): 60–76. http://journals.ed.ac.uk/hydra/article/viewFile/720/1002.

Thielen, B. 2010. 'The Change of Messages in Dancehall'. Essays from the University of Vermont Class, Rhetoric of Reggae Music. Dread Library: University of Vermont https://debate.uvm.edu/dreadlibrary/thielen.html.

Zindi, F. 2014. 'Dancehall Slackness Unacceptable'. *The Herald*, 15 September. http://www.herald.co.zw/dancehall-slackness-unaceptable/.

Conclusion

Luis Gimenez Amoros

This book examines how music takes place under different historical, social, cultural and political circumstances in Zimbabwean society. In addition, it offers a conscious involvement of Zimbabwean scholars in reconsidering the country's music and nationhood, providing a foundational pillar for future studies on Zimbabwean music. Throughout the book, the meaning of music is interpreted in multiple ways that emphasise the importance of the semiotic interaction between music and society. This interaction has been focal in this transdisciplinary study – even a musicological study, such as the one by Perminus Matiure on *mbira* music, provides an understanding of how rural musical culture has been spread through rural to urban migration as a result of wage labour and other forms of industrialisation. Therefore, in this book, the understanding of Zimbabwean music is not only based on musical aesthetic values, but also on its interaction and interconnectedness with Zimbabwean society.

The scholars who have contributed to this book perceive the notion of Zimbabweanness. For instance, Innocent Tinashe Mutero's chapter on the use of *chinyambera* dance provides a valuable criticism of censorship and cultural resistance against government cultural control. Mutero's criticism questions the centralisation of the government towards cultural production in Zimbabwe. Bridget Chinouriri and Munyaradzi Nyakudya demonstrate another clear example of cultural control by the government, showing that even in positive movements towards equality, such as agrarian reform, music was used by the ruling Zimbabwe African National Union – Patriotic Front (ZANU–PF) to promote the reform, while also capturing the votes of indecisive Zimbabweans during the 2000s. In other words, Chinouriri and Nyakudya show that the use of music during the agrarian reform was a strategy by the government to regain control and not necessarily to fairly develop an equalitarian and independent society. The notion of nationhood is highly contested in most of the chapters of this book.

Making a significant contribution to postcolonial literature, this book also touches on the artificial borders of Zimbabwe, as they stretch over the Shona people of Mozambique in the east and the Tonga people of Zambia to the west. Equally importantly, the book draws attention to the cultural and musical similarities between these southern African countries. The possibility of knowing how music circulates beyond colonial borders earmarks new forms of transdisciplinary studies that may lead to new analyses of Zimbabwean music in relation to neighbouring states. This exploration of Zimbabwean musical culture thus reveals that music transcends borders in southern Africa and shows that both people and music constantly move along precolonial geographical spaces.

Contemporary studies on the youth in urban spaces are also an important aspect of this book, through the study of Zimdancehall, which provides evidence that the youth in Zimbabwe is seemingly distinctly separated, apparent through linguistic and ethnicised demarcations of Shona and Ndebele. In addition, the analyses of Zimdancehall also bring to the fore the patriarchal inclinations that permeate certain musical lyrics, such as those that perpetuate the objectification of women as docile, sexual objects and voiceless. Such criticism of Zimdancehall by Zimbabwean scholars offers a positive input onto the music genre dominated by the youth and offers views on both the lack and presence of constructive content in the genre towards an equalitarian society. Furthermore, given that the origins of Zimdancehall are attributable to Jamaica, the study of this musical style provides a valuable criticism with regard to the notion of blackness for youth from the global South and how it is dominated by patriarchal discourses from outside Africa and not primarily local values. As demonstrated by the Zimbabwean scholars in this book, the analysis of Zimdancehall serves to underline internal and external forms of patriarchal behaviour inherent in the production of this musical genre. In contrast, Renias Ngara and Doreen Sibanda have provided an analysis of how gender equality is promoted in Tsonga and Karanga culture in southern Zimbabwe through dance and musical styles such as *xinombela*. The gender analyses in this book offer multiple and differing opinions regarding rural dances that are considered educative or urban music as influenced by external musical styles from African Americans from Jamaica or the United States.

An exploration of the Zimbabwean music industry provides a clear reference on how the interaction between musicians and other agents is sustained and affected by the economy. Examining the interaction between Zimbabwean musicians and promoters, record labels, CD piracy or the government is essential to understanding how artists navigate Zimbabwean society.

On the other hand, the analyses of how *mbira* music is mythologised as the Zimbabwean instrument par excellence by the political elite and, as a result, by Zimbabwean society. *Mbira* music has been exported as 'the music of Zimbabwe' in the world music industry in the global North – perhaps making it the most researched and valued instrument from Zimbabwe globally. In particular, there has been a homogenisation of the *mbira* instrument through the *mbira nhare* (or *dzavadzimu*) and the *karimba* (or *nyunganyunga*) globally. However, other *mbiras* from Zimbabwe such as the *mbira ndau*, the *mbira njari* or *mbira matepe* are not as popular as these *mbiras*. Such a reality demonstrates that the impact of certain *mbiras* around the globe, or the ones promoted by the Zimbabwean education system, favour the homegenisation of the *mbira nhare* and the *karimba* in Zimbabwean society and consequently in the world music industry. Furthermore, this book opens up the evolution and creativity of instrument making through Matiure's chapter, in which he highlights how scholars are able to participate in the evolution of *mbira* musical culture in Zimbabwe.

This book thus presents a wide range of critical questions pertaining to the study of Zimbabwean music that need to be developed in the future, in areas such as historical studies, gender interactions, power struggles, the migration of music from rural to urban spaces as a result of ongoing industrialisation and labour demands and the sustainability of the music industry in Zimbabwe. This book therefore provides an in-depth and important overview of how different aspects of the Zimbabwean music play out through the academic lenses of the contributing scholars. Fundamentally, the objective of this book is to provide a solid foundation of multidisciplinary studies on Zimbabwean music and the notion of Zimbabweanness for future scholars.

Contributors

Sandra Bhatasara is a senior lecturer in the Department of Sociology at the University of Zimbabwe. She writes on gender and women's issues, among other things.

Victoria Blessing Butete is a lecturer in the Department of Music Business, Musicology and Technology at Midlands State University in Zimbabwe. She is a PhD candidate at the University of South Africa. Her research interests include popular music, popular culture, music marketing and management, media relations, audience reception, copyright law and music journalism, creative economy, creative industries and cultural policy.

Vimbai Chamisa is a lecturer in the Department of Music Business, Musicology and Technology at Midlands State University in Zimbabwe. She studied ethnomusicology and popular music and her research interests lie in music and identity, indigenous music and sustainable development, as well as music as it relates to politics. She is conducting doctoral research on *sungura* music in Zimbabwe at the University of South Africa.

Bridget Chinouriri is an ethnomusicologist, creative writer, culture consultant and scientist. She is a senior lecturer in the Department of African Languages and Literature, University of Zimbabwe. She did her Master's at the University of Ghana (J.H. Kwabena Nketia) and PhD at the University of Pretoria (Meki Nzewi). Her interests include indigenous knowledge systems, expressive arts, land, cultural science and gender studies.

Manase Kudzai Chiweshe is a senior lecturer in the Institute of Lifelong Learning and Development Studies at Chinhoyi University of Technology and winner of the 2015 Gerti Hessling Award. He is the author of the book *The Peoples' Game: Football Fandom in Zimbabwe* (2017). His work revolves around the sociology of everyday life in African spaces.

CONTRIBUTORS

Luis Gimenez Amoros is a research fellow at the Centre for Humanities Research at the University of the Western Cape. He has researched transcultural music, postcolonial studies and new/old mobilities in precolonial music in Algeria, Western Sahara, Mali, Zimbabwe, Zambia and South Africa, as well as India and Spain. He is also a composer and has released solo albums and performed with numerous international artists.

Barbara Mahamba has a Master's in African history from the University of Zimbabwe and a PhD on mission and education history from the University of Wales. She is a lecturer in the History Department at the University of Zimbabwe. Her research interests are in African women's history, gender, mission and education history, the history of Asians in Zimbabwe and various aspects of social history in Zimbabwe and Africa.

Ruby Magosvongwe has a doctorate from the University of Cape Town, and is an associate professor in the Department of English, University of Zimbabwe, and the current chair of the department. She is editor-in-chief of the University of Zimbabwe's journal of humanities, *Zambezia*. She has compiled and co-edited a number of books, most recently *Africa's Intangible Heritage and Land: Emerging Perspectives* (2016).

Zifikile Makwavarara, a full professor and the founding and current director of the Postgraduate Centre at the University of Zimbabwe, has a Doctor of Philosophy degree from the University of Cape Town. Her research interests and publications include comparative and diasporan literature, literature and gender, culture and development, indigenous knowledge and technology, and land and indigenisation.

Rekopantswe Mate is a senior lecturer in the Department of Sociology at the University of Zimbabwe. She recently developed an undergraduate course on 'Popular Culture and Society', which she also teaches. She holds a PhD in Development Studies, specialising in youth studies, from the International Institute of Social Studies, Erasmus University, Rotterdam (EUR), in the Netherlands.

Perminus Matiure teaches ethnomusicology, video documentation, *mbira* playing and instrument construction and is currently chairperson of the Department of Music and Musicology at Midlands State University. Through research and experience in *mbira*, he designed four *mbira* innovations and founded an *mbira* ensemble called Zvirimudeze, which has recorded one album. He holds a PhD from the University of KwaZulu-Natal.

Innocent Tinashe Mutero holds a PhD in Peace Studies and a Master's in Applied Ethnomusicology. Mutero's research interests include community engagement and shared agency, arts for social change and conflict transformation. He is a part-time *mbira* lecturer at the University of KwaZulu-Natal and a guest contributor for the Music in Africa online portal, @263chat, and *The Herald*. Above all, he is a community artist.

Itai Muwati is executive dean of the Faculty of Arts at the University of Zimbabwe. He has a PhD from the University of South Africa, where he is also a research fellow. He obtained his Master's from the University of Zimbabwe. He is an associate professor of African literature and culture and has published widely. He has edited several books on gender and cultural studies, endangered languages and music and politics.

Tinotenda Mwamuka is studying for a Master's degree in financial analysis at La Trobe University in Australia. He is also a teaching assistant at the same university. He did his BA Honours degree at the University of Zimbabwe.

Renias Ngara holds a Master's in Music from the University of Fort Hare. He is a junior lecturer of ethnomusicology at Great Zimbabwe University and a PhD candidate in Applied Ethnomusicology at the University of Pretoria. His dissertation, on the induction of Shangwe chiefs, proposes a theoretical and practical model that may be adapted to preserve musical arts heritage, create employment and promote rural development.

Munyaradzi Nyakudya is a lecturer in the Department of History at the University of Zimbabwe. He has published on Zimbabwean history, the land question and the war of national liberation, among others. His publications include the co-edited books *Victors, Victims and Villains: Women and Musical Arts in Zimbabwe – Past and Present* (2018) and *Resilience under Siege: The Zimbabwe Economy, Politics and Society* (2016).

CONTRIBUTORS

Albert Nyathi is a poet and musician who has performed his poetry and music far and wide. He has published six books: *The Third Dimension* (1994), with Danish authors; *Echoes from Zimbabwe* (2010); *My Daughter* (2012); *My Son* (2016), co-written with Ignatius Mabasa; *Ten Conversations to End AIDS* (2016), co-written with Dr Daniel Low-Beer and *Ten Conversations on Health* (2017), also with Dr Daniel Low-Beer.

Urther Rwafa is a lecturer and associate professor in the Department of Film and Theatre Arts Studies at Midlands State University. He is also a Research Fellow at the University of South Africa (UNISA), attached to the Department of English Studies. Professor Rwafa has written extensively on film and cultural identity, film censorship, film and the representation of Rwandan genocide and music as popular culture.

Doreen Sibanda holds a Bachelors of Arts degree, with Music as a major subject of specialisation from Great Zimbabwe University. She also has a Postgraduate Diploma in Education from the same university. Sibanda is currently doing Special Honours in Music at Great Zimbabwe University.

Charles Tembo is an associate professor and chairperson of the Department of African Languages and Culture at Midlands State University. His research interests are in African literary studies, Afrocentricity and African Renaissance studies. He holds a BA (Hons) in African Languages and Culture from Midlands State University, a Master's in African Languages and Literature (University of Zimbabwe) and a PhD in African Languages (UNISA).

Azon Twala has a BA Honours degree in history from the University of Zimbabwe. He lives in Harare and has a strong interest in writing and researching on social histories, including leisure and entertainment. He also uses his intellectual energy to research and write on social problems and solutions affecting his country, Africa and the globe. In addition, he is interested in systems of governance and local and international current affairs.

Maurice T. Vambe is a professor of African Literature in English in the English Studies Department at the University of South Africa. He has published extensively on song, film and African literature in English and the Shona languages. His book

Genocide in African Fiction will be published in June 2018 by the Africa Institute for Culture, Peace, Dialogue and Tolerance Studies in collaboration with Africa World Press.

INDEX

'Abafundisi' (song: Pastors) 320–1
Acts of Parliament
   Access to Information and Privacy Protection (2002) 223–4
   Broadcasting Services (2001) 190, 223 n.4, 290
   Censorship and Control (2001) 57
   Censorship and Entertainment Act (1967) 162, 164
   Copyright and Neighbouring Rights (2000) 63
   Hall Hiring 162
   Land Acquisition (1992) 216
   Land Apportionment (1931) 161, 202
   Land Husbandry (1951) 202
   Land Tenure (1969) 202
   Law and Order Maintenance (1966) 164
   Matrimonial Causes and Maintenance (1985) 279
   Municipal Areas Act (1897) 162
   Public Entertainment Act (1965) 162
   Public Order and Security (2002) 57, 222–4
African Music Union 157
All Mills Brothers 149
Allan Ranks (performer) 252
'Amai' (song: Mother) 126–7, 128, 129
'Amasela Emzilikazi' (song: Thieves of Mzilikazi) 315–16
ancestors 2, 28, 31, 32, 97, 98, 99, 100, 105, 113, 114–15, 133, 137, 195–6, 210, 293, 294, 297–8

'Ancient Voices' (song) 131–3
'Ane Zihombe' (song: He Has a Huge One) 314
applied ethnomusicology 13–14, 25
Assegai Crew 186, 189

'Babe Wakachipa' (song: You Are Loose) 265
'Baby Help' (song) 274–6
Bacossi (Basic Commodities Supply Side Intervention) 265 n.5
bands 156, *see also* names of individual groups
Bantu Actors (formerly Expensive Bantus) 149, 150, 156
Bantu Social and Cultural Centre (Mbare) 150
'Bas Ah Blunk' (song) 317, 318
Beatles 159
beer halls 152, 158, 161
Bemba people (Zambia) 49
bembera (public ridicule) 60
'Bhendakunge Banana' (song: Bend Like a Banana) 262
Black & White Band 154, 155, 156
Black Roots 253
Blair, Tony 200
'The Blair That I Know Is a Toilet' (song) 219–20
bongo flava (East Africa) 234
Booker T (performer) 252, 290

'Boom Bye-Bye' (song by Buju Banton) 263
Born Free Crew 240
Bounty Lisa (performer) 269
Bovas (performer) 314
Brazzaville 147–8
British American Tobacco 157
Brown, Andy 225
Bulawayo 16, 30, 35, 112, 179–81, 182–3, 184, 185, 309, 312, 313, 317–18, 323
'Bvuma' (song: Admit) 224

Calaz, Seh (Tawanda Mumanyi) 231, 238, 241, 246, 247, 254, 266, 267, 268
'Calaz Ndakamukwapaidza' (song: I Beat up Calaz) 266–7
Cde Chinx *see* Makoni, Dickson Chingaira
Central African Broadcasting Station 34
'Chamba' (song: Marijuana) 268
Chambwera, Decent 37
'Chaminuka Ndimambo' (song: Chaminuka Is King) 131, 132, 133
'Chamunorwa' (song: Why the Fighting) 123–4, 125, 126, 127–8, 129, 130
'Chauraya Nyika' (song: What Has Destroyed Our Nation?) 222
Chavhunduka, J.J. 151
Chawasarira, Chaka 17, 30, 37
'Chemutengure' (song: Wagon Wheels) 38–9, 120, 130
Chewa people (Malawi) 54
Chibaya, Amos 59, 67, 68, 72
chiefs 76–7, 78, 80, 81–2, 84, 85–6
Chifunyise, David 258
Chigamba, Irene 30
Chihota, Ezekiah 149
Chikomo, Elijah 37, 40
Chikunguru (singer) 221, 222, 223
Chikupo, Tinei 196
Chillspot (studio) 254

Chimbetu, Simon 8, 194, 196–7, 198, 202, 203, 204, 213, 220
Chimedza, Albert 33
chimurenga
    first (1896–7) 196 n.1, 203
    music 60–1, 116 n.7, 163, 194–5, 196–7, 198, 204, 212–13, 219
    second (1964–79) 112, 162–3, 196 n.1, 198, 203, 209–10, 211–12
    third (2000–) 196 n.1, 198, 203, 219, 220, 222
Chingaira, Chix 170
chinyambera (dance) 6, 56, 60, 61, 62–3, 68–73
Chipanga, Hosiah 213, 221, 225
'Chipindura' (song: Answer) 126, 127
Chiredzi 43
Chirisa, Donald (Sniper Storm) 253
Chirumiko, Wallace *see* Winky D
Chishawasha mission school 144, 150
Chisvo, Adam 120
Chitengo, Guido 150
'Chitima Nditakure' (song) 128
Chiweshe, Stella 33, 34, 258
choirs 143, 149, 161
City Quads 150, 158, 160, 164
City Rhythms 157
City Slickers 150, 157
Coca-Cola Bottling Company 157
Coloured Arcadia Rhythm Lads 154
corruption 197, 208–9, 304, 305, 320
Crucial Mix 253
cultural nationalism 217
Culture T (performer) 252, 290

Dabengwa, Dumiso 197
dancehall *see* Jamican dancehall; Zimdancehall
dandaro ceremonies 14–17, 29, 33, 34, 40

Dat Studio 34–5
David, *Mr* 146, 149
De Black Evening Follies (aka De Pitch Black Evening Follies) 148, 149, 150, 154, 155, 156, 157, 158
death 45, 85, 115 n.6, 221, 319
detention 164
Dhadza D (performer) 263
'Dhodhi Reguava' (song) 269
Diamond Studio 35
digital technology 234
Doke, Clement xiv
Dos Santos, João 2
drums 71, 77–8
Dudz (performer) 252
Dumbutshena, Enoch 150
Dutiro, Chartwell 33
Dyoko, Beauler 33, 34
Dzimbahwe 35

Enharira, Mawungira 35
Environmental Management Agency 30
Epworth Singers 151
Epworth Theatrical Strutters 160
ethnicity xiv, xvi, xvii

families 278–81, 282–3, 286
famine 83–5
fashion 159
fast track land reform programme (FTLRP) *see* land
female sexuality 99, 101–7, 108, 109
film 93, 95–7
folktales and songs 15, 16, 46, 63, 87, 94–7, 100–1, 104–6
forests 99, 101, 201–2
Freeman (performer) 253

'Gal fi Beg' (song by Buju Banton) 255
Gary B (performer) 253
Gerrie B (performer) 290
ghetto culture 232, 238, 240–1, 243, 244–5, 247
Gokwe 6, 43, 53, 76, 77, 84
Golden Brothers 157, 163
Golden City Dixies 154, 155, 156
Gora, Sekuru 33
gospel music 257–8
Gospel Train Records 34
Gotora, Samuel 149
Gramma Records 34
Gukurahundi massacre xvii, xviii, 59, 197
'Gumkum' (song: Iguana) 262
Gwaze, Ernest 149
Gweru 13, 14, 16, 24, 30, 35, 36, 56, 58–9, 68, 73, 182, 183, 185

Hadebe, Josaya 149
'Hakuna asingade' (song: Everyone Wants Sex) 264
Harare 13, 14, 16, 24, 30, 33, 35, 36, 143–4, 179, 186
Harare Hot Shots 150
'Hatimisike' (song: We Are Unstoppable) 231, 242, 245
hip-hop 25, 184, 234, 255, 258
Hitler, Adolf 57–8
HIV and AIDS 95, 258, 262, 311, 315, 322–3
'Hondo Yeminda' (song: War for Land) 122, 220
hosho (musical instrument) 32
human security 218–19, 226
Hwedza 33

If Vagina Had Teeth (film) 98–9, 100, 101–7, 108, 109

'In My Dreams' (song) 253
indigenous knowledge 43, 49, 50, 78
Ink Spots 149
'Ivhu Ramakafira Nderipi?' (song: Which Soil/Land Did You Die For?) 221–2

Jackie Bango (performer) 253
Jamaican dancehall 237, 238, 255, 260, 262, 267–8, 289, 290, 291, 311, 313, 314, 315
jazz 25, 154
Jerusarema (dance) 148
jichi (fertility dance) 43, 52, 53, 54
Jones, Rennie 157
Judgement Yard (sound system) 253

Kabila, Laurent 235
'Kamwe Kabhebhi' (song: Another Girl) 275
Kandido Sabau 155
kanindo-rhumba (beat) 155, *see also sungura*
Karanga people 68, 69, 87, 89–90, 326
karimbaduriro (*mbira* instrument) 22
karimbamutatu (*mbira* instrument) 18–19
karimbanhovapasi (*mbira* instrument) 22–3
karimbashauro (*mbira* instrument) 21
kasi music 309
Kassim, Elisha 149, 156
Kaufman Centre (Mbare) 156, 158
Khoisan people xiii
'Khonapho Khonapho' (song: There and Then) 319–20
Killer T (performer aka The Chairman) 254, 261, 285
King Labash (performer) 253
Kingstons Music 35
Kinnah (performer) 254
Kombayi, Patrick 59

Korekore people 99–100, 106
Kroonvale (South Africa) 136 n.28
'Kubasa' (song: My Workplace) 265
'Kudzidza Kwakanaka' (song: Education Is Good) 160
kukiya-kiya (scamming) 239
'Kukunakidza' (song: It's Exciting) 275
Kumbula, Musekiwa 151
Kumuzi (community arts group) 63
kurhendzeleka see xinombela (fertility dance)
'Kusarima' (song) 134, 135
'Kutapira' (song: Sweet) 121–2
kwaito 234, 309
Kwanongoma College of Music 18 n.1, 30–1, 157–8
'Kwatinobva' (song: Where We Come From) 231, 246
kwela 154

Lady Bee (performer) 269, 310, 312
Lady Squanda (performer) 254, 268, 269, 310
lamellophones *see mbira* music
land 4, 8, 161, 202–4, 216–17, 218, 219, 220, 221, 222, 224, 225, 226
Lebakeng, Shirley 178
Lee, Boss 186
leisure 147–8, 163–4
Look East Policy 294, 295
'loxion kulture' (South Africa) 240 n.3

'Ma Babe Anoita' (song: Fine Women) 269–70
Mabhatimani (Batmen, Special Force) 163
Machinga (*mbira* instrument maker) 30
Madonna 254
Madzore (singer) 221, 223, 225
'Mafira Kureva' (song: Kill the Messenger) 268

Mafusire, Moses Mphahlo 156
Magaya, Cosmas 30, 33, 34
Magumede, Emma 152
Maguraushe, Wonder 37, 40
mahobo parties 147, 151–2, 160
Mai Musodzi Hall (Mbare) *see* Recreational Hall
Major E (performer) 252, 253, 290
Makamure, Obey *see* Tocky Vibes
Makoni, Dickson Chingaira (Cde Chinx) 220, 258
Makwembere, Bethel 59
Malvern S (performer) 253
'Mama' (song) 274–5, 277–8, 279–80
Mamaala people (South Africa) 100
'Mamisa' (song: To Cause Someone to Mess Themselves up) 312
Mangethe, Beater 318
'Manhanga Kutapira' (song: Sweet Pumpkins) 135, 136
Manhattan Brothers 154
Manjalima, Fred (Kapfupi) 186
Mapfumo, Thomas 60, 113, 115–16, 120, 125, 128, 129–30, 163, 170–1, 196, 197, 212, 213, 223, 225
marabi music 153
Maraire, Chiwoniso 113, 121, 123, 126–7, 129, 137, 258
Maraire, Dumisane 37
Maraire, Linda Nemarundwe 126, 127 n.20
Marariromba, Tevasiira Samson 79
Marley, Bob 252, 268
marokesheni (locations) 239
Marondera 32
marriage 43, 44, 46, 47–52, 53–4, 256
Mashonaland Melodians 158
Masike, Hope 258
Maskiri (performer) 245

Masuka, Dorothy 153
Matingwina, Mitchel 64
Matiure, Perminus 37, 40
Matiure, Sheasby 29, 36
Mattaka, Kenneth 149, 150
Mattaka, Lina 157
Matumba Emhondoro 35
Mauch, Carl 2
Mawungira Enharira 35, 36
Mazabane, Remington 149
Mazura, Benedict 151
Mbare (Harare) 3–4, 7, 112, 143–4, 145–7, 148, 149, 150–3, 154, 155–6, 158, 160–2, 163
Mbira Centre (Harare) 33
Mbira Dzenharira 21, 29, 35, 36, 37
mbira music 2–3, 5, 7, 13–15, 113–16, 118–19
  adaptation 16–17, 24–6, 31–2, 36, 40, 111, 112–13, 116–17, 118, 119–38, 158, 325
  audiences 37
  commercialisation 32–4, 327
  ensembles 35–6
  instruments 14, 15, 17–23, 24, 26–30, 31, 33, 37–8, 327
  international impact 31, 33, 36, 327
  recorded and broadcast 33–5
  songs 32
  teaching of 30–1, 37–40
  and women 258, 270
mbiragita (*mbira* instrument) 20
media 223 n.5
memory 97, 208, 209
Methodist Church (Mbare) 156, 158
Metro Studios 34
'Mhai' (song: Mother) 231, 244, 265, 280, 282, 283

Mhembero 35
Mhondoro 33
Mhuri yekwaChigamba 33
Mhuri yekwaRwizi 33
Mhuri yekwaZambuko 33
middle class 143, 144–7, 148, 149, 150–3, 155–6, 158–61, 164–5
Mills Bothers 154
Milton Brothers Band 159, 164
mime 69–70, 95
Miss Harare Pageant 156–7
mitila see *xinombela* (fertility dance)
Mkuzo, Nomzamo 178
Mkwesha, Virginia 258
Mnangagwa, Emmerson xviii
'Morefire' (song) 268
Mosia, Stan 178
Movement for Democratic Change (MDC) 4, 59, 60, 66, 68, 136, 181, 217, 218, 221
Moyo, Jonathan 191
Moyo, Tongai 186
Mozambique 93–4, 97–9, 102
Mphahlo, Moses 150, 153
Mtukudzi, Oliver 170, 196, 212, 213, 224, 225, 258
Muatengo, Taona 36, 40
Muchawaya, Ketai 196–7, 198
Mude, Hakurotwi 34
Mudenge, Stanislaus 163
Mugabe, Robert xvii, xviii, 196, 220, 221, 224, 240
Mujuru, Ephat 33, 34
Mujuru, Fradreck 124 n.17
Mujuru, Joyce 224
Mujuru, Samuel 30, 33
'Mukatiende' (song: Get up and Let's Go) 163
Mukombe, Mukudzei (Jah Prayzah) 186

mukwerera (fertility ceremony) 52, 76, 77, 78–82, 84, 85, 86, 87, 88, 89, 90–1
Mumanyi, Tawanda see Calaz, Seh
'Mumota Menyu Muri Kubvira' (song: There Is Something Burning in Your Car) 268
'Munotidako' (song) 190
'Mupunduru' (song: Buttocks) 269
'Murume' (song: A Husband) 312
Murwira, Emmanuel 150
Musarurwa, Isaac 156
'Musemwa Wee!' (song) 87–9
music
  backyard studio 189, 243, 254, 289, 310
  broadcast 152–3, 154, 171–2, 187–8, 189, 190, 191, 240, 243, 310
  Cameroon 255
  censorship and control of 4, 6, 57, 63, 162, 164, 170–1, 190, 224–5, 226, 232–3, 235, 240, 247, 296, 310, 325
  China 255
  and Christianity 245–6, 257–8
  and corruption 171–2, 187–8, 191
  Côte d'Ivoire 234
  cross-cultural composition 116–18, 123, 154, 170
  Democratic Republic of Congo 78, 235
  Dominican Republic 255
  and drugs 268–9, 311
  facilities 170, see also names of specific venues
  funding of 181
  hate 217–18, 219–22, 226
  and homosexuality 247, 262–4
  international tours 179
  Jamaica see Jamaican dancehall
  Kenya 235
  Laos 77–8

and liberation struggle *see chimurenga*, music
lyrics 185, 189–91, 236, 240, 241, 245, 247, 251, 258, 259–60, 261, 262, 277, 311, 312, 314, 315
Malawi 255
and nationalism 161, 162, 163, 165
nature of 254
and newspaper coverage 157, 187–8, 190, 243
and patriarchy and misogyny 94, 102, 103, 104–5, 108, 251, 254–9, 260–1, 262, 264, 265–6, 268–71, 326
piracy 189, 243
promotion 167, 168–9, 172–9, 182, 183–4, 185–9, 191–2, 326–7
and protest 57, 58, 60–1, 65, 68, 69, 70, 72–3, 95, 102, 116, 136, 160–1, 195, 203, 207–8, 212, 213, 225, 236, 290–3, 298–307, 310, 315, 316–17, 323
recording of 33–5, 112, 153, 189
royalties and payment 123 n.16, 137, 182–3, 185
Senegal 234
social context and role 168–70, 171, 172, 180–1, 182, 184, 186, 189, 191, 312, 315, 325
South Africa 255, 309
southern Africa 326
subversive and anti-establishment *see* music, censorship
Tanzania 234
teaching 30–1
Uganda 77
and violence 266–8
and women 95, 99, 100, 101–6, 108, 257–8, 260–1, 264–6, 269–71, 274–6, 277, 279–80, 282, 285, 286, 310, 314, 326

see also specific music genres
musical concerts 143, 145, 146–7, 148, 149, 150, 151, 152–3, 154, 156, 157, 158–63, 164–5
Musodzi, Mai 151, 158
Musvarwe, Oliver 156
Mutare 30, 183, 185, 186–7
Mutavati, Absolom 37
Muzanga, Elijah 155
Muzenda, Simon 59
Muzengeri, Robert 154–5
'Mzii' (song: Marijuana) 268
Mzilikazi xv, xvi
Mzingeli, Charles 149–50

Nasty Trix (performer) 256
National Arts Council of Zimbabwe (NACZ) 168, 175, 185, 186, 188–9
Nazarite religion (South Africa) 121
Ncube, Busi 258
Ncube, Welshman 68
Ndakabata Mic (album) 253
'Ndarangarira Gamba' (song) 198, 204–7, 213
'Ndatadza Kurima' (song: I Have Failed to Plough/Grow Crops) 87
'Ndazokundikana' (song) 280–1
Ndebele people and language xv–xvi, xvii, xviii, 53, 309–10, 312–14, 317, 323
'Ndezve Varume Izvi' (song: This Is for Men) 260
'Ndini Uyauya' (song: I Am the One) 265
'Ndinochema' (song: I Cry/I Am Crying) 231
'Ndinokuda Sechamba' (song: I Love You Like Marijuana) 268
'Ndinomira Semukono' (song: I Will Stand Like a Man) 265
'Ndinoputa' (song: I Smoke) 268

'Ndiratidze Zvaunoita' (song: Show Me What You Can Do) 262
'Ndiri Rasta' (song: I Am a Rasta) 268
'Ndiro Diro' (song: It Is a Baboon) 89
Ndivhurei Maziso (album: Enlighten/Guide Me) 283
Ndlovu, Eliot 30
Ndlovu, Madinda 318
Ndlovu, Peter 318
ndombolo (DRC) 234, 235
'Ndopisa Ngochani' (song: I Burn Gays) 263
Ndoro, Joyce 157
'Ndoshandira Iwe' (song: I Work for You) 275
Nehanda, Mbuya 297, 298
Nevana 77, 78, 79, 80, 81–2, 85–6, 89, 90, 91
Ngavongwe 34
Ngoma Ndaimba (I Have Poured My Heart out into/Given My Best in This Album) 283
'Nhai Ishe!' (song: Oh Chief!) 82
'Nhamo Yaive Nava Agrippa' (song: The Trials and Tribulations of Mr Agrippa) 155
'Nhemamusasa' (song: Temporary Shelter) 39, 119, 120, 121, 123
Ninja Lipsy (performer) 268
Nyakura, Mura 155
'Nyamaropa' (song) 26, 27–8, 119 n.12, 128
'Nyamboro' (song) 103
Nyathi, Albert 220, 225
Nyerere, Julius 58
'Nyika Dzapera Nevarungu' (song: The Europeans Have Taken Over the Countries) 161
nyunganhare (*mbira* instrument) 18
Nzou, Murenga Sorore 195

OK Success 155
Operation Murambatsvina 59, 221, 294, 296–7

'Pane Vasipo' (song) 198, 207–8, 209–10, 211, 212, 213
pastors 320, 321–2
patriarchy 94, 99, 256, 257–8, *see also* music, and patriarchy and misogyny
Perfect Works (community arts group) 63–4
'Pfuma Ndakabvisa' (song: I Paid Lobola) 265
Phiri, Charlotte 157
police 61–2, 161–2, 302–5, 307, 320
Port Elizabeth 178, 181–2, 183, 185, 191
Potato (performer) 252
Pringo (performer) 186
public holidays 208
'Public Image' (song) 298–302
pungwes (nocturnal political meetings) 162–3, 196

Qonfused (performer) 268

rainmaking 7, 52, 76–7, 78–82, 83, 84, 85–6, 87–91, 94, 97–8, 99–100, 101, 102, 103, 104, 105, 107–8, 113
Ranks, Shabba 252
rap 234, 254
rape 160, 262
Ras Pompy (performer) 265–6
Recreational Hall (Mbare, later Mai Musodzi Hall) 151, 156, 158, 159, 160
reggae 25, 236, 251, 252, 253, 260, 268
Rhodesia Broadcasting Corporation 34, 171
riddims 236–7, 243, 254
rock 25
Rogers, Jimmy 154

Rolling Stones 254
RTP Records 35
Rumors (club, Red Fox) 253
Rwanda genocide 96, 210–11

Sadza, Jack 151
Safe Brothers 157, 163
Saidi, William 159
'Sakunatsa' (song) 223
Salisbury African Male Voice Choir 149
'Sauro' (song: Saul) 246
'Sauro Une Pamutauro' (song: Soul Jah Love, You Are Troublesome) 267
Senko (performer) 312–14, 315–17, 318
'Seunononga' (song: Like You Are Bending) 262
Shamhuyarira, Nathan 151
Shangwe people 43, 45, 46–8, 49, 50, 52, 53, 54, 76–7, 78, 80, 81–4, 88–91
Sheba, Thandi 157
Shed Studio 34
Shinsoman (performer) 253, 274–6, 277–8, 279, 285, 306, 307
Shoko, *Mr* 146
Shona people and language xiii–xv, xvii, xviii, 7, 15–16, 25, 32, 48, 65, 78, 79–81, 90, 93–4, 97–9, 111, 113–15, 221, 257, 276, 277, 280, 283, 285, 294, 297–8, 309, 326
'Shumba' (song: Lion) 115
Sibanda, Marko 196–7, 198
Simson, Robert 18 n.1, 30
'Simudza Maoko' (song: Raise up Your Hands) 231, 245, 246, 281–2
skokiaan 144, 145, 151, 152, 155, 160
'Skokiaan' (tune) 153
Slaggy Yout (performer) 253
Sniper (performer aka Soldier) 261

Snipers (community arts group) 63
'Soja Riripo' (song: A Soldier Is Here) 266
Solomon, *King* 285
songs *see* folktales and songs
Soul Jah Love (performer aka Chibaba) 254, 261, 262, 263, 265, 266–7, 268
Spears, Britney 254
Star FM 242–3
'kuState House Kure' (song: The Journey to State House Is Very Far) 220
statutes *see* Acts of Parliament
Stereo One (sound system) 253
Stodart Hall (Mbare) 156, 158
Stunner (performer) 256
subalternity 233
sungura 256, 257, 258, 269, 270
'Survivor' (song) 305–7

'Taireva' (song) 124–5
'Tavaona' (song) 67–8
Tavirima 6, 56–7, 58, 60, 61, 62, 63, 64, 65, 66–9, 70–3
Taylor, Herbert 152
'tea parties' 155
Teal (later Gramma) Records 34
Templeman (performer) 253
Tempo Man (performer) 290
Thomas Mapfumo and the Blacks Unlimited 33
'Timonemone' (song: Let us Roll the Marijuana) 268
'Titambire' (song: Dance for Us) 135–6
'Tocky Aenda Nenyika' (song: Tocky Has Made It to the Top) 265
Tocky Vibes (Obey Makamure) 231, 238, 244, 280–3, 285, 301, 307
'Tombana' (song: Toddler) 221
'Tondobayana' (song: We Will Fight) 163

'Tondogare Kupiko?' (song: Where Are We Going to Live?) 84, 86–7
totems 32, 47
'Tozeza Baba' (song: We Are Scared of Father) 258
Tracey, Hugh 34
traditional leaders *see* chiefs
Transit Crew 253
tsava-tsava 155
Tsonga people 43, 45–53, 54, 326
Tsvangirai, Morgan 67–8, 220
Tuku Music 35

ubuntu 19, 46, 48, 53, 65
'Uchaenda Riini Mugabe?' (song: When Are You Dying Mugabe?) 221
'Umqombothi' (song by Yvonne Chaka Chaka) 96
Umzabalazo (community arts group) 63
'Unodazvinhu' (song) 264–5
'Unozoona Kukosha Kwechikorobho Warasa Mvura' (song: You Will Discover the Invaluable Worth of My Advice When It Is Too Late) 283–5
urban grooves 184, 234, 256–7, 258, 275, 289–90, 310
urban migration 16–17, 24–5, 111
'Usakanda Mapfumo Pasi' (song: Do Not Give Up) 265
Utsiwegota, Innocent 253

'VaChibanya' (song: Mr Chibanya) 85
'Vaigara Mumakomo' (song: They Stayed in Mountains) 155
'Vakafa Havana Chavakaona' (song: Those Who Are Dead Are Missing Out) 262–3
'VaMayaya' (song) 302–4, 305

'Vana Venyuvakura' (song: 'Kurauone', Your Children Have Grown) 64–5
'Vanhu Vakuru' (song: Big People) 258
'Vashakabvu' (song: The Departed) 293–4, 297–8
Vigilance Band 292
Viomak (singer) 221
Vito, Bernard 163

Wappy (performer) 252
West African literature and film 106
'When Will the Day of Freedom Come' (song) 164
White, John 149
Winky D (Wallace Chirumiko aka Big Man and Ninja President) 238, 240, 241, 244, 247, 253, 258, 261, 266, 268, 290, 292–3, 295–6, 297–8, 300, 301, 307, 311, 315

xinombela (fertility dance) 43, 44–6, 47, 48, 49–50, 51–3, 54, 326

Yappie Banton (performer) 252
young people 43, 44, 45–7, 49–53, 64–5, 232–3, 234, 235–6, 237, 238, 239, 240, 244–6, 247–8, 251–2, 280, 281, 282, 283, 285, 286, 290–1, 307, 310–11, 314–15, 326

Zebrons Band 157
Zhakata, Leonard 170, 212, 213, 223, 225
Zhou, Gilbert 56, 73
Zimbabwe
    Constitution 61
    currency 295–6, 322
    decade of crisis 288–9, 294–5, 297–8, 318–19

elections 59, 60, 65–6, 67–8, 72, 136, 298
history xiii–xviii
liberation movements and struggle xvi–xvii, 4, 94, 112, 162, 195–7, 199–201, 204, 205–6, 209, 212
natural resources 30
post-liberation 197–8, 199, 209, 213, 217, 320, *see also* Zimbabwe, decade of crisis
religion 320–2
structural readjustment 197
unemployment 311
Unity Accord xvii
'Zimbabwe' (song) 130
Zimbabwe African National Liberation Army (ZANLA) 94
Zimbabwe African National Union (ZANU) xvii
Zimbabwe African National Union – Patriotic Front (ZANU–PF) 4, 57, 58, 60, 61, 62, 66, 73, 112, 136, 181, 195, 196, 198, 205–6, 212–13, 217, 218, 222, 294, 300, 325
Zimbabwe African People's Union (ZAPU) xvii, 181, 195, 196, 206, 213
Zimbabwe Broadcasting Corporation 225
Zimbabwe Broadcasting Holdings 171
'Zimbabwe Iyoyi' (song) 198, 199–201, 202, 203–4, 213
Zimbabwe Music Company 34
Zimbabwe Music Rights Association (ZIMURA) 168, 177, 188
Zimdancehall 8–9, 25, 184, 231–3, 238, 239–40, 241–4, 246–8, 251–4, 258–63, 264–71, 274–8, 279–86, 288, 289–91, 296, 298–304, 305–7, 309, 310, 311–17, 319–22, 323, 326
Zimunya Danger Group 156
zouglou (Côte d'Ivoire) 234
Zvirimudeze Mbira Ensemble 13–14, 21, 24, 32, 35, 36–7, 40